The first edit[...] Carter, with [...] Vickerman. [...] Tricia and Bo[...] the fourth by ~~Henry Steaman~~ and this fifth edition by Joel Newton.

KEITH CARTER'S interest in the great outdoors was kindled on a school trip to Snowdonia which hooked him for life. Work became what he did between walks and he has since explored almost every corner of the British Isles with occasional forays into France, Austria and the USA. He is co-author of *The Pennine Way*, also from Trailblazer.

JOEL NEWTON'S passion for walking national trails was ignited in 2007 when he tackled the 630-mile South-West Coast Path. Despite ill-fitting shoes that caused blisters and a bag that was far too heavy, that journey was the inspiration for many more on the long-distance paths of Britain. He's since completed Offa's Dyke Path, West Highland Way, Great Glen Way, Hadrian's Wall Path, Cotswold Way and most of the Pennine Way. He is the author of *Thames Path* and co-author of the *South West Coast Path* series, all from Trailblazer.

Authors

Offa's Dyke Path
First edition: 2004; this fifth edition: 2019

Publisher: Trailblazer Publications (🖥 www.trailblazer-guides.com)
The Old Manse, Tower Rd, Hindhead, Surrey, GU26 6SU, UK

British Library Cataloguing in Publication Data
A catalogue record for this book is available from the British Library

ISBN 978-1-912716-03-6

© **Trailblazer** 2004, 2007, 2011, 2015, 2019: text and maps

Series Editor: Anna Jacomb-Hood **Editor**: Clare Weldon **Cartography**: Nick Hill
Proofreading: Jane Thomas **Layout**: Nick Hill **Index**: Anna Jacomb-Hood
Illustrations: © Nick Hill (pp71-74) **Photographs (flora)**: © Bryn Thomas
All other photographs: © Joel Newton (unless otherwise indicated)

The maps in this guide were prepared from out-of-Crown-
copyright Ordnance Survey maps amended and updated by Trailblazer.

Acknowledgements
Thanks to my parents, Jane and Paul Newton, for the company (and the lifts & accommodation) around Welshpool & Llanmynech, and thanks to my brother, Jamie, for collecting a
weary walker from Prestatyn during a heat-wave. Thanks to Nick Phillips and Pete Whaley
for the introduction to mango cider in Bodfari, and the company between Llandegla and
Prestatyn. I'm grateful to the staff at the Offa's Dyke Centre in Knighton who answered my
questions and also to the many campsites along the trail that helped me out and offered invaluable advice. And not forgetting a big thank you to the readers who have sent in suggestions
for this new edition – Mark & Liz Adams, Luc Barbe, Karen Besant, Lara Clough, Mike Fox,
Stephen Funnell, Stuart Greig, John Haley, Lara Pugh, Philip Scriver, David Smith, Pam &
Stephen Turner, Floortje Verhoek & Erik Weug and Dr Leszek Zdunek. Thanks, as ever, to all
at Trailblazer: Clare Weldon for editing, Nick Hill for maps and layout, Jane Thomas for
proofreading and Anna Jacomb-Hood for additional research and the index.

Dedication – From Joel: For Michela Prescott, for accompanying me to Chepstow, Tintern,
Devil's Pulpit and Hay-on-Wye; and for Graeme Quinnell and Jos Smith, with whom I first
'conquered' Offa's Dyke a decade ago.

A request
The author and publisher have tried to ensure that this guide is as accurate and up to date as
possible. Nevertheless, things change. If you notice any changes or omissions that should be
included in the next edition, please contact us at Trailblazer (🖥 info@trailblazer-guides.com).
A free copy of the next edition will be sent to persons making a significant contribution.

Warning: hill walking can be dangerous
Please read the notes on when to go (pp14-16) and health and safety (pp80-2). Every effort
has been made by the author and publisher to ensure that the information contained herein
is as accurate and up to date as possible. However, they are unable to accept responsibility
for any inconvenience, loss or injury sustained by anyone as a result of the advice and information given in this guide.

Updated information will shortly be available on: 🖥 **www.trailblazer-guides.com**

Photos – Front cover and this page: Traversing Hatterall Ridge between Hay-on-Wye
and Pandy. **Previous page**: The view from Cefn Du in the Clwydian Range. **Overleaf**: The
stage between Buttington and Llanymynech is by far the flattest on the path.

Printed in China; print production by D'Print (☎ +65-6581 3832), Singapore

Offa's Dyke
PATH

98 large-scale maps & guides to 52 towns and villages
PLANNING – PLACES TO STAY – PLACES TO EAT

CHEPSTOW TO PRESTATYN &
PRESTATYN TO CHEPSTOW

KEITH CARTER

WITH ADDITIONAL INFORMATION BY COLIN VICKERMAN

FIFTH EDITION RESEARCHED AND UPDATED BY

JOEL NEWTON

TRAILBLAZER PUBLICATIONS

Contents

APPENDICES

Contents

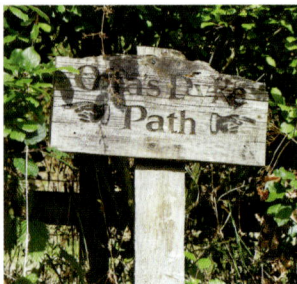

ABOUT THIS BOOK

This guidebook contains all the information you need. The hard work has been done for you so you can plan your trip without having to consult numerous websites and other books and maps. When you're all packed and ready to go, there's comprehensive public transport information to get you to and from the trail and detailed maps (1:20,000) to help you find your way along it.

● Where to stay – from campsites to B&Bs, hostels and hotels
● Walking companies if you want an organised tour and baggage-carrying services if you just want your luggage carried
● Itineraries for all levels of walkers
● Answers to all your questions: when is the best time to walk, how hard is it, what to pack and the approximate cost of the trip
● Walking times in both directions; GPS waypoints as a back-up to navigation
● Availability and opening times of cafés, pubs, tea-shops, restaurants, and shops/supermarkets along the route
● Rail, bus and taxi information for the towns and villages on or near the path
● Street maps of the main towns and villages
● Historical, cultural and geographical background information

❑ MINIMUM IMPACT FOR MAXIMUM INSIGHT

Man has suffered in his separation from the soil and from other living creatures ... and as yet he must still, for security, look long at some portion of the earth as it was before he tampered with it.
        Gavin Maxwell, *Ring of Bright Water*, 1960

Why is walking in wild and solitary places so satisfying? Partly it is the sheer physical pleasure: sometimes pitting one's strength against the elements and the lie of the land. The beauty and wonder of the natural world and the fresh air restore our sense of proportion and the stresses and strains of everyday life slip away. Whatever the character of the countryside, walking in it benefits us mentally and physically, inducing a sense of well-being, an enrichment of life and an enhanced awareness of what lies around us.

All this the countryside gives us and the least we can do is to safeguard it by supporting rural economies, local businesses, and low-impact methods of farming and land-management, and by using environmentally sensitive forms of transport – walking being pre-eminent.

In this book there is a detailed and illustrated chapter on the wildlife and conservation of the region and a chapter on minimum-impact walking, with ideas on how to tread lightly in this fragile environment; by following its principles we can help to preserve our natural heritage for future generations.

INTRODUCTION

Wherever I have been in Wales, I have experienced nothing but kindness and hospitality, and when I return to my own country, I will say so.

George Borrow *Wild Wales* 1862

For 177 miles (285km), between Chepstow in the south of Wales and Prestatyn in the north, the Offa's Dyke Path winds along the English–Welsh border, roughly following the line of the 1200-year-old frontier earthwork for which it is named. This magnificent long-distance footpath ranges over terrain **This magnificent footpath ranges over terrain as diverse as any you will find in Britain** as diverse as any you will find in Britain; it traverses the whaleback ridges of the Clwydian Hills, follows canal towpaths and old drovers' roads, goes beside the banks of the meandering Severn and Wye rivers, through the Shropshire hills and over the Black Mountains. The Border Country is the land of Merlin and Arthur, a land of history and legend, from which sprang Owain Glyndwr and the *Lord of the Rings*. To journey through it on foot is the finest way to discover one of Britain's best-kept secrets.

There are good reasons for walking the trail in either direction (see p31) so this book has been researched and written to be used by

Heading south through the Clwydian Hills towards Llandegla.

This simple stone and plaque, overlooking the River Severn at Sedbury Cliffs (see p86), marks the southern end of the walk.

St Cadoc's Church at Llangattock-Lingoed.

One of the most visible sections of the Dyke, just after the turn-off to Montgomery on the way to Brompton Crossroads.

both south-to-north walkers (starting in Chepstow) and north-to-south walkers (starting in Prestatyn). In the text and maps, **N FROM CHEPSTOW** look for the N↑ symbol which indicates information for those walking **from Chepstow to Prestatyn S FROM PRESTATYN** and the S↓ symbol with shaded text (also on the maps) for those walking **from Prestatyn to Chepstow**.

If you choose to walk north, you leave the South Wales coastline at Sedbury Cliffs, pass through Chepstow and by Tintern Abbey, climbing the River Wye's wooded slopes to Monmouth which is well worth exploring. On towards Pandy, you pass through a hidden world of intimate villages and quiet byways where you're likely to meet only livestock and farm people.

The trail climbs over the Hatterrall Ridge following the spine of this fine massif to Hay Bluff. Hay-on-Wye, with its 20 or so second-hand book shops, is a welcome stop for a night. Then it's on to Kington after the Hergest Ridge, a place of heather, gorse and wild ponies, with extensive views of Housman's 'blue-remembered' hills of Shropshire and the Black Mountains of the Brecon Beacons National Park. The halfway mark is at Knighton, 'the town on the dyke'. After the aptly-named Switchbacks you continue across the Severn Plain on a more modern man-made embankment with panoramic views of the Breidden Hills and then go up to the Iron Age hill-fort of Beacon Ring with its crown of trees.

After the inspiring views of the Marcher castle of Chirk you leave the Dyke itself and soon cross the magnificent Pontcysyllte Aqueduct, following the canals. The nearby festival town of Llangollen is well worth visiting before you enter a region that might be part of Tolkien's Middle Earth, the limestone cliffs and screes of Stack Rocks (Eglwyseg Crags) to reach Llandegla. Then come the splendid ridges of the Clwydian Range followed by the small lanes and hedgerows of the Vale of Clwyd. After a bracing walk over the Prestatyn hillside with its awesome views of the mountains of Snowdonia you descend to Prestatyn.

Ambling along the Llangollen Canal (see p203) makes a pleasant change from the gradients of the path's hills and mountains.

History

The Offa's Dyke Path was the fourth of 15 national trails to be established in England and Wales, with a further four in Scotland. The first of these trails, the Pennine Way, was opened in 1965 but it was not until 1971 that Lord Hunt, of Everest fame, officially opened the Offa's Dyke Path.

The path was originally the responsibility of the Countryside Commission, but as the path crosses the English/Welsh border many times, two-thirds being in Wales and one third in England, the responsibility for it passed to the Countryside Council for Wales in 1991. It is managed and maintained by the Offa's Dyke Path

Chepstow Castle (see p87) dates back to 1067.

The path passes over Monnow Bridge in Monmouth (see p102), the only intact example of a 13th-century fortified bridge in Britain.

Management Service based in Knighton, with the close co-operation of the local authorities through whose land it passes.

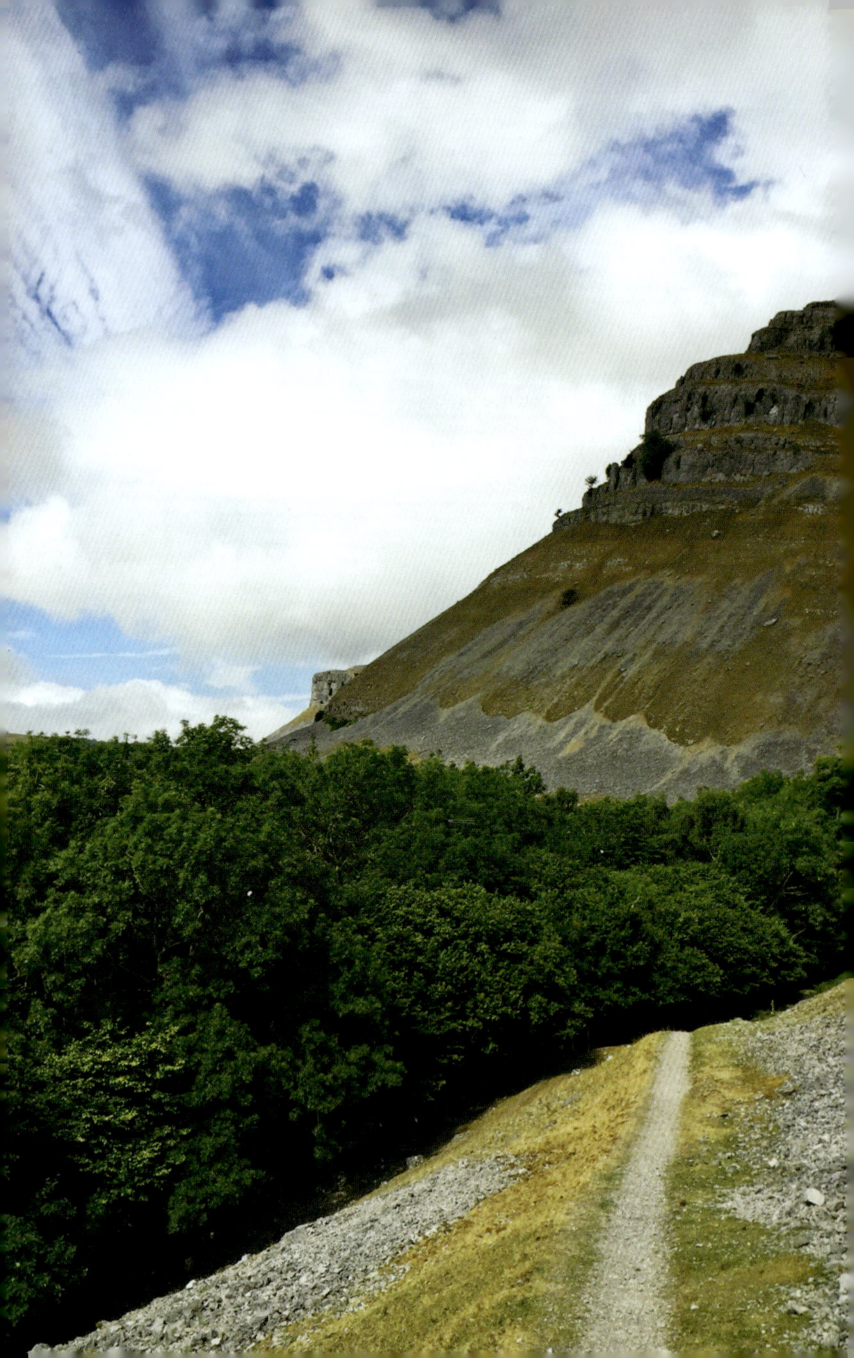

Strangely, the distance covered by the path is a matter for conjecture: you will see various figures given for the length of the path – 182 miles according to the sign in Chepstow, 177 miles according to the official National Trail website and 168 miles if you believe what is written at Sedbury Cliffs.

How difficult is the Offa's Dyke Path?

Do not be deceived into thinking this is an easy walk. A level of fitness and walking competence is required for most sections of the Offa's Dyke Path. It's 177 miles end to end and assuming you have two weeks available this will require an average of nearly 15 miles a day, based on 12 days of walking plus a day to get to the start and a day to get home. That's about five to seven hours' walking every day. On at least three days you will probably have to walk 17 miles; quite a tall order and you are going to feel a certain amount of tiredness at the end of the walking day. Are you up to it?

There are three severe and testing sections. First up, the so-called 'Switchbacks' (see north and south of Knighton, pp160-71). While most of the ups and downs on this section are par for the course, others, particularly north of the town, will pose a considerable challenge for many Dyke walkers.

The other two challenging sections involve exposed crossings well away from human habitation. First is the section along Hatterrall Ridge in the Black Mountains (see pp120-37) between

© Bryn Thomas

Plas Newydd, Llangollen (see p209).

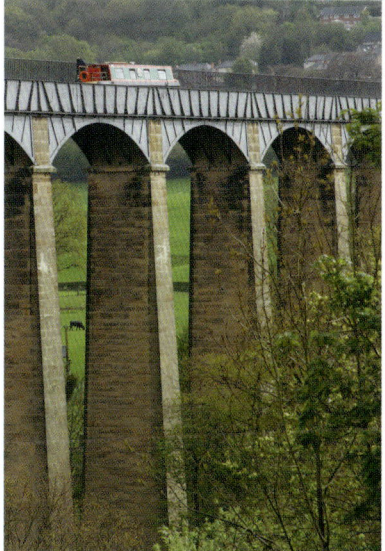

© Jim Manthorpe

Left: Eglwyseg Crags loom above you as you pass along the trail above Llangollen.

Crossing the River Dee high above it on the Pontcysyllte Aqueduct is one of the highlights of the walk (see p204).

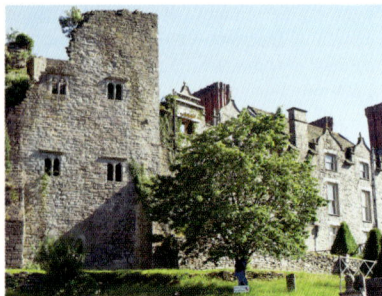

The partly ruined castle in the book town of Hay-on-Wye (see p132) also houses a bookshop.

Hay-on-Wye and Pandy. It's a distance of 17½ miles (28km) through exposed country, the highest point being 703m (2306ft), and can take up to 10 hours. There is little shelter and only a few escape routes although the journey could be broken at Capel-y-ffin or Llanthony. You will need to think carefully about how you are going to tackle this arduous crossing.

The crossing of the Clwydian Range (see pp223-30) between Bodfari and Clwyd Gate involves several climbs and descents as well as some incomparable ridge walking. On a fine day you will romp it but in bad weather it can be a severe test of endurance. Luckily there are several escape routes enabling you to arrange a pick-up, possibly by your B&B host for the night.

That said, anyone possessing basic outdoor competence should find themselves coping perfectly well even with these challenging sections but don't underestimate any part of the route; it is not a doddle.

How long do you need?

Possibly the finest pub on the trail – the Boat Inn at Redbrook (see p102).

This is the great imponderable. Can the path be walked from end to end in a fortnight's holiday? The answer is yes, definitely, but a lot will depend on your travelling time. If you have just 14 days but need two of those for the journey to and from the trail, you'll have to get a move on and it won't leave you much time to stop and stare. No time to visit Chirk Castle, see Llangollen, go into Montgomery, call in at the Offa's Dyke Centre in Knighton, shop for second-hand books in Hay-on-Wye, have a pint at the Boat Inn at Redbrook or the Three Tuns in Bishop's Castle. This is good country and it deserves more than a hurried glance.

The walk will be much more enjoyable if you can spare a full 14 (or even 15) days walking, plus a day or two for travelling to and from home, so if your fortnight's holiday incorporates three weekends, you're in luck. If not, you could leave out one or two of the less-inspiring sections without losing any of the essential character of the route. Llanymynech to Castle Mill (pp192-201), Bodfari to Prestatyn (pp230-5) and the section along the Severn plain (pp184-8) are all contenders for omission if you're in a hurry, as is the southernmost section of the walk: Sedbury Cliffs and Chepstow (pp85-6). See also suggested itineraries (p37).

If you can't spare the time to walk from end to end in one go you could undertake the walk over several shorter

Left: Looking south from Hatterrall Hill towards Pandy. You'll meet a lot of sheep on this walk!

Canoeists on the River Wye, seen from Hay Bridge (see p131). A day with a paddle is a great way to spend a rest day; you get a different perspective on the river and its wildlife.

trips, gradually accumulating the miles until the great day comes when you have completed it in its entirety. Another option is simply to sample the highlights of the route on day walks and weekend trips; see pp35-8 for recommended sections.

When to go

SEASONS

The months when the weather is less likely to be inclement are May to September, although April and October often bring days that are bright and breezy when the walking and the surroundings are at their best. Typically, the seasons are likely to present the following conditions:

Spring

The weather in spring is as unpredictable as the rest of the year. In **April** it can be warm and sunny on odd days, but seldom for sustained periods. Conditions are more likely to be changeable, with blustery showers and cold spells reminding you that winter has only just passed. On the other hand, less rain falls on average in spring than at any other time of the year. This, coupled with the milder weather of **May** and **June**, and the proliferation of wild flowers early in

the year, makes it one of the best times to tackle the trail.

Summer

July and **August** are the traditional holiday months and the conditions are usually good for walking with a greater likelihood of long periods of warm settled weather and many hours of daylight. Unlike many parts of Britain the Border Country is not afflicted by mass tourism. Thankfully there's no need to worry about crowds apart from when passing through the tourist hotspots of Prestatyn,

Glimpsed through the trees from the path high above the River Wye: the ruins of Tintern Abbey (see p95).

Hay-on-Wye and Llangollen. You can lord it over the daytrippers with your rucksack and big boots: let them look and wonder. Once you're back out among the fields and hills you can leave the hordes behind.

Autumn

Late **September** and **October** are a good time to get out on the trail to appreciate the full benefit of the autumn colours in the woodland and the leaves underfoot. Although the air temperature should remain relatively mild, October can see the first frosts, and rain is an ever-present threat, intensifying as the year draws to its close. Nevertheless, many connoisseurs consider autumn, especially early autumn, the best time of year for walking.

Below: Prestatyn, the northern terminus of the path, seen from the Bryn Prestatyn Hillside.

On Hatterrall Ridge. You need to be well prepared for this stage between Pandy and Hay-on-Wye as it's 17½ miles (28km) through exposed country.

Winter

Only the hardiest of souls will attempt the walk in winter. Once the days have shortened you will want to be at your day's end by 4-5pm. Colder days, wind and driving rain are not the best accompaniment for a good day on the path although you can hit lulls when the sun comes out and you imagine things are improving. Some winters see continuous rain for several months with severe flooding when parts of the path become impassable and others see plenty of snow.

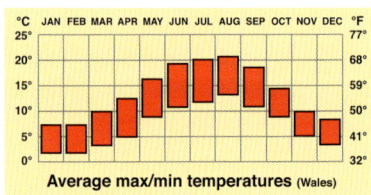

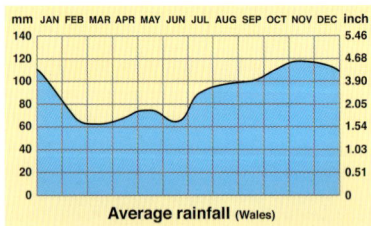

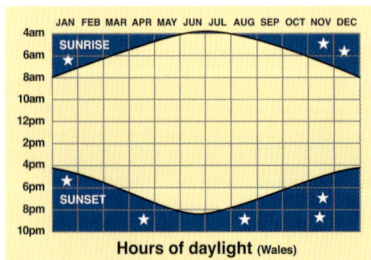

Average max/min temperatures (Wales)

Average rainfall (Wales)

Hours of daylight (Wales)

DAYLIGHT HOURS

If walking in autumn, winter and early spring, you must take account of how far you can walk in the available daylight. It will not be possible to be out for as long as you would in the summer. The table below gives the sunrise and sunset times (Greenwich Mean Time) for the middle of each month at latitude 52° North which runs through Wales, giving a reasonably accurate picture of daylight hours for the Offa's Dyke Path. Depending on the weather, you should get a further 30-45 minutes of usable light before sunrise and after sunset.

See p27 for **annual events and festivals** taking place in the area.

PLANNING YOUR WALK

1

Practical information for the walker

ROUTE-FINDING

The trail is generally waymarked with scrupulous attention to detail with only a few areas where more work is needed to avoid ambiguity in route-finding. The path was devised and initiated by a band of devotees who were at pains to ensure that those who came after them could find their way. It's waymarked with the national trail symbol: an acorn. This is supplemented with finger posts and guide posts which are frequently engraved, often in English and Welsh, and many stiles have the symbol of a coin of Offa's reign. Occasionally you'll come across older engraved stone markers, and more recent variations include the 'tombstone' markers on the Hatterrall Ridge. Arrows indicating the direction of the trail are nearly always marked 'Offa's Dyke', which helps to distinguish them from other way-marked trails sharing a similar route.

Aided by the waymarks and following the trail maps in this book, the walker is unlikely to get lost to any great degree. A word of advice is not to make assumptions. If the broad inviting path ahead of you looks the obvious route, it does not necessarily follow that it is your route. Look for the waymark, especially where the path changes direction, and take particular care when crossing fields if the trail exit is not entirely clear.

It isn't safe to assume the path follows the line of the Dyke in every case. There are places where the right of way diverges from the line of the Dyke; this is true on Hawthorn Hill (Map 38, p153) between Dolley Green and Knighton and over Baker's Hill (Map 63, p197) between Racecourse Common and Castle Mill. Check the trail maps regularly and keep your eyes open when walking through towns, where waymarking can be somewhat haphazard; the area east of Chepstow is particularly poor in this respect.

The path itself is in an impressive condition, though it didn't happen overnight. A full survey of the route was undertaken by the National Trails officer in summer 2007, with a view to preparing a three-year plan to bring the trail into line with new National Trail standards for both England and Wales. In 2009 parts of the Hatterrall Ridge underwent path improvement works. Further work has taken place – and continues to take place – to combat erosion along the length of the path.

The trail is well waymarked with the familiar acorn symbol. This is the mid point.

GPS

I never carried a compass, preferring to rely on a good sense of direction ... I never both-ered to understand how a compass works or what it is supposed to do ... To me a compass is a gadget, and I don't get on well with gadgets of any sort. **A Wainwright**

While modern Wainwrights will scoff, more open-minded walkers will accept GPS technology as an inexpensive, well-established if non-essential, naviga-tional aid. To cut a long story short, within a minute of being turned on and with a clear view of the sky, GPS receivers will establish your position and altitude in a variety of formats including the British OS grid system (see p242), any-where on earth to an accuracy of within a few metres. These days, most **smart-phones** have a GPS receiver built in and mapping software available to run on it (see box p43).

One thing must be understood however: **treating GPS as a replacement for maps, a compass and common sense is a big mistake**. Although current units are robust, it only takes the batteries to go flat or some electronic mal-function to leave you in the dark. GPS is merely a **navigational aid or backup** to conventional route finding and, in almost all cases, is best used in conjuction with a paper map. All a GPS does is stop you exacerbating navigational errors or save you time in correcting them.

Newer units may come with some inbuilt mapping, but while it's possible to buy **digital mapping** (see box p43) to import into a regular GPS unit with sufficient storage capacity, it might be considered as practical as having inter-net on a mobile phone – you still end up scrolling and zooming across a tiny screen.

Using GPS with this book

It's anticipated you won't tramp along day after day, ticking off the book's **way-points** as you pass them because the route description and maps are more than adequate. Only when you're **unsure of your position** or which way to go might you feel the need to turn on the unit for a quick affirmation.

Most of the book's maps feature numbered waypoints from Sedbury to Prestatyn. These correlate to the list on pp242-5 which gives the longitude/lat-itude position in a decimal minute format as well as a description. You can either manually key the nearest presumed waypoint from the list in this book into your unit as and when the need arises. Or, much less laboriously and with less margin for keystroke error, download the complete list for free as a GPS-readable file (but not the descriptions) from the Trailblazer website. You'll need the right cable and adequate memory in your unit (typically the ability to store 200 waypoints or more). This file, as well as instructions on how to interpret an OS grid reference, can be found at: 🖥 **trailblazer-guides.com/gps-waypoints**.

It's worth repeating that most of the people who've ever walked the Offa's Dyke Path did so without GPS so there's no need to rush out and buy one. Your spending priorities ought to be on good waterproofs and a sturdy pair of boots. However, all those thousands will have had their frustrating moments of navigational uncertainty and reliable technology now exists to reduce mistakes.

ACCOMMODATION

The path is well served with both camping and bed-and-breakfast-style accommodation (as well as a few hostels and bunkhouses), allowing for some flexibility in itineraries. A comprehensive selection of places to stay along the full length of the trail is given in each section of the route guide, Part 4, though it's worth noting that pubs in particular tend to change hands with almost alarming frequency.

Always **book your accommodation**, ideally at least the night before, but for peak periods – and even weekends – considerably earlier. Not only does this ensure that you have a bed for the night but it also gives you a chance to find out more about the place, check tariffs and see what's included. If you have to cancel, phone your hosts: it will save a lot of worry and allows them to provide a bed for someone else. In some cases, particularly in more upmarket establishments, you may be liable for the cost of the room if you don't give sufficient notice of cancellation. Many B&Bs and guesthouses/hotels require a deposit, though this will mostly be refunded if you give sufficient cancellation notice.

Many walkers opt for booking their accommodation during the planning stage of their walk. The key to selecting in advance where to stay lies in anticipating your daily mileage (many walkers work on an average of 12-14 miles a day). The suggested itineraries in the box on p37 will be of help here, too.

Camping
Man is born free under the stars, yet we lock our doors and creep to bed.
Robert Louis Stevenson

There's a reasonable number of official campsites along Offa's Dyke Path but it isn't as well served as some of the other popular long-distance footpaths. Don't let this put you off. It is still perfectly possible to backpack the route from end to end, pitching where enterprising B&B owners have made space on their lawn, letting campers use a shower and offering meals as well. Almost every village has at least one place where this is possible although it can occasionally be embarrassing if you have to pitch your tent right outside the family lounge with the family sitting around watching television. The charge is between £3 and £10 per person so this is by far the most economical way to walk the trail.

For those who are never happier than when pitching their tent behind a hedge and striking camp in the morning dew before the world is up, we salute you, but Offa's Dyke Path is not ideal for what you want. Farmers used to be very amenable to the odd inconspicuous tent being pitched in a field corner but

PLANNING YOUR WALK

❏ B&B-style accommodation

What to expect For most long-distance walkers, tourist-board recommendations and star-rating systems have little meaning. At the end of a long day you'll simply be glad of a place with hot water and a smiling face to welcome you. If there's somewhere to hang your wet and muddy clothes, so much the better. It is these criteria that have been used for places mentioned in this guide, rather than whether a room has tea- and coffee-making facilities, a shaver point or colour TV, though most establishments do have these.

Rooms Single rooms are usually poky 'box' rooms and are rarely available. **Twin rooms** have two single beds while a **double** is supposed to have one double bed though sometimes has two single beds that are pushed together to make a double when required. **Triples** generally have a double and a single, or three single beds, and **quads** often have a double bed with bunk beds, or four single beds. A triple or quad room can therefore also be used as a double or twin.

Facilities An **en suite** room attracts a premium although often this can be just for a cramped shower cubicle squeezed in next to a loo in a corner of the room. So don't automatically turn your nose up at a **bathroom** across the corridor, which is often more spacious with a deep, inviting bath just waiting for you to turn the taps on and ease away the aches with a long hot soak. In some places the bathroom is shared with other rooms (**shared facilities**), so you may have to wait your turn, but in others it may be for the sole use of the guests in a particular room (**private facilities**).

Some B&Bs, but more usually guesthouses/hotels, also have a **sitting room** (lounge) exclusively for guest use, a real bonus at the end of a day when retiring to your room instead of relaxing in a comfy chair can seem something of an anti-climax. It also gives you the opportunity to talk to the other guests.

Most guesthouses/hotels offer an **evening meal** as do the more isolated B&Bs, though you should always pre-book this. Ring ahead if you have been delayed on the trail since meals may be served at a set time. Alternatively, B&B/guesthouse hosts may be willing to drive you to the nearest pub if it is too far to walk.

Rates Proprietors either quote rates on a per room or a per person basis. In this guide we quote rates on a **per person** (pp) per night basis based on two sharing a room; a typical B&B will range in price from £30 to £35pp for a nice room and £30-40pp for a room with en suite facilities, though a lot depends on location and facilities. Guesthouses will charge £35-45pp and hotels are likely to charge £40pp or more. Bear in mind that hotel rates do not always include breakfast so check in advance. See also p84.

Lone walkers occupying a twin or double room will typically be expected to pay a **single occupancy rate** which is usually £5-15 less than the rate for two occupants. In the height of the season, and at weekends, at some places if you want to book in advance you could even be expected to pay the full room rate as they can usually be sure to fill the room with two people. If you turn up and there is availability on the day they may just charge a single occupancy rate. If the rate quoted is for a room (not per person) it will almost definitely be the same whether one, two or more share.

It is often necessary to pay a deposit when making your **booking**; this will usually be refunded if you cancel at least 48 hours in advance but is sometimes non refundable.

since the catastrophic foot-and-mouth epidemic in 2001 attitudes changed. However, some farmers are now happy enough to let you camp but others less so. Always find the landowner and ask permission before camping (see p77).

A few places now offer upmarket camping – '**glamping**' – options. These may range from basic wooden camping pods to better appointed and more comfortable shepherd's huts.

Hostels and bunkhouses

Cheap **hostel**-style accommodation is severely limited along the path: there is only one YHA hostel (at Kington) actually on the trail itself, with just two more YHA hostels (Clun and St Briavels) and two independent hostels (at Chepstow and Llangollen) within relatively easy reach of the trail. However, if you have the energy to walk the extra distance you are assured of a cheaper night's accommodation than the average B&B. All have self-catering facilities; some provide good-value evening meals too but only YHA St Briavels is open all year.

YHA stands for Youth Hostel Association: however, 'Youth Hostel' is something of a misnomer as visitors of any age are welcome. Membership of the **Youth Hostels Association** (freephone ☎ 0800-019 1700, or ☎ 01629-592700, 🖳 www.yha.org.uk) for an individual is £15 per year if paying by direct debit (£20 by credit card). It's possible to join in advance of your stay or when you arrive at a hostel. If you are not a member you can still stay at a YHA hostel but generally you will be charged an additional £3 per night. Bedding is provided; towels aren't but can generally be hired for £2.

As a rule, it's more efficient to make **reservations** using the central phone number or via the YHA website (see above), rather than contacting the individual hostels direct, though the contact details for these are given in Part 4. For details of pricing, see under Budgeting, pp30-1.

There's also a scattering of **bunkhouses** with dormitory accommodation; in some you will pay less if you bring your own bedding. Also be aware that some are booked by groups for sole occupancy.

Bed and breakfasts (B&Bs)

Staying in B&Bs (see also box opposite) has its own particular appeal. For anyone unfamiliar with the concept, you get a bedroom in someone's home along with a cooked breakfast the following morning. The accommodation is invariably clean and comfortable, traditionally with the emphasis on floral patterns and chintz, and it can be excellent value for money. One night you may be in a bijou bungalow, the next on a working hill farm to be woken by the crowing of a cock. The attraction lies in the variety, which gives you a unique insight into the local culture.

Transport offered by B&B hosts As many of the places offering accommodation are not right on the Offa's Dyke Path B&B owners are often happy to collect walkers at an agreed rendezvous and deliver them back to the trail in the morning. Since this is a service of mutual benefit it's one which B&B owners may provide free of charge, but do check first. Of course, the benefit to the walker is that there is no added mileage at the end of the day to reach the accommodation. It is important to agree lift arrangements with your host at the time of making the booking. Mobile phone users would find it useful to ring ahead to give their host warning of their impending arrival at the pick-up point – though plan this in advance because reception on the path is not always good.

Pubs and inns
Many rural pubs and inns (and even a couple of restaurants in Montgomery and Monmouth) offer B&B accommodation at similar prices to more homely establishments, and some have seized the challenge enthusiastically, supplying every modern convenience including, in extreme cases, four-poster beds or a pool. At least you do not have far to go to reach the bar. But the idea fails where the proprietor, with every good intention, has nevertheless to mind the bar and restaurant, so the personal touch can be lost. Pubs can also be quite noisy for those who retire early so choose carefully if you intend staying on the premises.

Guesthouses
Guesthouses (see also box on p21) are more impersonal and don't have that private life of their own that is characteristic of good B&Bs, although they can be perfectly acceptable and well run. The best guesthouses are those that 'cater for walkers', which means they understand the way walkers think and are happy to accommodate the problems walkers can bring with them; wet gear, dirty boots, huge rucksacks and a tendency to invade the place like an army on the march.

Hotels
Many walkers are prejudiced against staying in hotels, reluctant to pay the higher prices and believing, perhaps wrongly, that walkers are unwelcome in more genteel surroundings. You may want to treat yourself to one really luxurious night, possibly to mark the halfway point or to celebrate at the finish, in which case you may well choose to stay in more upmarket accommodation.

Airbnb
The rise and rise of Airbnb (🖥 airbnb.co.uk) has seen private homes and apartments opened up to overnight travellers on an informal basis. While accommodation is primarily based in cities, the concept is spreading to tourist hotspots in more rural areas, but do check thoroughly what you are getting and the precise location. While the first couple of options listed may be in the area you're after, others may be far too far afield for walkers. At its best, this is a great way to meet local people in a relatively unstructured environment, but do be aware that these places are not registered B&Bs, so standards may vary, yet prices may not necessarily be any lower than those of a regular B&B.

FOOD AND DRINK

Breakfast and lunch
A full fry-up of bacon, eggs and sausages is considered de rigueur by many walkers but remember when in Wales to ask for a 'full Welsh' **breakfast** rather

than a 'full English'! (The main difference being that laver bread, see box below, may be offered in a Welsh breakfast.) Others prefer a somewhat lighter continental breakfast which will almost always be available.

You will need to plan what to do for **lunch**. The easiest option is to get a packed lunch: most B&B hosts (and some hostels) will provide you with one for around £5-6; B&B hosts may also be happy to fill your flask with coffee or tea. If you don't fancy breakfast, or want an early start, it's worth asking if you could have a packed lunch instead. Alternatively you could pick up the makings of a packed lunch at village shops along the trail, thus contributing to the local economy: rolls and cheese are good for a day while apples and cereal bars survive well in a rucksack for a couple of days.

Be careful to plan ahead, though, as shops in rural areas are becoming more scarce and there'll be sections of the walk when you won't come across anything at all. In any event, you should always carry some form of emergency rations (see p82).

Evening meals
The Offa's Dyke Path is abundantly supplied with **pubs** and **inns**, which are a good choice for an evening meal. Many have restaurants but most walkers will be happy with a bar meal. Some establishments offer a wide and imaginative selection of hot meals, including vegetarian options where required, but in others vegetarians are going to find themselves struggling.

In the towns along the path there are also good **cafés** and **restaurants** as well as the usual choice of **takeaways**: Chinese and Indian cuisine has reached even the remotest outposts of civilisation.

Self-catering
There are enough shops along the path to allow you to buy food supplies frequently. You should not need to carry food for longer than one day.

❏ **Welsh specialities**
● **Laver bread** Seaweed with oatmeal fried in bacon fat and served for breakfast. Even supermarkets stock it now.
● **Bara brith** A traditional rich cake made with marmalade, mixed fruit, spices, egg and flour, not unlike fruit loaf.
● **Welsh cakes** Tasty cakes full of currants and sultanas. You can find them in supermarkets and in most tea shops and cafés.
● **Welsh rarebit** Melted cheese with a hint of mustard poured over buttered toast, though recipes vary.
● **Leek and parsley broth** (*Cawl cennin a phersli*) A traditional broth made from beef and lamb, root vegetables, herbs and leeks.
● **Tregaron granny's broth** (*Cawl mamgu Tregaron*) Another soup full of vegetables with beef and bacon.
● **Wyau mon** Eggs in cheese sauce with potatoes and leeks.
● **Miner's delight** (*Gorfoledd y glowyr*) A rabbit casserole dish.
● **Oggy** The Welsh equivalent of the Cornish pasty containing Welsh beef, leeks, potato, onions and gravy in a thick pastry crust; originally the standard lunch for miners.

❏ **The perfect pint**
Much of the beer found in pubs along the path is pasteurised and manufactured in millions of gallons and distributed throughout Britain. Known as keg beer, it has been reviled by real ale drinkers in its time but is invariably smooth and tastes the same wherever you are. However, traditional **real ale**, the product of small-scale local breweries, is always in demand. Real ale continues to ferment in the cask so can be drawn off by hand pump or a simple tap in the cask itself. Keg beer, on the other hand, has the fermentation process stopped by pasteurisation and needs the addition of gas to give it fizz and sparkle.

Keep an eye out for pubs with the CAMRA sticker which shows they have been selected by the **Campaign for Real Ale** (🖳 camra.org.uk). This invaluable organisation has been largely responsible for the survival of independent brewers in the UK and deserves our plaudits. Keen beer drinkers will be on the lookout for rare or unusual beers only available regionally, some even brewed on the premises of the pub where they are served. Examples of this are in Bishop's Castle, just off-route, where in-house beers are brewed at **The Three Tuns** (see p166); their Cleric's Cure, a light malty beer at 5% ABV, is well worth seeking out.

You could also try something from **Offa's Dyke Brewery**, a micro brewery at the Barley Mow in Trefonen (see p195). The brewery opened in 2003 when a local farmer bought the pub and satisfied his interest in real ale by starting to make his own beer, including the very delicious Gold.

Another local brewer near the path is **Llangollen Brewery** (see p214; 🖳 llangol lenbrewery.com), located just a few yards from Eliseg's Pillar. At the moment they do four beers including the very popular dark Welsh Black Bitter (5.8%).

Local brews well distributed in mid-Wales and the Welsh Borders are those by **Brains of Cardiff** (🖳 sabrain.com) and **Wye Valley Brewery** (🖳 wyevalleybrew ery.co.uk) from Stoke Lacy. All create good pints but try the brews above 4% ABV for better taste and flavour. From the Hereford-based Wye Valley Brewery try Dorothy Goodbody's which has a lovely crisp finish, or Butty Bach.

Lovers of good beer will no doubt sniff out their own choice brews, the Welsh Borders area giving plenty of opportunity to keep their love alive. Hwyl! (Cheers!)

Village shops, where they still exist, are open throughout the year and on Monday to Saturday most open 8am to 8pm or even later to take full advantage of casual trade and the sale of alcohol, though they may open only for the morning on Sundays and may close early on one day during the week. Fuel for camp stoves may not always be available although Camping Gaz and meths can usually be found.

Drinking water
When walking it is recommended that you drink at least two litres of water a day. On a hot day you will need to increase this to replace the fluids lost through sweating. Though it's tempting, don't drink from streams or rivers as they are likely to be laden with harmful chemical contaminants picked up from fields, roads and housing. Either carry enough for the day or fill up at public toilets or outside taps marked on the trail maps in Part 4. Alternatively, ask at a farm, bar or shop if they would mind filling up your water bottle for you; most people are happy to do so, though it's only fair to buy something first in a pub or café.

MONEY

Plan your money needs carefully. It would be sensible to carry a float of **cash** with you for day-to-day spending although **debit** and **credit cards** are widely accepted, including in pubs and in all but the smallest village shops. B&Bs, though, rarely have facilities for paying by credit or debit card, but they will usually accept a cheque so take a **cheque book**. Campsites are most easily paid for in cash because of the smaller amounts involved. Hostels usually accept cards.

If you're planning to stick to cash, start with about £200 and expect to replenish your funds in towns along the way. All the towns you pass through have banks, most of them with cashpoints. As long as you buy something most supermarkets offer a **cashback service** whereby they charge your debit card and give you cash from the till.

Even though no charge is made to withdraw money from most **ATMs** (unless a credit, store or charge card is used) some (even on the LINK network) are 'pay to use'. However, charges have to be clearly displayed both outside the machine and on the screen and customers have the right to cancel the transaction if they decide they don't want to pay the charge. Cash can also be drawn at **post offices** if you have a debit card. For further details see 🖳 postoffice.co.uk and click on Products & Services and then Branch and banking services.

For more on money, see pp42-3; for budgeting, see pp30-1.

WI-FI AND INTERNET ACCESS

Pretty much everywhere offers wi-fi free to visitors, though it's not 100% guaranteed in some of the more remote places on the route. Pubs in particular usually have a wi-fi connection, though this may in certain instances be only in the bar itself and not in the rooms. If an internet connection is vital to you, do ask beforehand to make sure your B&B is online.

WALKING COMPANIES

For walkers wanting to make their holiday as easy and trouble-free as possible there are several specialist companies offering a range of services from baggage carrying and/or accommodation booking to self-guided or fully inclusive tours.

Baggage transfer
The thought of carrying a heavy pack puts a lot of people off walking long-distance trails. A baggage-carrying service will deliver your bags to your accommodation each night, leaving you free to walk unencumbered. This obviously works out much cheaper if you are walking with other people.

● **Byways Breaks** (☎ 0151-722 8050, 🖳 byways-breaks.co.uk; Liverpool) Cost depends on distance and the size of the group, but expect to pay at least £25-30 per day for a small group. They also prefer luggage not to weigh more than 18-20kg; more smaller bags are better than a few larger ones.
● **Drover Holidays** (☎ 01497-821134, 🖳 droverholidays.co.uk; Hay-on-Wye) For a bespoke quote contact them direct.

If you are having problems carrying your bags for a day or two some of your B&B hosts may be happy to do the transporting for a small charge. Likewise some of the **taxi** firms listed (see Part 4) can provide a similar service within a local area. Prices vary, depending on the mileage involved and the individual concerned, but for the most part you can expect to pay a minimum of £15.

Accommodation booking

If you prefer to know that your accommodation is booked for the whole of your walk but you don't have time to book it yourself you may like to use one of these companies.

● **Byways Breaks** (see p25) Provide a flexible route planning, accommodation booking and baggage transfer service, along the whole path, or any section of it and in either direction.

● **Drover Holidays** (see p25) For a bespoke quote contact them directly.

● **Welshpool Tourist Information Centre** (see p181; ☎ 01938 552043, 🖳 visit welshpool.org.uk) Offer an accommodation booking service for the whole path or part of it and booking fees are applicable.

Self-guided holidays

The following companies provide customised packages for walkers which usually include detailed advice and notes on itineraries, maps, accommodation booking, daily baggage transfer and transport at the start and end of your walk. These companies can also usually arrange for you to have extra nights in towns along the way if you want time to explore them, and a break from walking. Some companies offer the walk all year but some only between late March and October.

● **Absolute Escapes** (☎ 0131-610 1210, 🖳 absoluteescapes.com; Edinburgh) Can arrange the full walk, either south to north or north to south, or half the walk, and can tailor to suit individual requirements.

● **British and Irish Walks** (☎ 01242 254353, 🖳 britishandirishwalks.com; Cheltenham) Offer the complete trail in 15 days and any variation.

● **Byways Breaks** (see p25) Flexible walking holidays, over any number of days, over the whole path or just part of it, with flexible daily distances. They will also organise the walk in either direction.

● **Celtic Trails** (☎ 01291-689774, 🖳 celtictrailswalkingholidays.co.uk; Chepstow) Arrange holidays for any length of time and in a range of accommodation standards. Their main office is in Chepstow, which is close to the beginning of the path.

● **Contours Walking Holidays** (☎ 01629-821900, 🖳 contours.co.uk; Derbyshire) They can arrange the full walk from Chepstow to Prestatyn (12-16 days) or either the southern or northern sections (6-10 nights); walking north to south is also possible.

● **Discovery Travel** (☎ 01983-301133, 🖳 discoverytravel.co.uk; Isle of Wight) The walk can be arranged in either direction and either as the full walk (about 15 days) or just half the walk or any number of days to suit the client's requirements.

● **Drover Holidays** (see p25) Are based on the path and offer the whole walk in either direction in 12- and 14-night itineraries or half the walk, and shorter breaks, and can tailor to suit requirements. Dogs can be accommodated.
● **Explore Britain** (☎ 01740-650900, ▢ explorebritain.com; Co Durham) Walks (4-19 nights) are mostly from south to north though they also offer north to south.
● **Let's Go Walking** (☎ 01837-880075, ▢ letsgowalking.com; Devon) Offer the whole walk from south to north or north to south, as well as half the walk. Can tailor to meet requirements.
● **Northwestwalks** (☎ 01257-424889, ▢ northwestwalks.co.uk; Wigan) Offer the full walk from 13 nights/12 days' walking to 16 nights/15 days as well as in two halves. They do north to south and south to north, and can tailor-make as required.
● **Sherpa Expeditions** (☎ 020-8875 5070, ▢ sherpa-walking-holidays.co.uk; London) Offer the first 80 miles of the walk from Chepstow to Knighton in 7 nights/8 days. Can tailor to suit requirements.
● **The Walking Holiday Company** (☎ 01600-713008, ▢ thewalkingholiday company.co.uk) Their office is in Monmouth, which is on the path, and they offer the walk in various itineraries, from south to north and north to south, and can tailor to suit requirements.
● **Wales Walking Holidays** (☎ 01248-713611, ▢ waleswalkingholidays.com) Offer the north and south sections in 8 nights/7 days and the full path in 15 nights/14 days, in either direction. Can tailor-make as required.

PLANNING YOUR WALK

❏ **Annual events**
The following events may need to be considered when planning your walk especially as accommodation in the area is often booked up months in advance.
● **Hay Festival of Literature, Hay-on-Wye** The famous book and literary festival (▢ hayfestival.com) held in the **last week in May**, with talks and readings all week from top names in the world of writing. It is an opportunity for readers to meet their favourite authors and the town's streets are thronged with visitors – although the events themselves are held in a series of marquees set up outside the town.
● **International Musical Eisteddfod, Llangollen** This major festival of music and the performing arts to which groups and individuals come from all over the world is held in the **first or second week in July**. For further information see ▢ internation al-eisteddfod.co.uk.
● **Royal Welsh Show, Builth Wells** The **last week in July** is a big date in the farming calendar for the whole of mid and south Wales, as this show (▢ rwas.wales) attracts visitors and competitors from a huge area. Kington and Hay-on-Wye are the two centres on the path most likely to be affected.
● **Knighton Show** The **last Saturday in August** is an important day for the local community. The show includes horticultural and floral exhibitions, vintage cars, food stalls and dog shows. See ▢ visitknighton.co.uk for details.
● **Presteigne Festival** A festival (▢ presteignefestival.com), **held over six days in late August**, which specialises in promoting contemporary classical music.

Group/guided walking tours

Fully guided tours are ideal for individuals wanting to travel in the company of others and for groups of friends wanting to be guided. Packages usually include meals, accommodation, transport arrangements, minibus back-up and baggage transfer, as well as a qualified guide.

● **Drover Holidays** (see p25)   Drover offers bespoke guided itineraries for small groups.

● **HF Holidays** (☎ 0345-470 8558, 🖥 hfholidays.co.uk; Herts)   Offer a two week guided holiday along the complete trail.

❑ **Information for foreign visitors**

● **Currency/money**   The British pound (£) comes in notes of £50, £20, £10 and £5, and coins of £2 and £1; even though £50 notes are available they are not often seen in circulation. The pound is divided into 100 pence (usually referred to as 'p', pronounced 'pee') which comes in silver coins of 50p, 20p, 10p, and 5p and copper coins of 2p and 1p.

Cash is the most useful form of payment but debit/credit cards are accepted in many places. Visit 🖥 xe.com/currencyconverter for the latest exchange rates; alternatively ask at banks, post office or travel agencies.

● **Business hours**   Most **shops and supermarkets** are open Monday to Saturday 8am-8pm (and sometimes up to 15 hours a day) and on Sunday from about 9am to 5 or 6pm, though again sometimes longer. Occasionally, especially in rural areas, you'll come across a local shop that closes at lunchtime on one day during the week, usually a Wednesday or Thursday.

Main **post offices** are open at least from Monday to Friday 9am-5pm and Saturday 9am-12.30pm. **Banks** typically open at 9.30am Monday to Friday and close at 3.30pm or 4pm though in some places they may open only two or three days a week and/or in the morning only; **ATMs** (**cash machines**) though are open all the time as long as they are outside; any inside a shop or pub will only be accessible when that place is open.

Pub hours are less predictable although many open Mon-Sat 11am-11pm and Sun to 10.30pm; often in rural areas, particularly in the winter months, pubs close in the afternoon (from 3pm to 5, 6 or 7pm). Last entry to most **museums and galleries** is half an hour, or an hour, before the official closing time.

● **National (bank/public) holidays**   Most businesses are shut on 1 January, Good Friday (March/April), Easter Monday (March/April), first and last Monday in May, last Monday in August, 25 December and 26 December.

● **School holidays**   State-school holidays in England and Wales are generally as follows: a one-week break late October, two weeks over Christmas and the New Year, a week mid-February, two weeks around Easter, one week at the end of May/early June (to coincide with the bank holiday at the end of May) and five to six weeks from late July to early September. Private-school holidays fall at the same time, but tend to be slightly longer.

● **EHICs and travel insurance**   Although Britain's National Health Service (NHS) is free at the point of use, that is only the case for residents. All visitors to Britain should be properly insured, including comprehensive health coverage. The European Health Insurance Card (EHIC) entitles EU nationals (on production of the EHIC card so ensure you bring it with you) to necessary medical treatment under the NHS while on a temporary visit here. For details, contact your national social security

● **Ramblers Walking Holidays** (☎ 01707-386800, 🖥 ramblersholidays.co.uk)
Offer 7-night guided holidays on the northern, southern and central sections of
the path, as well as hikes round the Wye Valley.

WALKING WITH A DOG   (see also pp245-7)

The Offa's Dyke Path is a dog-friendly path and most cafés and pubs welcome
dogs, and many B&Bs do too. Nevertheless, it's extremely important that dog
owners behave in a responsible manner. Dogs should always be kept on leads
while on the footpath to avoid disturbing wildlife, livestock and other walkers.

institution. However, this is not a substitute for proper medical cover on your travel
insurance for unforeseen bills and for getting you home should that be necessary.
Also consider cover for loss and theft of personal belongings, especially if you are
camping or staying in hostels, as there may be times when you'll have to leave your
luggage unattended.

If you're walking Offa's Dyke Path any time after March 2019 do check, too,
what the latest rules are, for Britain will have left the EU that March and you can
expect some changes to the legislation.

● **Weights and measures** In Britain milk is sold in pints (1 pint = 568ml), as is beer
in pubs, though most other liquid including petrol (gasoline) and diesel is sold in
litres. Distances on road and path signs are given in miles (1 mile = 1.6km) rather
than kilometres, and yards (1yd = 0.9m) rather than metres.

The population remains divided between those who still use inches (1 inch =
2.5cm), feet (1ft = 0.3m) and yards and those who are happy with millimetres, cen-
timetres and metres; you'll often be told that 'it's only a hundred yards or so' to somewhere, rather than a hundred metres or so.

Most food is sold in metric weights (g and kg) but the imperial weights of
pounds (lb: 1lb = 453g) and ounces (oz: 1oz = 28g) are frequently displayed too. The
weather – a frequent topic of conversation – is also an issue: while most forecasts pre-
dict temperatures in Celsius (C), many people continue to think in terms of
Fahrenheit (F; see the temperature chart on p16 for conversions).

● **Smoking** The ban on smoking in public places relates not only to pubs and restaurants, but also to B&Bs, hostels and hotels. These latter have the right to designate
one or more bedrooms where the occupants can smoke, but the ban is in force in all
enclosed areas open to the public – even if they are in a private home such as a B&B.

Should you be foolhardy enough to light up in a no-smoking area, which includes
pretty well any indoor public place, you could be fined £50, but it's the owners of the
premises who carry the can if they fail to stop you, with a potential fine of £2500.

● **Time** During the winter, the whole of Britain is on Greenwich Mean Time (GMT).
The clocks move one hour forward on the last Sunday in March, remaining on British
Summer Time (BST) until the last Sunday in October.

● **Telephone** The international country access code for Britain is ☎ 44 followed by
the area code minus the first 0, and then the number you require.

If you're using a **mobile (cell) phone** that is registered overseas, consider buy-
ing a local SIM card to keep costs down. See also box p42.

● **Emergency services** For police, ambulance, fire and mountain rescue dial ☎ 999,
(or the EU standard number ☎ 112).

PLANNING YOUR WALK

Your dog needs to be extremely fit to complete this walk. You may not believe it as you watch it haring around the fields but dogs do have a finite amount of energy, so consider whether yours really is up to walking for 10-20 miles a day.

DISABLED ACCESS

While many areas of the trail are inaccessible to the majority of wheelchair and scooter users, either because of the terrain or not inconsiderable number of stiles and kissing gates to be negotiated, some sections are more forgiving, particularly where the path runs alongside the canals. For more on access for the disabled, contact the Disabled Ramblers (🖳 disabledramblers.co.uk).

Budgeting

Your budget will depend largely on the type of accommodation you use and your eating habits as well as your travel costs to and from the start/end of your walk.

If you camp and cook your own meals you will be able to keep costs to a minimum. These escalate as you go up the accommodation and dining scales and will also be affected by the extent to which you use the services offered to guests, such as transportation of luggage, packed lunches and other refinements.

Camping
You can get by on as little as £12-15 per person (pp) per day, pitching your tent at official sites and where B&Bs allow camping in their garden or land and cooking your own food. Typically, camping costs £4-10pp per night, sometimes plus an extra 20/50p (and sometimes £3!) for the use of a shower.

Most walkers will find it hard to live that frugally and will indulge in the occasional cooked breakfast when it's offered (from around £5), the odd pint of beer (upwards of £3.50) and a pub meal after a long hard day (£8-12). It's probably more realistic to budget on around £20-25pp per day.

Hostels and bunkhouses
Rates for YHA hostels vary according to the season and the type of room and can start at £15pp but be as high as £23pp. Typically rates in the summer season are about £2 higher than the base rate. Where YHA hostels offer catering, you can expect to pay around £10 for an evening meal; £5 for breakfast and £5 for a packed lunch. Independent hostels charge a similar rate to YHA hostels while the more basic bunkhouses can be as little as £15pp .

B&Bs and hotels
You should allow £35-40 per person (pp) for an overnight stay and breakfast plus a further £12-16 for an evening meal. If you include a packed lunch (about £5) as well you won't be far wrong on £55-65pp per day; these figures assume two people sharing a room. If you're travelling alone, unless the B&B has single rooms, you will probably be charged a supplement of £10-20 for single

occupancy. Guesthouses are likely to be a bit more expensive so budget for about £55-65pp per day.

The tariff for hotels is likely to be £40 and upwards per person with some saving for two people sharing a room. Some hotels have adopted the continental system of charging for the room only rather than per person, which for a couple doing the walk together may prove an economical proposition when you consider that two people paying £60 for the room will be the same as £30 each, not much more than the rate of an average B&B. However, the room rate may not include breakfast. If the hotel charges a room rate lone walkers may have a discount. Watch out for the extras though, such as service charge and VAT, which can add to the bottom line when the bill is presented.

Extras
Don't forget to set some money aside for the inevitable extras, such as batteries, postcards, buses, taxis, drinks, snacks, phone calls and entrance fees – or, rather more crucially, any changes of plan. Around £100 should be about right.

Itineraries

PLANNING
All walkers are individuals. Some like to cover large distances as quickly as possible. Others are happy to amble along, stopping whenever the whim takes them. You may want to walk the Offa's Dyke Path in one go, tackle it in a series of days or weekends, or use the trail for a series of linear day walks; the choice is yours. To accommodate these different options, this guide has not been divided up into strict daily sections, which could impose too rigid a structure on how you should walk. Instead it has been devised for you to plan an itinerary that suits you.

The **planning map** opposite the inside back cover and **table of village and town facilities** on pp32-5 summarise the essential information for you to make a plan. To make it even easier, look at the **suggested itineraries** (see box p37) and simply choose your preferred speed of walking. There are also suggestions on p35 for those who want to experience the best of the trail over a day or a weekend. The **public transport map and table** (pp49-53) will also help.

Having made a rough plan, turn to **Part 4** where you will find summaries of the route, full descriptions of accommodation options, places to eat and other services in each town and village, with detailed trail maps.

Which direction?
That's entirely up to you. There are good reasons for walking in either direction so this book has been written to be used by both south-to-north walkers (starting in Chepstow) and north-to-south walkers (starting in Prestatyn). In the text

  and maps, look for the **N↑** symbol which indicates information for those walking **from Chepstow to Prestatyn** and the **S↓** symbol with shaded text (also on the maps) for those walking **from Prestatyn to Chepstow**.

(*cont'd on p34*)

VILLAGE AND TOWN FACILITIES
Chepstow to Prestatyn – Walking North N↑ FROM CHEPSTOW

PLACE*	DISTANCE* MILES/KM	BANK (ATM)	POST OFFICE	TOURIST INFO*	EATING PLACE*	FOOD SHOP	CAMP-SITE	BUNK/HOSTEL*	B&B* HOTEL
Sedbury Cliffs Start walk			✔			✔			
Chepstow 1.5/2.5		✔	✔	TIC	✔✔	✔		H	✔✔
(Tintern)					✔✔				✔✔
Brockweir 6/9.5					✔		✔		
Bigsweir 3.5/5.5									✔✔
(St Briavels)					✔			YHA	✔✔
Redbrook 6/9.5			✔		✔	✔			✔
Monmouth 3.5/5.5		✔	✔	TIC	✔✔	✔	✔		✔✔
The Hendre 3.5/5.5							✔		✔
Caggle Street 8.5/13.5									
Llangattock-Lingoed 2.5/4					✔		✔		✔
Pandy 2.5/4					✔	✔	✔	B	✔✔
(Longtown)			✔		✔	✔	✔	G	✔
(Llanthony)					✔		✔	B	✔
(Capel-y-ffin)							✔	G	✔
Hay-on-Wye 17.5/28		✔	✔	TIC	✔✔	✔	✔		✔✔
(Clyro)					✔		✔	H	✔
Newchurch 6.5/10.5					✔ (limited)				
Gladestry 3.5/5.5					✔		✔		✔
Kington 4.5/7		✔	✔	TIC	✔✔	✔	✔	YHA	✔✔
Discoed 8.5/13.5							✔		
(Presteigne)		✔	✔	TIC	✔✔	✔			✔
Knighton 5/8		✔	✔	TIC/ODC	✔✔	✔	✔		✔✔
Newcastle-on-C 7.5/12					✔				✔
(Clun 3 miles off route)				TIP	✔✔	✔	✔	YHA	✔✔
(Bishop's Castle)		✔	✔	TIC	✔	✔		G	✔
Brompton Xroads 7/11.5							✔		✔✔
(Montgomery)		✔	✔		✔✔	✔			✔✔
Kingswood/Forden 6.5/10.5					✔		✔	B	✔
(Welshpool)		✔	✔	TIC	✔✔	✔	✔		✔✔
Buttington 6/9.5					✔	✔	✔	B (groups)	✔
Pool Quay 2/3					✔				✔
Four Crosses 7/11.5					✔	✔	✔		✔
Llanymynech 2.5/4			✔		✔✔	✔			✔✔
Nant-Mawr 3/5									
Trefonen 2/3			✔		✔	✔			✔
Ty'n-y-Coed 1.5/2.5									
Racecourse C 2/3									
Around Baker's Hill ½/1							✔		
(Oswestry 2½ miles off route)		✔	✔	TIC	✔✔	✔			✔

*NOTES

PLACE   Places in brackets eg (Llangollen) are a short walk off the route.

DISTANCE   Distances given are between places directly on the route.
(cont'd on p34)   (from Buttington to Pool Quay, for example, is 2 miles/3km)

PLANNING YOUR WALK

VILLAGE AND TOWN FACILITIES
Prestatyn to Chepstow – Walking South S ↓ FROM PRESTATYN

PLACE*	DISTANCE* MILES/KM	BANK (ATM)	POST OFFICE	TOURIST INFO*	EATING PLACE*	FOOD SHOP	CAMP-SITE	BUNK/HOSTEL*	B&B/HOTEL
Prestatyn	Start walk	✔	✔	TIP	✔✔✔	✔	✔		✔✔✔
Rhuallt	8/13				✔		✔		✔
Sodom	3/5								
Bodfari	1/1.5				✔		✔		✔
(Llangynhafal)					✔		✔		✔
(Cilcain)					✔				
(Llanferres)					✔				✔
Clwyd Gate	11/18								
(Llanarmon-yn-Ial)					✔		✔		✔✔
Llandegla	6/9.5		✔		✔	✔	✔		
(Llangollen)		✔	✔	TIC	✔✔✔	✔	✔	H	✔✔✔
Trevor	11/18				✔	✔(limited)			
(Froncysyllte)			✔		✔				
Irish Bridge area	1.5/2.5								✔✔
(Chirk)		✔	✔		✔✔				
Castle Mill (& Bron-y-garth)	4.5/7						✔2019 only		✔
Craignant	2/3								
(Sellatyn)									
Around Baker's Hill	2/3						✔		
(Oswestry 2½ miles off route)		✔	✔	TIC	✔✔✔	✔			✔✔
Racecourse C	½/1								
Ty'n-y-Coed	2/3								
Trefonen	1.5/2.5		✔		✔	✔			✔✔
Nant-Mawr	2/3								
Llanymynech	3/5		✔		✔✔✔	✔			✔✔✔
Four Crosses	2.5/4				✔	✔	✔		✔
Pool Quay	7/11.5				✔				✔
Buttington	2/3				✔	✔	✔	B (groups)	✔
(Welshpool)		✔	✔	TIC	✔✔✔	✔	✔		✔✔✔
Kingswood/Forden	6/9.5				✔✔		✔		✔✔
(Montgomery)		✔	✔		✔✔✔	✔			✔✔✔
Brompton Xroads	6.5/10.5						✔		✔✔✔
(Bishop's Castle)		✔	✔	TIC	✔✔	✔		G	✔✔
(Clun 3 miles off route)				TIP	✔✔✔	✔	✔	YHA	✔✔✔
Newcastle-on-C	7/11.5				✔				✔✔
Knighton	7.5/12	✔	✔	TIC/ODC	✔✔✔	✔	✔		✔✔✔
(Presteigne)		✔	✔	TIC	✔✔✔	✔			✔✔
Discoed	5/8						✔		
Kington	8.5/13.5	✔	✔	TIC	✔✔✔	✔	✔	YHA	✔✔✔
Gladestry	4.5/7				✔		✔		✔✔

TOURIST INFO — TIC/TIP = Tourist information centre/point ODC = Offa's Dyke centre
EATING PLACE — ✔ = one place ✔✔ = two ✔✔✔ = three or more
BUNK/HOSTEL — YHA = YHA hostel H = independent hostel B = bunkhouse G = glamping
B&B/HOTEL — ✔ = one place ✔✔ = two ✔✔✔ = three or more   (cont'd on p35)

PLANNING YOUR WALK

(*cont'd from p32*)

VILLAGE AND TOWN FACILITIES
Chepstow to Prestatyn – Walking North N↑ FROM CHEPSTOW

PLACE*	DISTANCE* MILES/KM	BANK (ATM)	POST OFFICE	TOURIST INFO*	EATING PLACE*	FOOD SHOP	CAMP-SITE	BUNK/ HOSTEL*	B&B* HOTEL
(Sellatyn)									
Craignant	2/3								
Castle Mill (& Bron-y-garth)	2/3						✓2019 only		✓
(Chirk)		✓	✓		✓✓	✓			
Irish Bridge area	4.5/7								✓✓
(Froncysyllte)			✓		✓				
Trevor	1.5/2.5				✓	✓(limited)			
(Llangollen)		✓	✓	TIC	✓✓	✓	✓	H	✓✓
Llandegla	11/18		✓		✓	✓	✓		
(Llanarmon-yn-Ial)					✓		✓		✓✓
Clwyd Gate	6/9.5								
(Llanferres)					✓				✓
(Cilcain)					✓				
(Llangynhafal)					✓		✓		✓
Bodfari	11/18				✓		✓		✓
Sodom	1/1.5								
Rhuallt	3/5				✓		✓		✓
Prestatyn	8/13	✓	✓	TIP	✓✓	✓	✓		✓✓

*NOTES

PLACE   Places in brackets eg (Llangollen) are a short walk off the route

DISTANCE   Distances given are between places directly on the route (from Rhuallt to Prestatyn, for example, is 8 miles/13km)

Currently, walking from south to north – Chepstow to Prestatyn – seems to be marginally more popular than doing the walk in the other direction. The reason for doing this is the view that it is easier with the sun and prevailing wind at your back. The reason for walking the path in the opposite direction (from north to south) is that the route, arguably, improves in quality as you move south. As you progress south you will get fitter and should be in fine fettle by the time you have to tackle the Switchbacks and the Black Mountains. Alternatively, if you tackle these tougher stretches as you progress north, you will be prepared for the Clwydian Hills, which are no cinch either.

Whichever way you choose to tackle Offa's Dyke Path you'll have fine scenery and challenging walking in both North and South Wales, so it may simply come down to which end of the trail it is most practical for you to start from and finish at, where you can book accommodation, and how long you have got.

The route guides and maps in Part 4 give an overview and timings for both directions. As route-finding instructions are written onto the maps rather than in the text, you will easily be able to follow this guidebook in either direction.

(cont'd from p33)

VILLAGE AND TOWN FACILITIES
Prestatyn to Chepstow – Walking South S ▼ FROM PRESTATYN

PLACE*	DISTANCE* MILES/KM	BANK (ATM)	POST OFFICE	TOURIST INFO*	EATING PLACE*	FOOD SHOP	CAMP-SITE	BUNK/HOSTEL*	B&B/HOTEL
Newchurch	3.5/5.5				✔(limited)				
(Clyro)					✔✔		✔	H	✔✔
Hay-on-Wye	6.5/10.5	✔	✔	TIC	✔✔✔	✔	✔		✔✔✔
(Capel-y-ffin)							✔	G	
(Llanthony)					✔✔		✔	B	✔✔
(Longtown)			✔		✔	✔	✔	G	✔✔
Pandy	17.5/28				✔✔	✔	✔	B	✔✔✔
Llangattock-Lingoed	2.5/4				✔		✔		✔✔
Caggle Street	2.5/4								
The Hendre	8.5/13.5						✔		✔✔
Monmouth	3.5/5.5	✔	✔	TIC	✔✔✔	✔	✔		✔✔✔
Redbrook	3.5/5.5		✔		✔✔	✔			✔✔
(St Briavels)					✔			YHA	✔✔✔
Bigsweir	6/9.5								✔
Brockweir	3.5/5.5				✔	✔			
(Tintern)					✔✔✔				✔✔✔
Chepstow	6/9.5	✔	✔	TIC	✔✔✔	✔		H	✔✔✔
Sedbury Cliffs	1.5/2.5		✔			✔			

TOURIST INFO	TIC/TIP = Tourist information centre/point ODC = Offa's Dyke centre
EATING PLACE	✔ = one place ✔✔ = two ✔✔✔ = three or more
BUNK/HOSTEL	YHA = YHA hostel H = independent hostel B = bunkhouse G = glamping
B&B/HOTEL	✔ = one place ✔✔ = two ✔✔✔ = three or more

PLANNING YOUR WALK

THE BEST DAY AND WEEKEND WALKS

Day walks

● **Chepstow Bridge to Bigsweir Bridge or v/v** This 9-mile (14.5km) walk includes a visit to the ruins of Tintern Abbey, stunningly located below the heavily wooded slopes of the Wye Valley, a perfect spot for lunch and a chance to visit the abbey. It begins or ends at Chepstow Bridge from where the castle can be seen to dramatic effect. There are good transport links to Chepstow but buses no longer stop at Bigsweir Bridge. See pp90-4.

● **Monmouth to Redbrook via The Kymin and return along the River Wye** Outstanding 6½-mile (10.5km) circular walk with a climb to the top of The Kymin with fantastic views over Monmouth and the hidden country beyond, followed by a proper pint at The Boat Inn at Redbrook and return along the silvery Wye. A great walk with loads of variety (see p101). Both Monmouth and Redbrook are fairly well served by buses.

● **Hay-on-Wye to Newchurch or v/v** North along the Wye at first then through the mysterious glade of Bettws Dingle, this 6½-mile (10.5km) ramble gives a taste of the countryside which Francis Kilvert writes about in his diary (see box p136), including the chance to see Emmeline's Grave at the pretty church of Newchurch. Hay-on-Wye is fairly well served by buses but you would probably have to get a taxi back to Hay-on-Wye from Newchurch; see p137-40.

● **Kington to Gladestry and back** A superb 9-mile (14.5km) traverse of Hergest Ridge with views to the Shropshire Hills and the Black Mountains. Great walking on springy sheep-cropped turf through bracken and gorse. By doing the return trip after a pint at the Royal Oak in Gladestry you get a double helping of a marvellous area. See p148. Kington is on several useful bus routes.

● **Circular 15-mile walk from Bishop's Castle** Follow the Shropshire Way to its junction with Offa's Dyke Path at the tiny church at Churchtown, an ideal spot for a picnic. Then walk north along Offa's Dyke Path to where it meets the Kerry Ridgeway and back along quiet lanes to Bishop's Castle. This 15-mile (24km) ramble allows you to experience the hidden countryside of the Border Country and shows you the Dyke at its best. See p165 in conjunction with Ordnance Survey map Explorer 216. Bishop's Castle is fairly well served by buses.

● **The Switchbacks** The 12-mile (19.5km) section of Dyke between Selley Cross near Knighton and Brompton Crossroads is characterised by a series of ascents and descents to navigate the hilly country known as The Switchbacks. It makes a challenging day walk and will involve a lift at the start, no local transport being available. The distance is made to feel longer by the constant ups and downs but the country is quintessential Welsh Borders, secretive, remote and populated just by cows, sheep and mewing buzzards. See pp146-71.

● **Llanymynech to Pool Quay/Buttington Bridge or v/v** Starting with a stretch of the Montgomery Canal, this 8-mile (13km) walk joins the River Severn where the path follows a man-made embankment to Pool Quay (see p187). You can extend this walk with $2^{1}/_{2}$ miles (4km) of canal walking to Buttington Bridge (see p185). Llanymynech (p190) and Buttington are served by buses (Mon-Sat); Welshpool (p182), a further $1^{1}/_{2}$ miles (2.5km) on from Buttington Bridge, has both rail and bus connections.

● **Llangollen to Trevor via the Panorama route, returning along the canal** A gentle 6-mile (9.5km) circular walk with varied scenery and much of interest along this bustling stretch of inland waterway. See pp201-8. There are good public transport links to both Llangollen and Trevor.

● **Llandegla to Clwyd Gate or v/v** A pleasant stroll through the meadows from the charming village of Llandegla (see p218) followed by fine hillwalking over the southern outliers of the Clwydian Hills make this 6-mile (9.5km) walk an excellent one with wide views of the Vale of Denbigh. There are bus services to Llandegla but not Clwyd Gate.

● **Clwyd Gate to Bodfari or v/v** A challenging high-level walk of 11 miles (18km) through the exposed Clwydian Hills with views on a fine day to Snowdonia and the sea (see pp223-30). There are bus services to Bodfari (Mon-Sat only) but not Clwyd Gate.

● **Prestatyn to Rhuallt** An exhilarating 8-mile (13km) walk over the escarpment with great views of the North Wales coast, Snowdonia and the Clwydian Range.

PLANNING YOUR WALK

❏ SUGGESTED ITINERARIES

The itineraries below are suggestions only and should be adapted to suit your own preferences. **Don't forget** to add the travelling time before and after the walk.

ITINERARY FOR STEADY WALKERS

Walking 9-14.5 miles (14.5-23.5km) a day with a longer day of 17.5 miles (28km)

Day	Daily schedule	Miles/km (approx)	Nearest accommodation
1/15*	Sedbury Cliffs ⟷ Bigsweir	11/18	Chepstow, Tintern, Bigsweir
2/14*	Bigsweir ⟷ Monmouth	9.5/15	Monmouth
3/13	Monmouth ⟷ Llangattock-Lingoed	14.5/23.5	Llangattock-Lingoed
4/12	Llangattock-Lingoed ⟷ Longt'n	13.5/22	Llanthony, Longtown
5/11	Longtown ⟷ Hay-on-Wye	12.5/20	Hay-on-Wye
6/10	Hay-on-Wye ⟷ Gladestry	10/16	Gladestry
7/9	Gladestry ⟷ Discoed	13/21	Presteigne, Discoed (*campsite*)
8/8	Discoed ⟷ Newcastle-on-Clun	12.5/20	Clun, Newcastle-on-Clun
9/7	Newcastle-on-Clun ⟷ Kingsw'd	13.5/22	Kingswood
10/6	Kingswood ⟷ Llanymynech	17.5/28	Four Crosses, Llanymynech
11/5	Llanymynech ⟷ around Baker's Hill	9/14.5	Around Baker's Hill (*campsite*) Oswestry
12/4	Around Baker's Hill ⟷ Dinas Bran	13/21	Llangollen
13/3	Dinas Bran ⟷ Clwyd Gate	14/22.5	Llanarmon-yn-Ial, Llanferres
14/2	Clwyd Gate ⟷ Bodfari	11/18	Llangynhafal, Bodfari
15/1	Bodfari ⟷ Prestatyn	12/19.5	Prestatyn

* **Note**: if you have less time these two (first or last) stages could be combined into a long 20.5-mile/33km day.

ITINERARY FOR FAST WALKERS

Walking 12-14.5 miles (19.5-23.5km) a day with four longer days of up to 17-20.5 miles (27-33km)

Day	Daily schedule	Miles/km	Nearest accommodation
1/12**	Sedbury Cliffs ⟷ Monmouth	20.5/33	Chepstow, Monmouth
2/11	Monmouth ⟷ Pandy	17/27	Pandy
3/10	Pandy ⟷ Hay-on-Wye	17.5/28	Hay-on-Wye
4/9	Hay-on-Wye ⟷ Kington	14.5/23.5	Kington
5/8	Kington ⟷ Knighton	13.5/22	Knighton
6/7	Knighton ⟷ Brompton C'roads	14.5/23.5	Brompton C'roads, Montgomery
7/6	Brompton C'roads ⟷ Buttington	12.5/20	Welshpool, Buttington
8/5	Buttington ⟷ Nant-Mawr	14.5/23.5	Llanymynech, Trefonen
9/4	Nant-Mawr ⟷ Around Irish Bridge	12.5/20	Around Irish Bridge, Bron-y-garth
10/3	Around Irish Bridge ⟷ Llandegla	12.5/20	Llanarmon-yn-Ial, Llanferres
11/2	Llandegla ⟷ Bodfari	17.5/28	Llangynhafal, Bodfari
12/1	Bodfari ⟷ Prestatyn	12/19.5	Prestatyn

**Note that this is a long, tough first day, particularly if you're carrying a heavy pack.

See p240. There are good public transport links to Prestatyn but not to Rhuallt. There is accommodation at Rhuallt so you could make this a two-day walk.

Weekend walks

● **Monmouth to Sedbury Cliffs** A stunning walk of 18 miles (29km) following the winding course of the Wye Valley as the river snakes its way to the sea. There are plenty of places for refreshment, a chance to visit the atmospheric ruins of Tintern Abbey and to explore the characterful towns of Chepstow and Monmouth, both of which are well served by public transport; services to Sedbury operate Monday to Friday only. The best overnight stop is St Briavels, which is 2km off the path. See p101.

● **Monmouth to Hay-on-Wye or v/v** This is a great weekend leg-stretcher of 34 miles (54.5km) with a day wending through the by-ways of the Welsh Marches, followed by high-level walking along the spine of the Black Mountains, with a night in Pandy. On the way you pass lovely villages, country inns and the splendid ruin of the once-mighty White Castle. Hay-on-Wye and Monmouth are served by buses but services to Hay-on-Wye are more limited. See pp106-32.

● **Pandy to Kington or v/v** An outstanding 32-mile (51.5km) outing in classic Dyke Country. Start by walking along the grand sweep of the Hatterrall Ridge, stop for the night in the fascinating book town of Hay-on-Wye, then continue along the magnificent Hergest Ridge the next day. See pp119-43. Both ends can be reached by bus.

● **Llangollen to Llanymynech or v/v** A 24-mile (39km) walk of great variety taking in the aqueduct at Pontcysyllte, Chirk Castle, the secretive Morda Valley and the minor summit of Moelydd, criss-crossed by mountain-bike trails. See pp192-209. You can stay the night at one of the B&Bs around Irish Bridge; both ends of the walk are served by buses.

● **Llandegla to Bodfari or v/v** A spectacular 16-mile (26km) traverse of the entire Clwydian Range broken into two easy days by staying overnight at Llanferres (2 miles off the trail, see p225). There are bus services at both ends.

What to take

How much you take with you is a very personal decision which takes experience to get right. For those new to long-distance walking the suggestions below will help you strike a balance between comfort, safety and minimal weight.

KEEP YOUR LUGGAGE LIGHT

In these days of huge material wealth it can be a liberating experience to travel as light as possible to learn how few possessions we really need to be safe and comfortable. It is all too easy to take things along 'just in case' and these little items can soon mount up. If you are in any doubt about anything on your packing list, be ruthless and leave it at home.

CARRYING YOUR LUGGAGE

*I'm facing the wind
And I'm ready to fly
Anywhere my heart takes me tonight
I'm traveling light.*
Tom Shapiro and George Teren,
Traveling Light

The size of your **rucksack** depends on how you plan to walk. If you are camping along the way you will need a pack large enough to hold a tent, sleeping bag, cooking equipment and food: 65 to 75 litres' capacity should be ample. The pack should have a stiffened back system and either be fully adjustable or exactly the right size for your back. If you carry the main part of the load high and close to your body with a large proportion of the weight carried on your hips (not on your shoulders) by means of the padded hip belt you should be able to walk in comfort for days on end. Play around with different ways of packing your gear and adjusting all those straps until you get it just right.

It's also handy to have a **bum/waist bag** or a very light **daypack** in which you can carry your camera, guidebook and other essentials when you go off sightseeing.

If you are staying in bunkhouses you may want to carry a sleeping bag for which a 40- to 60-litre pack should be fine. If you are indulging in the luxury of B&Bs you should be able to get all you need into a 30- to 40-litre pack. Pack similar things in different coloured **stuff sacks** or plastic bags so they are easier to pull out of the dark recesses of your pack. Put these inside **waterproof rucksack liners**, or tough plastic sacks, that can be slipped inside your pack to protect everything from the inevitable rain.

Of course, if you decide to use a **baggage-transfer service** (see p25) you can pack most of your things in a suitcase and simply carry a small daypack with the essentials you need for the day's walking.

FOOTWEAR

Boots

Your boots are the single most important item of gear that can affect the enjoyment of your walk. In summer you could get by with a light pair of trail shoes if you're carrying only a small pack, although this is an invitation for wet, cold feet if there is any rain and they don't offer much support for your ankles. Some of the terrain is rough so a good pair of walking boots would be a safer option. They must fit well and be properly broken in. A week's walk is not the time to try out a new pair of boots. Refer to p80 for blister-avoidance strategies. If you plan to travel in spring, autumn or winter, good boots are essential. Fabric boots, unless with a layer of Gore-Tex or something similar, will soon become saturated and so will your socks unless you use Gore-Tex socks.

Socks

The traditional wearing of a thin liner sock under a thicker wool sock is no longer necessary if you choose a high-quality sock specially designed for walking. A high proportion of natural fibres makes them much more comfortable. If you're taking fabric boots, Gore-Tex socks will keep your feet completely dry. Whatever you take, three pairs of socks will be ample.

Extra footwear
Some walkers like to have a second pair of shoes to wear when not on the trail. Trainers, sport sandals or flip flops are all suitable as long as they are light.

CLOTHES

Wet and cold weather can catch you out even in summer and you should come prepared for the unexpected. Spring and autumn can also be glorious at times so clothes to cope with these wide variations are needed. Experienced walkers pick their clothes according to the versatile layering system: a base layer to transport sweat away from your skin; a mid layer or two to keep you warm; and an outer layer or 'shell' to protect you from the wind, rain and, at the worst, snow.

Base layer
Cotton absorbs sweat, trapping it next to the skin which will chill you rapidly when you stop exercising. A thin lightweight **thermal top** made from synthetic material is better as it draws moisture away, keeping you dry. It will be cool if worn on its own in hot weather and warm when worn under other clothes in cooler conditions. A spare would be sensible. You may also like to bring a **shirt** for wearing in the evening.

Mid layers
From May to September a woollen jumper or mid-weight polyester **fleece** will suffice. For the rest of the year you will need an extra layer to keep you warm. Both wool and fleece, unlike cotton, stay reasonably warm when wet.

Outer layer
A **waterproof jacket** is essential year-round and will be much more comfortable (but also more expensive) if it's also 'breathable' to prevent the build-up of condensation on the inside. This layer can also be worn to keep the wind off.

Leg wear
Whatever you wear on your legs it should be light, quick-drying and not restricting. Many British walkers find polyester tracksuit bottoms comfortable. Poly-cotton or microfibre trousers are excellent. Denim jeans should never be worn; if they get wet they become heavy, cold and bind to your legs. A pair of **shorts** should be carried for sunny days. Thermal **longjohns** or thick tights are cosy if you're camping and necessary for winter walking. **Waterproof trousers** are necessary most of the year but in summer could be left behind if your main

---

❏ **Outdoor clothing – cheaper alternatives**

Modern, synthetic outdoor clothing is light and quick-drying but doesn't come cheap. If you are new to walking and feel the expense of equipping yourself properly is prohibitive then of course you can get by with 'normal' cotton clothing under a good waterproof layer, especially in summer. However, if this is the case, you must carry a complete spare set of clothes that you should always keep dry. If this means pulling on the damp clothes you wore the day before do so.

pair of trousers is reasonably windproof and quick-drying. **Gaiters** are not essential but in very wet and muddy conditions can protect your boots and socks.

Underwear
Three changes of what you normally wear should suffice. Women may find a **sports bra** more comfortable because pack straps can cause bra straps to dig into your shoulders.

Other clothes
A **warm hat** and **gloves** should be carried at any time of the year. Take two pairs of gloves in winter. In summer you should carry a **sunhat** and possibly a **swimsuit**; there are a few swimming pools along the route which can be nice at the end of a hot day. A small **towel** will be needed if you are not staying in B&Bs.

TOILETRIES

Only take the minimum: a small bar of **soap** (unless staying in B&Bs) which can also be used instead of shaving cream and for washing clothes; a tiny tube of **toothpaste** and a **toothbrush**; one roll of **loo (toilet) paper** in a plastic bag. If you are planning to defecate outdoors you will also need a lightweight **trowel** for burying the evidence (see pp76-7 for further tips). A **razor**, **deodorant**, **tampons/sanitary towels** and a high-factor **sunscreen** should cover all your needs.

FIRST-AID KIT

Medical facilities in Britain are excellent so you only need a small kit to cover common problems and emergencies; pack it in a waterproof container. A basic kit will contain **aspirin** or **paracetamol** for treating mild to moderate pain and fever; **plasters/Band Aids** for minor cuts; '**moleskin**', **Compeed**, or **Second Skin** for blisters; a **bandage** for holding dressings, splints, or limbs in place and for supporting a sprained ankle; **elastic knee support** for a weak knee; a small selection of different-sized **sterile dressings** for wounds; **porous adhesive tape**; **antiseptic wipes**; **antiseptic cream**; **safety pins**; **tweezers**; and **scissors**.

GENERAL ITEMS

Essential
A **compass** should be carried, but it will be of no benefit to you without some familiarity with its use. You won't need it constantly but on the occasions when you do it can be invaluable, especially in poor visibility. A **GPS** (see pp18-19) could also be useful in an emergency, but not as an alternative to a compass: batteries have been known to fail at the crucial moment. An emergency **whistle** for summoning assistance; a one- or two-litre **water bottle or pouch**; a **torch** (flashlight) with spare bulb and batteries in case you end up walking after it's got dark; **emergency food** which your body can quickly convert into energy (see p820); a **penknife**; a **watch** with an alarm; and several **bags** for packing out any rubbish you accumulate (see pp75-6 for further information). If you're not carrying a sleeping bag or tent you should also carry an emergency plastic **bivvy-bag**.

PLANNING YOUR WALK

Useful

Many would list a **camera** as essential but it can be liberating to travel without one once in a while (and with most people carrying a smart phone with a built-in camera it's not as vital a piece of kit as it once was); a **notebook** can be a more accurate way of recording your impressions; a **book** to pass the time on train and bus journeys, or in the evening; a pair of **sunglasses**, particularly in summer; **binoculars** for observing wildlife; a **walking stick** or pole to take the shock off your knees (some walkers use two poles but this leaves no free hand); a **vacuum flask** for carrying hot drinks – your B&B host will probably be happy to fill it for you; and a **mobile (cell) phone** (see box below) and charger.

SLEEPING BAG

Unless you are camping there is no need to carry a sleeping bag. Hostels provide linen and do not allow you to use sleeping bags. Bunkhouses vary in their policy, some requiring you to bring your own bag, others providing bedding. If you intend to stay in them it would be worth phoning to check whether a sleeping bag is necessary or whether you could hire bedding for the night.

CAMPING GEAR

If you're camping you will need a decent **tent** (or bivvy bag if you enjoy travelling light) able to withstand wet and windy weather; a two- or three-season **sleeping bag**; a **sleeping mat**; a **stove** and **fuel** (there is special mention in Part 4 of which shops stock which fuel; bottles of meths and the various gas cylinders are readily available, Coleman fuel is sometimes harder to find); a **pan** with a lid that can double as a frying pan/plate is fine for two people; a **pan handle**; a **mug**; **cutlery**; and a wire/plastic **scrubber** for washing up.

MONEY

[See also p25] There are numerous banks in the towns along the path but you'll need to have an adequate supply of ready **cash**. A **debit card** is the easiest way to draw money either from banks, post offices or cash machines and can be used

---

❏ **Mobile phone network problems**

Many walkers carry **mobile phones** but it is important to remember that the network may not provide full coverage of the area through which you are walking due to the terrain. Mid Wales is poorly served by the networks and it is quite likely that you will be unable to make your call. Take the mobile by all means but don't rely on it.

Nor can you really rely on **phone boxes**, which have all but disappeared from the trail now, though you can still find the odd one en route and in towns, in case you have no signal at the crucial moment. Make sure that you always have 60p (the minimum needed for a call from a phone box; thereafter 10p a unit and no change is given). However, all BT public phones accept debit/credit cards.

While calls to the emergency services (☎ 999 or ☎ 112) are free of charge, it's an urgent call to book a night's accommodation that could catch you out.

to pay in larger shops, restaurants and hotels. It's also the ideal means of paying in supermarkets, which usually provide a **cashback** facility. A **cheque book** is useful for those with British bank accounts as a cheque will often be accepted where a card is not, particularly in B&Bs. However, note that supermarkets and many other retailers no longer accept cheques.

MAPS

The hand-drawn maps in this book cover the trail at a scale of 1:20,000; plenty of detail and information to keep you on the right track. The overview maps at the end of the book help to give you the wider picture.

Ordnance Survey (OS; 🖳 ordnancesurvey.co.uk) cover the whole route at a scale of 1:25,000 on the following seven maps: Explorer series (the ones with the orange cover) Nos 265, 256, 240, 216, 201, and Outdoor Leisure series (also orange, but double sided) OL13 and OL14. Not all of these are strictly necessary if you pay careful attention to the maps in this guide. This will come as a relief as all seven weigh about 2lb (1kg) and are expensive at £8.99 each. For the sake of safety you should carry the maps of the Clwydian Range (Explorer 265 and 256) and Brecon Beacons National Park (OL13) as the path crosses rugged and hilly terrain where visibility could be restricted. In such conditions

PLANNING YOUR WALK

❏ **Digital mapping**
Most modern smartphones have a GPS chip so you will be able to see your position overlaid onto the digital map on your phone. Almost every device with built-in GPS functionality now has some mapping software available for it. If you want a dedicated GPS unit, Garmin are the best known and have devices from £100.

There are numerous software packages now available that provide Ordnance Survey (OS) maps for a PC, smartphone, tablet or GPS. Maps are supplied by direct download over the Internet. The maps are then loaded into an application, also available by download, from where you can view them, print them and create routes on them. Alternatively, you could just get an annual subscription allowing use of all OS mapping.

Memory Map (🖳 memory-map.co.uk) currently sell OS 1:25,000 mapping covering the whole of Britain for £75.

Anquet (🖳 anquet.com) has the Offa's Dyke Path available for £25.85 using OS 1:25,000 mapping but they also offer subscriptions to all their mapping including OS 1:25,000 maps from £24 per year.

For a subscription of from £2.99 for one month or £19.99 for a year (on their current offer) **Ordnance Survey** (🖳 ordnancesurvey.co.uk) will let you download and then use their UK maps (1:25,000 scale) on a mobile or tablet without a data connection for a specific period.

Harvey (🖳 harveymaps.co.uk) sell their Offa's Dyke map (1:40,000 scale) as a download for £20.49 for use on any device.

Smartphones and GPS devices should complement, not replace, the traditional method of navigation (a map and compass) as any electronic device can break or, if nothing else, run out of battery. Remember that the battery life of your phone will be significantly reduced, compared to normal usage, when you are using the built-in GPS and running the screen for long periods.

❑ SOURCES OF FURTHER INFORMATION

Trail information

● **The National Trail website** (🖥 nationaltrail.co.uk/offasdyke) The official website for the trail with ideas on planning your trip (south to north) and a news page giving up-to-date information on any works or diversions on the trail. They also have Facebook and Twitter pages.

● **Offa's Dyke Association** (🖥 offasdyke.org.uk; West St, Knighton, Powys) This independent, voluntary organisation looks after the interests of walkers on the Offa's Dyke Path and maintains an excellent website.

Full membership, at £20 a year (£25 for a family), includes copies of their quarterly newsletter and an annual accommodation guide, and entitles the member to a 10% discount off anything bought from the association including maps. They are based at the tourist information centre in Knighton (see p158) and are unfailingly helpful and informative about every aspect of the path.

Tourist information

Tourist information centres (TICs) provide all manner of locally specific information for visitors. Some offer an accommodation-booking service (for which there is usually a £2 fee and 10% of the accommodation cost is taken as a deposit though this is deducted from the final bill) and also sell tickets for National Express coaches.

There are TICs on or near the path in: **Chepstow** (see p87), **Monmouth** (see p104), **Hay-on-Wye** (see p132), **Kington** (see p145), **Presteigne** (see p156), **Knighton** (see p158), **Bishop's Castle** (see p165), **Welshpool** (see p181) and **Llangollen** (see p209).

Tourist information points (TIPs) have leaflets but are generally not staffed; there is a TIP at **Clun** (see p164) and at **Prestatyn** (p235).

Tourist boards

The tourist boards produce glossy brochures on their region and can be a good source for general information. The relevant one for this area is the **Wales Tourist Board** (🖥 visitwales.com).

Organisations for walkers

● **Backpackers Club** (🖥 backpackersclub.co.uk) For people interested in lightweight camping. Members receive a quarterly magazine, access to a comprehensive information service (including a library), discounts on maps (see opposite) and a farm-pitch directory. Membership costs £15 per year, family £20, under 18s and retired individuals £8.50 (£12 for retired couples).

● **The Long Distance Walkers' Association** (🖥 ldwa.org.uk) An association of people with the common interest of long-distance walking. Membership includes a journal, *Strider*, three times per year giving details of challenge events and local group walks as well as articles on the subject. Information on over 730 paths is presented in their *UK Trailwalkers' Handbook*. Individual membership costs £18 per calendar year whilst family membership for two adults and all children under 18 is £25 a year. If you join on or after October 1st your membership will be valid for the following calender year.

● **Ramblers** (formerly Ramblers Association; 🖥 ramblers.org.uk) Looks after the interests of walkers throughout Britain. They publish a large amount of useful information including their quarterly *Walk* magazine (also available to non-members from newsagents etc). Membership costs £35.85/47.85 individual/joint and £23/30.75 individual/joint concessionary.

a map from which you can take compass bearings is essential. Enthusiastic map buyers can reduce the often considerable expense of purchasing them if they are a member of the **Backpackers' Club** (see box opposite) as they can buy maps at a significant discount through their map service. Alternatively, members of **Ramblers** (see box opposite) can borrow up to 10 maps for free, apart from the return postage cost. Public libraries in Britain often have OS maps and they can be borrowed for free by members.

Alternatively, OS now offers a **custom-made map service** where you choose the centre of the map and pick the scale and format and they print it up. You can even design the cover. While this service costs double the price of their standard maps, by carefully selecting where you centre your map you may find you can actually save money as you'll require fewer maps to cover the whole of your trek.

An option if you just wish to be able to see the path in an OS format but are not too concerned about what you can see a mile away is **AZ Adventure's** (🖵 az.co.uk; £8.95) *Offa's Dyke Path* booklet, which contains the whole path highlighted on OS maps to a 1:25,000 scale and an index.

RECOMMENDED READING

General guidebooks
There's the comprehensive *Wales: The Rough Guide;* Lonely Planet's *Wales* is also good.

Flora and fauna field guides
Any good guide will do; the range of field guides published by Collins is unfailingly practical.
● *Collins Bird Guide* by Lars Svensson (Collins, 2010)
● *British Wild Flowers (Collins Complete Guide)* by Paul Sterry (Collins, 2008) or *Collins Flower Guide (Britain and Ireland)* by David Streeter, Christina Hart-Davies, Audrey Hardcastle, Felicity Cole and Lizzie Harper (Collins 2010)
● *Insects of Britain and Western Europe* by Michael Chinery (A & C Black, 2012)
● *The Mammals of Britain and Europe* by David Macdonald and Priscilla Barrett (Collins, 2005)
● *Collins Field Guide – Trees of Britain and Northern Europe* by Alan Mitchell et al (Collins, 2001), or *Collins Tree Guide* by Owen Johnson (Collins 2006).

There are also several field guide **apps** for smartphones and tablets, including those that can aid in identifying birds by their song as well as by their appearance. One to consider is: 🖵 merlin.allaboutbirds.org.

History of Offa's Dyke
● *The Archaeology of the Welsh Marches* by S C Stanford (Collins, 1991)
● *Lordship and Military Obligation in Anglo Saxon England* by Richard P Abels (British Museum Publications, 1988)
● *Mercia: The Anglo-Saxon Kingdom of Central England* by Sarah Zaluckyj (Logaston Press, 2011)

PLANNING YOUR WALK

● *Offa's Dyke* by Sir Cyril Fox, British Academy (Oxford University Press, 1955). Written by the pioneering researcher into Offa's Dyke in the early 20th century.
● *Offa's Dyke – History and Guide* by David Hill and Margaret Worthington (Tempus, 2003). The must-read guide to research into the Dyke's history.
● *Offa's Dyke Reviewed* by Frank Noble, B A R British Series 114 (Oxford, 1983).

General reading

● *Offa's Dyke: A Journey in Words and Pictures* by Jim Saunders (Gomer Press, 2006) Written and photographed by a former trail officer of the Offa's Dyke Path.
● *Wild Wales* by George Borrow (Bridge Books, 2009) Quirky, opinionated yet irrepressible account of the author's visit to Wales in the mid-19th century. Not much about the areas you pass through though.
● *Kilvert's Diary* edited by William Plomer (Vintage Classics, 2012) Lovely man, curate of Clyro Church near Hay-on-Wye in the Victorian era. Well worth dipping into.
● *On the Black Hill* by Bruce Chatwin (Vintage Classics, 1998) Atmospheric, gives a good idea of what it was like to be a Welsh hill farmer after WWII.
● *Welsh Border Country* by Maxwell Fraser (Batsford, 1972) Sadly no longer in print but worth hunting for if you want a taste of this beautiful, secret area.
● *A History of Wales* by John Davies (Penguin, 2007) The best book on Welsh history from the Ice Age to the present. Honest, objective and packed with detail.
● *The Ladies of Llangollen – A Study in Romantic Friendship* by Elizabeth Mavor (Penguin, 2011) Intriguing account of the unconventional lives of the two devoted friends who set up home in Plas Newydd, attracting the greatest figures of the early 19th century to their door.
● *The Keys to Avalon – The True Location of Arthur's Kingdom Revealed* by Steve Blake and Scott Lloyd (Element, 2000) If you thought Avalon was in Cornwall or Glastonbury, here's another theory: Arthur was Welsh! This closely argued account also suggests the Romans built the Dyke; another of those ideas akin to spacemen building Stonehenge.
● *The Making of the English Landscape* by WG Hoskins (Little Toller Books, 2013) A classic work on how our countryside came to be as it is today and a provocative and eye-opening account which suggests that every change we have made to it has been for the worse.
● *Journey through Britain* by John Hillaby (Constable, 1968) The author's classic account of his walk from Land's End to John O'Groats in 1968. Some parts of Offa's Dyke are described.
● The Brother Cadfael books by Ellis Peters are a fictional account of a monk/sleuth who solves medieval mysteries in and around the abbey of Shrewsbury. You either love them or hate them but they are a good read, true to their time and place and specific to the area. Try *The First Cadfael Omnibus* (Sphere Paperbacks, 1990).

PLANNING YOUR WALK

Poetry

The poets that have relevance for visitors to the Border Country and North and South Wales include RS Thomas, AE Housman, John Ceiriog Hughes and Gerard Manley Hopkins, all of whose works will be found in anthologies. In Hay-on-Wye the works of these poets can be found in Poetry Bookshop (see p132).

Getting to and from the Offa's Dyke Path

Both Chepstow and Prestatyn, at each end of the trail, are easily reached by train, bus, National Express coach or car. In addition, several of the towns along the trail are also on the rail and coach networks. Where towns are not directly served by train or coach there will almost always be local buses to link you to the rail network. This makes getting to any of the major points along the Offa's Dyke Path by public transport relatively straightforward and this should always be the preferred mode of travel for walkers keen to put as much back into the countryside as they take out.

❏ **Getting to Britain**
● **By air** Most international airlines serve London Heathrow (🖥 heathrow.com) and London Gatwick (🖥 gatwickairport.com). A number of budget airlines fly from many of Europe's major cities to the other London terminals at Stansted (🖥 stanstedairport.com) and Luton (🖥 london-luton.co.uk).
　　There are also flights from Europe to Bristol (🖥 bristolairport.co.uk), Cardiff (🖥 cardiff-airport.com) and Birmingham (🖥 birminghamairport.co.uk), which are closer to the Offa's Dyke Path than London. For details of airlines and destinations served visit the website for the relevant airport.
● **From Europe by train** Eurostar (🖥 eurostar.com) operates a high-speed passenger service via the Channel Tunnel between Paris, Brussels, Amsterdam (and some other cities) and London. In London trains arrive and depart from St Pancras International. St Pancras has connections to the London Underground and to all other main railway stations in London. For more information about rail services from Europe contact your national rail operator, or Railteam (🖥 railteam.eu).
● **From Europe by coach** Eurolines (🖥 eurolines.eu) works with a huge network of long-distance coach operators connecting many cities in mainland Europe with London, where it links in with the British National Express network (see box p50). Flixbus (formerly Megabus; 🖥 flixbus.com) also provides services from destinations in mainland Europe to London.
● **From Europe by ferry (with or without a car)** Numerous ferry companies operate routes between the major North Sea and Channel ports of mainland Europe and the ports on Britain's eastern and southern coasts as well as from Ireland to both Wales and England. A useful website for further information is 🖥 directferries.com.
● **From Europe by car** Eurotunnel (🖥 eurotunnel.com) operates a shuttle train service for vehicles via the Channel Tunnel between Calais and Folkestone, taking one hour between the motorway in France and the motorway in Britain.

NATIONAL TRANSPORT

By rail
There are seven principal rail routes along the length of the walk with the towns on or close to the path highlighted. The most convenient stations are: Prestatyn; Chirk, which is two miles from Castle Mill or on a regular bus route to Llangollen; Welshpool, which is about 1¹/₂ miles off the route; Knighton; Abergavenny, which is six miles from Pandy; and Chepstow.

National Rail Enquiries (☎ 08457-484950, 🖳 nationalrail.co.uk) provides all timetable and fare information. Fares vary widely, but significant savings can be made by booking well in advance. You can purchase tickets: at railway stations in the UK, or by phone or online through the relevant company, or online through 🖳 thetrainline.com or 🖳 qjump.co.uk.

For details of the main operators and general frequency of service see the public transport services box, opposite.

By coach
National Express (see box p50) is the principal long-distance coach operator in Britain. Services of use to Offa's Dyke walkers include those to Prestatyn, Welshpool, Monmouth, and Chepstow. Travel by coach is usually cheaper than train but takes rather longer. As for travel by train the best fares are those bought at least a week in advance.

Megabus (🖳 uk.megabus.com) has services to Cardiff and Newport.

By car
Prestatyn has quick links to the motorway network via the A548 to the M56. Likewise Chepstow is just off the M48. Using the car is the most flexible way to travel but there are some notable problems. The first is how to get back to your car at the end of your walk. Unless you can arrange to leave a car at either end you will have to use a combination of public transport and taxis which can be a logistical nightmare.

The second problem is where to park the car safely while you are on the trail. Some B&Bs have sufficient space to let you park for the duration of your walk, usually without charge provided that you stay with them for a night or two. Public car parks are not usually geared for long-stay parking. The only other option is to park on the road but this means taking a security risk and is not recommended.

It may be easier after all, to leave the car at home and use public transport. You can then sit back and congratulate yourself on supporting local rural services and helping the environment.

LOCAL TRANSPORT

The maps on pp52-3 give an overview of the most useful bus and train routes for walkers; for contact details and the approximate frequency of services, see the public transport services box opposite and overleaf. The latest information on public transport can also be obtained from the national public transport information line, **traveline** (☎ 0871-200 2233, ⌨ traveline.info). Timetables can also be picked up at tourist information centres along the trail. A useful website for travelling along Offa's Dyke Path is ⌨ www.traveline.cymru; you will find an app available too.

The nature of the Border Country is such that bus services tend to be rather fragmented with different operators establishing routes on their own patch as local demand, particularly school bus services and shopping needs, dictates. Both timetables and operators, especially in rural areas, tend to change at short notice, and summer and winter services can vary quite considerably. Do check ahead to make sure that the service you want is running.

In rural areas many services operate on a hail and ride basis – the driver will stop to pick up or drop off as long as it is safe to do so.

❑ **PUBLIC TRANSPORT SERVICES – see maps on p52-3**

Train services (note: not all stops are listed and only direct services are included)
Transport for Wales (TfW; ⌨ tfw.gov.wales)
● Manchester to Llandudno Junction/Llandudno via Chester, **Prestatyn** & Rhyl, Mon-Fri 8/day, Sat 12/day, Sun 7/day
● Birmingham to Holyhead via Wolverhampton, Shrewsbury, Gobowen, Chirk, Ruabon, Wrexham & Chester, Mon-Sat 7/day, Sun 5/day
● Cardiff to Holyhead via Shrewsbury, Gobowen, Chirk, Ruabon, Wrexham & Chester, Mon-Sat 6/day, Sun 3/day
● Manchester Piccadilly to Milford Haven/Aberdaugleddau via Crewe, Shrewsbury, Ludlow, Leominster, Hereford, Abergavenny, Newport, Cardiff, Swansea & Carmarthen (some services continue to Milford Haven), Mon-Fri 1/hr, Sun 3/day
● Holyhead/Bangor to Swansea via Llandudno Junction, Chester, Wrexham, Shrewsbury, Craven Arms, Ludlow, Hereford, Abergavenny, Newport & Cardiff, Mon-Sat 6/day
● Birmingham to Aberystwyth via Shrewsbury & **Welshpool**, Mon-Sat 8/day, Sun 6/day
● Shrewsbury to Swansea via Craven Arms, **Knighton**, Llandrindod, Builth Road & Llanelli, Mon-Sat 4/day, Sun 2/day
● Cardiff to Cheltenham Spa via Newport, **Chepstow** & Gloucester, Mon-Sat 1-2/hr, Sun 5/day (some services continue to Birmingham)

Cross Country Trains (⌨ crosscountrytrains.co.uk)
● Nottingham to Cardiff via Derby, Birmingham, Cheltenham Spa, Gloucester, **Chepstow** (Mon-Sat only) & Newport, Mon-Sat approx 1/hr, Sun 8/day

GWR (⌨ gwr.com)
● London Paddington to Swansea via Swindon & Newport, Mon-Sat 1/hr, Sun 8/day
● London Paddington to Hereford via Reading, & Didcot Parkway, 4-5/day

London Northwestern Railway (⌨ londonnorthwesternrailway.co.uk)
● London Euston to Birmingham New St, Mon-Sat 2/hr, Sun 1/hr

Virgin (⌨ virgintrains.co.uk)
● London to Holyhead via Crewe, Chester, **Prestatyn**, Rhyl & Bangor, 3-4/day
● London to Wolverhampton, daily 1/hr (2/day continue to Shrewsbury)

(cont'd on p50)

PLANNING YOUR WALK

PUBLIC TRANSPORT SERVICES – see maps on p52-3 *(cont'd from p49)*

Train services (note: not all stops are listed and only direct services are included)
West Midlands Railway (⌨ westmidlandsrailway.co.uk)
● Birmingham New Street to Hereford, Mon-Sat 1/hr, Sun 6/day
● Birmingham to Shrewsbury, Mon-Sat 1/hr (see Transport for Wales for Sunday service)

Coach services
National Express (⌨ www.nationalexpress.com)
Note: only direct services are shown and not all stops are listed.
NX201 Brighton to Swansea via Gatwick Airport, Heathrow Airport, Reading & Chepstow, 1/day year-round plus up to 4/day
NX343 Birmingham to Cardiff via **Monmouth**, 1/day
NX375 Great Yarmouth to Bangor via Birmingham, Liverpool & **Prestatyn**, 1/day
NX409 London to Aberystwyth via Birmingham, Shrewsbury & **Welshpool**, 1/day
NX507 London to Swansea via **Chepstow** & Cardiff, 2/day
NX509 London to Cardiff via **Chepstow**, 1-2/day plus 5/day via Newport

Bus services
Note: not all stops are listed.

Arriva Bus (⌨ arrivabus.co.uk)
2   Wrexham to Oswestry via Ruabon, Chirk & Gobowen, daily 1/hr
2A   Wrexham to Oswestry via Ruabon & Chirk, Mon-Sat 1/hr
5   (Wrexham Express) Wrexham to Llangollen via Ruabon, Mon-Sat 2/hr
5E   Wrexham to Llangollen, Sun 5/day
11/11A Chester to Holywell, Mon-Sat (11) 2/hr, Sun (11A) 8/day
11G/11M Holywell to Rhyl via **Prestatyn**, Mon-Sat 2/hr, Sun 8/day
35 & 36 Rhyl to **Prestatyn** circular route, Mon-Sat 2/hr, Sun 7-8/day
            (the two services follow the same route but in the opposite direction)
51/51B Rhyl to Denbigh, Mon-Sat 3/hr, Sun 1/hr
X51   Wrexham to Denbigh via **Llandegla** & Ruthin, Mon-Sat 1/hr, Sun 4/day
740   Knighton to Ludlow, Mon-Sat 4/day

Celtic Travel (☎ 01686-412231, ⌨ celtic-travel.co.uk)
X75 Llanidloes to Shrewsbury via Newtown, Welshpool & **Buttington**, Mon-Sat 6/day

First (⌨ firstgroup.com)
7XP (Severn Express) Bristol to Newport via **Chepstow**, Mon-Sat 10/day
Bristol to **Chepstow** Sun 5/day (Severn Express)

James Bevan Coaches (☎ 01594-842859, ⌨ jamesbevancoaches.com)
761 **Chepstow** to Beachley via **Sedbury**, Mon-Sat 4-5/day

Lloyds Coaches (☎ 01654-702100, ⌨ lloydscoaches.com)
T3 Wrexham to Barmouth via Ruabon, **Trevor** & Llangollen, Mon-Sat 9/day, Sun 4/day
T12 Machynlleth to Wrexham via Newtown, Montgomery, **Forden**, **Kingswood**, Welshpool, **Four Crosses**, **Llanymynech**, Morda, Oswestry & Chirk, Mon-Sat 2/day (see Tanat Valley for additional services)

M&H Coaches (☎ 01745-730700, 🖥 mandhcoaches.co.uk)
1/X1 Mold to Ruthin via Llanferres & Llanarmon-yn-Ial,
     Mon-Sat 5-6/day (2/day start in Chester)
2 Mold to Ruthin via Llanarmon-yn-Ial, Mon-Sat 3-4/day

Minsterley Motors (☎ 01743-791208, 🖥 minsterleymotors.co.uk)
552/553 Shrewsbury to Bishop's Castle, Mon-Fri 6/day, Sat 4/day

Monmouthshire County Council (MCC; 🖥 monmouthshire.gov.uk)
65 **Chepstow** to **Monmouth** via Trellech, Mon-Fri 6/day, Sat 4/day

Newport Bus (☎ 01633-263600, 🖥 newportbus.co.uk)
60 **Monmouth** to Newport, Mon-Fri 7-8/day, Sat 6/day, Sun 2/day
73 Newport to **Chepstow** via Langstone, Mon-Fri 13/day, Sat 10/day
X74 Newport to **Chepstow** via Caldicot, Mon-Sat approx 1/hr
     (see Stagecoach for Sun service)

P&O Lloyd (☎ 01352-710682, 🖥 polloydcoaches.co.uk)
14 Mold to Denbigh via **Bodfari**, Mon-Sat 5/day

Phil Anslow (☎ 01495-775599, 🖥 philanslowcoaches.co.uk)
69 **Chepstow** to **Monmouth** via Tintern & Redbrook,
     Mon-Fri approx 1/hr, Sat 6/day

Sargeants (☎ 01544-230481, 🖥 sargeantsbros.com)
41 Kington to Knighton via Presteigne, Mon-Sat 5-6/day
461/462 Llandrindod Wells to **Kington** via Evenjobb, Mon-Sat 10-11/day
       Kington to Hereford, Mon-Sat 10-11/day

Stagecoach (🖥 stagecoachbus.com)
36 Hereford to **Monmouth**, Mon-Sat 6/day
     (connects with 34 Monmouth to Ross-on-Wye)
74 Newport to **Chepstow** via Caldicot, Sun 6/day (see Newport Bus for Mon-Sat)
83 **Monmouth** to Abergavenny, Mon-Sat 6/day, Sun 3/day
T14 Hereford to Cardiff via **Hay-on-Wye**, Clyro, Brecon & Merthyr Tydfil,
     Mon-Fri 3/day plus 2-3/day to Brecon and 1/day to Merthyr Tydfil,
     Sat 3/day plus to Brecon and 1/day to Merthyr Tydfil
X3 Hereford to Cardiff via **Pandy** & Abergavenny,
     Mon-Sat 5/day plus 4/day Abergavenny to Cardiff

Tanat Valley Coaches (☎ 01691-780212, 🖥 tanat.co.uk)
64 Llangollen to Llanarmon Dyffryn Ceiriog (aka Llanarmon DC) via
     Froncysyllte, Chirk & Glyn Ceiriog, Mon-Sat 3/day plus 2/day to Glyn
     Ceiriog
72 Oswestry to Llanfyllin via **Llanymynech**, Mon-Sat 2/day
74 Llanfyllin to Shrewsbury via **Llanymynech** & **Four Crosses**, Mon-Sat 2/day
79A Llangynog to Oswestry via **Trefonen** & Morda, Mon-Sat 1-2/day
558 Shrewsbury to **Montgomery**, Mon-Sat 4/day
T12 Machynlleth to Wrexham via Newtown, Montgomery, **Forden**, **Kingswood**,
     Welshpool, **Four Crosses**, **Llanymynech**, Morda, Oswestry & Chirk,
     Mon-Sat 2/day (see Lloyds Coaches for additional services)

Yeoman Travel (🖥 hayhobus.org.uk)
39A/Hay Ho! Hereford to **Hay-on-Wye**, Sun & Bank Hols Mon 3/day

PLANNING YOUR WALK

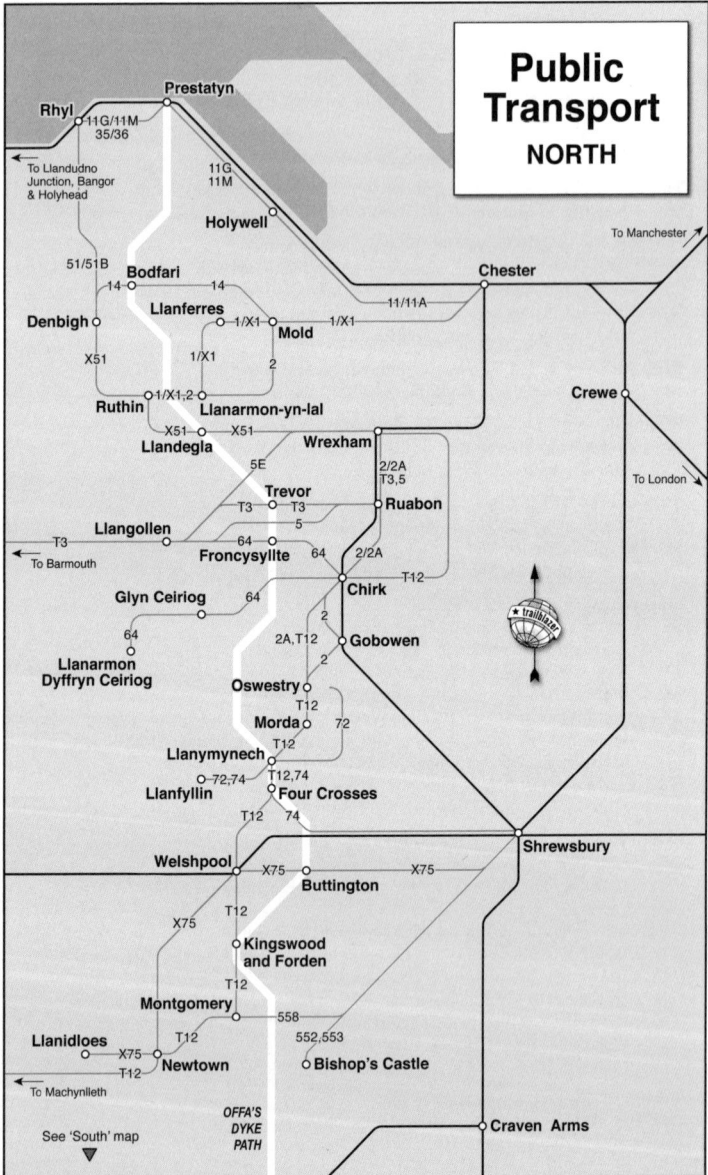

Public Transport NORTH

Rhyl 11G/11M 35/36
Prestatyn

To Llandudno Junction, Bangor & Holyhead

11G 11M

Holywell

To Manchester

51/51B
Bodfari 14
14
Llanferres
1/X1
Mold
1/X1
Chester
11/11A

Denbigh

X51
1/X1
2

Crewe

Ruthin 1/X1,2
Llanarmon-yn-Ial

To London

X51 X51
Llandegla
Wrexham

5E
2/2A T3,5
Trevor
T3 T3
Ruabon

Llangollen
5
T3
64
2/2A

To Barmouth
64
Froncysyllte
Chirk
T12

Glyn Ceiriog 64
2

Llanarmon Dyffryn Ceiriog
64
2A,T12
Gobowen
2

Oswestry
T12

Morda 72
T12

Llanymynech
72,74
T12,74
Four Crosses
74

Llanfyllin
T12
74

Welshpool X75
Buttington
X75
Shrewsbury

X75
T12

Kingswood and Forden
T12

Montgomery
558
552,553

Llanidloes X75
T12
Newtown
Bishop's Castle

To Machynlleth

See 'South' map ▽

OFFA'S DYKE PATH

Craven Arms

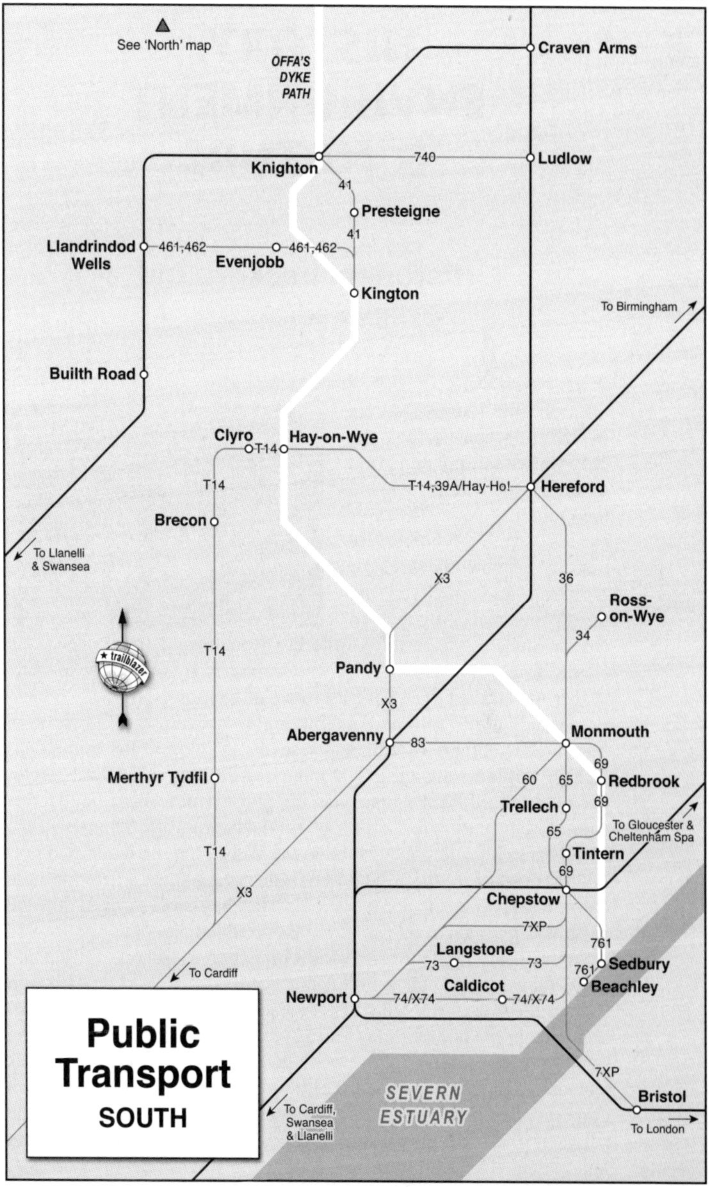

PLANNING YOUR WALK

Public Transport SOUTH

Craven Arms

OFFA'S DYKE PATH

See 'North' map

Knighton — 740 — Ludlow

41

Presteigne

Llandrindod Wells — 461,462 — Evenjobb — 461,462

41

Kington

To Birmingham

Builth Road

Clyro — T14 — Hay-on-Wye

T14,39A/Hay Ho! — Hereford

T14

Brecon

X3

36

Ross-on-Wye

34

T14

Pandy

X3

Abergavenny — 83 — Monmouth

69

60 65 Redbrook

Merthyr Tydfil

Trellech 69

65 To Gloucester & Cheltenham Spa

Tintern

T14

69

X3

Chepstow

7XP

Langstone 761

73 73 Sedbury

Caldicot 761 Beachley

To Cardiff

Newport — 74/X74 — 74/X74

SEVERN ESTUARY

7XP

To Cardiff, Swansea & Llanelli

Bristol

To London

To Llanelli & Swansea

To Cardiff

HISTORY, ENVIRONMENT & NATURE

Historical background

Colin Vickerman

Who was Offa?

Offa became king of Mercia in 757AD, when he took the crown after a turbulent period of civil war, which included the murder of his predecessor by his own bodyguard. He rose to become the greatest monarch and ruler of the most powerful kingdom in

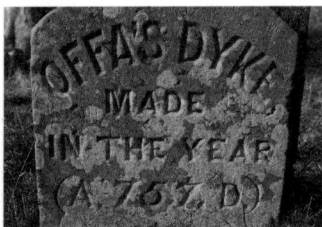

Britain since the departure of the last Roman soldiers in 406AD. Of all the Anglo-Saxon kings, he was surpassed by only one: his successor Alfred the Great. Like all rulers of his time, Offa was ruthless in defending himself and attempting to extend his kingdom of Mercia, the largest of England's seven kingdoms. He bullied his weaker neighbours to the extent of having the king of the East Angles put to death while the king was his guest. Under his rule, Mercia came to cover the greater part of England, from the Thames to the Humber. In his attempts to subdue the Welsh, too, he made two brutal invasions of southern Wales but failed to establish a firm foothold there. It was after the second attempt that he seems to have decided to build a permanent barrier along the troubled frontier.

For all his limitations it would be wrong to dismiss Offa as no more than a particularly brutal but successful war lord. Although written records of his reign are very scanty and (particularly unfortunate from the point of view of this guide) non-existent as far as the building of the Dyke is concerned, there is evidence to reveal him as a leading figure in the Western Europe of his day. In the first-known correspondence between any two European rulers about trade between their countries, the great Charlemagne addressed him uniquely as 'Dearest brother ... recognising you as not simply a most

strong defender of the holy faith ...'. Although relations between the two monarchs later broke down, Offa's concern with his kingdom's economic activity continued and he established a new coinage, the silver penny, intended to have full international standing. By the time of his death in 796AD he had earned the title which he had adopted and which appeared, abbreviated, on his later silver pennies: Rex Anglorum – 'King of the English'.

Coin (c790)

What is surprising is the way in which Offa's achievements were forgotten in the succeeding centuries. The long period after the exit of the Romans and the flood of Germanic settlers was written off as The Dark Ages, enlightened only by St Augustine's landing in Kent, leading eventually to the mutual recognition of the Church of Rome and the long-established Christians of the Celtic tradition. Then came King Arthur, an obscure Romano-British ruler who became the subject of legends and folk tales across Western Europe. Finally came Alfred the Great (King of Wessex from 871 to 899AD) and his struggle against the Norse/Vikings. As for Offa, he survived simply as the name given to an earthwork running somewhere along the English–Welsh border.

Anglo-Saxon England

Anglo-Saxon England was not, as is sometimes imagined, a remote backwater which, even 200 years after Offa, needed the Norman Conquest to drag it into the mainstream of European civilisation. The Anglo-Saxons had formed settled, agricultural peasant societies living under their local lords in villages often separated from their neighbours by forests. There was no individually owned land and each peasant cultivated his plots or strips in large communal fields, which was a step towards the open field system of medieval times. Their main crops were wheat and barley, which provided bread (their staple food) and ale (an essential drink, given the doubtful quality of much water). Given their local forests to provide fuel and building materials, they were, as a village, virtually self-sufficient and self-contained.

There were a few towns, with markets, craftsmen and traders, at least one church and perhaps even a bishop. Most would have a simple protective wall, but with their huddles of thatched-roof and wood buildings they were vulnerable to fire. Most were on navigable rivers and those on the east or south-east coasts would be ports trading with the Continent. The way of life in these times was not idyllic but it was one which we, even in the 21st century, can visualise and understand.

A fluctuating frontier During their time in Britain the Romans had pushed into much of Wales, with permanent forts and the mining of precious metals. Following their departure, Wales became, to some extent, a place of refuge for Romano-British people fleeing from the inroads of the Germanic invaders and settlers. Subsequently the frontier between the Anglo-Saxons and Welsh fluctuated with the varying strength and aggressiveness of the two sides and the volatile support of the minor princedoms along the border. The first half of the

8th century seems to have been a period of Welsh domination, as shown by the inscription on Eliseg's Pillar (see box p212), when Offa's predecessor, Aethalbald, had attempted but failed to set up Mercian settlements inside Welsh territory. Offa's two brutal forays into south Wales also failed, presumably leading to his decision to build the Dyke.

Were the Anglo-Saxons capable of building the Dyke? It has been argued that the Anglo-Saxons of Offa's time lacked the experience and the techniques to build such a major fortification and that the political and social organisation of Mercia was too primitive to be capable of rising to the task. Yet as far as expertise is concerned, the digging of a ditch and piling the turf and soil to one side to make a barrier is so basic as to require neither a model nor previous experience. In any case England and Wales abounded in hill-forts and fortified settlements relying on the ditch and dyke construction, and there are fortifications of this kind in the Saxons' homeland in Germany, in particular the Danevike dyke on the Jutland peninsula.

The centre of power in Mercia, as in other kingdoms, was the king himself with his court, supported by his council of senior officials (*ealdormen*); leading clergy and major land-holders (*thegns*) with an equal number of lesser land-holders, giving 50 or so members in all. The ealdormen were the king's chief territorial officials, directly answerable to him. Answerable to them in turn were the thegns who were obliged to give military or other assistance to their monarch as needed. The principle was well established by Offa's time that, in granting land to any of his followers, the king imposed on them the obligation to provide service in 'matters pertaining to expeditions and the construction of bridges and fortifications, which is necessary for the whole people and from which none ought to be excused'. In turn, the thegns could drum up the lesser land-holders and retainers, whose peasants would provide the rank and file of any military force – or the labour to build or repair fortifications.

How was it done?
A king of Mercia such as Offa clearly had the authority, the administrative structure and the manpower at his disposal to enable him to organise and direct the building of a major defensive earthwork along one of his kingdom's frontiers. But how did it work in practice? Using information from contemporary sources, a comprehensive and convincing reconstruction of the way in which the planning and building of the Dyke would have been carried out has been produced by Hill and Worthington (see p46). It has been summarised in a display at the Offa's Dyke Centre (see p158) in Knighton.

It has been estimated that the total labour force needed would have been in the order of 5000 men, with each village leader being given responsibility for completing individual sections of the dyke. The decision over the course of the Dyke would have taken into account the need to protect Mercian settlements as far as possible but also the best line of defence and surveillance of activity on the Welsh side of the Dyke, as can be seen by any walker along the Dyke today. In areas where relations with the local Welsh chieftains were reasonably good the Mercian officials would probably have been allowed discretion to negotiate with them over the final course of the Dyke, taking into account local settlements, trade and other contacts. The best ways of dealing with water courses and river crossings, steep hillsides and so forth also had to be decided, recognising that the best route might involve some increase in the length of the Dyke, again as one can easily make out as one walks along the path.

Building Once the exact line had been decided, using beacons to establish the correct alignment between adjacent sections, it would be marked out with stakes and finally a ploughed furrow. If the terrain made ploughing impossible

---

❏ Construction of the Dyke

Comparisons are inevitably made between Offa's Dyke and the much more famous Hadrian's Wall, even to the extent of suggestions that Offa took the Roman fortification as his model. However, there is virtually nothing in the Dyke to support this. The difference between the two kinds of fortification was emphasised by Bede in his *History of the English Church and People*, written 50 years or so before Offa became king of Mercia:

'*A wall is built of stone but an earthwork ... is built with sods cut from the earth and raised well above ground level, fronted by the ditch from which the sods were taken and topped by a strong timber palisade.*'

This is a fair description of the way in which Offa's Dyke was to be built (see diagram), although excavations have yet to reveal evidence of a palisade.

Offa's Dyke

Palisade   Dyke

Ditch

Roman (Hadrian's) Wall

Wall

Glassis
(60ft/18m)

Berm

Ditch

| 0 | 10 | 20 feet |
| 0 | 3 | 6 metres |

HISTORY, ENVIRONMENT & NATURE

the line would be shown by a low bank of stones. Finally, the organisers would decide the allocation of sections of the Dyke to the villages which were to provide the working parties of peasants to do the actual building. The volunteers, or conscripts, would have walked with their food supplies and implements, very probably using pack horses, to the section allocated to them. It is likely that the length of earthwork per man would have worked out at rather over 4ft/1.3m, so that a team of four men would cover about 16½ft/5m. Once they had completed their stint to the satisfaction of their overseer they would be free to go back home. (Although the Dyke was designed and built as an earthwork, there are signs here and there that stone was used if it was to hand – found, say, in the digging of the ditch. Walkers with a particular interest in the construction might keep an eye open for the occasional trace of this.)

Doubtless the operation would have been rather more complicated and certainly messier than this brief description might suggest, but it should show how a relatively simple society such as Offa's Mercia could have carried out what appears to have been a daunting task. As well as demonstrating the strength and capacity of Offa's kingdom, the building of the Dyke had a significant long-term outcome: it defined the frontier with Wales in a way which had never previously been attempted, or even contemplated. It also eliminated the possibility of any of the people living along the Welsh Marches gaining local independence.

The Dyke today
Systematic surveying of the Dyke effectively started with Cyril Fox in the first half of the 20th century and was eventually taken over in 1971 under the auspices of the newly formed Offa's Dyke Project, led by David Hill and Margaret Worthington. It is believed that the Dyke was a continuous defensive earthwork that covered some 59 of the 64 or so miles of Mercia's border with Powys at the time it was constructed. It is likely that when the Dyke was built a few guarded crossing points would have been included in the design, with armed forces sent to a particular section if there was an attack or the threat of some kind of incursion. In more peaceful times it might have been sufficient to send out occasional patrols on horseback able to call for support from local fortified settlements.

Even without regular patrolling the Dyke would have been a real obstacle for would-be raiders. In the first place it would not have been easy to cross the Dyke with a horse and much more difficult for a returning gang to drive, say, stolen cattle over the rampart, down into the ditch and then up the other side – particularly if angry Mercians were on their heels.

The existence of a palisade along the rampart would, of course, have made the crossing much more difficult – if a palisade was an original feature. All this can readily be envisaged by the walker along the many sections of the Dyke where both ditch and rampart are reasonably well preserved.

As can be seen as you halt to admire the view, the Dyke's winding course was carefully planned to take advantage of natural features and, in hilly areas, to combine the protection given by steep slopes with the best open views across Welsh territory to the west. There are, however, two places where instead of the usual sinuous course there is a curious almost right-angled bend. These are at the very southernmost end of the Dyke at Rushock Hill (Map 35, p150), near Kington, and at Hergan Corner (Map 44, p167), near Clun. Although early researchers suggested that this was to bring together two lines that were not otherwise going to meet, in each instance the course adopted was in fact the best way of dealing with the particular features. At Rushock it was to take advantage of the lie of the land and give the best views to the west; at Hergan Corner it was simply the need to negotiate a water-course gully. So we can give the Mercians credit for knowing exactly what they were doing.

For recommended reading on the history of Offa's Dyke, including books by the principal researchers, see pp45-6.

Conserving the Anglo-Welsh Border Country

It's the business of government to see that the countryside is preserved for the pleasure and sanity of all of us. The fatal mistake has been to imagine that the interests of the countryside are in some way different from the interests of farmers. The countryside can only be maintained by a healthy agriculture. If farming dies, a most precious part of Britain dies with it.
John Mortimer

Frequently we are made aware that hostile interests from construction, development and the transport infrastructure make demands on our woods and fields, replacing them with concrete and brick. In the words of Joni Mitchell, 'they paved paradise and put up a parking lot' (*Big Yellow Taxi*).

There are plenty of organisations that are determined not to let this happen, however, some of them listed on pp61-2. Thanks to the efforts of these groups, many of them voluntary, the fight-back is gaining ground. Despite the optimism, the struggle cannot be sustained without the active participation of people who care. This is where walkers can play their part. We are the ones who can see what's going on. We are the spies, the fifth column, the silent majority. We can go into the countryside with our eyes open and report back on what we see happening. If you see obvious examples of despoliation or threat to an area, let somebody know.

GOVERNMENT AGENCIES AND SCHEMES

Primary responsibility for countryside affairs in England rests with **Natural England** (🖥 gov.uk/government/organisations/natural-england); this organisation is responsible for enhancing biodiversity, landscape and wildlife in rural, urban, coastal and marine areas; promoting access, recreation and public wellbeing; and contributing to the way natural resources are managed. One of its roles is to designate national trails, national parks, areas of outstanding natural beauty (AONBs), sites of special scientific interest (SSSIs), and national nature reserves (NNRs), and to enforce regulations relating to all these sites. In 2013 the Countryside Council for Wales was renamed **Natural Resources Wales**

HISTORY, ENVIRONMENT & NATURE

(NRW; 🖥 naturalresources.wales); this is the government body responsible for conservation and landscape protection in Wales. NRW has also taken over the functions of Forestry Commission Wales and the Environment Agency in Wales and is also responsible for drawing up and reviewing the quality standards for National Trails in Wales. NRW and other agencies aim to give protection from modern development and to maintain the countryside in its present state.

National parks
National park status is the highest level of landscape protection available in Britain and recognises the importance of the area in terms of landscape, biodiversity and as a recreational resource.

The Offa's Dyke Path touches only one national park, the Brecon Beacons (🖥 breconbeacons.org), into which area the Black Mountains between Hay-on-Wye and Pandy fall. Although the Brecon Beacons is one of the lesser-known national parks, bank holidays and summer weekends can see the area choked with traffic and practically full to bursting with picnickers and day-trippers. Conservation in national parks is always a knife-edge balance between protecting the environment, the rights and livelihoods of those who live in the park and the needs of visitors.

Areas of outstanding natural beauty (AONBs)
Land which falls outside the remit of a national park but which is nonetheless deemed special enough for protection may be designated an AONB, the second level of protection after national park status. The Offa's Dyke Path crosses three AONBs: the Wye Valley, controlled by the Wye Valley AONB (🖥 wyevalley aonb.org.uk); the Shropshire Hills, under the care of the Shropshire Hills AONB Partnership (🖥 shropshirehillsaonb.co.uk); and the Clwydian Range, administered by Denbighshire Countryside Service (🖥 denbighshire.gov.uk/countryside).

Sites of special scientific interest (SSSIs; Triple SIs)
This is an important designation which affords extra protection to unique areas against anything that threatens the habitat or environment. Although SSSIs are not widely known, they range in size from small sites where orchids grow, or birds nest, to vast swathes of upland, moorland and wetland. The country of the Offa's Dyke Path has its share but they are not given a high profile for the very reason that this would draw unwanted attention when what is wanted is for them to be left undisturbed. 'Triple SIs' are managed in partnership with the owners and occupiers of the land who must give written notice of any operations likely to damage the site and who cannot proceed until consent is given.

National nature reserves (NNRs)
NNRs were set up to conserve the finest examples of wildlife habitats and geological features. There are 224 NNRs in England and 76 in Wales; all of them are also SSSIs. Natural England manages about two-thirds of the NNRs in England; about 30% of these are owned by them. Some of the NNRs in Wales are owned by NRW who select and designate them; there are 76 and NRW manages 58 of these, but others are managed by landowners or bodies such as

Wildlife Trusts, the RSPB or a local authority. **Local nature reserves** (LNRs) are designated by local authorities.

CAMPAIGNING AND CONSERVATION ORGANISATIONS

Voluntary organisations started the conservation movement back in the mid-1800s and are still at the forefront of developments. Independent of government but reliant on public support, they can concentrate their resources either on acquiring land which can then be managed purely for conservation purposes, or on influencing political decision-makers by lobbying and campaigning.

The **National Trust** (NT; ▢ nationaltrust.org.uk), with a membership of around four million, protects over 350 historic houses, gardens and ancient monuments as well as forests, woods, coastline, farmland, moorland and islands. NT properties on or close to the trail include Chirk Castle (p201), The Kymin (box p107) and Powis Castle & Garden (box p181).

Cadw: Welsh Historic Monuments (▢ cadw.wales.gov.uk) is the Welsh organisation that protects, conserves and promotes an appreciation of the built heritage of Wales.

Often seeming to overlap the work of the National Trust, **English Heritage** (▢ english-heritage.org.uk) looks after, champions and advises the government on historic buildings and places. Now a charitable trust which cares for over 400 historic buildings, monuments and sites with a central aim of ensuring that the historic environment of England is properly maintained.

The **Royal Society for the Protection of Birds** (RSPB; ▢ rspb.org.uk) and **RSPB Welsh Office** (▢ rspb.org.uk/whatwedo/wales) has over a million members and 200 nature reserves (covering almost 130,000 hectares), of which the nearest to the path is Lake Vyrnwy, some 20 miles from Welshpool.

Active support for conservation work and sustainability comes from a number of organisations: the **Council for the Protection of Rural England** (CPRE; ▢ cpre.org.uk) and its Welsh equivalent, **Campaign for the Protection of Rural Wales** (CPRW; ▢ cprw.org.uk); both aim to conserve the landscape and quality of life in rural areas; the **Inland Waterways Association** (▢ www.waterways.org.uk) looks after the interests of canal users; on Offa's Dyke

---

❑ **Other statutory bodies and countryside authorities**
● **Clwyd-Powys Archaeological Trust (CPAT**; ▢ cpat.org.uk) This organisation is one of the four Welsh archaeological trusts that works to help protect, record and interpret all aspects of the historic landscape.
● **Historic England** (▢ historicengland.org.uk) Created in April 2015 as a result of dividing the work done by English Heritage. Historic England is the government department responsible for looking after and promoting England's historic environment and is in charge of the listing system, giving grants and dealing with planning matters.
● **Forestry Commission England** (▢ forestry.gov.uk/england) Government department for establishing and managing forests for a variety of uses in England.
● **Natural Resources Wales** (▢ naturalresourceswales.gov.uk) See p59.

HISTORY, ENVIRONMENT & NATURE

❏ **Maintenance of Offa's Dyke Path**
The **Offa's Dyke Path Management Service** looks after the running of this national trail, fixing broken stiles and bridges, dealing with erosion and making sure the route is well signposted.

   Any problems encountered along the way should be reported to the trail officer, Rob Dingle (☎ 01597-827580, 🖳 rob.dingle@powys.gov.uk).

Path you'll walk beside the Llangollen Canal and Montgomery Canal for a distance; **The Wildlife Trusts** (🖳 wildlifetrusts.org) is an umbrella organisation that brings together the work of 47 individual Wildlife Trusts, of which there are six in Wales, and 36 across England; the trusts advise on wildlife-friendly land management; and the **Woodland Trust** (🖳 woodlandtrust.org.uk) aims to conserve, restore and re-establish trees, particularly broadleaved ones.

   Increasing interest in environmental issues both from the public and the media in recent years underlines a greater awareness that such issues affect us all, and should not just be left to government agencies. What is emerging is the most powerful lobbying group of all: an informed electorate.

Flora and fauna

Perhaps more than any other British national trail, the Offa's Dyke Path runs through a wide diversity of landscape and habitats that play host to a rich and varied wildlife. The path passes from wooded hillside to canal towpath, from the swooping ridges of the Clwydian Hills to the Severn plain. It therefore offers opportunities for seeing a wide range of wildlife and wild flowers, both familiar and unfamiliar.

   It would take a considerable library to do justice to the flora and fauna that you're likely to encounter on the way, so this can serve only as a brief introduction to the trail's most common species. Many of the B&Bs along the trail have field guides and environmental magazines that you can read at the end of the day's walk, while for additional input, the list of field guides on p45 should point you in the right direction.

   In order to understand an environment it is important to appreciate the interactions between the plants and animals that inhabit it – and the impact of man on this fragile relationship. If a greater awareness of these issues leads to an improvement in the way that we as walkers treat the countryside, and thus to our attitudes to conservation, that can only be a good thing.

TREES

It's encouraging to see the wide diversity of trees growing in areas alongside the Dyke, with efforts being made to replant cleared plantations by introducing local broadleafed species. On a less positive note, where felling takes place it can have the effect of obscuring the path and displacing waymarks.

Deciduous

Trees are abundant along the Welsh Borders with all the common indigenous species evident in large numbers. These include the oak, both **English oak** (*Quercus robur*) and **sessile oak** (*Quercus petraea*), the difference between them being that the leaves of the sessile have stalks and the acorns are unstalked; **sycamore** (*Acer pseudoplatanus*), **ash** (*Fraxinus excelsior*), **beech** (*Fagus sylvatica*), **birch** (*Betula pubescens*), **lime** or **linden** (*Tiliax vulgaris*), **horse chestnut** (*Aesculus hippocastanum*) and **hornbeam** (*Carpinus betulus*).

Amongst mixed woodland you will also see trees such as **rowan** or **mountain ash** (*Sorbus aucuparia*) with its bright red berries from August, a favourite

---

❏ Timber growing

Forest and woodland areas make up almost 14% of the land area of Wales, of which almost a third is taken up by the sitka spruce, grown primarily for newsprint: 'paper from sustainable forestry'. The Offa's Dyke Path goes through several such plantations, the largest of which is at Llandegla.

Originally oak and ash dominated the Welsh landscape until fast-growing conifers were introduced from America to produce pit props for the coal-mining industry. Even then, it was not until the latter part of the 20th century that large tracts of land were given over to conifer plantations, serving a massive softwood-processing industry that created thousands of jobs. Hand in hand with the new plantations went the desecration of moorland, blanketed with regimented rows of trees that became a familiar sight in Britain under the auspices of the Forestry Commission, supported by tax advantages that encouraged investment. These short-sighted policies produced the eyesores that defaced many a lovely valley, the effect of which is still felt today.

The negative visual impression caused by the plantations is as nothing compared with the ecological impact. Thousands of acres of species-rich moorland were ploughed up and replaced by a monoculture of conifers. With it go birds such as the merlin and the golden plover. Once mature the trees cannot support much wildlife as the close canopy allows little light to penetrate to the forest floor. Nothing else can grow and as a consequence few animals venture into this sterile environment. As with all monocultures, pests easily thrive and have to be controlled with chemical pesticides. The deep ploughing and use of heavy machinery damages soil structure and also leads to a higher risk of flash floods as drainage patterns are altered. It has also been found that acid rain gets trapped in the trees and is released into the streams during heavy rain to the detriment of fish and invertebrates.

Fortunately the policy of blanket planting of conifers has fallen out of favour as environmental issues have been taken on board and a more responsible approach has been adopted. Even in already-forested areas, new policy initiatives have been put in place to reduce this negative impact on the environment, while more generally the Welsh authorities have devised a woodland strategy for improved management and control. Mixed varieties of trees are being planted to cover areas blighted by industry and mining, and to restore an appropriate habitat, with the aim of creating multi-purpose woodlands that will benefit tourism, agriculture and the environment.

food for birds, **silver birch** (*Betula pendula*), **aspen** (*Populus tremula*), **alder** (*Alnus glutinosa*), **wych elm** (*Ulmus glabra*), **poplar** (*Populus alba*) and **hazel** (*Corylus avellana*). The **English elm** (*Ulmus procera*) has been virtually wiped out by Dutch elm disease.

The willow most commonly seen along riverbanks and streams is the **crack willow** (*Salix fragilis*) which is often pollarded to encourage growth. The tree on which catkins appear is the **goat** or **pussy willow** (*Salix caprea*).

Conifers
The Welsh Borders are not afflicted by the mass planting of conifers to anything like the same extent as Scotland, the Lake District and Northumberland although there are some stretches of the trail where the dark, silent environment of closely planted conifers can be rather dispiriting.

The most common plantation trees are the **sitka spruce** (*Picea sitchensis*) introduced from North America and capable of 1.5m (approx 5ft) growth a year, **Norway spruce** (*Picea abies*) which can reach a height of 40m (131ft), the **European larch** (*Larix decidua*) and the **Scots pine** (*Pinus sylvestris*).

WILD FLOWERS
Hedgerows and field boundaries
In spring and early summer the variety of wild flowers in the hedgerows and along the verges of the minor roads and lanes which you will walk along will be rich indeed.

Even those with no knowledge will soon learn to recognise the commoner species such as **red campion** (*Silene dioica*), **cowslip** (*Primula veris*), **primrose** (*Primula vulgaris*), **birdsfoot trefoil** (*Lotus corniculatus*) or 'bacon and eggs', **common speedwell** (*Veronica officinalis*) which can cure indigestion, gout and liver complaints, **bugle** (*Ajuga reptans*), **tufted vetch** (*Vicia cracca*) and **common dog violet** (*Viola riviniana*), all of which are easy to spot. Banks of the white **greater stitchwort** (*Stellaria holostea*) enliven the dullest stretch, often interspersed with **bluebells** (*Endymion non-scriptus*).

Later, from May to September, these will be joined by **buttercup** (*Ranunculus acris*), the flowers of which when rubbed on a cow's udders were said to improve the milk, **yellow pimpernel** (*Lysimacia nemorum*), **golden-rod** (*Solidago virgaurea*) used in folk medicine to treat wounds, **viper's bugloss** (*Echium vulgare*), **harebell** (*Campanula rotundifolia*), **herb Robert** (*Geranium robertianum*), **foxglove** (*Digitalis purpurea*) which is poisonous and from which the drug Digitalin is extracted to treat heart disease, **field poppy** (*Papaver rhoeas*) and **ox-eye daisy** (*Leucanthemum vulgare*), also known as dog daisy or marguerite. The tall white flowering heads of members of the carrot family such as **cow parsley** (*Anthrisus sylvestris*), **yarrow** (*Achillea millefolium*), and upright **hedge parsley** (*Torilis japonica*) will be obvious along with, occasionally, **hogweed** (*Heracleum sphondylium*) which can grow to 1.75m (6ft) high.

Summer is when the climbers and ramblers come into their own. No introduction is needed for the common **bramble** (*Rubus fruticosus*) sought out in autumn by blackberry pickers. **Honeysuckle** (*Lonicera periclymenum*), also

Common Vetch
Vicia sativa

Harebell
Campanula rotundifolia

Red Campion
Silene dioica

Lousewort
Pedicularis sylvatica

Germander Speedwell
Veronica chamaedrys

Common Dog Violet
Viola riviniana

Common Fumitory
Fumaria officinalis

Heather (Ling)
Calluna vulgaris

Bell Heather
Erica cinerea

Foxglove
Digitalis purpurea

Rosebay Willowherb
Epilobium angustifolium

Early Purple Orchid
Orchis mascula

Gorse
Ulex europaeus

Meadow Buttercup
Ranunculis acris

Marsh Marigold (Kingcup)
Caltha palustris

Bird's-foot trefoil
Lotus corniculatus

Water Avens
Geum rivale

Tormentil
Potentilla erecta

Primrose
Primula vulgaris

St John's Wort
Hypericum perforatum

Honeysuckle
Lonicera periclymemum

Common Ragwort
Senecio jacobaea

Hemp-nettle
Galeopsis speciosa

Cowslip
Primula veris

Rowan (tree)
Sorbus aucuparia

Dog Rose
Rosa canina

Forget-me-not
Myosotis arvensis

Scarlet Pimpernel
Anagallis arvensis

Self-heal
Prunella vulgaris

Herb-Robert
Geranium robertianum

Ramsons (Wild Garlic)
Allium ursinum

Common Hawthorn
Crataegus monogyna

Bluebell
Hyacinthoides non-scripta

Common Knapweed
Centaurea nigra

Yarrow
Achillea millefolium

Hogweed
Heracleum sphondylium

known as woodbine, makes its appearance growing through hedges from June to September, the fruits ripening to red in the autumn.

Hedge bindweed (*Calystegia sepium*), with its white trumpet-shaped flowers, and the related pink **field bindweed** (*Convolvulus arvensis*) are a common sight during summer months, as is the pale pink **dog rose** (*Rosa canina*), which later produces rosehips, an excellent source of vitamin C when taken as a syrup.

Woodland

In late spring, deciduous woodlands are often carpeted deep blue by **bluebells** (*Endymion non-scriptus*), while in others the air is pungent with the smell of densely packed white **ramsons** (*Allium ursinum*), widely known as **wild garlic**. Equally common are two flowers whose petals close up at night and in bad weather: the **wood anemone** (*Anemone nemorosa*), and the smaller **wood-sorrel** (*Oxalis acetosella*), with its soft, light-green leaves.

From April to June **early purple orchids** (*Orchis mascula*) are occasionally to be seen, often growing with bluebells, while far more in evidence from May onwards is the poisonous **bittersweet** or **woody nightshade** (*Solanum dulcamara*).

❏ BUTTERFLIES AND DRAGONFLIES

Butterflies
Given the numerous factors that militate against the survival of butterflies including high winds and heavy rain throughout the year, the use of pesticides and loss of habitat and the removal of hedgerows and intensive farming, it is surprising how often one does see butterflies whilst on the trail during the summer months.

Breeding in nettle patches left alone by most grazing animals, the nettle feeders include **peacock** (*Inachis io*), **tortoiseshell** (*Aglais urticae*), **red admiral** (*Vanessa atalanta*) and **painted lady** (*Cynthia cadui*). They are in colourful contrast to the **meadow brown** (*Maniola jurtina*), **wall** (*Lasiommata megera*) and **small heath** (*Coenonympha pamphilus*), all of which are likely to be seen on warm, sunny days. **Large whites** (*Pieris brassicae*) and **small whites** (*Artogeia rapae*) are common everywhere but should not be disregarded, having their place in the ecological chain. Although rarer nowadays you could still see the **common blue** (*Polyommatus icarus*), the **orange tip** (*Anthocaris cardamines*) and the **green-veined white** (*Artogeia napi*), especially in areas such as the disused quarries on Llanymynech Hill and along Montgomery Canal.

Dragonflies
The commoner dragonflies fall into two groups: hawkers and darters. **Hawkers** restlessly patrol their territory by a river, lake or canal which the male, much more brightly coloured than the female, defends against intruders; most common is the **brown aeshna**, the wingspan of which is 10cm (4in) **Darters** are less restless than hawkers and have a sturdier body, spending time clinging to vegetation and making occasional darts after prey. The males have a blue bloom on their bodies.

Opposite, top The Hatterrall Ridge is ideal terrain for wild ponies as well as hikers. Behind them the road leads to Llanthony via Gospel Pass. **Centre:** Much of this walk is through or near farming communities and you'll attract friendly interest from most of the locals. **Bottom**: You may also see red deer (left) but the stag (right) is one of the sculptures near Mellington Hall Hotel (Map 47, p170).

It is always a pleasure to see wild fruit growing. **Wild strawberry** (*Fragaria vesca*) and to a lesser extent **wild raspberry** (*Rubus idaeus*) can be spotted in wooded areas. Other berries will be dark-blue sloes on the **blackthorn** (*Prunus spinosa*) bushes, the clustered heads of the **elderberry** (*Sambucus nigra*), and occasionally **bilberry** (*Vaccinium myrtillus*) – although this last is far more common on open moorland.

Moorland

Bracken and **gorse** (*Ulex europaeus*) are everywhere on the trail, but especially over the exposed open moorland of the Clwydian Hills, the Hergest Ridge and the Black Mountains, where you will also see **heather** or **ling** (*Calluna vulgaris*) and the gentle **broom** (*Cytisus scoparius*) with its characteristic seed-pods in the autumn. Here, too, you'll find great expanses of **bilberry** (*Vaccinium myrtillus*) among the heather, its tiny red bell-shaped flowers in evidence from April to July, followed in summer by blackberries.

Riverbanks and wet areas

Lady's smock (*Cardamine pratensis*) and **ragged robin** (*Lychnis flos-cuculi*) are two pink flowers that are often seen in damp areas. **Watermint** (*Mentha aquatica*), **meadowsweet** (*Filipendula ulmaria*), which medicinally has the same properties as aspirin, and the poisonous **water-crowfoot** (*Ranunculus aquatilis*) make canals and ponds their habitat.

Sometimes the prolific **policeman's helmet** (*Impatiens glandulifera*), distinctive by the shape of its flowers, will be found colonising riverbanks.

Rough ground and waste land

Uncultivated areas such as land that has been cleared of buildings or disturbed by construction seems to attract certain plants which move in and sometimes take over the whole area. These include the ubiquitous **rosebay willowherb** (*Epilobium angustifolium*), **ragwort** (*Senecio jacobaea*) which is poisonous to horses, **dandelion** (*Taraxacum officinale*) and **groundsel** (*Senecio vulgaris*).

You will also see **Aaron's rod** (*Verbascum thapsus*) which used to be smoked like tobacco in a pipe, **rape** (*Brassica napus*), **knotgrass** (*Polygonum aviculare*), **field scabious** (*Knautia arvensis*) and **valerian** (*Valeriana officinalis*), the smell of which cats are said to love.

MAMMALS

The **rabbit** (*Oryctolagus cuniculis*) is abundant along the Dyke and is indeed responsible in part for the erosion of the earthwork in which it makes its burrows. Rabbits are responsible for an estimated £100,000,000 damage a year to crops and in spite of being prey to buzzards, foxes, feral cats, stoats and man, they are able to replenish their numbers rapidly, bucks mating at four months old and does at three-and-a-half months. Rabbits may appear to be delightful creatures but to the countryman they are a pest.

The **brown hare** (*Lepus europaeus*) is bigger than the rabbit with large powerful hind legs and very long black-tipped ears. They are common on

❏ Cattle

Apart from the breeds common to the British Isles generally, you will almost certainly come across the **Welsh Black** when walking in the Border Country. A native British breed descended from cattle of pre-Roman origin, they are entirely black in colour, and are ideally suited to the rough upland country characteristic of the area. Bred for beef production, they are hardy and adapted to a rough environment and can be out-wintered. Prolific milkers, they thrive on poor pasture. They make excellent mothers and grow heavier and more quickly than most other British breeds.

Elsewhere on the trail you may come across unusual breeds such as **Red Poll**, a breed of rich brown cattle without horns; an excellent cheese is made from their milk. Around the site of the vanished Grace Dieu Abbey (p107) is a herd of rare **White Park** cattle, said to have similarities to the famed white Chillingham herd, the oldest breed still surviving. They look like the Texas Longhorns from cowboy films, with black noses and wide horns that you wouldn't want to get too near. Beautiful-looking beasts though they are, give them a wide berth.

Walking through fields of cattle

It is very rare that cows will attack walkers but it does happen and people have been trampled to death. Cows get particularly nervous when dogs are about so if you are walking with a dog be aware of this. Cows with calves can be even more twitchy. But don't get alarmed; a walk along the length of Offa's Dyke Path will involve walking through dozens and dozens of fields with cattle in them. Most of the time they will just watch you pass. Cattle are usually docile animals. If you walk calmly past they will invariably ignore you. If you feel nervous or unsure about a herd, you are entitled to walk round the edge of the field to avoid them and rejoin the path later. Very rarely they will wander over out of curiosity but if they do you should be on your guard. Ramblers (see box p44) offer the following guidelines:

● Try not to get between cows and their calves.
● Be prepared for cattle to react to your presence, especially if you have a dog with you.
● Move quickly and quietly, and if possible walk around them; if that's not possible it's best to wait for the cattle to move.
● Keep your dog close and under proper control.
● Don't hang onto your dog. If you are threatened by animals – let it go as the cow will chase after that.
● Don't put yourself at risk. Find another way round the cows and rejoin the footpath as soon as possible.
● Don't panic! Most cows will stop before they reach you. If they follow just walk on quietly. Don't forget to report any problems to the highway authority.

Beware of the bull! Sometimes a field full of cows will be accompanied by their lord and master, a bull. This is in fact in contravention of the law, especially if they endanger the public. In theory, bulls aged more than 10 months must not be allowed in a field through which a public footpath passes.

In practice, if the farmer decides to let his bull in a field there's not much you can do about it. The best thing you can do if you spot one is give it a wide berth. Keep to the edge of the field and keep a healthy distance between it and you. If it seems to be taking notice of you, quicken your exit from the field without delay.

❏ Sheep

Since sheep are the one animal you are likely to see every single day of your walk it is worth trying to recognise the diverse breeds that graze in the Welsh Borders. Because of the widespread crossing of breeds most animals you will see will be cross-breeds, usually referred to as mules, and reared for their meat. Fleeces no longer command a price in today's markets and sheep reared solely for their wool are a rarity.

Among the different varieties which may be noticed look out for the following:

● **Black Welsh Mountain** Small, black sheep with no wool on their face or legs below their knee and hock. Rams are typically horned and ewes hornless. The meat obtained is of premium quality and much prized.

● **Balwen Welsh Mountain** With a white blaze on its face, white feet and a white tail, the Balwen is said to have been placed as a landmark on the hills in order to help the farmer to recognise his flock. It's a small, hardy breed which can get by on very little when food is scarce.

● **Welsh Mountain Badger Faced** Ancient breed, once common, it has a distinctive broad stripe on its face with a black band from its jaw extending under the belly to the tail. The fleece is used mainly for the carpet industry.

● **Kerry Hill** A well-balanced, sturdy sheep with ears set high and free from wool, a black nose and sharply defined black and white markings on its head and legs. The ewe is a perfect mother, adaptable and a good forager producing strong, lean lambs.

● **Shropshire** A sheep with a gentle disposition, the Shropshire has a white fleece and black face with wool on its head. The lambs are hardy, vigorous and meaty and the ewes make wonderful mothers.

● **Hill Radnor** A hill or mountain breed found in Powys and Gwent; a hardy sheep with a grey aquiline nose and a tan face and legs. Rams have long curved horns and ewes are hornless.

● **Clun Forest** A hardy animal that breeds well; many flocks have been kept for years in the hills of the Clun Forest area. It has a long clean dark brown face, free from wrinkles with bold, bright eyes. Its head is covered in wool and its ears are set well to the top of its head.

farmland and rough grazing and rely for escape on their great acceleration, being capable of attaining speeds of up to 45mph (70km/h). In upland areas the **mountain hare** (*Lepus timidus*) replaces the brown, being distinguishable by its slightly blue colour that blends more easily with rocky terrain. In winter in mountain country they adopt a white coat, supposedly for camouflage in the snow, although it has been suggested that the white fur offers a thermal advantage, creating a greenhouse effect on the outer layers of the skin.

Badgers (*Meles meles*) are nocturnal animals and rarely seen during the day, lying up in their underground burrows known as setts. Litters of cubs are born in February. Badgers, too, are responsible for undermining the Dyke – you'll see heavy excavation work in some places along the trail – but unlike rabbits they are a protected species and cannot be destroyed. There is also some suggestion that cattle can catch the TB virus through contact with badgers which has led to them being culled in some areas.

Red foxes (*Vulpes vulpes*) are becoming common in spite of occasional persecution by man, and our murderous roads. Readily identifiable by their colour and bushy tail, foxes are shy animals that come out mainly at night to hunt for food. Their habit of killing all the hens in a coop and taking only one is apparently not the result of vicious rage but done to take advantage of abundance while it is available to compensate for times when food is scarce. Although the issue remains controversial, a ban on fox hunting was implemented in 2005.

The **red squirrel** (*Sciurus vulgaris*) is the only squirrel indigenous to the British Isles and is protected by law. There are only a few thousand left in Wales, primarily in coniferous woodland. The species is threatened with extinction for a number of reasons, including disease, loss of habitat and the dominance of the grey squirrel. Active during the day, the red squirrel is recognised by its colour which varies from deep brown to chestnut to grey brown but its size and tufted ears easily distinguish it from the much larger grey. The **grey squirrel** (*Sciurus carolinensis*) was introduced to this country from North America in the 19th century and is an altogether more robust species than the red, adaptable to the changing habitat of our woodland and perfectly at home in parks and domestic gardens.

The **weasel** (*Mustela nivalis*) is one of our smaller carnivores, found in a wide range of habitats and not a protected species. It is considered an enemy of gamebirds and is sometimes trapped and killed by gamekeepers. Mainly nocturnal and preferring dry areas, the weasel is smaller than the **stoat** (*Mustela erminea*), the tip of whose tail is always black.

It is possible that you may catch sight of an **otter** (*Lutra lutra*) along one of the riverbanks, where they live their secretive semi-aquatic life, as the species is increasing in numbers after an alarming decline. They eat mainly fish but will take moorhens and their chicks, and in spring frogs are an important food item. Litters of cubs can be born at any time of the year. Their dens, or holts, are usually in holes in riverbanks or under a pile of rocks. Not dissimilar at first glance is the smaller, darker **American mink** (*Mustela vison*), an escapee from fur farms in the 1950s which gained a hold on British rivers. Recent sightings have been reported in the Welsh Borders area of two rare animals: the **pine marten** (*Martes martes*) and the **polecat** (*Mustela putorius*), both similar in size to the mink, and the latter with a distinctive white 'face mask'.

The species of deer you are most likely to see is the **roe deer** (*Capreolus capreolus*); these are quite small with an average height of 60-70cm (about 2ft) at the shoulder. They are reddish brown in summer, grey in winter and have a distinctive white rear end which is conspicuous when the deer is alarmed. Males have short antlers with no more than three points. Abundant in mixed coniferous and deciduous woodland, they are active at dawn and dusk and can sometimes be heard barking. If you come across a young kid apparently abandoned, leave it alone and go away; it's normal behaviour for the mother to leave her kid concealed while she goes off to feed.

REPTILES

The **adder** (*Vipera berus*) is the only venomous snake in Britain but poses very little risk to walkers and will not bite unless provoked; if you're lucky enough to see one, don't disturb it. You are most likely to encounter them in spring when they come out of hibernation and during the summer, when pregnant females warm themselves in the sun. They are easily identified by the striking zigzag pattern on their back and a 'V' on the top of their head behind their eyes. The venom is designed to kill small mammals such as mice and shrews; human deaths are rare.

Grass snakes (*Natrix natrix*) are Britain's largest reptile, growing up to a metre in length. They prefer rough ground with plentiful long grass in which to conceal themselves, laying their eggs in warm, rotting vegetation such as garden compost heaps, the young hatching in August. They are sometimes killed by people mistaking them for adders but are neither venomous nor aggressive and should be left alone. The grass snake's body has vertical black bars and spots running along the sides and usually has a prominent yellow collar round its neck.

The **slow worm** (*Anguis fragilis*) looks like a snake but is actually a legless lizard. It has no identifying marks on its body, which varies in colour from coppery brown to lead grey, and is usually quite shiny in appearance. Like lizards, they are able to blink; snakes have no eyelids. Slow worms are completely harmless, love to sun themselves and are found in old buildings under stones or discarded roofing sheets.

BIRDS

Streams, canals, rivers

The familiar sight of a **swan** (*Cygnus olor*), **mallard** (*Anas platyrhynchos*), **coot** (*Fulica atra*) or **moorhen** (*Gallinula chloropus*) may be all that is immediately apparent to the walker following the path along water courses but there will be occasional surprises to add to your enjoyment of the natural environment. The **grey heron** (*Ardea cinerea*) is a striking sight as it takes off on its ungainly and unhurried flight or is spotted standing sentinel at the water's edge.

A **kingfisher** (*Alcedo atthis*) is a rare sighting since they fly at great speed; often all that's spotted is a flash of blue, there one minute and gone the next. The **grey wagtail** (*Motacilla cinerea*) and the **dipper** (*Cinclus cinclus*) are two delightful birds which can be seen year-round bobbing up and down on boulders in fast-flowing streams. With a blue-grey head and bright-yellow underside the grey wagtail is the most striking of the wagtails. The dipper's flight is unmistakable, with its rapid wingbeat, white bib and tail held upright all helping in identification. These two are joined in summer by the **common sandpiper** (*Tringa hypoleucos*), a long-legged long-billed wader whose characteristic stance is with the body tilted forward, head lowered and the tail bobbing up and down almost continuously.

Swallows (*Hirundo rustica*), **house martins** (*Delichon urbica*) and **swifts** (*Apus apus*) love to swoop low over water to drink or take flies. The swift cannot perch like the swallow and martin: its legs are mere hooks and it is unable to walk. The less-common **sand martin** (*Riparia riparia*) nests in colonies in holes in steep riverbanks and has a curious low buzz for its call. The **reed bunting** (*Emberiza schoeniclus*) frequents reed beds and is recognisable by its white collar, black hood and bib.

SWALLOW
L: 190MM/7½"

Woodland

The familiar woodland residents such as **chaffinches** (*Fringilla coelebs*), **robin** (*Erithacus rubecula*), **blue tit** (*Parus caeruleus*) and **great tit** (*Parus major*), **song thrush** (*Turdus philomelos*) and **blackbird** (*Turdus merula*) are joined by birds that are less common in our gardens, including the **coal tit** (*Parus ater*) which has a black head with white on the cheeks and nape of the neck; it's often seen in coniferous woodland. Its relative, the **long-tailed tit** (*Aegithalos caudatus*), is smaller in size and has a very long tail which distinguishes it from other tits; it tends to frequent woodland fringes and clearings.

HOUSE MARTIN
L: 140MM/5½"

In spring the very different songs of the almost identical **willow warbler** (*Phylloscopus trochilus*) and **chiffchaff** (*Phylloscopus collybita*) ring across the Welsh valleys, the descending trill of the willow warbler contrasting with the sharp, mechanical chiffchaff of the bird of the same name. The chiff-chaff is generally rather browner than the willow warbler and its legs are blackish. The **whitethroat** (*Sylvia communis*) is easier to identify since its characteristic behaviour is its constant activity, never keeping still. You may also see the **pied flycatcher** (*Ficedula hypoleuca*) which prefers deciduous woods, especially oak, and darts after insects in the air, seldom returning to the same perch after an aerial sally.

SWIFT
L: 200MM/8"

The **green woodpecker** (*Picus viridis*) is a striking bird with its bright green body and red head and its curious call, a kind of laughing cry that carries a long way. Its near kindred, the **great spotted woodpecker** (*Dendrocopos major*), with its striking black-and-white plumage, and the smaller **lesser spotted woodpecker** (*Dendrocopos minor*), both habitually drum on trees, usually to mark their territory and extract insects rather than to bore holes for a nest site.

Of the finches, the **greenfinch**, **goldfinch** and **linnet** are relatively common. Thanks to the conifer plantations which are their habitat you might also spot the **siskin** (*Carduelis spinus*); it has similar greenish plumage to the greenfinch but is much smaller and more streaked. The **brambling** (*Fringilla mon-*

HISTORY, ENVIRONMENT & NATURE

❏ The Raven

There are said to be about 7400 breeding pairs of ravens in the British Isles, with Wales home to the largest population, supposedly thanks to upland farmers leaving their sheep out all winter. Ravens feed mainly on carrion and seem to be particularly partial to sheep carrion, which gets them through the winter. Ravens are territorial and having once adopted a territory they stick to it. They can be seen year-round in many of the areas through which Offa's Dyke Path passes, particularly where crags are in evidence, their favourite nesting places. When fully grown the mature raven measures 60cm (2ft) from beak to tail, much larger than its cousin the carrion crow with which it is sometimes confused. Its call is a deep-throated croak: once heard, never forgotten or mistaken for that of the lightweight crow. Ravens breed early in the year, making a flimsy nest of twigs lined with moss and sheep wool, usually high on a ledge on a cliff-face or quarry wall. The birds are often seen in pairs although they can sometimes gather in quite large numbers, with first-year birds usually flocking together. In the early months of the year ravens perform aerial acrobatics, swooping and diving and looping the loop in an extraordinary display which is part of their courting ritual.

RAVEN
L: 650mm/25"

tifringilla) often mixes with chaffinches in winter but is easily distinguished from them by its distinct white upper rump. The **bullfinch** (*Pyrrhula pyrrhula*) has a slow and deliberate movement and a rosy red underside as it feeds on berries, buds and seeds in the trees and bushes. A much smaller bird is the **goldcrest** (*Regulus regulus*) which is the smallest European bird, recognised by its yellow crown with black edges.

A darting movement on the trunks of trees may reveal the **treecreeper** (*Certhia familiaris*), a small brown bird with a curved bill which creeps spirally up trees searching for insects, dropping down to the bottom of another one when one is explored, or the **nuthatch** (*Sitta europaea*) which has a bluish-grey upper side and is very acrobatic, often climbing down tree trunks head first which woodpeckers cannot do.

It is highly likely that the **magpie** (*Pica pica*) will be seen and the **jay** (*Garrulus glandarius*) is becoming more common everywhere; both are highly efficient at cleaning eggs out of birds' nests and even taking young birds.

Less often seen and not heard as much now is the **cuckoo** (*Cuculus canorus*), which is grey or very occasionally brown in colour which makes it easy to confuse with birds of prey such as kestrels and sparrowhawks.

Among the dove family, **wood pigeons** (*Columba palumbus*) and **collared doves** (*Streptopelia decaocto*) are seen everywhere but you may try to distinguish the **stock dove** (*Columba oenas*) which is a darker, smaller bird than the wood pigeon, nesting in holes.

Open farmland and upland areas

The two birds you're most likely to see are the **wheatear** (*Oenanthe oenanthe*), the male of which has a steel grey back and crown and often bows and flicks its tail and perches on walls or rocks, and the **stonechat** (*Saxicola torquata*), much smaller and darker in plumage and identifiable by its call, a single sharp 'teck'.

SKYLARK
L: 185MM/7.25"

Among the smaller birds seen on open moorland are the **meadow pipit** (*Anthus pratensis*) and the **skylark** (*Alauda arvensis*), which is often heard long before it is seen, its clear song delivered as it soars overhead. You may also see the **ring ouzel** (*Turdus torquatus*) which looks like a blackbird but with a white bib. In autumn huge flocks of **redwings** (*Turdus iliatus*) and **fieldfares** (*Turdus pilaris*) fly over from Scandinavia to feed on the berries.

Pheasants (*Phasianus colchicus*), **partridges** (*Perdix perdix*) and **lapwings** (*Vanellus vanellus*) are likely to be seen practically everywhere. In summer in upland areas the bird whose bubbling call will first alert you before you spot its characteristic flight is Britain's largest wader, the **curlew** (*Numenius arquata*), a large brown bird with a long down-curved bill that is as at home in moorland as on the coast.

LAPWING/PEEWIT
L: 320MM/12.5"

The **oystercatcher** (*Haematopus ostralegus*) is another perhaps surprising wader that is quite common in the breeding season, with its distinctive black-and-white plumage and orange pointed bill and legs. You may also put up a **snipe** (*Gallinago gallinago*), which has a zig-zag flight when flushed, or in wooded areas the **woodcock** (*Scolopax rusticola*), easily distinguished from the snipe by its larger size and more rounded wings. Its camouflage makes it difficult to observe during the day.

Much larger than the **carrion crow** (*Corvus corone corone*), the **raven** (*Corvus corax,* see box opposite) is now quite common in upland areas.

Most conspicuous of the birds of prey are the **kestrel** (*Falco tinnunculus*), the **sparrowhawk** (*Accipiter nisus*) and the much larger **buzzard** (*Buteo buteo*), with its brown colouring and cruel yel-

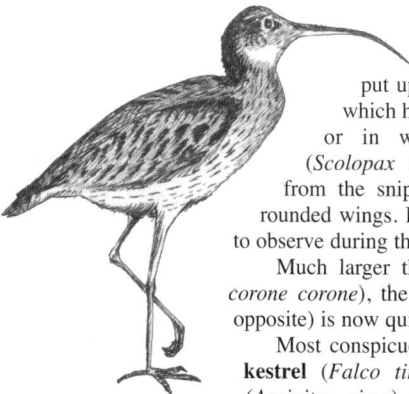

CURLEW
L: 600MM/24"

HISTORY, ENVIRONMENT & NATURE

❑ The Red Kite

RED KITE
L: 650MM/25"

Red kites were common throughout Britain centuries ago and were known to scavenge the streets of London but they have since been shot, trapped or poisoned to the extent that by the end of the 19th century they had retreated to a tiny colony in Wales. They were saved from extinction by a dedicated group of conservationists and, with the help of the Nature Conservancy Council, the Joint Nature Conservation Committee and the RSPB, they were re-introduced from 1989 onwards. The project was a great success and the latest figures we have are that there are now 1800 breeding pairs in the UK.

Although it is commonly believed that kites feed on lambs, they do not have the strength to tear the carcass of a lamb, let alone kill a live animal. They will feed on scraps left by crows and buzzards but wait their turn, knowing better than to get involved with these fiercer birds. The main prey of kites is small mammals, insects and earthworms: it has been estimated that a growing kite consumes the equivalent each day of a small rabbit.

Offa's Dyke walkers will have no trouble spotting a kite – they're quite numerous in the skies above the path these days. The main problem is actually distinguishing them from the even more common buzzard, a similar-sized bird though one that looks heavier and is less graceful in flight. Get a close enough view of the kite and you'll also be able to spot its distinguishing features, namely its deeply forked tail and the reddish-brown-to-dull-orange plumage. Nevertheless, the RSPB continues to put the red kite on its 'amber' list, meaning it's a species with an 'unfavourable conservation status in Europe', largely due to its historical decline.

For further information see 🖥 welshkitetrust.wales.

low talons. **Red kites** (*Milvus milvus*) can now be seen once again in mid-Wales; their forked tails distinguish them quite clearly from other birds of prey in flight; see also box above.

If you're very lucky you may even spot the **merlin** (*Falco columbarius*) which has a darkish bluish back and tail and flies fast and low over the ground chasing pipits and larks.

There's also a large population of **redstarts** (*Phoenicurus phoenicurus*) in Wales and you may see the tell-tale flash of the male's orange tail as it flits amongst hedgerows and bushes, especially near Eglwyseg Crags.

Disgwylfa Hill is a gift from God
Or whomever you believe in
Please cherish it as we do
Don't dump your scrap or tin

We wish to preserve the beauty
Of this green and pleasant land
So don't be selfish have a heart
And help us make a stand

This is a heartfelt message
To all you lazy dumpees
Take away your rubbish and litter
Don't leave it here, PLEASE

For those of you who do not care
And ignore our message too
Just remember that these hills
have eyes
And they are watching YOU.
Posted on a stile on the trail

HISTORY, ENVIRONMENT & NATURE

MINIMUM IMPACT & OUTDOOR SAFETY

Minimum-impact walking

Walk as if you are kissing the Earth with your feet
Thich Nhat Hanh *Peace is every step*

The countryside through which you pass when walking the Offa's Dyke Path holds a fascination and an appeal that has attracted visitors since tourism first began. Perhaps its juxtaposition of attractive towns and easily accessible countryside makes it an ideal area for a short or long visit to recharge your batteries and call a temporary halt to the pace of life. However, as more and more people enjoy the freedom of open country so the land comes under increasing pressure and the potential for conflict with other land-users is heightened. Everyone has a right to this natural heritage but with it comes a responsibility to care for it too. By following some simple guidelines while walking you can have a positive impact, not just on your own well-being but also on local communities and the environment, thereby becoming part of the solution.

ENVIRONMENTAL IMPACT

By choosing a walking holiday you have already made a positive step towards minimising your impact on the wider environment. By following these suggestions you can also tread lightly along the path.

Use public transport whenever possible

Using public transport rather than private cars benefits both visitors and locals, as well as the environment. Unfortunately, while local buses (see pp50-1) serve many of the villages through which you pass, it's only occasionally possible to use them at the end of a day (or several days) on the trail to get back to a convenient point. To fill in the gaps, local taxi firms and some B&B proprietors are happy to ferry walkers and/or their luggage around (though this is, of course, the more expensive option). Doing this boosts the local economy too.

Never leave litter

Leaving litter shows a total disrespect for the natural world and others coming after you. As well as being unsightly, litter kills wildlife, pollutes the environment and can be dangerous to farm animals.

Please carry bags so you can dispose of your rubbish in a bin in the next village. It would be very helpful if you could pick up litter left by other people too.

● **Is it OK if it's biodegradable?** Not really. Apple cores, banana skins, orange peel are all unsightly, encourage flies and wasps and ruin a picnic spot for others.

● **The lasting impact of litter** A piece of orange peel left on the ground takes six months to decompose; silver foil 18 months; a plastic bag 10 years; clothes 15 years; and an aluminium drinks can 85 years.

Buy local

Look and ask for local produce to buy and eat. Not only does this cut down on 'food miles' (the amount of pollution and congestion that the transportation of food creates), it also ensures that you are supporting local farmers and producers.

Erosion

● **Stay on the waymarked trail** The effect of your footsteps may seem minuscule but when they are multiplied by several thousand walkers each year they become rather more significant. Avoid taking shortcuts, widening the trail or creating more than one path; your boots will be followed by many others. The principal causes of erosion to the Offa's Dyke earthwork are agriculture, burrowing animals and tourism and these have to be balanced against its practical purposes, namely as a boundary, a wildlife corridor, a local landmark and a lane or footpath. There are conflicting demands made on Offa's Dyke and conservationists and those responsible for its preservation have a difficult task in steering the most appropriate course to ensure that future generations will be able to experience the same degree of interest and enjoyment from it as we do today.

● **Consider walking out of season** Maximum disturbance by walkers coincides with the time of year when nature wants to do most of its growth and repair. In high-use areas, like that along much of the path, the trail is often prevented from recovering. Walking at less busy times eases this pressure while also spreading the income for the local economy. Not only that, but it may make the walk a more relaxing experience for you as out of season there are fewer people on the path and there's less competition for accommodation.

Respect all wildlife

Care for all wildlife you come across on the path; it has just as much of a right to be there as you. Tempting as it may be to pick wild flowers, leave them so the next person who passes can enjoy them too. Don't break branches off or damage trees in any way. If you come across wildlife keep your distance and don't watch for too long. Your presence can cause considerable stress particularly if the adults are with their young or in winter when the weather is harsh and food scarce. Young animals are rarely abandoned. If you come across deer calves or young birds that are apparently alone, keep away so that their mother can return.

The code of the outdoor loo

'Going' in the outdoors is a lost art worth relearning, for your sake and everyone else's. As more and more people discover the joys of the outdoors this is becoming an important issue. Human excrement is not only offensive to our senses but, more importantly, can infect water sources.

● **Where to go** Wherever possible wait until you can **use a toilet**. Public toilets are marked on the trail maps in this guide and you will also find facilities in pubs or cafés and on campsites.

If you do have to go outdoors choose a site at least **30m away from running water**. Carry a small trowel and, as long as you are sure the land is not of specific historical or archaeological interest, **dig a small hole** about 15cm (6") deep in which to bury your excrement. It decomposes quicker when in contact with the top layer of soil or leaf mould. Use a stick to stir loose soil into your deposit as well as this speeds up decomposition even more. Do not squash it under rocks as this slows down the composting process. If you have to use rocks to hide it make sure they are not in contact with your faeces.

● **Toilet paper and tampons** Toilet paper takes a long time to decompose whether buried or not. It is easily dug up by animals and could then blow into water sources or onto the trail. The best method for dealing with it is to **pack it out**. Put the used paper inside a paper bag which you place inside a plastic bag (or two). Then simply empty the contents of the paper bag at the next toilet you come across and throw the bag away. You should also pack out **tampons** and **sanitary towels** in a similar way; they will almost certainly be dug up and scattered about by animals and they take years to decompose.

Wild camping

Wild camping is not permitted anywhere along the Offa's Dyke Path. Carrying a tent is no problem since there are many campsites, both purpose-built and those in the gardens of B&Bs and pubs. It goes without saying that you should leave your pitch exactly as you found it: unmarked, without litter and without any obvious signs that you have been there.

ACCESS

Much of the route which walkers on Offa's Dyke Path follow is through farmland, frequently passing farm buildings and grazing livestock to the point that it is impossible to be unaware of the business of farming. Farmers are faced with a harsh environment, a short grazing season and severe weather conditions; so let's not add the nuisance of long-distance walkers to their problems.

The landscape of the countryside and its wildlife has been created to a large extent by farming. Centuries of grazing by sheep has created the close-cropped grassy hillsides characteristic of the Clwydian Hills and the Black Mountains and hill farming has shaped the land and made for us the special identity which is so appealing to walkers and visitors. The hill farm helps sustain a service and supply industry, from feed suppliers to transport, fuel, machinery, farm labour, fencing and walling, vets and auction marts. It should be seen as a part of the vital rural infrastructure rather than an isolated farmstead at the end of a long and winding road.

Rights of way

As a designated national trail, Offa's Dyke Path is a public right of way, a path that anyone has the right to use on foot provided that they stay on the path and do not cause damage or obstruct it in any way. Broadly, public rights of way in Britain fall into one of three (colour-coded) categories:

● A **footpath** (yellow) is open to walkers only, not to cyclists, horse-riders or vehicles.

● A **bridleway** (blue) is open to walkers, horse-riders and cyclists.

● A **byway** (red) is open to motorised traffic as well as to walkers, riders and cyclists.

That said, not all footpaths are necessarily rights of way. Some canal tow-paths, for instance, aren't official rights of way but their use for this purpose is more or less taken for granted. Sometimes a landowner will allow a path across his land to be used for the convenience of walkers although it may not be recog-nised as a right of way. This is known as a **permissive path**.

The maintenance of rights of way is down to the landowner in conjunction with the county council through whose area it passes and sometimes the local authority. Farmers and land managers must ensure that paths are not blocked by crops or other vegetation, or otherwise obstructed, that the route is identifiable, and that the surface is restored soon after cultivation. If there are crops growing over the path, you have every right to walk through them, following the line of the right of way as closely as possible. Should you find a path blocked or impassable, report it to the appropriate highway authority.

'Right to roam'

Walkers can be forgiven for being confused by all the talk about where they can and can't go in the countryside. What is meant by 'the right to roam'? Where do we stand with the legislation? Has anything changed?

Well, yes. Following a concerted effort by groups such as Ramblers (see box p44) and the British Mountaineering Council, the countryside is finally being opened up under the Countryside and Rights of Way Act 2000, affection-ately known as CroW. In Wales the act came into effect in full in May 2005 and in England in October 2005, creating a new right of access to the English and Welsh coun-tryside for recreation on foot. There are restrictions, of course: some land (such as gar-dens, parks and cultivated land) is excluded, and high-impact activities such as driving a vehicle, cycling, and horse-riding may not be permitted.

The act also gives greater protection to SSSIs (see p60), and new powers to set up conservation boards to manage AONBs (see p60); it lists habitats and species important to biological diversity in England; and it covers the conduct of those walking with dogs (see pp245-7). While much of this is only of

> ❏ **Lambing**
> This takes place from mid-March to mid-May and is a critical economic time for the hard-pressed hill farm-ers. Please do not interfere with livestock farming in any way. If a ewe or lamb seems to be in distress con-tact the nearest farmer. **Dogs** should be kept off land where sheep are grazing throughout this season so that pregnant ewes are not disturbed.

❏ The Countryside Code

The Countryside Code, originally described in the 1950s as the Country Code, was revised and relaunched in 2004, in part because of the changes brought about by the CRoW Act (see opposite); it was updated again in 2012, 2014 and also 2016. The Code seems like common sense but sadly some people still appear to have no under-standing of how to treat the countryside they walk in. An adapted version of the 2016 Code, launched under the logo 'Respect. Protect. Enjoy.', is given below:

Respect other people

● **Consider the local community and other people enjoying the outdoors** Be sensitive to the needs and wishes of those who live and work there. If, for example, farm animals are being moved or gathered keep out of the way and follow the farmer's directions. Being courteous and friendly to those you meet will ensure a healthy future for all based on partnership and co-operation.

● **Leave gates and property as you find them and follow paths unless wider access is available** A farmer normally closes gates to keep farm animals in, but may sometimes leave them open so the animals can reach food and water. Leave gates as you find them or follow instructions on signs. When in a group, make sure the last person knows how to leave the gate. Follow paths unless wider access is available, such as on open country and registered common land (known as 'open access land'). Leave machinery and farm animals alone – if you think an animal is in distress try to alert the farmer instead. Use gates, stiles or gaps in field boundaries if you can – climbing over walls, hedges and fences can damage them and increase the risk of farm animals escaping. If you have to climb over a gate because you can't open it always do so at the hinged end. Also be careful not to disturb ruins and historic sites.

Stick to the official path across arable/pasture land. Minimise erosion by not cutting corners or widening the path.

Protect the natural environment

● **Leave no trace of your visit and take your litter home** Take special care not to damage, destroy or remove features such as rocks, plants and trees. Take your litter with you (see pp75-6); litter and leftover food doesn't just spoil the beauty of the countryside, it can be dangerous to wildlife and farm animals.

Fires can be as devastating to wildlife and habitats as they are to people and property – so be careful with naked flames and cigarettes at any time of the year.

● **Keep dogs under effective control** This means that you should keep your dog on a lead or keep it in sight at all times, be aware of what it's doing and be confident it will return to you promptly on command.

Across farmland dogs should always be kept on a short lead. During lambing time they should not be taken with you at all. Always clean up after your dog and get rid of the mess responsibly – 'bag it and bin it'. (See also box opposite and pp245-7).

Enjoy the outdoors

● **Plan ahead and be prepared** You're responsible for your own safety: be prepared for natural hazards, changes in weather and other events. Wild animals, farm animals and horses can behave unpredictably if you get too close, especially if they're with their young – so give them plenty of space.

● **Follow advice and local signs** In some areas there may be temporary diversions in place. Take notice of these and other local trail advice.

background interest for those walking the Offa's Dyke Path, it will have a significant impact on the future of walking in the countryside generally.

Full details are given on the 'Access and rights of way' page on 🖳 gov.uk/ government/organisations/natural-england, or the 'Days out' page on 🖳 natural resources.wales for Wales.

Health and outdoor safety

HEALTH

Preventative measures

Water and dehydration You need to drink lots of water while walking: 2-4 litres a day depending on the weather. If you're feeling drained, lethargic or just out of sorts it may be that you haven't drunk enough. Thirst is not a reliable indicator of how much you should drink. The frequency and colour of your urine is better; the maxim, 'a happy mountaineer always pees clear' is worth following.

Sunburn Even on overcast days, the sun still has the power to burn. Sunburn can be avoided by regularly applying sunscreen, remembering your lips and ears, and by wearing a hat to protect your face and the back of your neck. Those with fair skin should consider wearing a light, long-sleeved top and long trousers rather than T-shirt and shorts.

Blisters You will prevent blisters by wearing worn-in, comfortable boots and looking after your feet. How many people set out on a long walk in new boots and live to regret it!

Look after your feet: air them at lunchtime, keep them clean and change your socks daily. If you feel any 'hot spots' on your feet while you are walking, stop immediately and apply a few strips of zinc oxide tape and leave them on until it is pain free or the tape starts to come off.

If you have left it too late and a blister has developed you should surround it with 'moleskin' or any other 'blister kit' to protect it from abrasion. Popping it can lead to infection. If the skin is broken, keep the area clean with antiseptic and cover with a non-adhesive dressing material held in place with tape.

Joints and muscles If you're susceptible to joint problems – in particular knees and ankles – do invest in a pair of walking poles and use one or both of them, especially during steep ascents or descents. Properly used, they can lessen the impact on your joints during long-distance walking, and thus can help to prevent injury. Even the fittest athlete warms up before exercise and stretches afterwards – and so should you. It's surprising how much easier it is to set off in the morning without aching muscles, and this, too, lessens the risk of injury.

More serious problems

Hypothermia Hypothermia, or exposure, occurs when the body can't generate enough heat to maintain its core temperature. Since it is usually as a result of being wet, cold, unprotected from the wind, tired and hungry, it is easily avoided by wearing suitable clothing (see pp40-1), carrying and eating enough food and drink, being aware of the weather conditions, and checking on the morale of your companions.

Early signs to watch for include feeling cold and tired with involuntary shivering; find shelter as soon as possible and warm the person up with a hot drink and chocolate or other high-energy food. If possible, give them another warm layer of clothing and allow them to rest.

If the condition is allowed to worsen, strange behaviour, slurring of speech and poor co-ordination will become apparent and the victim can quickly progress into unconsciousness, followed by coma and death. Quickly get the victim out of the wind and rain, improvising a shelter if necessary.

Rapid restoration of body warmth is essential and best achieved by bare-skin contact: someone should get into the same sleeping bag as the patient, both having stripped to their underwear, with any spare clothing laid under and over them to build up heat. This is an emergency: send for help.

Hyperthermia At the other end of the scale, hyperthermia occurs when the body is allowed to overheat. **Heat exhaustion** is often caused by water depletion and is a serious condition that could eventually lead to death. Symptoms include thirst, fatigue, giddiness, a rapid pulse, raised body temperature, low urine output and, later on, delirium and coma. The only remedy is to re-establish the balance of water. If the victim is suffering severe muscle cramps it may be due to salt depletion.

Heat stroke is caused by failure of the body's temperature-regulating system, and is extremely serious. It is associated with a very high body temperature and an absence of sweating. Early symptoms can be similar to those of hypothermia, such as aggressive behaviour, lack of co-ordination and so on. Later the victim goes into a coma or convulsion, and death will follow if effective treatment is not given. Sponge the victim down or cover with wet towels, then vigorously fan them. Get help immediately.

Dealing with an accident
● Ensure that both you and the casualty are out of further risk of danger, but otherwise do not move someone who may be seriously injured.

● Use basic first aid to treat the injury to the best of your ability.

● Work out exactly where you are in case you have to send for the emergency services, and write down the details.

● Try to attract the attention of anybody else who may be in the area. The **emergency signal** is six blasts on a whistle, or six flashes with a torch.

● If you have to go for help, ideally leave someone with the casualty. If there is nobody else, make sure that the casualty is warm, sheltered and as comfortable as possible, and leave spare clothing, water and food within easy reach, as well as a whistle and/or torch for attracting attention.

● Telephone ☎ 999 and ask for the police or other rescue service.

● Report the exact position of the casualty and his or her condition.

OUTDOOR SAFETY

Avoidance of hazards

The Offa's Dyke Path is not a hazardous undertaking and should not put the average walker to any greater risk than he or she would encounter on an average day's ramble in the countryside. Always make sure you have sufficient clothes to keep you warm and dry, whatever the conditions, and a spare change of inner clothes. A **compass**, **whistle**, **torch** and **first-aid kit** should also be carried and you should know how to use them.

Take enough **food** to sustain you during the day and always set out with at least one litre of **water**. Drinking from streams is not recommended since they are likely to contain traces of pesticides and other chemicals used on the land. You will find that you will eat more than normal because you are using up more energy. High-energy snacks are worth considering, either proprietary brands or chocolate, nuts and dried fruit.

Stay alert and try to keep track of exactly where you are throughout the day. The easiest way is to use the map, or GPS if you have it, to **check your position**. If bad weather comes in, you will then be able to make a sensible decision on what action to take based on your location.

If you enjoy **walking alone** you must appreciate and be prepared for the increased risk. You should tell someone where you are going. One way of doing this is to telephone your booked accommodation and let them know you are walking alone and what time you expect to arrive. If you leave word with someone else, don't forget to let them know you have arrived safely.

Safety in wild country

There are parts of the Offa's Dyke Path that fall into the category of wild country, particularly in the Clwydian Hills (north of Llangollen) and the Black Mountains (south of Hay-on-Wye). These parts can feel quite remote and you should always have the means to protect yourself from the worst weather conditions. Besides **extra food** (high-energy snacks are best here), **water** as well as **map(s) and a compass**, you should also carry a **hat** and **gloves** and possibly a **survival bag**. Anyone tackling the route in winter must have sufficient experience to know when not to go out on the hill. Low-level walking in bad weather should not be a problem for the experienced.

Weather information

Anyone familiar with the British weather will know that it can change quickly. What started out as a warm sunny day can be chilly and wet by lunchtime, so don't be fooled. The daily newspapers, television and radio will always give the forecast for the day ahead and local people will have plenty of advice on the subject. You can get an online forecast at 🖥 metoffice.gov.uk or 🖥 bbc.co.uk/weather. Pay close attention to it and contemplate altering your plans for the day accordingly.

That said, even if the forecast is for a bright sunny day do consider packing some wet-weather gear – just in case.

ROUTE GUIDE & MAPS   4

Using this guide

The route guide and maps have not been divided into rigid daily stages since people walk at different speeds and have different interests. Some sections fall naturally into full days such as between Kington and Knighton but more often the choice is up to the walker.

The **route summaries** describe the trail between significant places and are shown twice: for walking the path south to north and for walking the path north to south. To enable you to plan your own itinerary **practical information** is presented clearly on the trail maps. This includes walking times, waypoints, places to stay, camp and eat, as well as shops where you can buy supplies. Further service details are given in the text under the entry for each place.

For **map profiles** see the colour pages and **overview maps** at the end of the book. For an overview of this information see 'Itineraries' pp37 and the 'Village and town facilities' table on pp32-5.

TRAIL MAPS

Direction
(See p31 for a discussion of the pros and cons of walking north to south or south to north). In the text and maps that follow, look for the
N↑ symbol which indicates information for those walking **from Chepstow to Prestatyn** and the **S↓** symbol with shaded text (also on the maps) for those walking **from Prestatyn to Chepstow**.

Scale and walking times
The trail maps are to a scale of 1:20,000 (1cm = 200m; $3^1/_8$ inches = one mile). Walking times are given along the side of each map and the arrow shows the direction to which the time refers. Black triangles indicate the points between which the times have been taken. **See note on walking times in the box below**. The time-bars are a tool and are not there to judge your walking ability. There are so

---

❏ **Important note – walking times**
Unless otherwise specified, **all times in this book refer only to the time spent walking**. You should add 20-30% to allow for rests, photos, checking the map, drinking water etc, not to mention time simply to stop and stare. When planning the day's hike count on 5-7 hours' actual walking.

many variables that affect walking speed, from the weather conditions to how many beers you drank the previous evening. After the first hour or two of walking you will be able to see how your speed relates to the timings on the maps.

Up or down?
The trail is shown as a dotted line – – –. An arrow across the trail indicates the slope; two arrows show that it is steep. Note that the arrow points towards the higher part of the trail. If, for example, you are walking from A (at 80m) to B (at 200m) and the trail between the two is short and steep it would be shown thus: A– – – >> – – – B. Reversed arrow heads indicate downward gradient.

Other features
Features are marked on the map when pertinent to navigation. In order to avoid cluttering the maps and making them unusable, not all features have been marked each time they occur.

ACCOMMODATION
Accommodation marked on the map is either on or within easy reach of the trail. The details for each place are given in the accompanying text.

The number of **rooms** of each type is stated, ie: **S** = Single, **T** = Twin room, **D** = Double room, **Tr** = Triple room and **Qd** = Quad. Note that most of the triple/quad rooms have a double bed and one/two single beds (or bunk beds). Consequently for a group of three or four, two people would have to share the double bed but it also means the room can be used as a double or twin.

Rates quoted for B&B-style accommodation are **per person (pp)** based on two people sharing a room for a one-night stay; rates are usually discounted for longer stays. Where a single room **(sgl)** is available the rate for that is quoted if different from the rate per person. The rate for single occupancy **(sgl occ)** of a double/twin may be higher, and the per person rate for three/four sharing a triple/quad may be lower. At some places the only option is a **room rate**; this will be the same whether one or two people (or more if permissible) use the room. See box p20 for more information on rates.

The text also mentions whether the bedrooms are **en suite**, or whether **facilities** are **private** or **shared** (in either case this may be a bathroom or shower room just outside the bedroom). In the text ♥ signifies that at least one room has a **bath** – either in an en suite bathroom or in a separate bathroom – for those who prefer a relaxed soak at the end of the day.

Also noted is whether the premises have: **wi-fi** (WI-FI); if **dogs** (🐾 – see also pp245-7) are welcome in at least one room (often places only have one room suitable for dogs), or at campsites, subject to prior arrangement, and any associated requirements; and if **packed lunches** (Ⓛ) are available (these must almost always be requested in advance – ie by, or on, the night before).

If arranged in advance many B&B proprietors are happy to collect walkers from the nearest point on the trail and deliver them back again next morning; they may also be happy to transfer your luggage to your next accommodation place on the map. Some may make a charge for either or both of these services.

The route guide

N↑ **FROM CHEPSTOW** If you're doing this walk in a **northerly direction** (starting in Chepstow and ending in Prestatyn) follow the maps below in an ascending order (from 1 to 86) and the text as below, looking for the **N↑** symbol on overview text and on map borders.

S↓ **FROM PRESTATYN** If you're walking in a **southerly direction** (Prestatyn to Chepstow) follow the maps in a descending order (from 86 to 1) and the text with a **grey background**, looking for the **S↓** symbol on overview text and on map borders. **Turn to p240 to start your walk in this direction**.

SEDBURY CLIFFS TO CHEPSTOW   MAP 1, p86

The initial **1½-mile (2km, 30-45mins)** stretch from Sedbury Cliffs to the outskirts of Chepstow is a rather ignominious introduction to this superb walk and should certainly not be taken as any indication of what is to come.

In the shadow of the Severn Bridge sits the stone that marks the symbolic beginning of your 177-mile odyssey. Despite the stone stating that there are 168 miles between here and Prestatyn, where via riverbank, hill and towpath your journey will end, be assured – there are 177 miles to go.

Choosing to start at the southern end of the path means that you are immediately astride the Dyke (unlike the northern end where you won't see evidence of the Dyke until Castle Mill) and the trail teases you; conspiring with the ancient rampart to take you through fields and past **Buttington Tump** before anti-climatically entering suburbia – although, be assured, once you clear Chepstow and its environs, things will dramatically liven up. Be sure to follow closely either the maps in this book or the acorns dotted on lampposts and gates along this initial stretch as once you re-enter civilisation following this briefest of dices with the Dyke the path can catch you out if you're not vigilant.

Sedbury is on James Bevan Coaches' No 761 bus route (see pp49-53) and there is a Spar (Mon-Sat 7am-11pm, Sun 8am-10.30pm) with a post office but little else.   [*Next route overview p90*]

CHEPSTOW (*CAS-GWENT*)
Map 1a, p88

He who by land would enter
Chepstow Town
Must quit his horse, and
lead him gently down (Engraved in the paving just below the Town Arch)

If Chepstow is your first port of call on Offa's Dyke Path then take inspiration from those you see arriving from the North; if that is you, then journey's end is in sight. If

you've walked all the way from Prestatyn you should feel in tune with the engraving on the pavement by Chepstow's Town Arch, which manfully resists the traffic pollution as it has done for four hundred years. A good bypass keeps through traffic away from the town centre, where a one-way system circulates around a central pedestrian area.

Chepstow offers everything the overnighter could need, from accommodation to

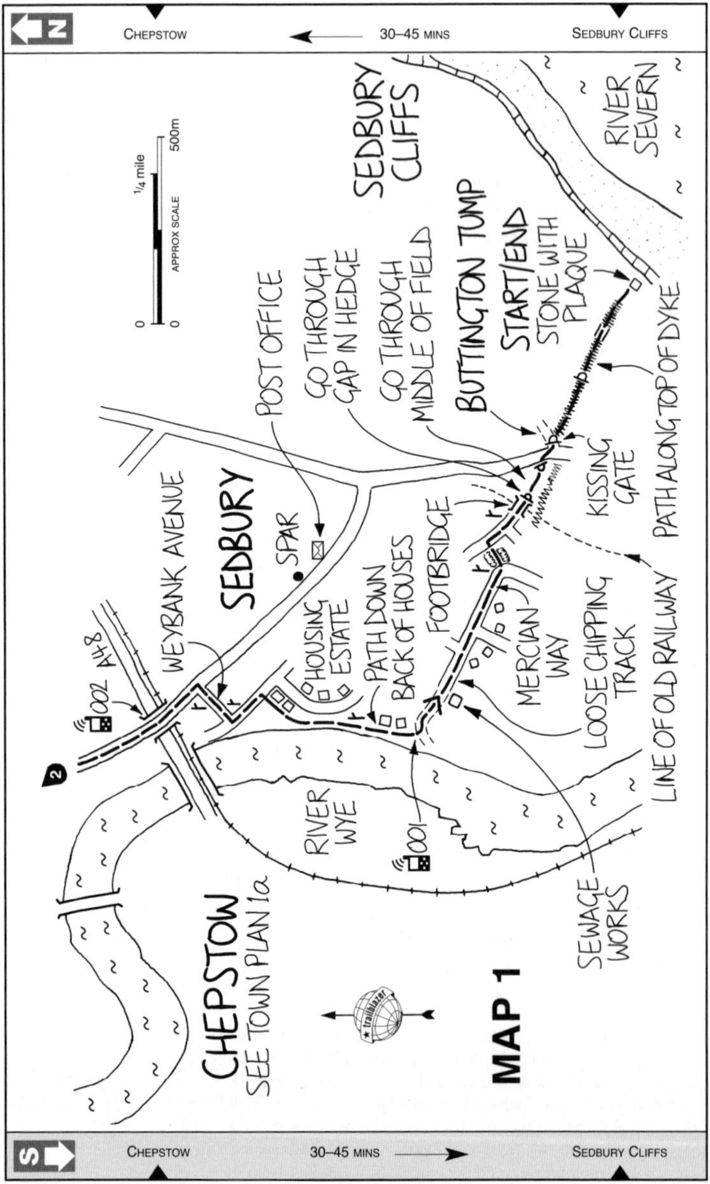
N
CHEPSTOW
30–45 MINS
SEDBURY CLIFFS
1/4 mile
0
0
APPROX SCALE
500m
SEDBURY CLIFFS
RIVER SEVERN
POST OFFICE
GO THROUGH GAP IN HEDGE
GO THROUGH MIDDLE OF FIELD
BUTTINGTON TUMP
START/END
STONE WITH PLAQUE
PATH ALONG TOP OF DYKE
KISSING GATE
WEYBANK AVENUE
SEDBURY
SPAR
HOUSING ESTATE
PATH DOWN BACK OF HOUSES
FOOTBRIDGE
MERCIAN WAY
LOOSE CHIPPING TRACK
LINE OF OLD RAILWAY
002
A48
2
RIVER WYE
001
SEWAGE WORKS
CHEPSTOW
SEE TOWN PLAN 1a
trailblazer
MAP 1
S
CHEPSTOW
30–45 MINS
SEDBURY CLIFFS

> ❏ **Chepstow Castle**
> Standing stark and solid on the cliffs above the River Wye, Chepstow Castle (☎ 01291-624065, 🖳 cadw.wales.gov.uk/daysout/chepstow-castle; Mar-Jun & Sep-Oct daily 9.30am-5pm, Jul-Aug 9.30am-6pm, Nov-Feb Mon-Sat 10am-4pm, Sun 11am-4pm; admission £6.90) has a commanding presence over the town.
> The castle was built by the Norman baron William Fitzosbern as a base for subduing South Wales, with work starting in 1067, the year after the Battle of Hastings. It was constructed of stone, a considerable improvement on the old earth-and-timber motte-and-bailey castles, which had been adequate until the introduction of cannon and gunpowder. The building was progressively improved and strengthened during the 12th and 13th centuries when it changed hands many times, although resisting an assault by Owain Glyndwr. By the time of the English Civil War it was held by the Royalists, but was surrendered in 1645 to the Parliamentarians, who used it mainly as a prison. By the end of the 17th century it had begun to fall into disrepair.

efficient rail and road links. There's a good selection of places to eat and things to do and see, including an impressive castle to add to your list. Most places of interest to the visitor lie within the old city walls, below the Town Arch, focusing on the river and the **castle** (see box above).

The **museum** (☎ 01291-625981, 🖳 monmouthshire.gov.uk/chepstow-museum; daily 11am-4pm; entry free), on Bridge St, has displays on the town's history and its shipbuilding and fishing heritage.

Transport
[See pp49-53] Chepstow **railway** station is a shadow of its former self, with absolutely no facilities – not even a ticket office. Nevertheless, Cross Country and Transport for Wales services call here and the journey from London (change at Newport) takes only 2½ hours.

Several National Express **coach** services call here: NX201 (Brighton to Swansea via Heathrow & Gatwick airports); NX507 (London to Swansea); and NX509 (London to Cardiff).

Useful **bus** services include: First's 7XP and Newport Bus's No 73 & X74 (the latter is Stagecoach's No 74 on Sun) to Newport; Monmouthshire CC (No 65) and Phil Anslow Coaches (No 69) to Monmouth – the latter goes via Redbrook and Tintern; and James Bevan Coaches operate the No 761 to Sedbury.

For a **taxi** contact Abbey Taxis (☎ 01291-625847).

Services
The **tourist information centre** (☎ 01291-623772; open summer daily 10am-5pm, rest of year daily 10am-3pm) is located just off Bridge St by the car park. They provide accommodation booking (see box p44), a left-luggage service (£3 per day) and book tickets for National Express coaches (normal booking fee payable). A useful website is 🖳 chepstow.co.uk.

For anyone in need of extra cash, the town is liberally supplied with **cashpoints** from most of the main high street banks and there is a **post office** on Welsh St. For health needs, there is a **hospital** (☎ 01291-636636), which is out of town on the A466, and **pharmacies** in town which include Boots and the in-store department at Tesco. Although **early closing** day is Wednesday, most shops remain open, including the huge Tesco **supermarket** (Mon-Fri 24 hours, Sat to 10pm, Sun 10am-4pm) in front of the station. There's also a branch of M&S Food Hall (Mon-Sat 8am-8pm, Sun 10am-4pm) at the southern end of town.

Where to stay
Chepstow has a reasonable choice of accommodation, which can get booked up in the high season due to its prominent position as the gateway to Wales.

ROUTE GUIDE & MAPS

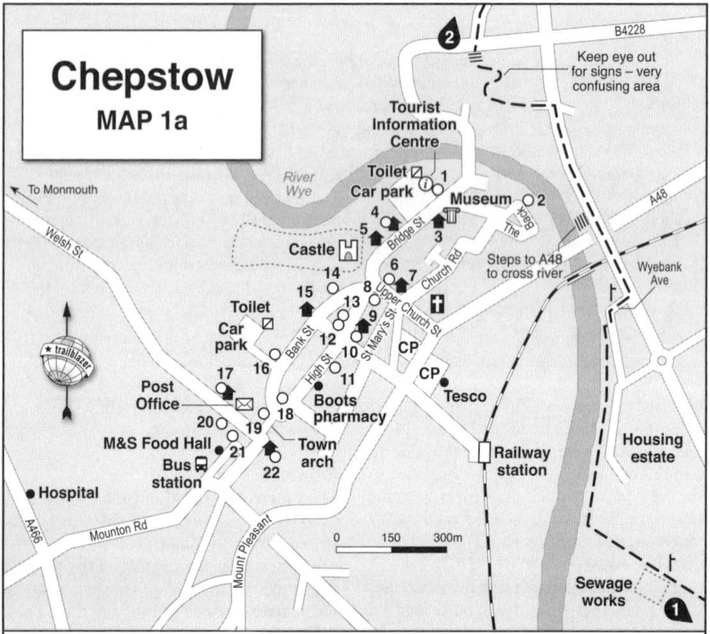

Chepstow
MAP 1a

B4228

Keep eye out for signs – very confusing area

To Monmouth

River Wye

Tourist Information Centre

Toilet ☑ 1
Car park ⓘ

Museum ○ 2

Welsh St

Bridge St

Castle 🏰
14

5

3

The Back

A48

Steps to A48 to cross river

Wyebank Ave

6 7
Toilet ☑
Car park

15
13
8
12
10
9
11

Upper Church St

Church Rd

St Mary's St

CP

Bank St

High St

Post Office ✉
20
19
17
16
18

CP

Tesco

Boots pharmacy

M&S Food Hall
21
22
Bus 🚌 station
Town arch

Railway station

Housing estate

● Hospital

A46

Mounton Rd

Mount Pleasant

0   150   300m

Sewage works

Where to stay
3 Woodfield Arms
4 Three Tuns Inn
5 Ty'r Castell B&B
7 The First Hurdle
9 The Beaufort Hotel
15 Greenman Backpackers
17 Coach & Horses
22 The George

Where to eat and drink
1 Panevino
2 Riverside Wine Bar
3 Woodfield Arms
4 Three Tuns Inn
6 Stone Rock
8 The Bell Hanger
10 Coffee #1
11 Greggs Bakery
12 Picnic

13 Lime Tree
14 The Orange Crate
16 Red Lantern
17 Coach & Horses
18 The Peppermill
19 Pye Corner &
   White Lion
20 Mythos
21 No 12 Fish 'n' Chips
22 The George

For those on a budget, *Greenman Backpackers* (☎ 01291-626773 or 07870-611979, 🖥 greenmanbackpackers.co.uk/chepstow-accommodation; WI-FI), 13 Beaufort Sq, is ideal. As well as dorm beds (2 x 6, 2 x 4, all shared facilities, 1 x 5 en suite; £22pp; sgl occ of dorm from £30) there are also three double en suite rooms (£65 per room) and two twin rooms (can be Tr/Quad) with private facilities (£55-75 per room). All prices include a self-service continental breakfast and there is a large TV

lounge and a bar (Thur-Sat noon-11.30pm) to relax in.

B&B-wise, *The First Hurdle Guest House* (☎ 01291-622189, 🖥 thefirsthurdle .com; 5D/5T/2S, all en suite; ✆; WI-FI), 9-10 Upper Church St, is a deceptively spacious establishment where B&B costs from £35pp (sgl occ £70).

Closer to the river and with views of the castle, *Ty'r Castell* (☎ 01291-627191 or ☎ 07977-038027 or ☎ 07958-207580, 🖥 tyrcastellbandbchepstow.co.uk; 1D en suite,

1D private facilities; 🐾; WI-FI; ☞; Ⓛ; £37.50pp, sgl occ £65), 45 Bridge St, is a Grade-II listed town house that will provide transport to Sedbury by arrangement.

A great option for walkers is the 550-year-old but recently renovated *The Coach and Horses Inn* (☎ 01291-622626, 🖳 the coachandhorseschepstow.co.uk; WI-FI in some areas; 🐾; Ⓛ) on Welsh St. There are two en suite double rooms which can be twin or family rooms (£75 per room); one double, and one twin (both en suite; £35pp, sgl occ £55) and a family wing which consists of two single rooms and a double (all of which share a bathroom; £120) and can be rented separately: the double for £25pp, and the singles for £35 – very reasonable indeed. Rates are room only (£7 extra for a full-English breakfast) but all of the rooms are that dog-friendly they stay for free.

Two other pubs worth considering are *The Three Tuns Inn* (☎ 01291-645797; 3D/1T, mixture en suite & private facilities; WI-FI; 🐾; Ⓛ; £42.50pp, sgl occ £57.50) and *The Woodfield Arms* (☎ 01291-620349, 🖳 thewoodfieldarms.com; 2S/10D all en suite; ☞; WI-FI; 🐾; from £45pp, sgl/sgl occ £60/70); both are on Bridge St.

The town centre has two hotels: *The George* (☎ 01291-625363, 🖳 georgehotel chepstow.co.uk; 6D or T/6D, all en suite; ☞; WI-FI), with accommodation including breakfast from £27.50pp (sgl occ full room rate); and *The Beaufort Hotel* (☎ 01291-622497, 🖳 beauforthotelchepstow.com; 4S/8D/9T/3Tr, all en suite; ☞; WI-FI; Ⓛ) which is a little smarter but pricier too; rooms cost from £42.50pp (sgl from £50), excluding breakfast which is an extra £5.55-6.95.

Approximately one mile north of Chepstow (along Offa's Dyke Path; Map 2) is *Broad Rock* (☎ 01291-794375, ☎ 07786-242565, 🖳 broadrock.co.uk; 3D can be T or Tr en suite; ☞; WI-FI; from £49.50pp, £105-115 for three sharing): a fine option for making your first – or final – full day on the trail a couple of hours shorter.

Where to eat and drink

There's plenty for the hungry to choose from in Chepstow.

Picnic (☎ 01291-621112; Mon-Sat 8am-3.30pm) is a take-out sarnie shop which can make you a packed lunch (around £4-5). There's a branch of *Gregg's* bakery in the town centre. Nearby, *Coffee No 1* (☎ 01291-630490; Mon-Sat 7.30am-6pm, Sun 8.30am-5.30pm) has gourmet coffee, and *The Orange Crate* (☎ 01291-630153; Mon-Sat 8.30am-4.30pm), serves detoxifying juices and freshly made smoothies.

Pye Corner and The White Lion (☎ 01291-630886; food is served in Pye Corner, daily 9am-6pm) has a good lunch menu but they also do afternoon teas (noon-4pm) and light bites during the day. Next door is The White Lion, a 17th-century inn (daily noon-midnight).

Other pubs to try are *Coach and Horses Inn* (see Where to stay; food Mon-Fri noon-2.30pm & 6-9pm, Sat noon-9pm, Sun noon-5pm), and closer to the castle and river, *The Three Tuns Inn* (see Where to stay; food daily noon-3pm). All can be trusted to fill your belly and serve you ale at a reasonable price. *The Woodfield Arms* (see Where to stay) is an option for Sunday lunch only (approximately £15).

The George (see Where to stay; 🐾 in the conservatory only; food served Mon-Thur 8am-9pm, Fri & Sat 8am-8pm, Sun 8am-5pm) has little character but the most expensive item on the menu is £7.95; breakfasts are £5-6.50. Likewise, *The Bell Hanger* (☎ 01291 637360), part of the Wetherspoons chain, is short of personality but you can take advantage of their very cheap meal deals (eg steak and a drink for around £6-7) and they have real ales on tap.

Award-winning artisan pizza (£7-14; eat-in or takeaway) can be found at *Stone Rock* (☎ 01291-621616, 🖳 stonerockpiz za.co.uk; Tue-Thur noon-3pm & 5-9pm, Fri to 9.30pm, Sat & Sun noon-9.30pm); meanwhile, for a far more extensive Italian menu head to *Panevino* (☎ 01291-409568, 🖳 panevino-restaurantchepstow.com; Mon-Sat 11am-11pm, Sun 11am-9pm), at the bottom of Bridge St. Mains cost approximately £10-20.

Keeping it continental, superbly located by the river is *Riverside Wine Bar* (☎

01291-628300, 🖥 theriversidewinebar.co
.uk; Mon-Thur 10.30am-11pm, Fri & Sat to
midnight), a Spanish tapas bar with dishes
for £3.95-5.95. Main meals such as Brazilian
spicy prawns (£13.95) are also an option.

Centrally, *Lime Tree* (☎ 01291-
620959; Mon-Fri 9am-9pm, Sat & Sun
8.30am-9pm) has an interesting and diverse
menu (for example, Pimm's salad for £8),
well worth checking out, and *The
Peppermill* (☎ 01291-630572, 🖥 pepper
millchepstow.co.uk; Sun noon-3pm, Mon-
Fri noon-2pm, Sun–Fri 6-10pm, Sat noon-
10pm) is also worth considering (steaks
£14.95-24.95).

If you fancy something different, head
for *Mythos* (☎ 01291-627222, 🖥 themythos
.co.uk; Tue-Thur noon-midnight, Fri & Sat
noon-2am, Sun 5pm-midnight) and feast on
Greek specialities such as moussaka (£11.95);
the rest of the menu is magnificent too.

If you just want a chippie, you'll find
No 12 Fish 'n' Chips (Mon-Sat opens
11.30am, closes Mon 10.30pm, Tue &
Thur 10pm, Wed 9.30pm, Fri & Sat midnight, Sun noon-9pm) next to the bus station and there's a Chinese, *Red Lantern* (☎
01291-627726; daily 5.30-11.15/30pm)
centrally too.

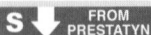

S ⬇ FROM PRESTATYN   CHEPSTOW TO SEDBURY CLIFFS   MAP 1, p86

The final 1½ miles (2km, 30-45mins) from the bridge over the A48 to Sedbury
Cliffs gets off to a poor start, a rather ignominious end to a superb walk. The
trail takes you along suburban streets, past a sewage works and into more
streets, before eventually emerging in fields at **Buttington Tump**. From here,
though, you are back on top of the Dyke, able to celebrate the last few yards
with a triumphant, albeit often muddy, climb to the edge of the Severn Estuary
and the stone that marks the symbolic end of your 177-mile journey – even if
the engraving on the stone states that you've completed just 168 of them! If
you've carried a pebble all the way from Prestatyn, toss it into the estuary from
the top of the cliffs – a fence bars your way down to the foreshore and there's
little to draw you down there.

Sedbury is on James Bevan Coaches' No 761 bus route (see pp49-53) and
there is a Spar and a post office but little else. So, unless you just happen to
have a bottle of champagne and a picnic in your rucksack, you'll probably want
to return to the pubs of Chepstow to celebrate your achievement and contemplate the ups and downs, literal and metaphorical, of this magnificent walk.

N ⬆ FROM CHEPSTOW   CHEPSTOW TO MONMOUTH   MAPS 1-10

[*Route section begins on Map 1, p86*] This **16½-mile (27km, 9hrs 25mins-
10hrs 10mins)** section is long and can be arduous. Don't forget that the walk
from Sedbury Cliffs (see p85) will make this an 18-mile opener to Offa's Dyke
Path, and with that in mind and despite your thirst to trek northwards, as your
first day on the trail you may wish to split this into two stages in order to ease
in your ankles and ameliorate your calves. Tintern is a fine option for an
overnight stop. Stopping there, you may feel that you have not ambled overly
far, but this feeling will soon dissipate as the path sucks you in: don't forget that
there are some long, hard – but ultimately, rewarding – days to come, and that
this early stop may be the decision that ensures your success in completing the
whole trail.

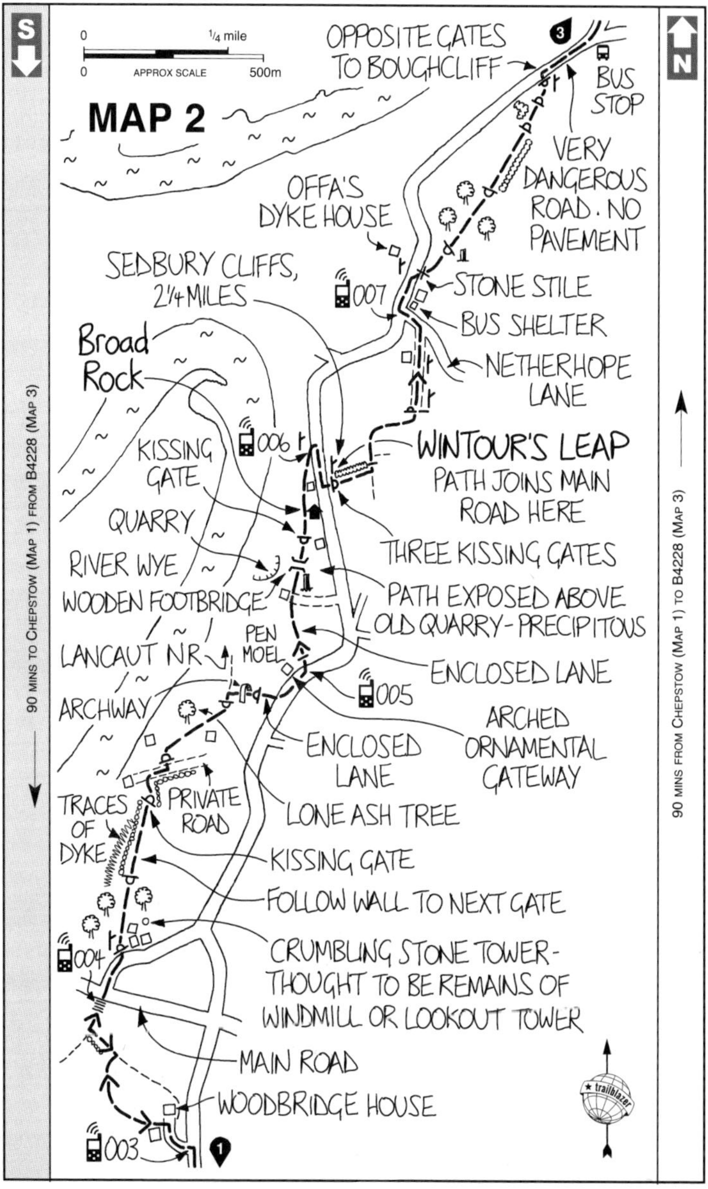

MAP 2

0 ———— 1/4 mile
0 ———— APPROX SCALE 500m

OPPOSITE GATES TO BOUGHCLIFF

3

BUS STOP

VERY DANGEROUS ROAD. NO PAVEMENT

OFFA'S DYKE HOUSE

SEDBURY CLIFFS, 2¼ MILES

007

STONE STILE

BUS SHELTER

NETHERHOPE LANE

Broad Rock

006

KISSING GATE

WINTOUR'S LEAP PATH JOINS MAIN ROAD HERE

QUARRY

RIVER WYE

THREE KISSING GATES

WOODEN FOOTBRIDGE

PATH EXPOSED ABOVE OLD QUARRY - PRECIPITOUS

LANCAUT NR

PEN MOEL

ENCLOSED LANE

ARCHWAY

005

ENCLOSED LANE

ARCHED ORNAMENTAL GATEWAY

TRACES OF DYKE

PRIVATE ROAD

LONE ASH TREE

KISSING GATE

FOLLOW WALL TO NEXT GATE

004

CRUMBLING STONE TOWER - THOUGHT TO BE REMAINS OF WINDMILL OR LOOKOUT TOWER

MAIN ROAD

WOODBRIDGE HOUSE

003

1

90 MINS TO CHEPSTOW (MAP 1) FROM B4228 (MAP 3)

90 MINS FROM CHEPSTOW (MAP 1) TO B4228 (MAP 3)

ROUTE GUIDE & MAPS

The path stealthily avoids Chepstow, weaving its way back and forth across the B4228, before arriving at **Wintour's Leap** (Map 2). From here some splendid woodland walking leads you to **Devil's Pulpit** (Map 3), with its magnificent view of Tintern Abbey and the **River Wye**.

Campers, content with what they have already achieved on this first day's trek, should leave the path where it joins the track (WPT 013; Map 4) and go to

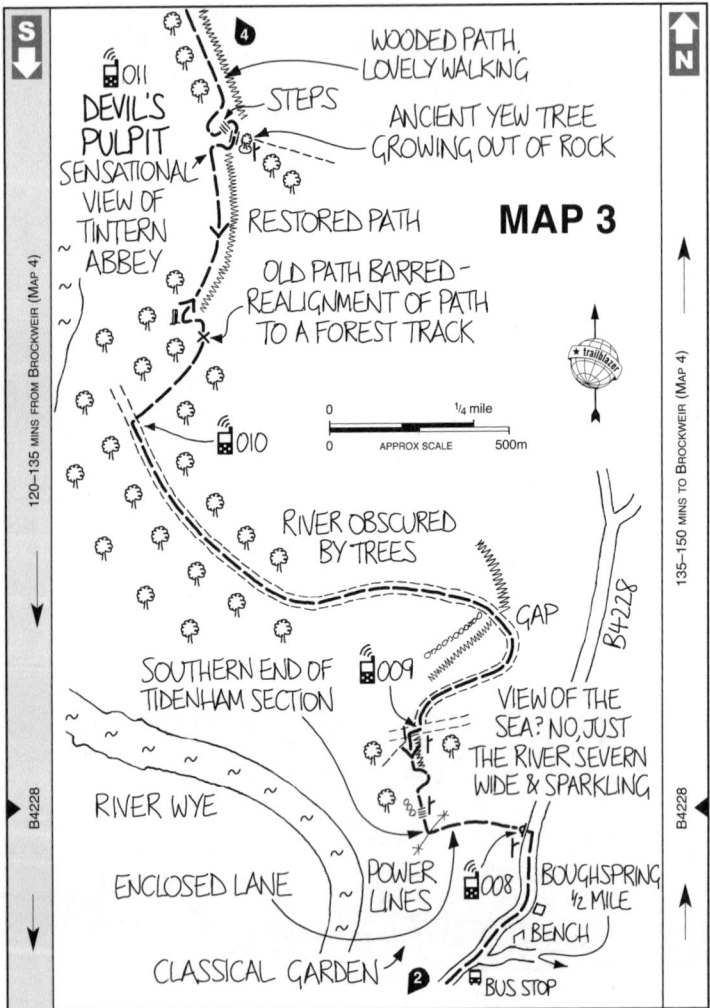

S

N

📱 011
DEVIL'S
PULPIT
SENSATIONAL
VIEW OF
TINTERN
ABBEY

WOODED PATH,
LOVELY WALKING

STEPS

ANCIENT YEW TREE
GROWING OUT OF ROCK

RESTORED PATH

MAP 3

OLD PATH BARRED –
REALIGNMENT OF PATH
TO A FOREST TRACK

trailblazer

📱 010

0 .... ¼ mile
0 .... 500m
APPROX SCALE

RIVER OBSCURED
BY TREES

GAP

SOUTHERN END OF
TIDENHAM SECTION

📱 009

VIEW OF THE
SEA? NO, JUST
THE RIVER SEVERN
WIDE & SPARKLING

RIVER WYE

ENCLOSED LANE

POWER
LINES

📱 008

BOUGHSPRING
½ MILE

BENCH

CLASSICAL GARDEN

2

BUS STOP

B4228

120–135 MINS FROM BROCKWEIR (MAP 4)

135–150 MINS TO BROCKWEIR (MAP 4)

B4228

B4228

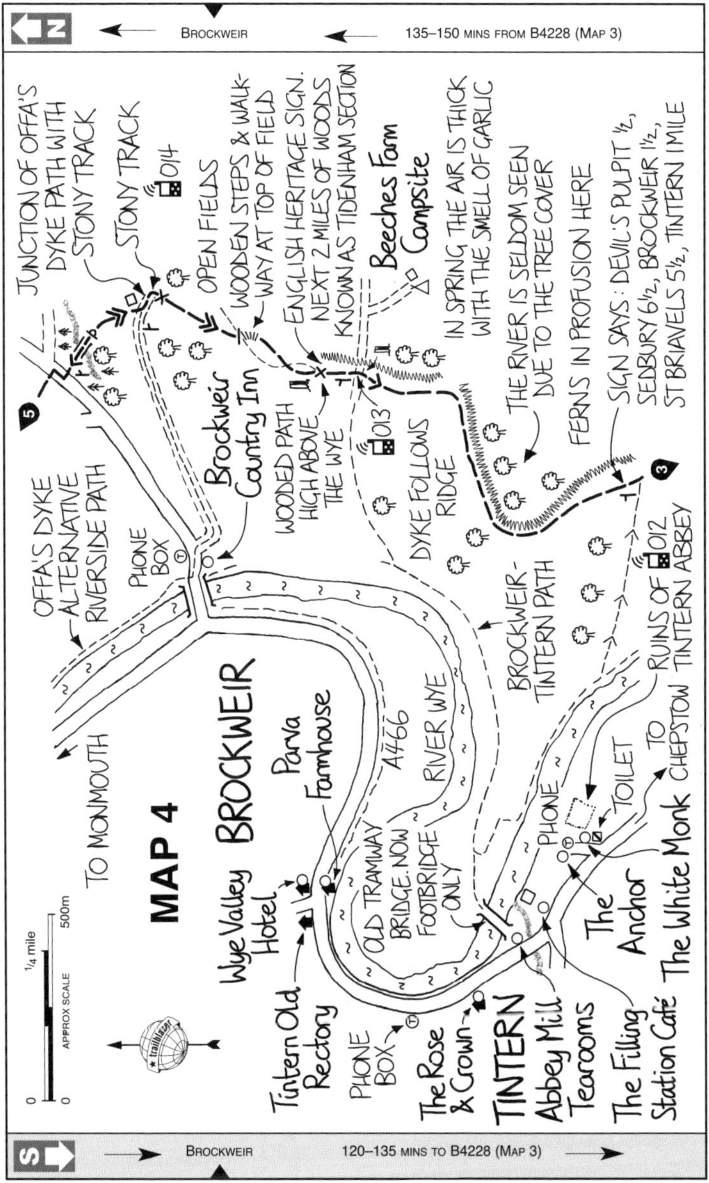
N
BROCKWEIR
135–150 MINS FROM B4228 (MAP 3)
JUNCTION OF OFFA'S DYKE PATH WITH STONY TRACK
STONY TRACK
014
OPEN FIELDS
WOODEN STEPS & WALK-WAY AT TOP OF FIELD
ENGLISH HERITAGE SIGN. NEXT 2 MILES OF WOODS KNOWN AS TIDENHAM SECTION
Beeches Farm Campsite
IN SPRING THE AIR IS THICK WITH THE SMELL OF GARLIC
THE RIVER IS SELDOM SEEN DUE TO THE TREE COVER
FERNS IN PROFUSION HERE
SIGN SAYS: DEVIL'S PULPIT ½, SEDBURY 6½, BROCKWEIR 1½, ST BRIAVELS 5½, TINTERN 1 MILE
5
Brockweir Country Inn
WOODED PATH HIGH ABOVE THE WYE
013
DYKE FOLLOWS RIDGE
3
OFFA'S DYKE ALTERNATIVE RIVERSIDE PATH
PHONE BOX
BROCKWEIR-TINTERN PATH
RUINS OF 012 TINTERN ABBEY
MAP 4
BROCKWEIR
TO MONMOUTH
Parva Farmhouse
A466
RIVER WYE
OLD TRAMWAY BRIDGE. NOW FOOTBRIDGE ONLY
PHONE
TOILET
TO CHEPSTOW
The Anchor
The White Monk
Wye Valley Hotel
Tintern Old Rectory
PHONE BOX
The Rose & Crown
TINTERN
Abbey Mill Tearooms
The Filling Station Café
¼ mile
500m
APPROX SCALE
0
0
trailblazer
S
BROCKWEIR
120–135 MINS TO B4228 (MAP 3)

Beeches Farm Campsite (☎ 07791-540016, 🖥 beechesfarmcampsite.co.uk; 🐾 ; Apr-Oct though dependent on the weather), Miss Graces Lane. They charge £8pp for **campers**; each pitch boasts a fire pit for which they sell wood (£4.50 per bag). They also have **static caravans** (£50-70; sleeping up to five people). There are toilet and shower facilities; the latter costs £1 for four minutes.

Whichever route you choose to take at this crossroads: whether to stay with the devil in the woods or to descend to those more heavenly at the abbey, when you reach the path's junction for **Brockweir** (WPT 014; Map 4), you have a more practical decision to make. Between Brockweir and **Bigsweir** the original route of the trail follows the beautiful **Wye Valley**, characterised by densely wooded slopes high above the gently flowing river, and as such there is an **alternative route** that you can opt to follow along the river. Purists will stick to the woods, settling for glimpses of the Wye through the trees, in part for the solitude but also because this is the route of the Dyke; however, for those fancying a far gentler day's walk, especially in anticipation of what is to come, the path along the river is a more-than-worthy alternative and many will find it a more enjoyable walk.

The paths re-join at Bigsweir Bridge (Map 7; although, the river can in fact be followed all the way to Monmouth via the Wye Valley Walk) before some tremendous trekking marches you on up through **Cadora Woods** and **Highbury Wood**, before you descend via a fine view of the Wye, to **Redbrook** (Map 9) and one of the path's best pubs. If you have the chance, it's well worth indulging in a pint at ***The Boat Inn*** (see p102) before you continue up again to **The Kymin** (see box p107), where more views await, before the final descent of the stage leads you over the river and into **Monmouth (Map 10, 101)**.

[*Next route overview p106*]

TINTERN   Map 4, p93

The romantic riverside ruins of **Tintern Abbey** (see box opposite) are one of the highlights of the walk, glimpsed through the trees from the path high above the Wye. It's just over a mile (1.6km) off route, though, so those short of time or energy may have to dispense with a closer look.

A clear signposted path leads down through the thickly wooded hillside to the riverside path which takes you to the old tramway bridge across the Wye. Once over the plank-boarded (but safe) bridge, turn left along the road; the abbey ruins are a quarter of a mile (400m) away. There are several hotels here as well as cafés, pubs and various souvenir-type shops, all well frequented, for this is a favourite venue for coach trips.

At the old stone-built ***Parva Farmhouse*** (☎ 01291-689411, 🖥 parva farmhouse.co.uk; 4D/2T/2Tr, all en suite; 🍴; WI-FI; Ⓛ), B&B costs £45pp (sgl occ £70; three sharing a room £120); an evening meal is offered Wed-Sat 7-8.30pm, £34 for 2 courses, £42 for 3 courses.

Overlooking the river is ***Tintern Old Rectory*** (☎ 01291-689920, 🖥 tinternold rectory.co.uk; 1D/2D or T/1Qd, all en suite, 🍴; WI-FI; 🐾; Ⓛ) with B&B for £40-50pp (sgl occ £30-40); you'll be hard-put to find a better breakfast.

More of a pub is ***Wye Valley Hotel*** (☎ 01291-689441, 🖥 thewyevalleyhotel.co.uk; 2S/2D/3D or T/1Tr, all en suite, 🍴; 🐾; WI-FI; Ⓛ) where B&B costs from £45pp (sgl/sgl occ from £70; Tr/Qd £95-125).

❑ Tintern Abbey

Tintern Abbey (☎ 01291-689251, 🖳 cadw
.wales.gov.uk/daysout/tinternabbey; Jul-
Aug daily 9.30am-6pm, Mar-Jun & Sep-
Oct daily 9.30am-5pm, Nov-Feb Mon-Sat
10am-4pm, Sun 11am-4pm; admission
£6.90) was founded in 1131 by Cistercian
monks, the most successful of the various
monastic orders of the period. The name
comes from their first establishment at
Citeaux in France, Cistercium in Latin,
established in 1098. Known as the White monks from their custom of wearing habits
made from undyed cloth, they followed a regime of strict abstinence, forsaking personal possessions and any unnecessary ornamentation. They sought out remote places
far away from the concourse of men and it was this that brought them to beautiful
river valleys such as Tintern, Grace Dieu (see p107) and Strata Marcella (see p180),
all on Offa's Dyke Path. At their height there were over 500 foundations spread right
across Northern Europe, 85 of them in Britain alone.

At the time of the Dissolution of the Monasteries by Henry VIII the monastery
at Tintern had declined and was reduced to only a few monks, and after they were
expelled it fell into ruin and destitution. However, the area was known for iron working and the ruins were soon appropriated as dwellings by the iron workers.

Wordsworth came here twice as a tourist and the scene of romantic desolation
soon had him reaching for his pen, composing the long poem *Lines Written a Few
Miles Above Tintern Abbey* in 1798. Tintern isn't mentioned but the poet was obviously impressed by the scenery:

> *How oft, in spirit, have I turned to thee*
> *O sylvan Wye! Thou wanderer through the woods*
> *How often has my spirit turned to thee!*

Food is available here (Mon-Sat noon-
2.30pm & 6-9pm, Sun noon-3.30pm &
5.30-8.45pm).

Closer to the bridge and abbey and
with outdoor seating by the river the food
can be highly recommended at *The Rose
and Crown* (☎ 01291-689254, 🖳 roseand
crowntintern.co.uk; food Wed-Fri noon-
2.30pm, Tue-Fri 6-8.30pm, Sat & Sun noon
-8.30pm), a friendly place where you'll get
a main meal (including specials) for less
than a tenner; **B&B** is also available (2D/
2T, shared facilities; £30pp, sgl occ £60).

The Anchor (☎ 01291-689582, 🖳
theanchortintern.co.uk; bar Mon-Sat
11.30am-11pm, Sun 11.30am-10.30pm)
serves food (Mon-Sat noon-9pm; Sun

noon-8pm) in their bar and restaurant, or
you can opt to eat at their outdoor seating
with views of the abbey. It's well produced
pub-grub (average price for a main £10)
and the service is efficient; the desserts
(£5.50) are well worth sampling if you
fancy a breather with a view of the abbey.

There are several cafés and tearooms
near the abbey too, including *Abbey Mill
Tearooms*, in the Abbey Mill complex by
the river, *The White Monk Tearoom*, with
an outside terrace, and *The Filling Station
Café*, by the main road.

Phil Anslow Coaches' No 69 **bus**
between Monmouth and Chepstow calls here.
See public transport map and table, pp49-
53.

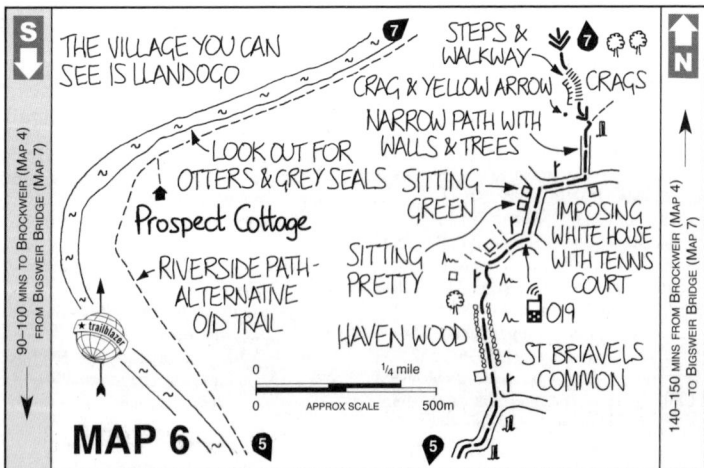

MAP 5

90–100 MINS TO BROCKWEIR (MAP 4) FROM BIGSWEIR BRIDGE (MAP 7)

140–150 MINS FROM BROCKWEIR (MAP 4) TO BIGSWEIR BRIDGE (MAP 7)

ROUTE GUIDE & MAPS

018
KISSING GATE IN HEDGE

DENEHURST
KISSING GATE IN WALL

HOUSE
STABLES

STONE GATE POST 017

PATH MEETS LANE

STONY PATH

POWER LINES

HILGAY COTTAGE

RIVERSIDE PATH – ALTERNATIVE O/D TRAIL

016

0   ¼ mile
0   APPROX SCALE   500m

STONY LANE

PENLLYN

BROOK HOUSE

ROCK FARM

FOOTBRIDGE
015

MAP 6

90–100 MINS TO BROCKWEIR (MAP 4) FROM BIGSWEIR BRIDGE (MAP 7)

140–150 MINS FROM BROCKWEIR (MAP 4) TO BIGSWEIR BRIDGE (MAP 7)

THE VILLAGE YOU CAN SEE IS LLANDOGO

STEPS & WALKWAY

CRAG & YELLOW ARROW
CRAGS

NARROW PATH WITH WALLS & TREES

LOOK OUT FOR OTTERS & GREY SEALS

Prospect Cottage

SITTING GREEN

RIVERSIDE PATH – ALTERNATIVE O/D TRAIL

SITTING PRETTY

IMPOSING WHITE HOUSE WITH TENNIS COURT

019

HAVEN WOOD

ST BRIAVELS COMMON

0   ¼ mile
0   APPROX SCALE   500m

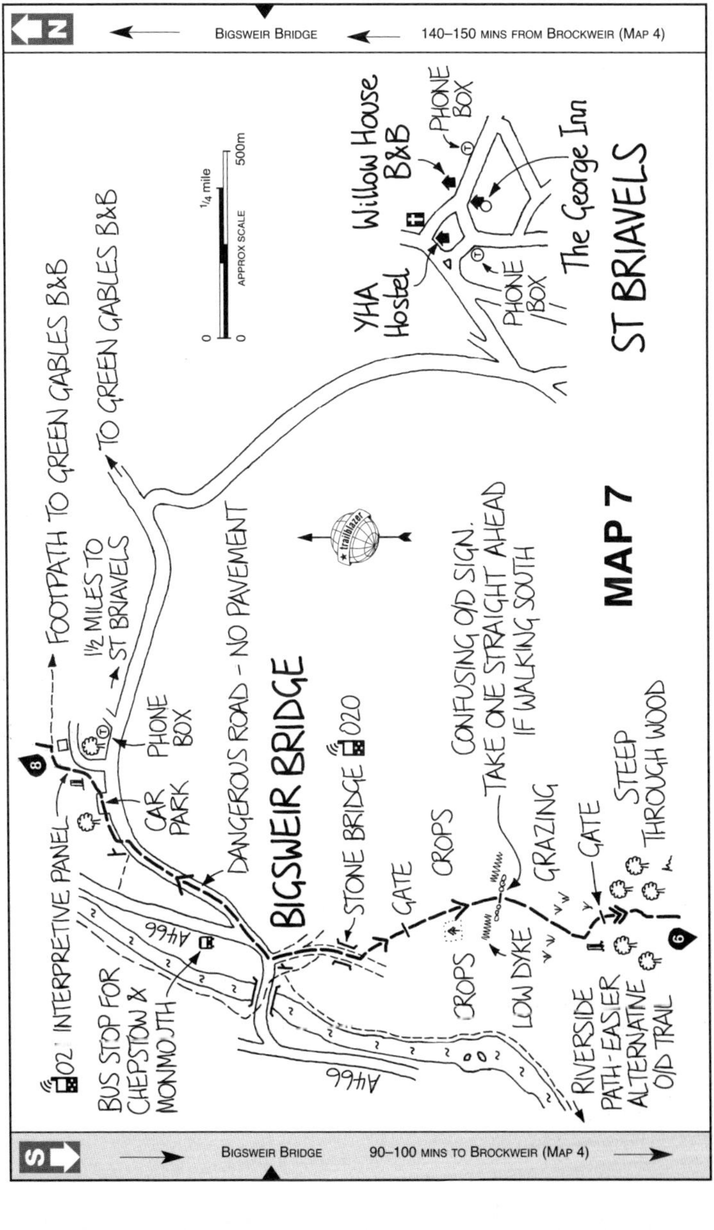

ROUTE GUIDE & MAPS

Map content (labels):

BIGSWEIR BRIDGE ← 140–150 MINS FROM BROCKWEIR (MAP 4)

Willow House B&B
PHONE BOX
The George Inn
YHA Hostel
PHONE BOX
ST BRIAVELS

FOOTPATH TO GREEN GABLES B&B
TO GREEN GABLES B&B
1½ MILES TO ST BRIAVELS

MAP 7

¼ mile
500m
APPROX SCALE

CONFUSING O/D SIGN. TAKE ONE STRAIGHT AHEAD IF WALKING SOUTH

DANGEROUS ROAD – NO PAVEMENT

BIGSWEIR BRIDGE

STONE BRIDGE 020

PHONE BOX
CAR PARK

INTERPRETIVE PANEL
BUS STOP FOR CHEPSTOW & MONMOUTH

A466

CROPS
CROPS
LOW DYKE
GRAZING
GATE
GATE
STEEP THROUGH WOOD

RIVERSIDE PATH – EASIER ALTERNATIVE O/D TRAIL

BIGSWEIR BRIDGE → 90–100 MINS TO BROCKWEIR (MAP 4) →

BROCKWEIR   Map 4, p93

Brockweir marks one end of the alternative
route along the River Wye. From here,
walkers head back into the woods to continue the trail high above the river. The village itself has a quay that is used by
canoeists to get their boats out of the river.
For walkers its main attraction is *The
Brockweir Country Inn* (☎ 01291-689548,
bar Mon 6-10pm, Tue-Sat 6-11pm, Wed-
Sat noon-2.30pm, Sun noon-6pm; **food**
served Wed-Sat noon-2pm, 6.30-9pm, Sun
to 4pm) which serves standard pub fare
(mains £8.50-14.50) and a roast on Sunday
lunch (booking recommended). Pensioners
can take advantage of the two courses for
£8.95 deal (Tue & Thur lunch) and there's
open-mic folk-based singing on the first
Tuesday of every month.

Close to the trail is *Beeches Farm
Campsite*, see p94 for details.

BIGSWEIR   Map 7, p97

From its vantage point above the Wye, the
comfortable and stylish *Prospect Cottage*
(Map 6; ☎ 01594-530566, 🖳 prospectcot
tage.com; 1D/1Tr, both with private facilities; 🛏; WI-FI; Ⓛ) charges £42.50pp (sgl
occ from £45-50) for **B&B** and there's
plenty of pampering, making it a good
choice for a celebratory last (or first) night.
An evening meal is available if requested in
advance (two courses; £15). The owners
will transport you to/from Sedbury and collect you/drop you off/from further along the
trail should you opt to stay for two or more
nights. A great option, especially considering that otters are regularly spotted (and
less often grey seals) frolicking along the
banks of the Wye below.

ST BRIAVELS   Map 7, p97

This unusual hilltop village is 1½ miles
(2km) off route but notable for the YHA
hostel *YHA St Briavels Castle* (bookings ☎
0800-019 1700 or ☎ 01629-592700 or
online, general ☎ 0845-371 9042, 🖳
yha.org.uk/hostel/st-briavels; 71 beds – 1 x
4 beds, 3 x 6, 1 x 8, 1 x 10, 1 x 12 & 1 x 14;
Ⓛ; open year-round); the castle was once
used as a hunting lodge by King John. Beds
cost from £15pp (private rooms from £35).
There's a licensed restaurant here so all
meals are available; there are also self-
catering facilities, a drying room and cred-
it/debit cards are accepted. The hostel is
often booked by groups, so it's important to
phone ahead rather than turning up on spec.

Close by, *The George Inn* (☎ 01594-
530228, 🖳 georgeinnstbriavels.co.uk; bar
Mon-Fri noon-3pm & 5.30-11pm, Sat &
Sun noon-11pm; 1T/2D, all en suite; 🛏;
WI-FI; 🐾; Ⓛ) has a reputation for providing
home-made local **food** (served summer
daily noon-2.30pm & 6-8.30pm, Sun to
8pm; in the winter they may close at lunch
on Mon) and traditional ales. B&B costs
£40pp (sgl occ £60). It's an interesting
place to stay, off the beaten track.

Opposite the pub is *Willow House* (☎
01594-531280, 🖳 stbriavelsbandb.co.uk;
2D/1T, mix of en suite and private facilities; 🛏; WI-FI; 🐾; Ⓛ; £35pp, sgl occ £40);
well-behaved dogs are welcome, although
expect to be charged should they leave any
damage behind them.

A 10- to 15-minute walk from the path,
but 20-25 minutes from the pub, evening
meals (2 courses £16; unlicensed) are available at *Green Gables* (☎ 01594-531039, 🖳
greengablesmork.com; 1D/1T/1D, T or Tr;
both en suite and private facilities; 🛏; WI-
FI; 🐾; Ⓛ; from £42.50pp, sgl occ £50),
Mork (north of St Briavels). The owners
will drop off baggage or indeed walkers for
£15 either north or south. Give them a call
about the footpath that leads directly to
them if you wish to avoid walking along the
road.

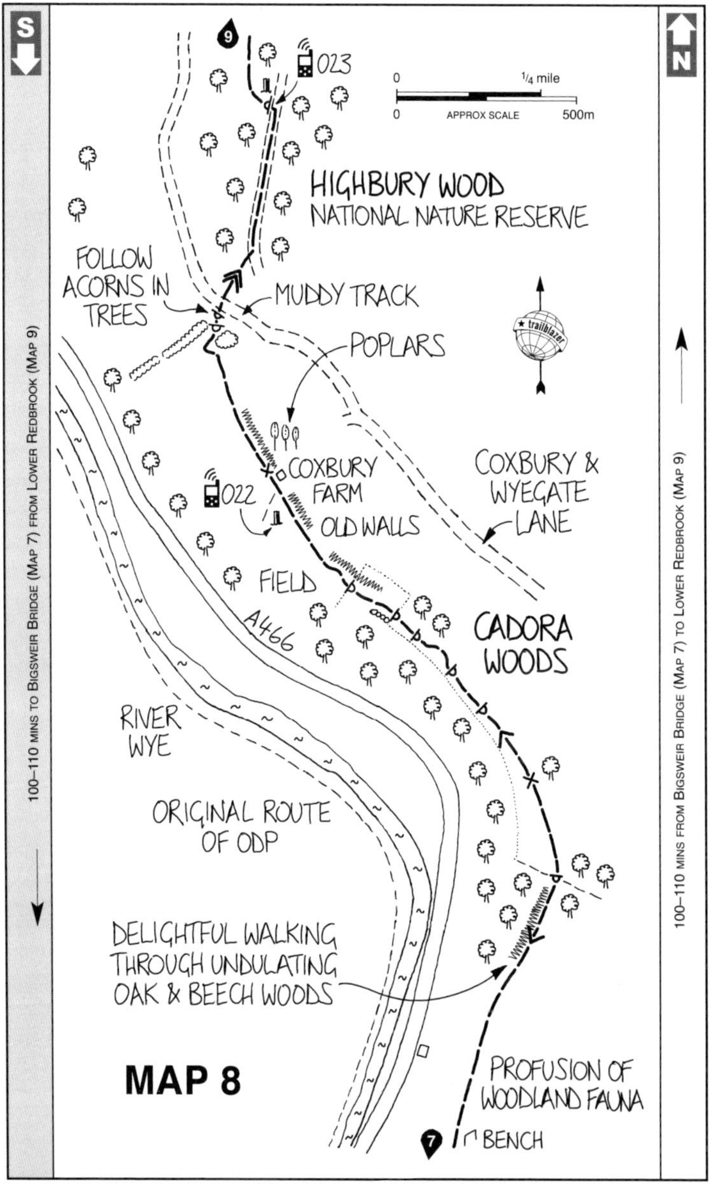

S ⬇

N ⬆

9

023

1/4 mile

0 — 500m

APPROX SCALE

HIGHBURY WOOD
NATIONAL NATURE RESERVE

FOLLOW
ACORNS IN
TREES

MUDDY TRACK

POPLARS

trailblazer

COXBURY &
WYEGATE
LANE

022

COXBURY
FARM
OLD WALLS

FIELD

A466

CADORA
WOODS

RIVER
WYE

ORIGINAL ROUTE
OF ODP

DELIGHTFUL WALKING
THROUGH UNDULATING
OAK & BEECH WOODS

MAP 8

PROFUSION OF
WOODLAND FAUNA

7 ⌐ BENCH

100–110 MINS TO BIGSWEIR BRIDGE (MAP 7) FROM LOWER REDBROOK (MAP 9)

100–110 MINS FROM BIGSWEIR BRIDGE (MAP 7) TO LOWER REDBROOK (MAP 9)

ROUTE GUIDE & MAPS

MAP 9

S

N

105–120 MINS FROM WYE BRIDGE (MAP 10)

100–110 MINS TO WYE BRIDGE (MAP 10)

LOWER REDBROOK

100–110 MINS TO BIGSWEIR BRIDGE (MAP 7)

100–110 MINS FROM BIGSWEIR BRIDGE (MAP 7)

10

LOOK OUT
FOR DOVES

DUFFIELD'S
FARM

026
HOUSE

UPPER
REDBROOK

INCLINE
BRIDGE

RIVER
WYE

A466

PATH RUNS
ABOVE
HOUSES
& CUTS OFF
THE CORNER

Inglewood
House

LOWER
REDBROOK

Tresco

PHONE BOX

Boat Inn

SHOP
& PO

PARK AREA

025 STEPS, PLENTY OF 'EM

024

The Bell Inn

ORIGINAL ROUTE
OF ODP

HIGHBURY
FARM

WALKING ON TOP OF
STEEP WOODED BANK

HIGHBURY WOOD

8

trailblazer

0   ¼ mile
0   APPROX SCALE   500m

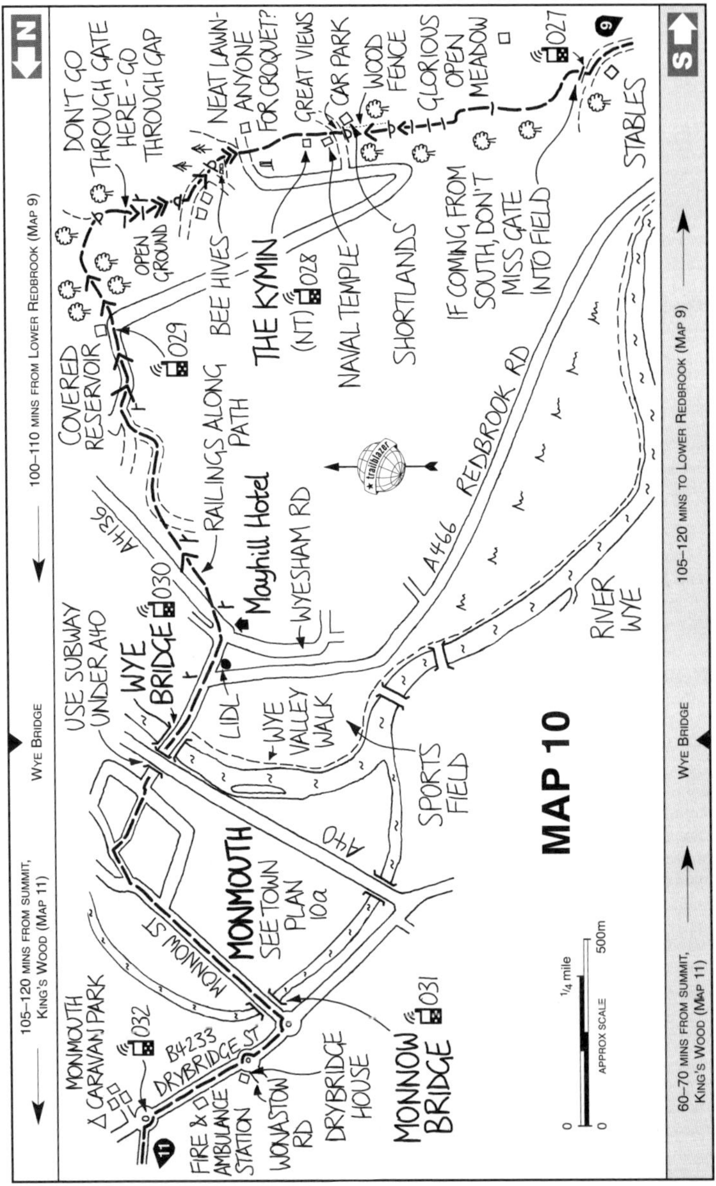
MAP 10
105–120 mins from summit, King's Wood (Map 11)
Wye Bridge
100–110 mins from Lower Redbrook (Map 9)
60–70 mins from summit, King's Wood (Map 11)
105–120 mins to Lower Redbrook (Map 9)
Monmouth Caravan Park
032
B4233 Drybridge St
Fire & Ambulance Station
Wonastow Rd
Drybridge House
Monnow Bridge
031
Monnow St
Monmouth
See town plan 10a
A40
Use subway under A40
Wye Bridge
030
Lidl
Wye Valley Walk
Sports Field
Mayhill Hotel
Wyesham Rd
A4136
Railings along path
Covered Reservoir
029
Open Ground
Don't go through gate here - go through gap
Bee Hives
Neat lawn - anyone for croquet?
The Kymin (NT)
028
Great views
Naval Temple
Car Park
Shortlands
Wood Fence
Glorious open meadow
If coming from south, don't miss gate into field
027
Stables
A466 Redbrook Rd
River Wye
Approx scale
0
¼ mile
500m
trailblazer
N
S
11
9

REDBROOK   **Map 9, p100**
Redbrook Village Stores and post office
(Mon-Fri 7.30am-7.30pm, Sat 8am-7pm,
Sun 9am-4pm) has all the basics.

A candidate for the trail's best pub,
The Boat Inn (☎ 01600-712615, ☐ the
boatpenallt.co.uk; **bar** daily all day from
noon, **food** served daily noon-2.30pm &
Tue-Sat 6.30-8.30pm), a delightful establishment with wood-burning stove and
wooden benches by the river, is reached by
crossing an iron footbridge over the Wye
from the recreation park alongside the main
Monmouth–Chepstow road. It's a busy, no-
frills pub with a selection of ciders and ales,
including Wye Valley Butty Bach, straight
from the cask, and is popular with canoeists
as well as walkers. **Meals** are enterprising
and original – try pan haggarty, a Scottish
dish made with layers of potatoes, onions,
garlic and cheese, great value at £9.45.
Note that their opening hours do depend on
demand so check in advance if you know
you want to visit here.

If you haven't time to cross the river,
The Bell Inn (☎ 01600-713612; WI-FI; 🐾)
is minutes from the trail on the eastern

bank. As well as **food** (Tue-Sun 11.30am-
2.30pm, daily 6.30-9pm), **B&B** (1T/1D/1D
or T, all en suite; from £35pp, sgl occ £50)
is available. It's a vibrant place with music
at the weekends so it's worth calling to
check what's on before booking to avoid a
poor night's sleep. The food is homemade
pub-grub (mains £10-12).

Towards the northern end of the village peaceful B&Bs can be found at either
Tresco (☎ 01600-712325; 1S/1D shared
facilities & 1D/Tr en suite; 🐾; Ⓛ; from
£37.50pp, sgl £35), or *Inglewood House*
(☎ 01600-228975, ☐ inglewoodhousewye
valley.co.uk; 2D/1Tr/one suite; mixture of
en suite and private facilities; 🐾; WI-FI; Ⓛ;
£45-60pp). The suite at the latter is either
hired as a double, a triple, or, if you're one
big group, as both rooms together, meaning
it can accommodate up to five (£125 without breakfast; £160 with breakfast). The
breakfasts are superb.

Phil Anslow Coaches operate the No
69 **bus** which stops here en route between
Monmouth and Chepstow; see public transport, pp49-53.

MONMOUTH *(TREFYNWY)* Map 10a
Monmouth is a delightful town set in the
heart of the Wye Valley. It was the birth-
place of Henry V (see box p111) and has
links to Nelson, but is perhaps best known
for the 13th-century Monnow Bridge which
compares with that in Cahors, France, in
having a fortified tower. Those who are
walking south to north may well make this
their first night's stopover, although to walk
more than 17 miles (28km) on the first day
may be a severe test of character.

It's worth visiting one of the town's
two museums, both with free admission.
The **Castle and Regimental Museum** (see
box p104; ☎ 01600-772175, ☐ monmouth
castlemuseum.org.uk; The Castle; Mar/
Apr-Oct daily 2-5pm; admission free but
donations appreciated) has a fascinating
description of the Battle of Agincourt and
the English bowmen, many of whom came
from Monmouthshire. Don't be put off by
the barrier across the entrance on Castle

Hill; just walk around it. Close by, on
Priory St, is **Nelson Museum** (☎ 01600-
710630; daily 11am-4pm, Oct-May closed
Wed; admission free).

Savoy Theatre (☎ 01600-772467, ☐
monmouth-savoy.co.uk), on Church St, is a
charming small theatre that also shows
films; a nice place to while away an
evening.

Transport
[See pp49-53] Numerous **bus** services
link Monmouth with surrounding towns;
all the buses stop at the bus station on
Monnow St.

Stagecoach operates the No 36 to
Hereford and the 83 to Abergavenny.
Newport Bus run the No 60 to Newport and
Phil Anslow Coaches the No 69 service to
Chepstow via Tintern & Redbrook.
Monmouthshire CC operate the No 65 to
Chepstow via Trellech.

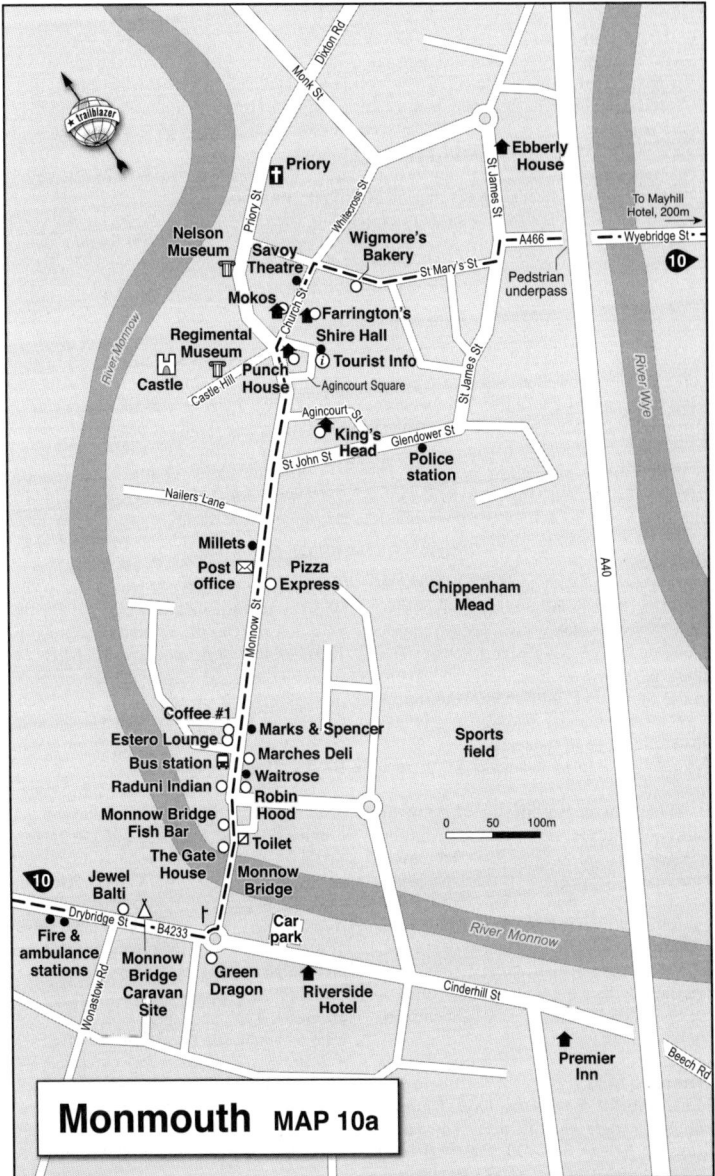

★ trailblazer

To Mayhill
Hotel, 200m
Wyebridge St
10

Dixon Rd

Monk St

Priory St

Whitecross St

St James St

✝ **Priory**

Ebberly House

Nelson Museum 🏛

Savoy Theatre

Wigmore's Bakery

St Mary's St

A466

Pedestrian underpass

Mokos ♠

Farrington's

Shire Hall

Church St

Regimental Museum 🏛

Castle 🏰

Castle Hill

Punch House ♠

ℹ **Tourist Info**

Agincourt Square

Agincourt St

King's Head ♠

St John St

Glendower St

Police station

St James St

River Monnow

River Wye

Nailers Lane

Millets ●

Post office ✉

Pizza Express ○

Chippenham Mead

Monnow St

Coffee #1 ○

Estero Lounge ○

Bus station 🚏

Raduni Indian ○

Marks & Spencer ●

Marches Deli ○

Waitrose ●

Robin Hood ●

Sports field

0   50   100m

Monnow Bridge Fish Bar ●

☑ **Toilet**

The Gate House ●

Monnow Bridge

10

Jewel Balti ●

Drybridge St

⛺

B4233

Car park

River Monnow

Fire & ambulance stations

Wonastow Rd

Monnow Bridge Caravan Site

Green Dragon ○

Riverside Hotel ⬆

Cinderhill St

Premier Inn 🏠

Beech Rd

A40

Monmouth MAP 10a

ROUTE GUIDE & MAPS

❏ The Longbow
The Castle and Regimental Museum has a reconstruction of a longbow, the decisive weapon used at the battles of Crecy (1346) and Agincourt (1415), when bowmen made up half the mass of the infantry in the English army. The longbow was traditionally made of yew, but as this depleted the churchyards, bowyers were ordered to make four bows of wych hazel, elm or ash to every one of yew.

Longbows were 5ft (1.5m) long and the shaft was a cloth yard, ie 27½inches (70cm). They had an accurate range of 300yds (275m) and six to ten arrows could be fired each minute, sometimes with devastating effect: in 1182 a Welsh archer in Abergavenny fired an arrow through a 4-inch-thick (10cm) door. In wet weather the archers kept the bowstrings dry under their Monmouth caps: conical hats of hard, boiled leather, which they preferred to metal helmets.

There is no railway station, the nearest being at Chepstow, but National Express has a daily **coach** service (NX343) between Birmingham and Cardiff that calls at Monmouth.

Taxi firms include Amber Cabs (☎ 01600-712200), Ace Taxis (☎ 07754-174 596) and Kenny's Taxis (☎ 07828-882432).

Services
Most of the services you will need are to be found on the main Monnow St, which runs uphill from the now-pedestrianised Monnow Bridge to Agincourt Square. This is where the town's heart beats and where, in the Shire Hall, **tourist information** (☎ 01600-775257; daily 9am-4pm, generally closed Sundays in winter) is to be found. Information is also available on 🖳 monmouth.gov.uk.

Stock up on groceries on Monnow St, either at Waitrose **supermarket** (Mon-Fri 7.30am-9pm, Sat to 8pm, Sun 10am-4pm), or at Marks & Spencer (Mon-Fri 8am-8pm, Sat 8am-7pm, Sun 10am-4pm). Basic **camping** and **outdoor gear** are available at Millets.

Most of the high street **banks** have branches with cashpoints along Monnow St. The **post office** and several **pharmacies** are along here, too.

Where to stay
Monmouth has a centrally located **campsite** that's right on the path. The small *Monnow Bridge Caravan Site* (☎ 01600-

714004; Drybridge St), only a two-minute walk from town, is happy to take tents and will always squeeze you in somewhere if you arrive late. Walkers pay £7/11 single/double tent; a shower costs 60p.

Slightly less central, *Monmouth Caravan Park* (Map 10; ☎ 01600-714745, 🖳 monmouthcaravan.co.uk; £8 per tent) also accepts campers; showers cost 20p.

Budget-priced B&Bs are thinly spread but there are a number of places where you will be comfortable and welcome. On the path and right in the centre of the town is *Farrington's Restaurant and B&B* (☎ 01600-712600, 🖳 farringtonsrestaurant.co.uk; 2T/3D, all en suite; ☞; WI-FI; Ⓛ), Church St; it is more of a restaurant with rooms than a B&B, charging from £50pp B&B (£75 sgl occ).

In the same area, and surprisingly affordable – though it could be noisy in the evenings – *The King's Head* (☎ 01600-710500, 🖳 jdwetherspoon.co.uk/home/pubs/the-kings-head; 4S/4T/11D/5Qd, all en suite; ☞; WI-FI), Agincourt Sq, charges from £45 per room: a bargain, if there's two of you. That's for the room only, but you can go through the hotel to the bar next door for breakfast (7am-noon); the menu options are extensive. The bar is open daily 7am to at least midnight; food is served all day.

B&B is offered by *Punch House* (☎ 01600-713855, 🖳 sabrain.com/pubs-and-hotels/south-wales/monmouthshire/punch-house-new; 1S/1T/8D/1Tr, all en suite; ☞; WI-FI; 🐾; Ⓛ) with pleasant staff and rooms for around £30pp (sgl occ from £60; three sharing a room from £90).

Rather quieter is *Ebberley House* (☎ 01600-713602, 🖳 ebberleyhousemon mouth.co.uk; 1D/1Tr, both en suite; ➡) where B&B costs from £32pp (sgl occ/ three sharing rates on request), St James Sq.

Mokos (☎ 01600-712001, 🖳 mokos mex.com; 2D, both en suite; WI-FI) a Mexican restaurant (see Where to eat) with rooms from £25pp (sgl occ £35).

Conveniently located on the path, as the A4136 turns uphill, is *Mayhill Hotel* (Map 10; ☎ 01600-712280, 🖳 themayhill hotel.com; 1S/1T/2D/2Tr, most en suite; WI-FI) though it suffers a little from traffic noise. B&B costs £34.50-39.50pp (sgl £64; three sharing rate on request), but for meals other than breakfast you'll have to go into Monmouth. Alternatively, at the other end of town and only a short walk away from the trail is *Riverside Hotel* (☎ 01600-715577, 🖳 riversidehotelmonmouth.co.uk; 1S/1OT/9D, all en suite; ➡; WI-FI; 🐾; from £39.50pp, sgl from £55) where evening meals can be arranged but only for groups of ten or more.

Monmouth has a branch of *Premier Inn* (☎ 03330-038101, 🖳 premierinn.com; rooms from £35), but this is a little further out of town.

Where to eat and drink

For a lunchtime take away, *Wigmores Bakery* (Mon-Thur 8am-3.30pm, Fri 7.30am-3.30pm, Sat 7.30am-2.30pm) on St Mary's St offers a good selection of baked products.

On Monnow St, *Marches Deli* (🖳 marchesdeli.co.uk; Tue-Sat 10am-5pm) sells far fancier fayre whilst *Coffee No 1* (Mon-Fri 7.30am-6pm, Sat 8am-6pm, Sun 8.30am-5pm) has gourmet lattes, salads, ciabattas, and gigantic almond croissants.

Recently renovated, *Green Dragon* (☎ 01600-712561), St Thomas Sq, is handy for those who have camped just down the road.

Guarding the other end of Monnow Bridge, you'll find *The Gate House* (☎ 01600-713890, 🖳 the-gate-house.com; food Mon-Thur noon-8pm, Fri-Sun noon-8.30pm, Sunday lunch noon-4pm), and our

favourite: the 15th-century *Robin Hood* (☎ 01600-713240; food served daily 11am-9pm; 🐾). Both provide good pub grub at reasonable prices; dogs are especially welcome at the latter.

Punch House (see Where to stay; bar daily all day), Agincourt Sq, serves food throughout the day (daily 8am-9pm). The menu is pretty standard and they have offers on during the week such as 50% off the pub classics section of their menu on a Monday.

Estero Lounge (☎ 01600-714164, 🖳 thelounges.co.uk/estero; food daily 9am-10pm), Monnow St, is the best place to go for vegan and gluten-free dishes; they have dedicated menus for both.

The pedestrianised Church St is a haven for foodies. Here Tex-Mex food – such as tequila chicken for £13.95 – at *Mokos* (see Where to stay; Mon-Sat 11am-2.30pm, Mon-Sun 6-10pm) rubs shoulders with the upmarket offerings at *Farrington's* (see Where to stay; food noon-2.30pm & 6-9.30pm, Sun noon-4pm): you'll not pay over £20 for one of their mouth-watering mains, unless you choose the 21-day matured Herefordshire rib-eye (£24) that is.

The King's Head (see Where to stay; bar daily till midnight or later) on Agincourt St is part of the Wetherspoons chain. You can get cheap food (daily till 11pm) and cheap ale here. Another chain, *Pizza Express*, is halfway down Monnow St.

Monmouth has a few good restaurants representing the East, the best of which is probably *Raduni Indian* on Monnow St, offering the usual enormous selection of Asian dishes. *Jewel Balti* is another option on the other side of the bridge.

If you're just plain hungry, you could do worse than *Monnow Bridge Fish Bar* (Mon-Sat noon-8pm), which has a seating area and serves considerably more than just fish & chips. There's plenty more to choose from, including **Indian** and **Chinese** restaurants and several **cafés**; Monmouth is not a place where you'll go hungry!

ROUTE GUIDE & MAPS

[*Route section begins on Map 10, p101*] This **16½-mile (27km, 8½-9¼hrs)** section is long and can be arduous as it is almost the last leg, but there are plenty of rewards to ease your way southwards. Many walkers divide it into two stages, stopping at Tintern.

The original route of the trail follows the beautiful **Wye Valley**, characterised by densely wooded slopes high above the gently flowing river. Although the solitude that you may have relished through the hidden country of the Borders is less likely to be found here, the steep and sometimes slippery climbs up into the woods do much to cushion the walker from the bustle of this tourist area, with its busy roads and hordes of visitors in season. The first of these climbs, out of Monmouth, leads up to **The Kymin** (see box opposite), where on a good day compensation for the tough ascent comes in the form of some magnificent views over Monmouth and the Wye Valley. From here you pass through **Redbrook** (Map 9), where you have the opportunity to stop for a pint at another one of the path's great pubs, The Boat Inn (see p102).

Purists will stick to the woods, settling for glimpses of the river through the trees, in part for the solitude but also because this is the route of the Dyke. For those wishing to spend time by the river, however, an easier alternative is now signposted along the Wye from **Bigsweir** (Map 7), with the two paths joining up again at **Brockweir** (Map 4), just north of Tintern Abbey (see p93).

Campers needing a break should leave the path where it joins the track (WPT 013, Map 4) and go to *Beeches Farm Campsite* (🖳 beechesfarmcampsite.co.uk; 🐾; Apr-Oct though dependent on the weather), Miss Graces Lane. They charge £8pp for **campers**; each pitch boasts a fire pit for which they sell wood (£4.50 per bag). They also have **static caravans** (£50-70; sleeping up to five people). There are also toilet and shower facilities; the latter costs £1 for four minutes. It's a lovely campsite though most people will want to push on through to Chepstow at this stage.

At **Devil's Pulpit** (Map 3) you should get a brilliant view of Tintern Abbey (see box p95) and from your first glimpse of the **River Severn** when you reach the road (B4228), it will be clear that the end is in sight.

A daunting vantage point over **Wintour's Leap** (Map 2) follows, but this last stretch is otherwise decidedly urban in parts, as the trail weaves back and forth across the B4228, stealthily avoiding **Chepstow (Map 1, p86)**, and frequently confusing the walker. [*Next route overview p90*]

[*Route section begins on Map 10, p101*] This **9-mile (14km, 4½-5¼hrs)** stretch is through undulating country, the ground ascending gradually towards the Black Mountains. The path meanders away from the Wye, leaving Monmouth in its wake. The trail follows Watery Lane (Map 11), skirting a housing estate before a pleasant stroll through fields leads you to **King's Wood**, a mixture of broadleaved trees and conifers where forestry operations are likely to be heard if not seen. Exiting the trees, you pass **The Hendre** (Map 12) before negotiating more fields and arriving at **Abbey Bridge**, the only obvious reminder of the Cistercian abbey of **Grace Dieu** founded in 1226 by John of Monmouth but destroyed by Henry VIII. Not a trace remains and you have to rely on your imagination to picture the site bustling with activity. For something more solid, just before the bridge, take a look at the rare **White Park cattle** (see box p67), an attraction in their own right.

If you are booked to stay at Penylan Farm (see The Hendre below) and have requested a lift from here you may want to call the proprietors.

A couple of fields after the bridge you join the **River Trothy** which accompanies you to **Llanvihangel-Ystern-Llewern** (Map 13). The tiny village church of St Michael is one of the many beautiful small churches that you will pass on Offa's Dyke Path, though sadly this one is kept locked.

From here cider-apple orchards and the B4233 see you safely to **Llantilio-Crosseny (Map 14, p112)**. *[Next route overview p114]*

❏ The Kymin
Long popular with picnickers for its superb views across the valley, The Kymin (see Map 10) is the site of a naval temple built in 1800 to celebrate the victories of the British Navy and its admirals. Rather more prominent is the Round House, a white, two-storey banqueting house built on the brow of the hill. During a visit in 1802, Nelson described the Wye as 'a little gut of a river' – hardly the words that spring to the mind for those who have followed its course along the Dyke!

Now owned by the National Trust (☎ 01600-719241, 🖳 nationaltrust.org.uk/the-kymin; grounds summer daily 7am-9pm, winter dawn to dusk, Round House late Mar-Oct Sat-Sun & Bank Hol Mons 11am-4pm), the grounds and temple are open to all-comers, but there's an admission fee of £3 for the Round House. For most visitors, the views from the lawns below are more than enough.

THE HENDRE   Map 12, p109
The Hendre itself is little more than a cross-roads some half a mile from the path, but B&Bs and camping are available, making this an attractive option for those who would rather not stay in Monmouth.

Right on the path is *Hendre Farmhouse Orchard Campsite* (☎ 01600-740484, ☎ 07974-393430, 🖳 hendrefarmhouseorchardcampsite.co.uk). **Campers** (£10/tent & two people, £5 per additional person) can have breakfast here for £7 (by prior arrangement); shower & toilet facilities are available, as are a fridge and microwave. B&B at *Old Hendre Farm* (☎ 01600-740447, 🖳 oldhendrefarm.com; 1S/ 1T/2D, all en suite, 🛁; 🐾 in boot room; WI-FI; Ⓛ) on the opposite side of the road costs from

£42.50pp (sgl/sgl occ £50), plus £8-20 for an evening meal if arranged in advance. Two self-catering studios are also available (£35-40 for two people or £29 for one.

Penylan Farm (☎ 01600-716435, 🖳 penylanfarm.co.uk; 1T/2D en suite; 🛁; WI-FI; Ⓛ) is around two miles from the path, but the owners are happy to collect walkers and return them the next day if arranged in advance. If you'd prefer to walk, think carefully; the obvious footpath – across the so-called Llymon Bridge – isn't in evidence on the ground and it's a long haul on the road. The rooms here seamlessly blend the traditional and the modern. B&B starts from £40-50pp (sgl occ £50) and if arranged in advance an evening meal costs £14-20.

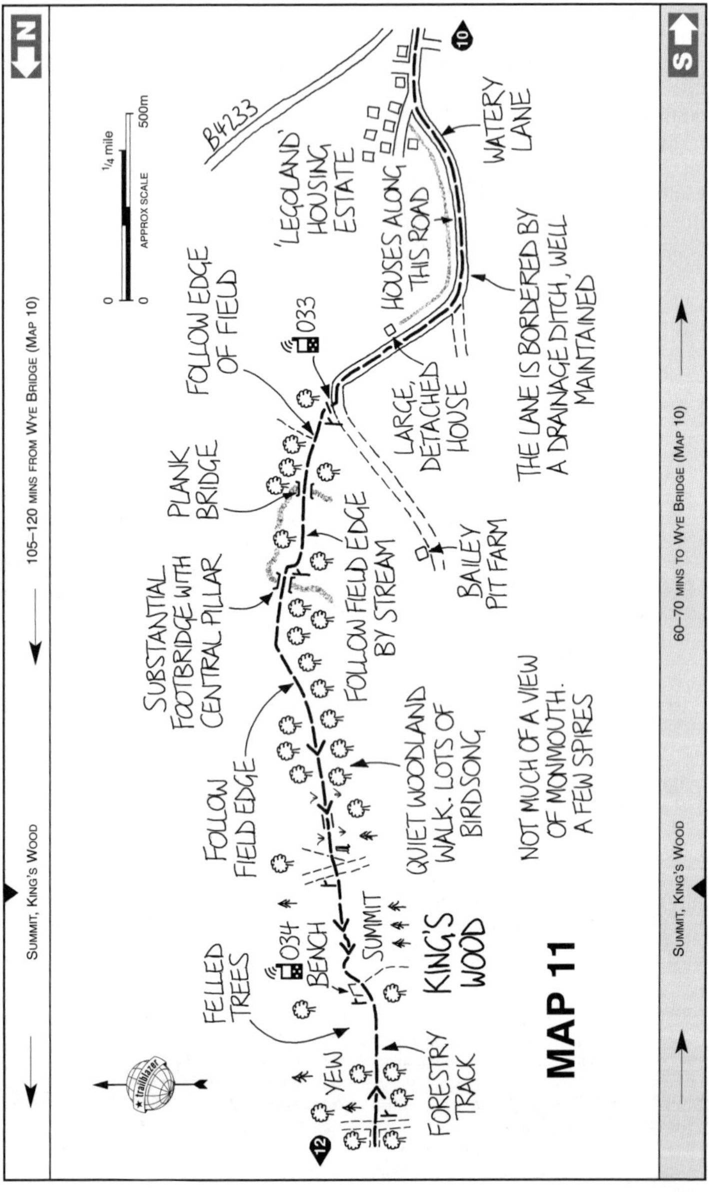

N

S

SUMMIT, KING'S WOOD ——— 105–120 MINS FROM WYE BRIDGE (MAP 10)

¼ mile

0
0   500m
APPROX SCALE

B4233

'LEGOLAND' HOUSING ESTATE

WATERY LANE

HOUSES ALONG THIS ROAD

FOLLOW EDGE OF FIELD

📷 033

THE LANE IS BORDERED BY A DRAINAGE DITCH, WELL MAINTAINED

PLANK BRIDGE

LARGE, DETACHED HOUSE

BAILEY PIT FARM

SUBSTANTIAL FOOTBRIDGE WITH CENTRAL PILLAR

FOLLOW FIELD EDGE BY STREAM

FOLLOW FIELD EDGE

QUIET WOODLAND WALK. LOTS OF BIRDSONG

NOT MUCH OF A VIEW OF MONMOUTH. A FEW SPIRES

FELLED TREES

📷 034

BENCH

SUMMIT

KING'S WOOD

YEW

FORESTRY TRACK

MAP 11

🧭 TrailBlazer

10

12

SUMMIT, KING'S WOOD ◄ ———   60–70 MINS TO WYE BRIDGE (MAP 10) ——— ►

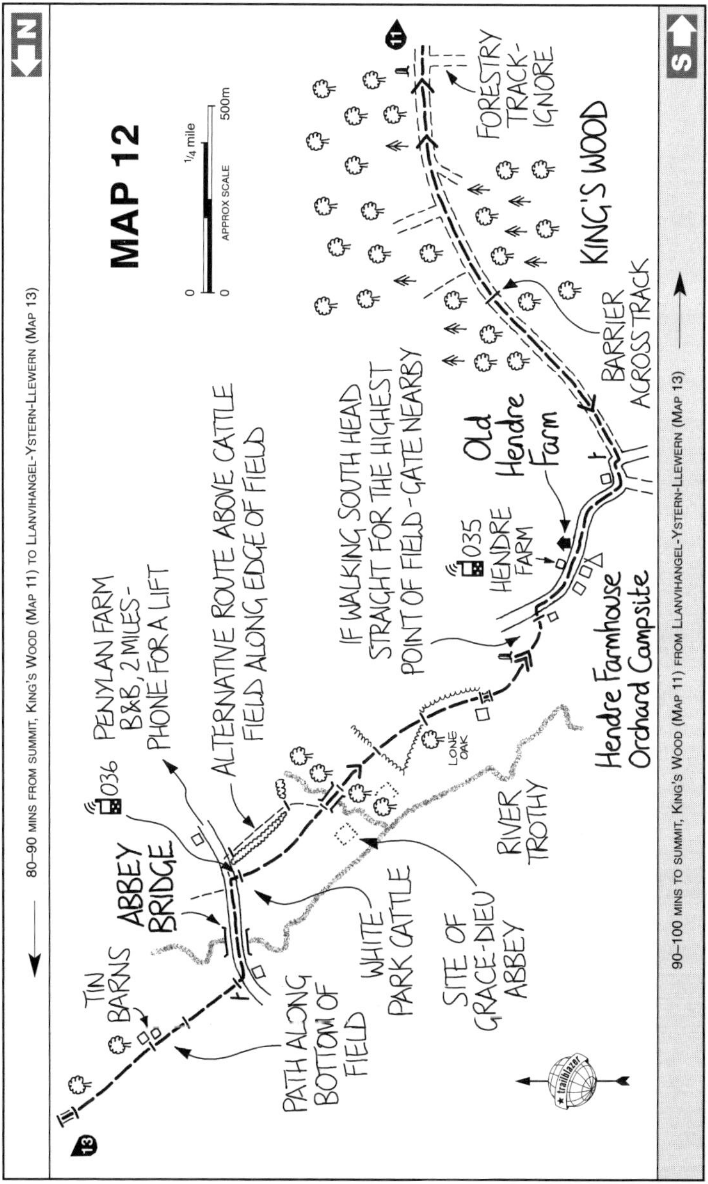

MAP 12

1/4 mile

500m

0

0

APPROX SCALE

80–90 MINS FROM SUMMIT, KING'S WOOD (MAP 11) TO LLANVIHANGEL-YSTERN-LLEWERN (MAP 13)

FORESTRY
TRACK-
IGNORE

FORESTRY
TRACK-
IGNORE

KING'S WOOD

BARRIER
ACROSS TRACK

Old
Hendre
Farm

IF WALKING SOUTH HEAD
STRAIGHT FOR THE HIGHEST
POINT OF FIELD - GATE NEARBY

035
HENDRE
FARM

PENYLAN FARM
B&B, 2 MILES -
PHONE FOR A LIFT

ALTERNATIVE ROUTE ABOVE CATTLE
FIELD ALONG EDGE OF FIELD

036

ABBEY
BRIDGE

TIN
BARNS

PATH ALONG
BOTTOM OF
FIELD

WHITE
PARK CATTLE

SITE OF
GRACE-DIEU
ABBEY

LONE
OAK

RIVER
TROTHY

Hendre Farmhouse
Orchard Campsite

90–100 MINS TO SUMMIT, KING'S WOOD (MAP 11) FROM LLANVIHANGEL-YSTERN-LLEWERN (MAP 13)

ROUTE GUIDE & MAPS

ROUTE GUIDE & MAPS

MAP 13

N

S

90–105 MINS TO LLANTILIO-CROSSENNY (MAP 14)

LLANVIHANGEL-YSTERN-LLEWERN

80–90 MINS FROM SUMMIT, KING'S WOOD (MAP 12)

85–95 MINS FROM LLANTILIO-CROSSENNY (MAP 14)

LLANVIHANGEL-YSTERN-LLEWERN

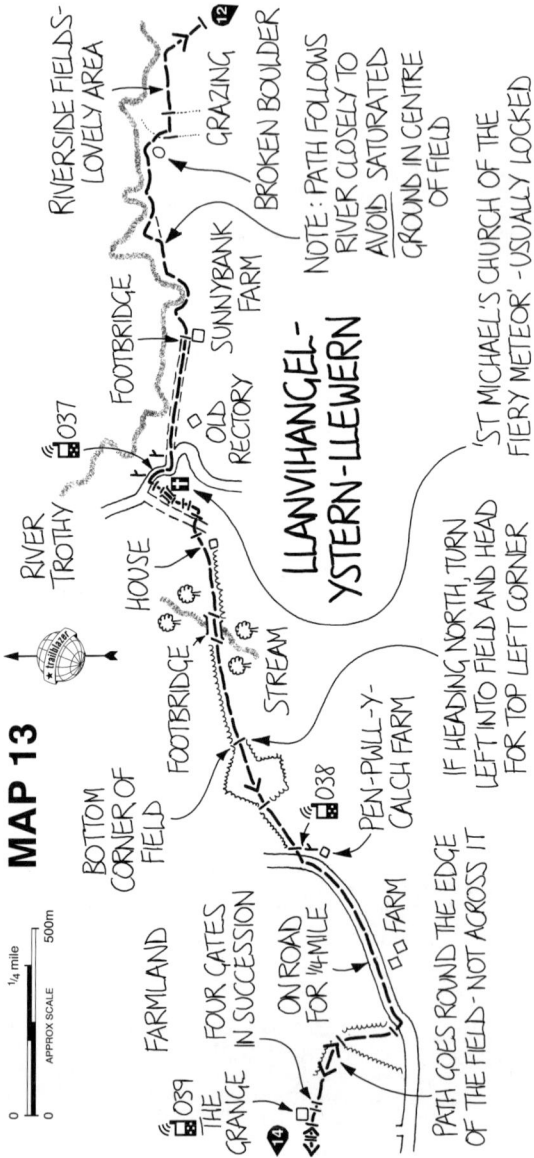

90–100 MINS TO SUMMIT, KING'S WOOD (MAP 12)

¼ mile

500m

APPROX SCALE

0

0

FARMLAND

THE GRANGE 039

FOUR GATES IN SUCCESSION

ON ROAD FOR ¼ MILE

14

FARM

PATH GOES ROUND THE EDGE OF THE FIELD - NOT ACROSS IT

BOTTOM CORNER OF FIELD

FOOTBRIDGE

STREAM

PEN-PWLL-Y-CALCH FARM 038

IF HEADING NORTH, TURN LEFT INTO FIELD AND HEAD FOR TOP LEFT CORNER

RIVER TROTHY

HOUSE

LLANVIHANGEL-YSTERN-LLEWERN

'ST MICHAEL'S CHURCH OF THE FIERY METEOR' - USUALLY LOCKED

037

OLD RECTORY

FOOTBRIDGE

SUNNYBANK FARM

RIVERSIDE FIELDS - LOVELY AREA

GRAZING

BROKEN BOULDER

NOTE: PATH FOLLOWS RIVER CLOSELY TO AVOID SATURATED GROUND IN CENTRE OF FIELD

12

❏ An alternative route?

To anyone who is particularly interested in the history and archaeology of the Dyke, it seems unfortunate that when Offa's Dyke Path was officially designated, it was given a somewhat north-westerly route from Chirk to Prestatyn. Perhaps the decision was influenced by Fox's conclusion (see Recommended reading, p46) that, although the construction of the Dyke had never been completed, it had been planned to run in a northerly direction to the sea coast. In fact, the Dyke was constructed beyond Chirk (Map 65, p200), following a more north-easterly course to end near Treuddyn.

From the historical and archaeological points of view, a more appropriate and interesting route for the Path would follow the Dyke through to its terminus near Treuddyn and then strike east for a few miles to join Wat's Dyke near its southern end, then running north, roughly parallel with the northern stretch of Offa's Dyke. The path could then run alongside Wat's Dyke through to Holywell and on to the Dee estuary at Basingwerk, a place of greater historical interest than (with all due respect to the popular holiday resort) Prestatyn. In taking this route, apart from following Offa's Dyke to its actual end, the walker would encounter some 19 miles of identifiable earthworks constructed earlier than Offa's Dyke itself.

That said, I must admit that the route actually followed by the officially designated path along the Clywdian range is better walking terrain. Perhaps the ideal solution would be to present a choice: 'walkers this way, historians and archaeologists that'.

There is no comparable controversy about the southern end of either the Dyke or the Path. It has been argued that various isolated earthworks were evidence that the Dyke had continued right down to the Severn estuary. It is, however, now generally agreed that the Dyke's southern end was near Kington at Rushock Hill (Map 35, p150), with its splendid view across to the west and the one-time threatening Welsh. Whichever end you choose to start from, you will be walking along the remains of a remarkable achievement by some of our early ancestors – one situated in some of our most attractive and varied scenery.   **Colin Vickerman**

❏ Henry V

In Shakespeare's *Henry V*, reference is made to Henry's connections with the Wye Valley in a conversation with the Welsh Captain Fluellen after the Battle of Agincourt. In it Fluellen reminds the king of the Battle of Crecy:

Fluellen: *... the Welshmen did good service in a garden where leeks did grow, wearing leeks in their Monmouth caps; which your majesty know, to this hour is an honourable badge of the service; and I do believe your majesty takes no scorn to wear the leek upon Saint Tavy's day.*
King Henry: *I wear it for a memorable honour;*
For I am Welsh, you know, good countryman.
Fluellen: *All the water in Wye cannot wash your majesty's Welsh blood out of your body, I can tell you that; God bless it and preserve it, as long as it pleases His Grace, and His Majesty too!*

It seems, however, that having left Wales as an infant Henry was not sufficiently attached to his place of birth to wish to return, for he never did.

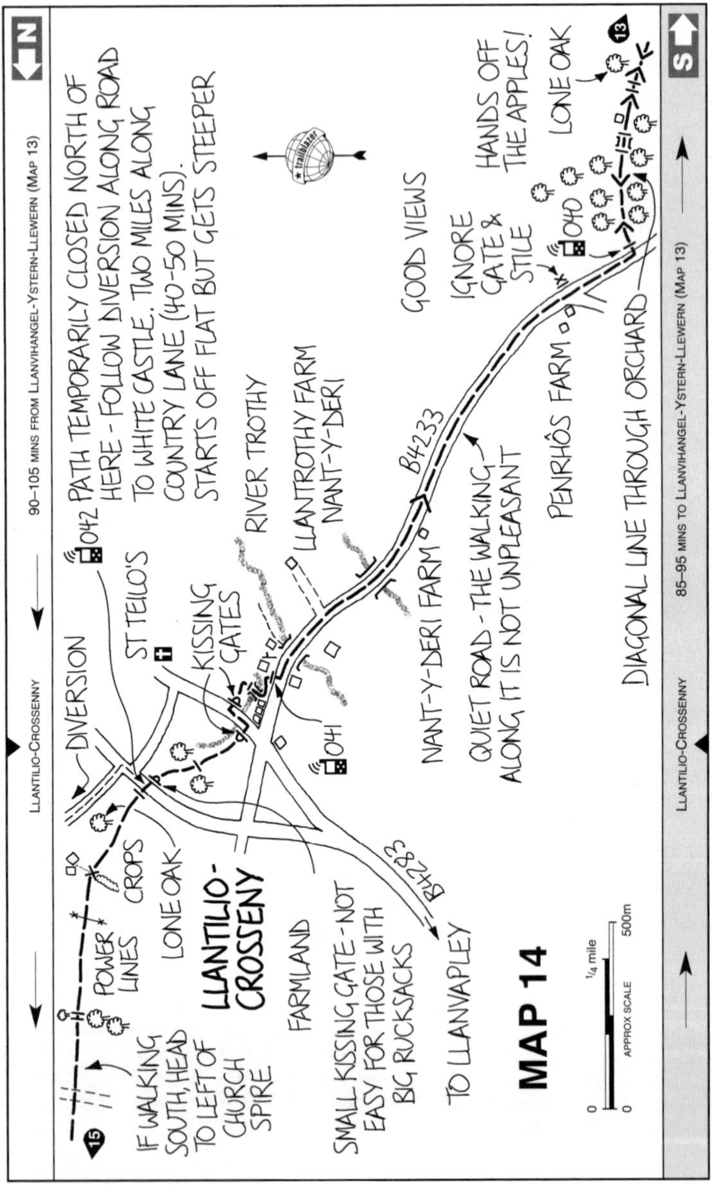

LLANTILIO-CROSSENNY

90–105 MINS FROM LLANVIHANGEL-YSTERN-LLEWERN (MAP 13)

85–95 MINS TO LLANVIHANGEL-YSTERN-LLEWERN (MAP 13)

LLANTILIO-CROSSENNY

DIVERSION

ST TEILO'S

042 PATH TEMPORARILY CLOSED NORTH OF HERE – FOLLOW DIVERSION ALONG ROAD TO WHITE CASTLE. TWO MILES ALONG COUNTRY LANE (40–50 MINS). STARTS OFF FLAT BUT GETS STEEPER

KISSING GATES

041

RIVER TROTHY

LLANTROTHY FARM NANT-Y-DERI

GOOD VIEWS

IGNORE GATE & STILE

HANDS OFF THE APPLES!

LONE OAK

13

B4233

NANT-Y-DERI FARM

PENRHÔS FARM

QUIET ROAD – THE WALKING ALONG IT IS NOT UNPLEASANT

DIAGONAL LINE THROUGH ORCHARD

POWER LINES

LONE OAK

CROPS

LLANTILIO-CROSSENNY

FARMLAND

IF WALKING SOUTH, HEAD TO LEFT OF CHURCH SPIRE

15

SMALL KISSING GATE – NOT EASY FOR THOSE WITH BIG RUCKSACKS

TO LLANVAPLEY

B4283

MAP 14

¼ mile

500m

0

0

APPROX SCALE

❏ **White Castle**   **Map 15, p114**
Once known as Llantilio Castle, the fortifications of White Castle earned their modern name from the white plaster rendering on the outer walls, still visible in places.

The castle has many distinctive features, not least the almost complete moat, still filled with water and in the summer a happy hunting ground for dragonflies. This is crossed by a wooden bridge to enter the outer ward through the 13th-century gate. The inner gateway has twin towers that can be climbed via a staircase to a gallery from which marvellous views can be enjoyed, including to the north the prominent scarp of The Skirrid (see box p115). The inner buildings are well preserved and include the remains of a chapel, a hall and the kitchens and there is a deep well covered by a grill from which the garrison would have drawn their water.

White Castle was one of three Marcher castles that formed a powerful defensive presence in mid-Wales, the other two being Skenfrith and Grosmont, neither as well preserved as White. The three are linked by the 'Three Castles Walk', for which signposting can be seen as you emerge on to the lane by the entrance.

S ⬇ FROM PRESTATYN **LLANTILIO-CROSSENNY TO MONMOUTH**
                                        MAPS 14-10

[*Route section begins on Map 14, opposite*] This **9-mile (14km, 3hrs 55mins-4hrs 25mins)** stretch is through undulating country, the ground descending gradually from the Black Mountains. The path sets off along the road (B4233) before heading up through cider-apple orchards and eventually joining the **River Trothy** at **Llanvihangel-Ystern-Llewern** (Map 13). The tiny village church of St Michael is another of the many beautiful small churches that you pass on Offa's Dyke Path, though sadly this one is kept locked.

The trail continues along the river valley, an area of sequestered calm where you will see hardly anyone and can enjoy the peace. **Abbey Bridge** (Map 12) is the only obvious reminder of the Cistercian abbey of **Grace Dieu** founded in 1226 by John of Monmouth but destroyed by Henry VIII. Not a trace remains and you have to rely on your imagination to picture the site bustling with activity.

For something more solid, take a look at the rare **White Park cattle** (see box p67) by the bridge, an attraction in their own right.

If you are booked to stay at Penylan Farm (see The Hendre, p107) and have requested a lift from here you may want to call the proprietors.

The patchwork of meadow and field divided up by broad hedgerows of blackthorn, hawthorn, elder, dogwood and maple merge with scattered woodland to create an area which grows on you as you move through it. At times it seems that it has been deserted, since its inhabitants are seldom seen apart from an occasional tractor or children getting off the school bus, but well-kept fields and neat farms bear witness to the agricultural importance of the area.

After passing through **The Hendre** (Map 12) you approach the town of Monmouth over the mound of **King's Wood**, a mixture of broadleaved trees and conifers where forestry operations are likely to be heard if not seen.

ROUTE GUIDE & MAPS

There is no sudden vista of Monmouth from the north and you pass along the edge of a succession of potato fields to reach Watery Lane (Map 11) which gradually leads into a mushrooming housing development and joins Drybridge St (B4233). Once you stand on Monnow Bridge in **Monmouth (Map 10, p101)**, however, you know you have arrived. Tomorrow the Wye Valley awaits.

[*Next route overview p106*]

N ↑ FROM CHEPSTOW **LLANTILIO-CROSSENNY TO PANDY   MAPS 14-18**

[*Route section begins on Map 14, p112*] This quiet **7½-mile (12km, 3½-4¼hrs)** section of the walk is mainly across agricultural land; however, when researched there was a diversion in place (off Maps 14 and 15) for the initial two-mile stretch to **White Castle** (*Castell Gwyn*; Map 15 and box p113; 🖥 cadw.wales.gov.uk/daysout/whitecastle; Apr-early Nov 10am-5pm; admission

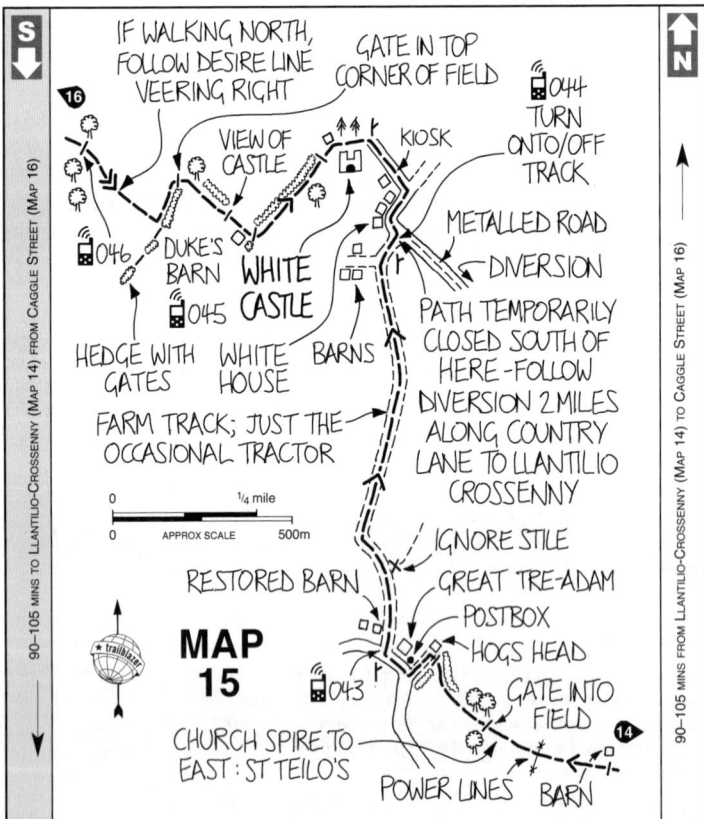

MAP 15

S ↓   N ↑

IF WALKING NORTH, FOLLOW DESIRE LINE VEERING RIGHT

GATE IN TOP CORNER OF FIELD

16

VIEW OF CASTLE

KIOSK

📱044 TURN ONTO/OFF TRACK

METALLED ROAD

📱046 DUKE'S BARN
📱045

WHITE CASTLE

DIVERSION

PATH TEMPORARILY CLOSED SOUTH OF HERE - FOLLOW DIVERSION 2 MILES ALONG COUNTRY LANE TO LLANTILIO CROSSENNY

HEDGE WITH GATES

WHITE HOUSE

BARNS

FARM TRACK; JUST THE OCCASIONAL TRACTOR

0   ¼ mile
0   APPROX SCALE   500m

IGNORE STILE

RESTORED BARN

GREAT TRE-ADAM

POSTBOX

HOGS HEAD

📱043

MAP 15

GATE INTO FIELD

14

CHURCH SPIRE TO EAST: ST TEILO'S

POWER LINES   BARN

* trailblazer

90–105 MINS TO LLANTILIO-CROSSENNY (MAP 14) FROM CAGGLE STREET (MAP 16)

90–105 MINS FROM LLANTILIO-CROSSENNY (MAP 14) TO CAGGLE STREET (MAP 16)

ROUTE GUIDE & MAPS

£3). The path will be returning to its original route but is currently diverted along a country lane to what is one of the best preserved of the Marcher castles and the perfect place to stop for a picnic. For updates on the path you can contact Offa's Dyke Centre (see p158), although the diversion is not an unpleasant walk. Water and confectionery are available at the ticket kiosk, beside which there's a single portaloo. Even if you don't go into the castle, do take the time to gaze at these massive towers dominating the surrounding countryside, a reminder of a more troublesome past.

Leaving the castle behind there's little of interest until you reach the charming village of **Llangattock-Lingoed** (Map 17), its few houses clustered near a cheerful pub and the whitewashed church of St Cadoc which is worth seeing. If you have no intention of walking from Monmouth to **Pandy (Map 18, p118)** in one go, or would prefer to stay outside the town, you might decide to break the journey here.   [*Next route overview p120*]

LLANGATTOCK-LINGOED
Map 17, p117

The small hamlet of Llangattock-Lingoed is an unassuming place hiding itself from the world. At its heart stands the medieval church of **St Cadoc** around which the houses have clustered since its earliest known dedication in the 6th century. The wall paintings in the church are well worth a look; there's a 15th-century painting of St George on horseback while the 300-year-old coat of arms of Queen Anne adorns the main arch and the intricate work of the rood beam across the nave is impressive.

You could pass through the settlement without seeing a soul yet you can stay here at either *The Old Rectory Guest House*

(☎ 01873-821326, 🖳 oldrectorystayin wales.co.uk; 3D/1T, en suite; ①; WI-FI; from £37.50pp, sgl occ from £45) or *Hunter's Moon Inn* (☎ 01873-821499, 🖳 hunters-moon-inn.co.uk; bar open daily from noon) where **B&B** (1T/1D, both en suite; WI-FI; ①) costs from £42.50pp (sgl occ £65). **Campers** are welcome and a pitch is free, though there are no outside facilities so you'll be relying on the toilets in the pub. They serve **food** (bar food daily noon-9pm, restaurant 6-9pm); the menu (mains typically £10-20) changes daily and the pub is a member of CAMRA. Well worth a stop for a local cider on your way, be you heading north or south.

❑ **The Skirrid (*Ysgyrid Fawr*)**
Dominating the view south of Pandy, the long whale-backed hill of the Skirrid, also known as St Michael's Mount or the Holy Mountain, has long been a place of superstition and pilgrimage. Rising to 486m (1595ft), the summit is encircled by an Iron Age hill-fort, a low rampart visible on the north side. The highest point is marked by an OS triangulation column.

Nearby, two square stones and a shallow depression mark the site of St Michael's Chapel, once used by persecuted Catholics for secret worship. The northern slope was created by an Ice Age landslip, although local superstition suggests it occurred at the very moment of the crucifixion.

❑ **Important note – walking times**
All times in this book refer only to the time spent walking. You will need to add 20-30% to allow for rests, photography, checking the map, drinking water etc.

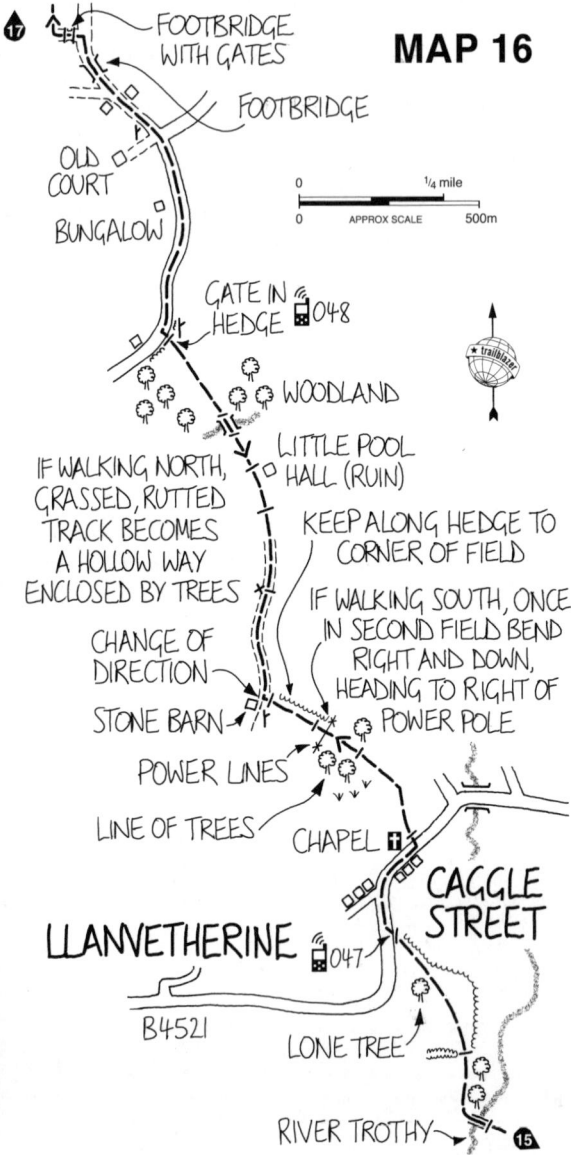

MAP 16

FOOTBRIDGE WITH GATES

FOOTBRIDGE

OLD COURT

BUNGALOW

0   ¼ mile

0   APPROX SCALE   500m

GATE IN HEDGE 📱 048

WOODLAND

LITTLE POOL HALL (RUIN)

IF WALKING NORTH, GRASSED, RUTTED TRACK BECOMES A HOLLOW WAY ENCLOSED BY TREES

KEEP ALONG HEDGE TO CORNER OF FIELD

IF WALKING SOUTH, ONCE IN SECOND FIELD BEND RIGHT AND DOWN, HEADING TO RIGHT OF POWER POLE

CHANGE OF DIRECTION

STONE BARN

POWER LINES

LINE OF TREES

CHAPEL ✝

CAGGLE STREET

LLANVETHERINE 📱 047

B4521

LONE TREE

RIVER TROTHY

60-75 MINS FROM LLANGATTOCK-LINGOED (MAP 17)

60-75 MINS TO LLANGATTOCK-LINGOED (MAP 17)

CAGGLE STREET

CAGGLE STREET

ROUTE GUIDE & MAPS

MAP 17

60–75 MINS TO PANDY (MAP 18)

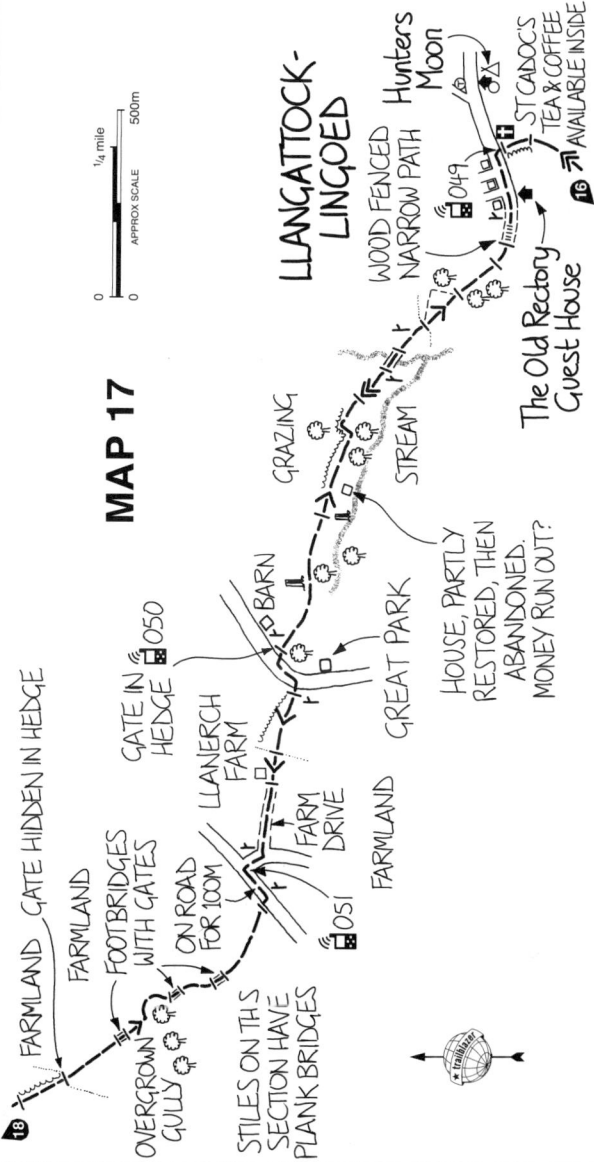

60–90 MINS FROM PANDY (MAP 18)

APPROX SCALE

¼ mile

500m

FARMLAND   GATE HIDDEN IN HEDGE

FARMLAND

FOOTBRIDGES WITH GATES

OVERGROWN GULLY

ON ROAD FOR 100M

STILES ON THIS SECTION HAVE PLANK BRIDGES

GATE IN HEDGE

050

LLANERCH FARM

FARM DRIVE

051

BARN

GRAZING

GREAT PARK

FARMLAND

HOUSE, PARTLY RESTORED, THEN ABANDONED. MONEY RUN OUT?

STREAM

LLANGATTOCK-LINGOED

WOOD FENCED NARROW PATH

Hunters Moon

049

ST CADOC'S TEA & COFFEE AVAILABLE INSIDE

16

The Old Rectory Guest House

ROUTE GUIDE & MAPS

PANDY   Map 18

Once you reach the busy A465 you are in Pandy. *Lancaster Arms* (☎ 01873-890699; 1D en suite/2T shared bathroom; ♥; WI-FI; 🐾; (L)) is no longer a pub having been reinvented as a guesthouse, with B&B from £33 to £35pp (sgl occ £40); evening meals cost from £8.25. They also do luggage transfer. It's pretty well right on the trail and, despite the noise from the main road, makes a convenient stopover.

Some 850 metres along the A465 – and thus from the path – is *The Old Pandy Inn* (☎ 01873-890208, 🖥 oldpandyinn.co.uk; one room sleeping up to six en suite, as well

as a bunkhouse; 🐾 in bar or bunkhouse only; WI-FI; (L)), which caters mainly for groups but will accept individual walkers when space allows. Walkers wishing to avoid a trek up the main road can take a quicker route to the inn via the back roads (see Map 18). It's a friendly and professionally run establishment, managed for many years by Alan Bridgewater. Accommodation in the **bunkhouse** (four rooms with six, eight and ten beds) costs from £27.95pp, including breakfast and bedding but not towels (£1.50 per stay to hire), while above the pub is a 'family'

ROUTE GUIDE & MAPS

S

135-150 MINS FROM PATH TO LLANTHONY (MAP 21)

PANDY

MAP 18   RIVER MONNOW

GRASSY BANKS OF FORT

19

055

SMALL ENCLOSURE OF SCOTS PINE

TO OLDCASTLE COURT FARM, 1½ MILES

054   GATE & STILE

Old Pandy Inn

BRACKEN

HEDGED PATH

INTERPRETIVE BOARD DESCRIBING HATTERALL HILL

SHORTCUT TO OLD PANDY INN

Brynhonddhu Country House

★ trailblazer

053

TROSTREY BARN

Lancaster Arms

MAST

PATH CUTS OFF CORNER THROUGH FIELD

PANDY

SIGN: UNSUITABLE FOR HEAVY GOODS

FARM

TWO METAL GATES

SPACE TO PARK TWO CARS

052

FIELD

OLD QUARRY FULL OF TREES

17

TO RISING SUN PUB, 5 MINS; SKIRRID INN & SHOP, 10 MINS & ABERGAVENNY

OLD STONE BARN

A465

N

0   ¼ mile
0   APPROX SCALE   500m

150-165 MINS TO PATH TO LLANTHONY (MAP 21)

PANDY

room with six beds (**B&B** costs £29.95pp).
Drying facilities are available. In the bar,
substantial main courses (food served daily
noon-3.30pm & 6-9.30pm) costing from
£9.45 (traditional Welsh faggots), washed
down with a pint or two of Wye Valley's
beer make for a satisfying end to a long
day.

The imposing *Brynhonddhu Country
House* (☎ 01873-890535, 🖳 brynhonddu
.co.uk; 1S/1T/2D, all en suite; ✆; WI-FI;
🐾; Ⓛ; from £40pp) also provides B&B as
does *The Rising Sun* (off Map 18; ☎
01873-890254, 🖳 therisingsunpandy.com;
2D/2Tr all en suite; ✆; WI-FI bar area only),
five minutes' walk down the main road.
B&B costs £40-45pp (sgl occ £55). You can
also **camp** (Mar-Oct) here: pitches are £8pp
and there are toilet and shower facilities.
Breakfast costs around £6.50 and it is best

to pre-order the night before. **Food** is
served (Mon-Sat noon-2.30pm & 6-
8.45pm, Sun noon-2pm) and the bar is generally open till 11pm. You'll get a large
hearty pub meal for less than £10.

A 10- to 15-minute stroll to
Llanvihangel Crucorney (off Map 18) will
lead you to *The Skirrid Inn* (☎ 01873-
890258, 🖳 skirridmountaininn.co.uk; 3D
all en suite; ✆; WI-FI; £45pp, sgl occ room
rate; food Tue-Sun noon-1.45pm & daily 6-
9pm) and what may be a very welcome
sight: a **shop** (Mon-Fri 7am-6pm, Sat &
Sun 7am-2pm); useful to stock up in as
your next such source of supplies won't be
until either Hay-on-Wye or Monmouth,
both approximately 17 miles away.

Stagecoach's X3 **bus** (Hereford–
Cardiff) stops here; see pp49-53).

PANDY TO LLANTILIO-CROSSENNY   **MAPS 18-14**

[*Route section begins on Map 18, opposite*]   After the long crossing of
Hatterrall Ridge comes a quiet **7½-mile (12km, 3½-4¼hrs)** section of the
walk, mainly across agricultural land.

Highlights start with the charming village of **Llangattock-Lingoed** (Map
17), its few houses clustered near a cheerful pub and the whitewashed church
of St Cadoc which is worth seeing. If you have no intention of walking from
Pandy to Monmouth in one go, or would prefer to stay outside the town, you
might decide to break the journey here. Failing this you'll have to walk on
beyond Llantilio-Crossenny to The Hendre (see p107; Map 12) as there's nothing of interest to trekkers at **Caggle Street** (Map 16) now nor at **Llantilio-
Crossenny** (Map 14). Another option if you have had enough is to call for a
taxi to ferry you on to Monmouth, back to Pandy or into Abergavenny; Lewis
Taxis (☎ 01873-859839) are reliable.

Assuming you continue to walk, the trail takes you up to the very walls of
White Castle (*Castell Gwyn*; Map 15 and box p113; 🖳 cadw.wales.gov.uk/
daysout/whitecastle; daily 10am-4pm; free), one of the best preserved of the
Marcher castles and the perfect place to stop for a picnic to take in the atmosphere. Water and confectionery are available at the ticket kiosk, beside which
there's a single portaloo. Even if you don't go into the castle, do take the time
to gaze at these massive towers dominating the surrounding countryside, a
reminder of a more troublesome past.

Finally, St Teilo's church at **Llantilio-Crossenny (Map 14, p112)** peeps
from amongst the trees as you approach, field by field, until at last you meet a
lane that takes you into the village. However, there are no services here.

[*Next route overview p113*]

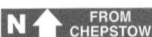

PANDY TO HAY-ON-WYE

[*Route section begins on Map 18, p118*] This **17½-mile (28km, 8¾-9¾hrs)** stretch of the walk takes in the long spine of the **Hatterrall Ridge** (Maps 22-24) and the highest point on Offa's Dyke Path, at 703m (2306ft). It is one of the most demanding days on the entire walk, but is also without doubt one of the most scenic – on a good day. While it can be enormously rewarding, it can equally be something of an endurance test so needs some thought before it is tackled. Food, drink (essential en route) and clothing must be adequate for the terrain: wild, open moorland at a continuous altitude of around 600m (2000ft) with hardly any shelter and relatively few options for escaping to the valleys to the east or west.

Most walkers will undertake the section between Pandy and Hay-on-Wye as a challenge for a single day and it is probably best treated as such rather than divided by an overnight stop. However, if the idea is too daunting, or the weather particularly bad, the crossing can be broken by an overnight stop at **Longtown** (off Map 20) to the east, **Llanthony** (Map 21) in the Vale of Ewyas to the west, or at **Capel-y-ffin** (off Map 22). The descent off the ridge in either direction presents no problem, but the climb back is a stiff test for your legs first thing the following morning. If planning on descending from the ridge you may wish to have an OS map (see p43) with you so that you can keep a close eye on your route.

The stage begins by leaving the A465 and cutting through fields and lanes before steadily climbing to the top of **Hatterrall Hill** (Map 19).

From here, the going underfoot is good, aided in many places by heavy mill flagstones laid end to end as part of an erosion-control programme by Brecon Beacons National Park Authority. These don't please everybody since they introduce a man-made element to what are natural surroundings, but they do help to address the steadily worsening erosion caused by both walkers and animals.

Once atop the ridge, and as long as the weather is clement, you'll experience arguably the finest walking and grandest views to be found on Offa's Dyke Path, and the sometimes-steep descent from **Hay Bluff** (Map 25) will leave you feeling your own descent into the holiday blues; should the weather be intolerable, you may never have been so relieved to see the end in sight! Either way, once you reach the valley road (Map 25) there are still a further four miles of moorland and farmland to go before you arrive in **Hay-on-Wye (Map 27, p131)**, so ensure you have the supplies left in your bag and the strength left in your legs to make it – just because the end of the ridge is in sight, the end of this lengthy stage is not.   [*Next route overview p137*]

❏ **Important note – walking times**
Unless otherwise specified, **all times in this book refer only to the time spent walking**. You will need to add 20-30% to allow for rests, photography, checking the map, drinking water etc. When planning the day's hike count on 5-7 hours' actual walking.

S ↕

N ↑↓

20

HEADING SOUTH THE PATH BEGINS TO DESCEND GRADUALLY

△ HATTERRALL HILL
531M/1743FT

RUTTED TRACK →

MILL SLAB PAVING HEREABOUTS

☎058 CAIRN & STONE MARKER, 'CWMYOY'. ODD NAME. IT MEANS HOLLOW SHAPED LIKE A YOKE

0 —————— 1/4 mile
0 —————— 500m
APPROX SCALE

PATH TO OLDCASTLE

STONE MARKER 'OLDCASTLE' ☎057

MAP 19

IF HEADING SOUTH YOU GET A STRONG SENSE OF THE RIDGE COMING TO AN END. THE CROSSING IS NEARLY OVER, PANDY IS IN SIGHT. IF HEADING NORTH YOUR JOURNEY IS ONLY JUST BEGINNING

TRIG POINT ☎056
464M/1522FT

△

PATH DIVIDES CONFUSINGLY, NO WAY MARKER. KEEP EAST, ALTHOUGH WEST SEEMS MORE APPEALING

STONE WALL WITH METAL RELIEF PLAQUE. WHAT DOES IT MEAN?

STRANGE WALLED ENCLOSURE- PROBABLY A SHEEPFOLD

QUICKEST ROUTE TO OLDCASTLE

BRACKEN

VIEW OF THE SKIRRID TO THE SOUTH ↓

STONE MARKER

18

ROUTE GUIDE & MAPS

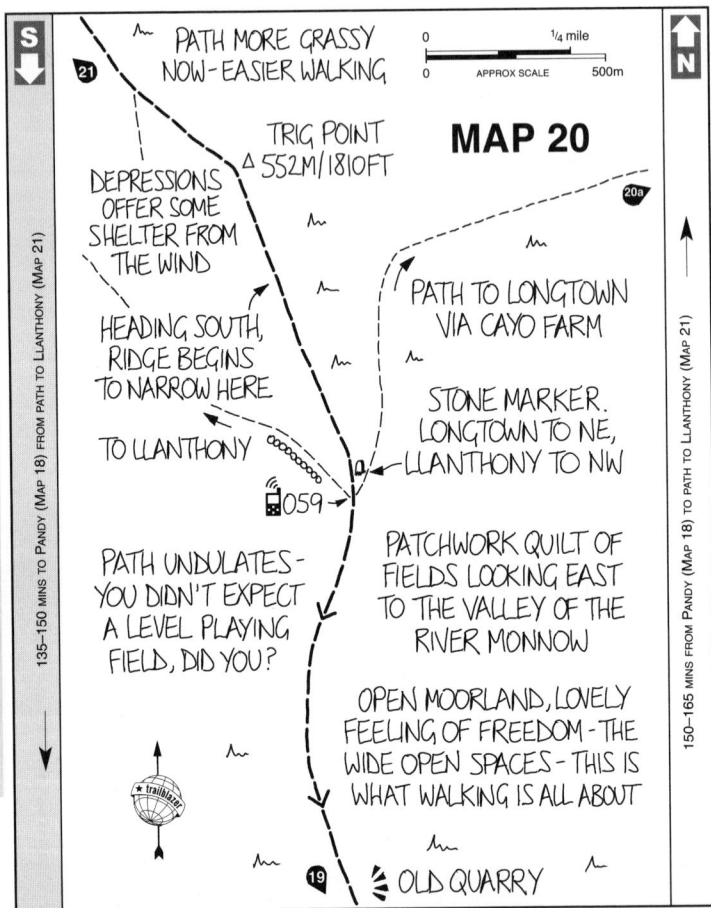

PATH MORE GRASSY NOW – EASIER WALKING

21

0   ¼ mile
0   APPROX SCALE   500m

TRIG POINT
△ 552M/1810FT

MAP 20

20a

DEPRESSIONS OFFER SOME SHELTER FROM THE WIND

PATH TO LONGTOWN VIA CAYO FARM

HEADING SOUTH, RIDGE BEGINS TO NARROW HERE

STONE MARKER. LONGTOWN TO NE, LLANTHONY TO NW

TO LLANTHONY

059

PATCHWORK QUILT OF FIELDS LOOKING EAST TO THE VALLEY OF THE RIVER MONNOW

PATH UNDULATES – YOU DIDN'T EXPECT A LEVEL PLAYING FIELD, DID YOU?

OPEN MOORLAND, LOVELY FEELING OF FREEDOM – THE WIDE OPEN SPACES – THIS IS WHAT WALKING IS ALL ABOUT

★ trailblazer

19   OLD QUARRY

LONGTOWN   Map 20a

Longtown – and it really is long! – is almost two miles (3km) off-route to the east of Hatterrall Ridge and has accommodation. To reach Longtown, take the path east from the stone marker (Map 20) then descend for half a mile on a clear green track with a wall on the right. Keep to the upper path above trees then swing right through fields to Cayo Farm. Follow the

concrete farm lane to reach a bridge over the Olchon Brook and follow the lane till you reach Longtown.

The **castle ruins** are managed by English Heritage (🖥 english-heritage.org.uk /visit/places/longtown-castle); you are free to walk around this 12th-century site at any time. There's a **shop** in the village: **Hopes** (☎ 01873-860444, 🖥 hopesoflongtown.co

.uk; Mon-Wed & Fri 7.30am-5.30pm, Thur to 7pm, Sat to 4pm, Sun 10am-2pm or to noon in winter) sells provisions as well as such trekking essentials as maps and blister plasters; the local **post office** (Mon-Fri 10.30am-3.30pm, Sat 9-11am) is also housed here. The owners of Hopes also operate *Tan House Farm* (☎ 01873-860221, or try the shop, 💻 camping4us.co .uk; 1Tr with private bathroom; 🛏; WI-FI; (L)), down the road by the River Monnow, where **B&B** costs from £40pp (sgl occ from £50), or you can **camp** (£5pp; 🐾); the rate includes a shower.

The Crown Inn (☎ 01873-860217, 💻 crowninnlongtown.co.uk; 1S/2D/2T/3Tr, bunk room sleeping 4, all en suite; 🛏; WI-FI; 🐾; (L)) offers **B&B** from £37.50pp (sgl occ £45) or on a room-only basis. Dogs are welcome but they have to sleep in a room downstairs. **Food** is served Mon-Fri noon-3pm & 6-9pm, Sat & Sun noon-9pm, closed Wed lunchtime. They also offer glamping (💻 offasdykeretreat.co.uk) in a number of pods and shepherds' huts sleeping between two and six people (£60-110 per pod/hut).

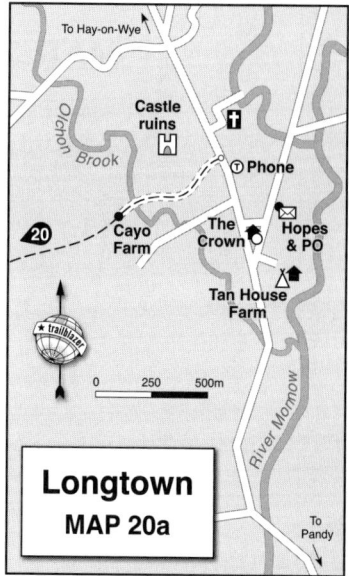

To Hay-on-Wye

Olchon Brook

Castle ruins

Phone

Cayo Farm

The Crown

Hopes & PO

Tan House Farm

trailblazer

0   250   500m

River Monnow

Longtown
MAP 20a

To Pandy

R O U T E   G U I D E   &   M A P S

☐ **The Vale of Ewyas**
Here, you feel, is the Glencoe of the Welsh Border, a place marked indelibly by conflict.
                              John Hillaby, *Journey through Britain*
The Vale of Ewyas in which Llanthony sits has attracted its share of dreamers. In 1807 the poet Walter Savage Landor bought an estate that cost him the then colossal sum of £20,000, hoping to create for himself an escape from the world but instead finding nothing but dispute, resentment and trouble with his neighbours. Washing his hands of it, he was left with a lifelong loathing for the Black Mountains.

At **Capel-y-ffin**, the building that used to be the YHA hostel was formerly acquired by one Father Ignatius who established a British order of Benedictine monks. As **Francis Kilvert** (see box p136), a regular visitor, testified, he laboured ceaselessly, but when he died in 1907 there was no one of sufficient energy to carry on his work. The estate was taken over in 1924 by Eric Gill, artist, sculptor and typographer of genius, and his extended family, who believed that the surroundings would help create a new life of harmony and creativity. Some of his best work was indeed done here but eventually his vision came to nothing. The only reminder of his time here are some headstones in the tiny **chapel of St Mary**, their bold sharp lettering speaking for the skill of the carver. Each of these visionaries was convinced that the landscape could help them to achieve great things; each was defeated by the harsh and unforgiving surroundings. Dreams are not enough.

MAP 21

0 — ¼ mile

0 — 500m APPROX SCALE

*trailblazer

22

SMALL TARN

PATH DOWN TO ROAD AT LITTLE DAREN FARM

STONE MARKER FOR RED DAREN 📱061

📱060

STONE MARKER TO LLANTHONY

CAIRN ⚬⚬⚬

SMALL STONE MARKER

LOXIDGE PATH TO LLANTHONY

HILL TO SOUTH IS SKIRRID

CULVERT

☼ **LOXIDGE TUMP**

SHELTER - A CHANCE TO GET OUT OF THE WIND

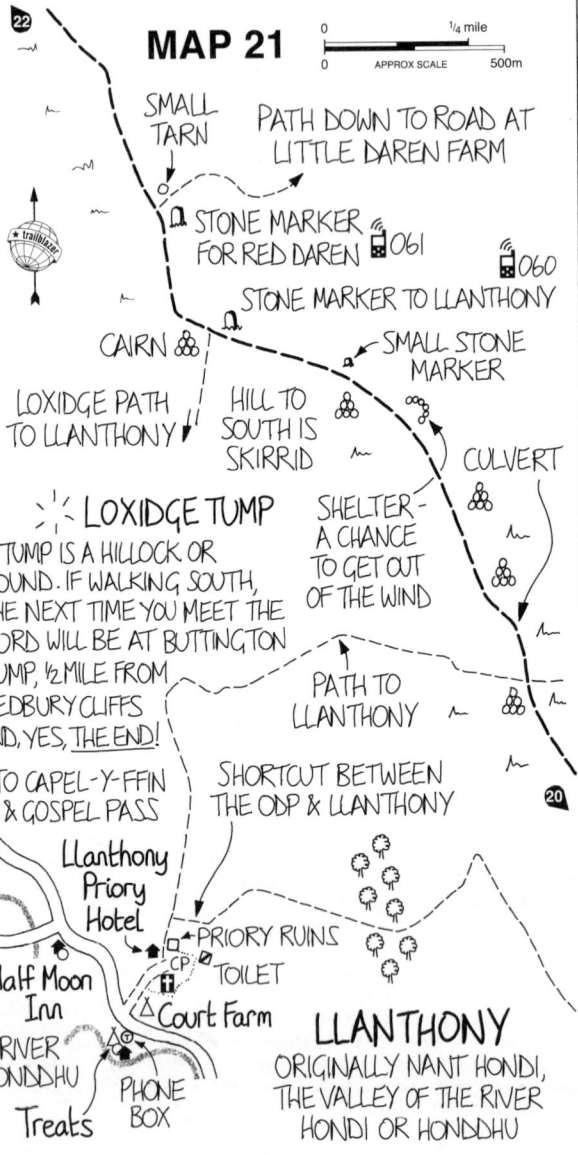

A TUMP IS A HILLOCK OR MOUND. IF WALKING SOUTH, THE NEXT TIME YOU MEET THE WORD WILL BE AT BUTTINGTON TUMP, ½ MILE FROM SEDBURY CLIFFS AND, YES, <u>THE END</u>!

PATH TO LLANTHONY

TO CAPEL-Y-FFIN & GOSPEL PASS

SHORTCUT BETWEEN THE ODP & LLANTHONY

20

Llanthony Priory Hotel

PRIORY RUINS

CP

TOILET

Half Moon Inn

Court Farm

RIVER HONDDHU

PHONE BOX

Treats

LLANTHONY

ORIGINALLY NANT HONDI, THE VALLEY OF THE RIVER HONDI OR HONDDHU

4 HRS 30 MINS–5 HRS FROM ROAD TO GOSPEL PASS (MAP 25)

PATH TO LLANTHONY

135–150 MINS TO PANDY (MAP 18)

4 HRS 30 MINS–5 HRS TO ROAD TO GOSPEL PASS (MAP 25)

PATH TO LLANTHONY

150–165 MINS FROM PANDY (MAP 18)

ROUTE GUIDE & MAPS

LLANTHONY   Map 21

Three miles (5km) or so further along the ridge are several paths west to the atmospheric **ruins of the 12th-century Augustinian Llanthony Priory** (🖳 cadw .gov.wales/daysout/llanthonypriory; daily 10am-4pm, admission free; no dogs). A side trip from the ridge to the priory takes about two hours.

The tiny *Llanthony Priory Hotel* (☎ 01873-890487, 🖳 llanthonyprioryhotel.co .uk; 2T/5D, shared facilities; ➡; Ⓛ) is romantically set right in the ruins of the priory; three of the rooms are in the tower and are accessed by a spiral staircase. **B&B** starts at £47.50pp (sgl occ £75) during the week rising to £50pp (sgl occ £80) at weekends. Both the hotel and the bar are closed on Mondays, except during the school summer holidays. From November to Easter the hotel and bar are open only at the weekend. In the summer food is served in the bar daily (11am-3pm & 7-9pm) but at weekends only in winter. See their website for details of the various opening hours.

As long as you're happy with basic facilities (cold water and toilets) you can **camp** in a field, set in a splendid location alongside the ruins, at the neighbouring *Court Farm* (☎ 01873-890359, 🖳 court-farm@llanthony.co.uk; £3pp a night). They also have a bunk barn though this is currently limited to group bookings only so if you're travelling solo or in a couple consider instead the excellent *Treats* (☎ 01873-890867, 🖳 llanthonytreats.co.uk; 12 beds; 🐾 as long as not left unattended in

bunkhouse; Ⓛ), a set of stables which have been converted into a **café**, which has a woodburning stove, and a **bunkhouse** of two en suite rooms (containing 2D and a single bunk bed over the top). The price is from £18pp if you bring your own towel and bedding, or from £20pp otherwise, both with breakfast included – terrific value. Alternatively you can **camp** (£5pp); there are three different private sites, the most popular being an idyllic spot by the river where guinea fowl may scratch around your tent. There is also a communal camping field (£3pp). However, book early for this spot in peak periods. The **food** (summer daily 8 or 9am-5pm, winter generally weekends only; evening meals, and winter opening, available subject to prior arrangement), is of great quality, all homemade and much of it locally sourced, including meat for the burgers from the cows just across the road!

Nearby is *Half Moon Inn* (☎ 01873-890611, 🖳 halfmoon-llanthony.co.uk; bar Thur-Tue noon-11pm; but hours can be variable due to weather so contact them; 2T/6D/1Qd, most share facilities; ➡; 🐾; limited WI-FI; Ⓛ), also in a stunning location. **B&B** costs from £35pp (sgl occ £50; four sharing from £95); the room with the bath costs an additional £10. **Food** is available (Thur-Tue noon-3pm & 6-8.30pm); contact them for details in the winter months but evening meals are always possible for guests. Luggage transfer (from £25) to your next stop is available.

❏ Stone waymarkers on Hatterrall Ridge

Between Hatterrall Hill (Map 19) and the Gospel Pass road (Map 25), Brecon Beacons National Park Authority has erected a series of waymarkers like gravestones with the acorn and directional details hand carved, as part of a European-funded project for the National Trail.

The design was based on traditional parish-boundary markers in the Black Mountains; the old red sandstone came from a quarry near Abergavenny. Local carvers employed to carve the stones have done a good job although it is to be feared that erosion will obliterate the text eventually; even now they are not particularly easy to read. Meanwhile they make a welcome addition to the multiplicity of waymarkings used on Offa's Dyke Path and chime well with the surroundings.

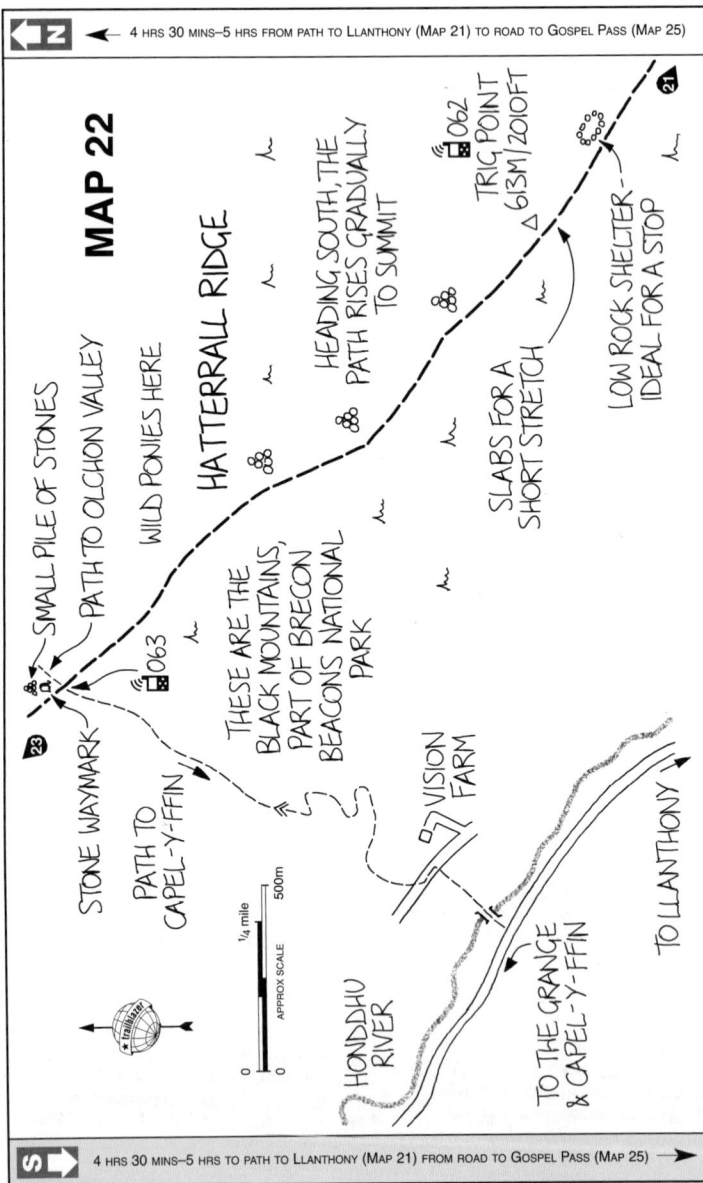

← 4 HRS 30 MINS–5 HRS FROM PATH TO LLANTHONY (MAP 21) TO ROAD TO GOSPEL PASS (MAP 25)

MAP 22

HATTERRALL RIDGE

SMALL PILE OF STONES

PATH TO OLCHON VALLEY

WILD PONIES HERE

HEADING SOUTH, THE
PATH RISES GRADUALLY
TO SUMMIT

062
TRIG POINT
△ 613M / 2010FT

21

LOW ROCK SHELTER –
IDEAL FOR A STOP

SLABS FOR A
SHORT STRETCH

23

STONE WAYMARK

063

THESE ARE THE
BLACK MOUNTAINS,
PART OF BRECON
BEACONS NATIONAL
PARK

PATH TO
CAPEL-Y-FFIN

VISION
FARM

¼ mile   500m

APPROX SCALE

0   0

HONDDU
RIVER

TO THE GRANGE
& CAPEL-Y-FFIN

TO LLANTHONY

4 HRS 30 MINS–5 HRS TO PATH TO LLANTHONY (MAP 21) FROM ROAD TO GOSPEL PASS (MAP 25) →

CAPEL-Y-FFIN   off Map 22

The first place with accommodation that you come to when traversing Hatterrall Ridge is here, in the Vale of Ewyas.

The Grange (☎ 01873-890215, 🖥 grangeguesthouse.co.uk; 3 rooms sleeping from one to four people, all en suite; shared bathroom; 🛏; 🐾; WI-FI) is a pony-trekking centre that offers **B&B** (£38pp), or **camping** at £6pp. There's also **a shepherd's hut** (1Tr) and a **camping pod** (1T) with electricity for which they charge £20pp. Subject to prior arrangement an evening meal is available for all guests for about £18. Breakfast is included for B&B guests but is available for everyone else for £8. Campers and hut/pod guests share the toilet/shower facilities.

To get here from the ridge, leave Offa's Dyke Path at the signpost pointing west to Capel and east to Olchon (see Map 22). The path descends the open hillside steeply, heading towards the farm buildings of **Vision Farm** where the path turns right to meet the road.

Right again along the road leads after a mile or so to a little cluster of buildings and **St Mary's Chapel** (see box p123), built in 1762 on an earlier site, the ancient yews in the churchyard shielding the tiny chapel from the elements.

The Grange is just before the chapel on the lane to the left. The climb back on to the ridge in the morning will be steep.

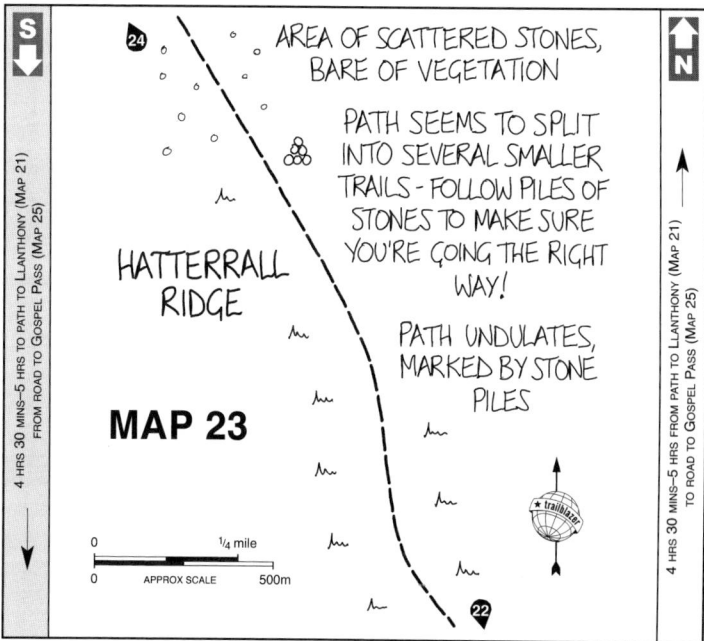

MAP 23

AREA OF SCATTERED STONES, BARE OF VEGETATION

PATH SEEMS TO SPLIT INTO SEVERAL SMALLER TRAILS - FOLLOW PILES OF STONES TO MAKE SURE YOU'RE GOING THE RIGHT WAY!

PATH UNDULATES, MARKED BY STONE PILES

HATTERRALL RIDGE

4 HRS 30 MINS–5 HRS TO PATH TO LLANTHONY (MAP 21) FROM ROAD TO GOSPEL PASS (MAP 25)

4 HRS 30 MINS–5 HRS FROM PATH TO LLANTHONY (MAP 21) TO ROAD TO GOSPEL PASS (MAP 25)

ROUTE GUIDE & MAPS

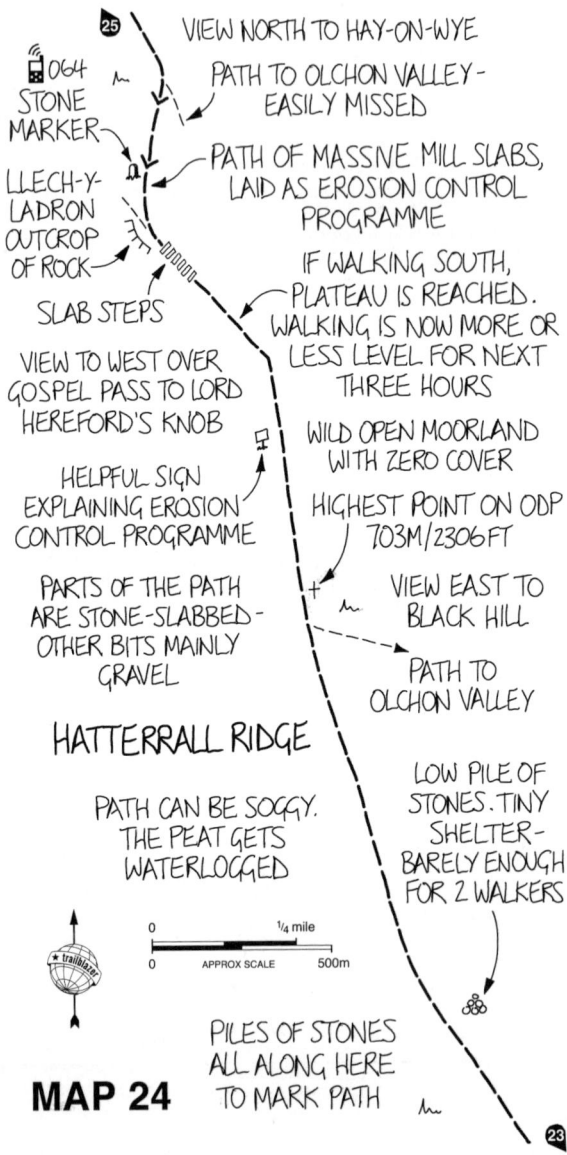

S ↓

N ↑

ROUTE GUIDE & MAPS

25

VIEW NORTH TO HAY-ON-WYE

📱064 STONE MARKER

PATH TO OLCHON VALLEY – EASILY MISSED

LLECH-Y-LADRON OUTCROP OF ROCK

PATH OF MASSIVE MILL SLABS, LAID AS EROSION CONTROL PROGRAMME

SLAB STEPS

IF WALKING SOUTH, PLATEAU IS REACHED. WALKING IS NOW MORE OR LESS LEVEL FOR NEXT THREE HOURS

VIEW TO WEST OVER GOSPEL PASS TO LORD HEREFORD'S KNOB

WILD OPEN MOORLAND WITH ZERO COVER

HELPFUL SIGN EXPLAINING EROSION CONTROL PROGRAMME

HIGHEST POINT ON ODP 703M/2306FT

PARTS OF THE PATH ARE STONE-SLABBED – OTHER BITS MAINLY GRAVEL

VIEW EAST TO BLACK HILL

PATH TO OLCHON VALLEY

HATTERRALL RIDGE

PATH CAN BE SOGGY. THE PEAT GETS WATERLOGGED

LOW PILE OF STONES. TINY SHELTER – BARELY ENOUGH FOR 2 WALKERS

★ trailblazer

0   ¼ mile

0   APPROX SCALE   500m

MAP 24

PILES OF STONES ALL ALONG HERE TO MARK PATH

23

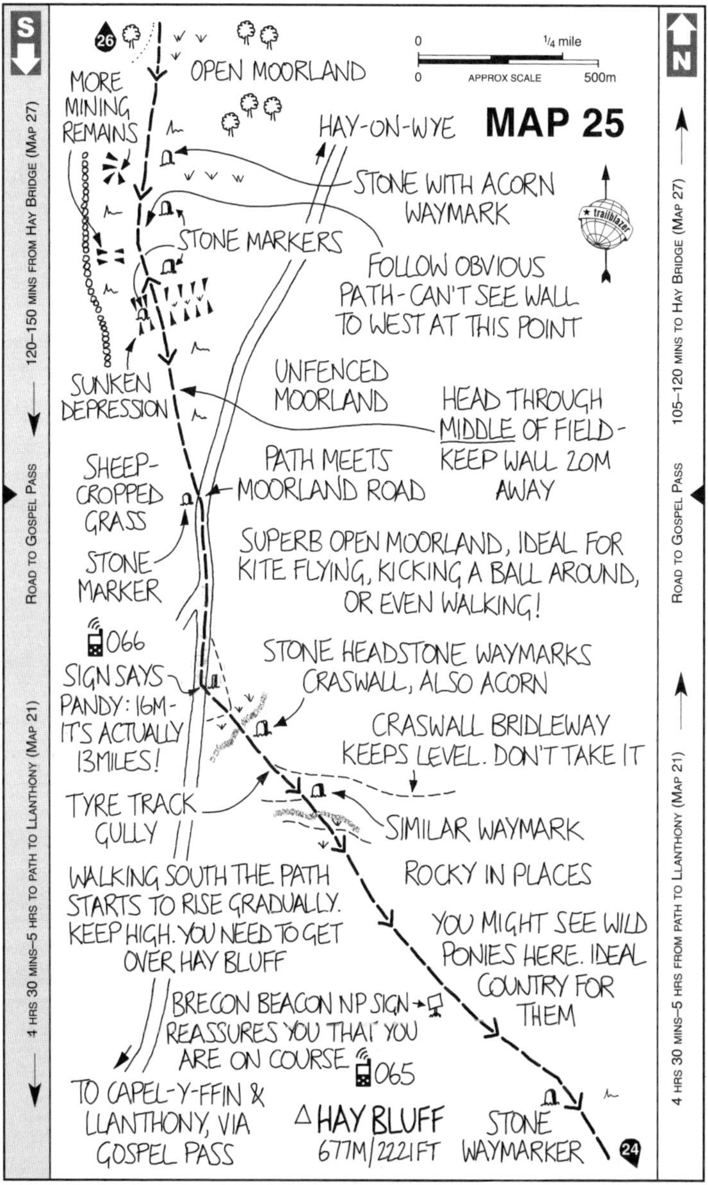
S
N
0
1/4 mile
0
APPROX SCALE
500m
MAP 25
120–150 MINS FROM HAY BRIDGE (MAP 27)
ROAD TO GOSPEL PASS
4 HRS 30 MINS–5 HRS TO PATH TO LLANTHONY (MAP 21)
105–120 MINS TO HAY BRIDGE (MAP 27)
ROAD TO GOSPEL PASS
4 HRS 30 MINS–5 HRS FROM PATH TO LLANTHONY (MAP 21)
26
OPEN MOORLAND
MORE MINING REMAINS
HAY-ON-WYE
STONE WITH ACORN WAYMARK
trailblazer
STONE MARKERS
FOLLOW OBVIOUS PATH - CAN'T SEE WALL TO WEST AT THIS POINT
SUNKEN DEPRESSION
UNFENCED MOORLAND
HEAD THROUGH MIDDLE OF FIELD - KEEP WALL 20M AWAY
SHEEP-CROPPED GRASS
PATH MEETS MOORLAND ROAD
STONE MARKER
SUPERB OPEN MOORLAND, IDEAL FOR KITE FLYING, KICKING A BALL AROUND, OR EVEN WALKING!
066
SIGN SAYS PANDY: 16M - IT'S ACTUALLY 13MILES!
STONE HEADSTONE WAYMARKS CRASWALL, ALSO ACORN
CRASWALL BRIDLEWAY KEEPS LEVEL. DON'T TAKE IT
TYRE TRACK GULLY
SIMILAR WAYMARK
WALKING SOUTH THE PATH STARTS TO RISE GRADUALLY. KEEP HIGH. YOU NEED TO GET OVER HAY BLUFF
ROCKY IN PLACES
YOU MIGHT SEE WILD PONIES HERE. IDEAL COUNTRY FOR THEM
BRECON BEACON NP SIGN REASSURES YOU THAT YOU ARE ON COURSE
065
TO CAPEL-Y-FFIN & LLANTHONY, VIA GOSPEL PASS
HAY BLUFF 677M/2221FT
STONE WAYMARKER
24

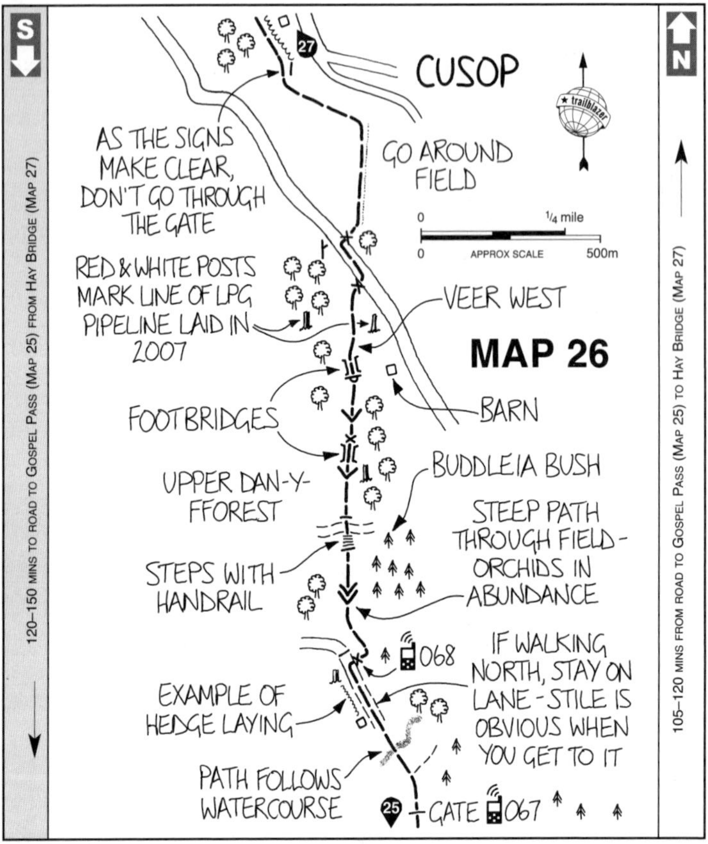
S
N
120–150 MINS TO ROAD TO GOSPEL PASS (MAP 25) FROM HAY BRIDGE (MAP 27)
105–120 MINS FROM ROAD TO GOSPEL PASS (MAP 25) TO HAY BRIDGE (MAP 27)
27
CUSOP
trailblazer
AS THE SIGNS MAKE CLEAR, DON'T GO THROUGH THE GATE
GO AROUND FIELD
0
1/4 mile
0
APPROX SCALE
500m
RED & WHITE POSTS MARK LINE OF LPG PIPELINE LAID IN 2007
VEER WEST
MAP 26
FOOTBRIDGES
BARN
BUDDLEIA BUSH
UPPER DAN-Y-FFOREST
STEEP PATH THROUGH FIELD - ORCHIDS IN ABUNDANCE
STEPS WITH HANDRAIL
068
IF WALKING NORTH, STAY ON LANE - STILE IS OBVIOUS WHEN YOU GET TO IT
EXAMPLE OF HEDGE LAYING
PATH FOLLOWS WATERCOURSE
25
GATE
067

❑ Felindre–Tirley gas pipeline

Just south of Hay-on-Wye, though you probably won't now know it, you'll cross a massive 115-mile (184km) gas pipeline which was installed in 2007. It's used to transport liquefied natural gas from Felindre in South Wales to Tirley in Gloucestershire, as part of the National Grid system.

Construction of the pipeline involved setting industrial diggers to work across 16 miles of the national park. Protests were long and fierce, not least from the park authorities themselves, but the national pressure for energy won the day. And this despite the area being a national park and thus having the highest form of environmental protection that can be afforded in Britain.

Stringent controls were placed on the National Grid to minimise the effect that the work would have on national park land and it has to be said that, cosmetically at least, the impact of the underground pipeline on the landscape has been minimal.

MAP 27

28

FARM TRACK

HIGH HEDGE

070

0   1/4 mile

0   APPROX SCALE   500m

PATH MEETS/
LEAVES RIVER

WOODED PATH
HIGH ABOVE
THE WYE

RIVER
WYE

Radnors End
Campsite

B4351

TO CLYRO

STEPS TO/
FROM ROAD

INTERPRETIVE
BOARD ABOUT
PATH

069

HAY BRIDGE

The Start

HAY-ON-WYE
SEE TOWN PLAN 27a

BUS
STOP

TOILETS

CP

POWER
LINES

PHONE BOX

SUCCESSION OF 3
KISSING GATES

THE KISSING
BRIDGE

BROOK

ATTENTION! IF COMING
FROM THE NORTH IGNORE
HAY BLUFF POINTER-
FOLLOW CUSOP

NOT THIS WAY

HAY BLUFF AHEAD/BEHIND

26

60–70 MINS FROM A438 (MAP 28)

HAY BRIDGE

120–150 MINS TO ROAD
TO GOSPEL PASS (MAP 25)

60–70 MINS TO A438 (MAP 28)

ROUTE GUIDE & MAPS

HAY BRIDGE

105–120 MINS FROM ROAD
TO GOSPEL PASS (MAP 25)

HAY-ON-WYE *(Y-GELLI)* Map 27a

Don't miss the opportunity of an overnight stay in one of the most interesting towns on your route. Hay-on-Wye was effectively rescued from obscurity by Richard Booth, the self-styled 'King of Hay' who resolved to turn a previously rundown town into the second-hand book capital of the Western world. He opened the first second-hand bookshop here in 1961 and despite the number of bookshops slowly diminishing over the years, there are still 18 within Hay, and 26 if you include the surrounding area. Bibliophiles and the curious can browse for hours, fascinated by the cornucopia of titles on sale, from cheap paperbacks to antiquarian rarities costing astronomical sums.

The **castle**, which Booth used to reside in, is currently being restored with no reopening date on the horizon; however, you can visit the castle's courtyard where the walls are lined with books at the single price of 50p.

One of the biggest **bookshops** is housed in the old **Hay Cinema** (☎ 01497-820071, 🖵 haycinemabookshop.co.uk; Mon-Sat 9am-6pm, Sun 11.30am-5.30pm though they are open for viewing from 10am; closed Christmas Day and Easter Sunday). Throughout the year it may be worth popping into **Poetry Bookshop** (☎ 01497-821812, 🖵 poetrybookshop.co.uk; Brook St; Mon-Sat 11am-5pm) and you'll also find bookshops dedicated to specific genres such as children's fiction or **Murder and Mayhem** (Mon-Sat 10.30am-5.30pm; some Sundays too), on Lion St, which specialises in detective novels, true crime and horror stories.

Each year in late May, the town hosts **Hay Festival of Literature** (see box p27) when the great and the good from the world of books visit to speak on their chosen subject or promote their latest publication.

Another busy period is in late July, during the **Royal Welsh Show** (see box p27) held at nearby Builth Wells. Both events make great demands on the accommodation available in the town and rates can double.

In 2007 Hay finally found another town wacky enough to be its twin. Rhodri Morgan, then First Minister of Wales, performed the ceremony, linking Hay with Timbuktu in Mali. Hay-on-Wye is now also twinned with La Redu in Belgium so they are more triplets than twins.

Despite its international reputation, Hay-on-Wye remains small and compact, with all facilities within easy walking distance of each other. If you're planning to take a day out along the trail, this is the place to do it.

A great option to include as part of a rest day in Hay-on-Wye is to see the River Wye from a different angle and hire canoes. Allowing the current to carry you with your feet finally inactive for a day surrounded by the river's resident birds and butterflies offers tremendous respite from the trail. **Want to Canoe?** (☎ 01497-820604, 🖵 canoehire.co.uk) offer 5¼-mile trips to Whitney from where they will collect you approximately 3 hours later (although you can take all day to get there if you wish) and transport you back to Hay-on-Wye. Highly recommended.

Transport

[See pp49-53] There is no rail link, the nearest station being about 20 miles (32km) away at Hereford, but there is a regular **bus** service, the T14, run by Stagecoach from Hereford. On Sundays and Bank Holiday Mondays Yeomans Canyon Travel operate the 39A/Hay Ho! service to/from Hereford.

You won't have any luck if you want a bus to Kington, which is a pity for those doing the trail in daily stages and thus trying to get back to their starting point. It will mean a taxi costing around £24-7. **Taxi** operators include: Hay Taxi Bus (☎ 07974-106656, ☎ 03311-39992, 🖵 haytaxibus.co .uk); Booktown Taxis (☎ 07881-726547); and Julie's Cabs (see p145).

Services

Hay is well supplied with all the services you're likely to need. The **tourist information centre** (☎ 01497-820144, 🖵 hay-on-wye.co.uk; Mon-Sat 10am-4.30pm, Sun 11am-2pm) is on Oxford Rd. They do accommodation booking for a fixed charge;

Hay-on-Wye MAP 27a

Where to stay	Where to eat and drink	
1 The Start	**2** The Globe at Hay	**12** Kilvert's
3 Rest for the Tired	**4** Hay Takeaway	**13** Oscars Bistro
5 Seven Stars	**6** The Granary	**14** Old Black Lion
12 Kilvert's	**7** Cinema Café	**17** Shepherds Parlour
14 Old Black Lion	**8** Chop Suey	**18** Sandwich Cellar
15 La Fosse	**9** Hay Delicatessen	**20** Red Indigo
16 Hay Stables	**10** Tomatitos	**21** Blue Boar
19 Belmont House	**11** St John's Place	**22** Swan at Hay

Internet access is also available here. There are **banks** in the town with **cashpoints** and the **post office** can be found on the narrow street called High Town.

The major **supermarket** chains are notable by their absence but you will find a branch of Spar (daily 7.30am-10pm) on

Castle St, and a Londis on High Town, with similar hours. A 10-minute walk along the B4350 is a well-stocked Co-op (Mon-Sat 6am-11pm, Sun 10am-4pm).

If you're short on **walking gear**, head for Golesworthy's by the clocktower; for **camping accessories**, including Camping

Gaz and Coleman fuel, try Jones Home Hardware on Church St. For medical needs, there's a **pharmacy** on Castle St and the **medical centre** is on Forest Rd. There's also a **launderette** (daily 8am-9pm) on Bell Bank. **Market day** is Thursday and **early closing** is on Tuesday.

Where to stay

As you'd expect, there's no shortage of accommodation and most of it is pretty central. However, if you are planning to be here around the time of the Literature Festival you will need to book well in advance. Also some places may only accept bookings for two nights at the weekend and in peak periods. That said, for the rest of the year the accommodation is surprisingly inexpensive and some of the best value on the trail.

Campers should head for *Radnors End Campsite* (Map 27; ☎ 01497-820780, 🖳 hay-on-wye.co.uk/radnorsend; 🐾; Mar-Oct), a 10-minute walk uphill from the bridge; they charge £8pp. The showers are a coin-in-the-slot system so have some 50p coins handy. They also have a tumble dryer (10p coins) which campers can use. The family who own and run the place are terrific and very helpful – really highly recommended.

For straightforward B&Bs, start at *The Start* (☎ 01497-821391, 🖳 the-start.net; 1T/1D/one suite, all en suite; ☛; WI-FI; Ⓛ). Set right by the River Wye, it's an attractive place, tastefully decorated and with hens and ducks in the garden (hence not accepting dogs!). B&B costs from £40pp (sgl occ £65). They have drying facilities and are happy to do luggage transfer.

Rest for the Tired (☎ 01497-820550, 🖳 restforthetired.co.uk; 1S/1T/2D/1Tr, all en suite; ☛; WI-FI), 6 Broad St, is above a second-hand bookshop. You'll know it by the bicycle-wheel sign, a relic from the days when the shop was a cherished café for cyclists. The tariff is £40pp (sgl occ £55, three sharing £90).

Continuing along Broad St, *The Seven Stars* (☎ 01497-820886, 🖳 theseven-stars .co.uk; 6D/1Tr/1Qd, all en suite; ☛; WI-FI; small 🐾; Ⓛ) boasts an indoor-heated pool and sauna, and offers B&B for £47pp (sgl

occ please apply for rates; £104/114 for three/four sharing).

Old Black Lion (☎ 01497-820841, 🖳 oldblacklion.co.uk; 2S/2T/6D, all en suite; ☛; WI-FI; Ⓛ), on Lion St, is very much still an inn, with B&B from £44.50pp (sgl from £50, sgl occ from £80).

On Oxford Rd, *La Fosse* (☎ 01497-820613, 🖳 lafosse.co.uk; 1T/2D, all en suite; small 🐾; WI-FI; Ⓛ) is good value and a friendly B&B charging from £35pp (sgl occ from £50).

Up the road you'll find *Hay Stables* (☎ 01497-820008, 🖳 haystables.co.uk; 1D/2D or T all en suite; 🐾; WI-FI), where B&B costs £37.50pp (sgl occ on request; higher rates may apply at bank holidays and weekends). Guests use a kitchen here to prepare their breakfast (ingredients are provided) and they can also use it to cook an evening meal and/or prepare a packed lunch.

At the end of Castle St, but on Belmont Rd, there's the white Georgian *Belmont House* (☎ 01497-820718, 🖳 hay-on-wye .co.uk/belmont; 1S/1T/3D/1Tr, some en suite and some with shared facilities; ☛; WI-FI; Ⓛ), charging £30-35pp (sgl £35).

If you prefer hotels to the more homely world of the B&B, *Kilvert's* (☎ 01497-821333, 🖳 kilverts.co.uk; 8D/2D or T/1Tr, all en suite; ☛; WI-FI in bar area; 🐾) is right in the middle of town and ideally placed to catch the buzz. B&B is from £40.50pp.

If all the accommodation is full you could head for **Clyro** (see p136).

Where to eat and drink

There are **cafés** and **tea shops** aplenty in the town.

Hay Delicatessen (☎ 01497-820708; Mon-Sat 9.30am-5.30pm), on Lion St, sells dried fruits, samosas and cakes.

The Granary (☎ 01497-820790; daily 9am-5pm; WI-FI; 🐾) on Broad St is all sophistication and style – and it's great for morning coffee and lunch. If it's just a sandwich you're after no-nonsense *The Sandwich Cellar* (daily from 7.30am), tucked away up the side of the Castle, is a safe bet and a local favourite. *Cinema Café* (☎ 01497-820405, 🖳 boothbooks.co.uk/

cafe.htm; Tue-Sat 9.30am-4.30pm, Sun 10.30am-3.30pm) has an imaginative breakfast and lunch menu (£4-12).

Moving to the pubs, *Blue Boar* (☎ 01497-820884; bar open daily 11am-11pm; food served Sun-Thur 9.30-11.30am & noon-9pm, Fri & Sat to 9.30pm; 🐾 bar only) is a welcoming pub and remains our favourite in Hay, sitting at the junction of Oxford Rd and Church St. The beers are Doom Bar and Timothy Taylor and they also serve Dunkerton's Cider on draught; the usual bar meals are provided (mains £12-17) but it's of a particularly high standard; well worth a visit. It is also one of the few pubs in town (Kilvert's is another – see below) where dogs are allowed in the bar (though not the garden).

Old Black Lion (see Where to stay; food daily Mon-Fri noon-2pm, Sat & Sun to 2.30pm, Sun-Thur 6.30-9pm, Fri & Sat to 9.30pm), serves top-class meals – their 2/3 courses for £29/36.95 (eg scallops followed by asparagus and white truffle oil risotto) may sound expensive but it's worth it, especially if you're there on a Friday for the live jazz.

The *Swan at Hay* (☎ 01497-821188, 🖥 swanathay.co.uk; daily noon-9.30pm serving a variety of menus) is a smart place with the food served at scrubbed wooden tables. The innovative menu includes 48-hour cooked pork belly with mashed potato, burnt apple and seasonal vegetables (£14).

Kilvert's (see Where to stay; bar daily 11am-11pm, food served daily 8-9.30am for breakfast, Mon-Sat noon-2.30pm & 6-8.30pm, Sun noon-6pm though hours vary depending on demand; 🐾), on Bull Ring, is a good bet for homemade pies and there's a variety of them on offer (all £9.95).

Away from the pubs, *Tomatitos* (☎ 01497-820772; Mon-Thur food noon-2.30pm & 6-9pm, Fri & Sat noon-3pm & 6-10pm,

Sun 4-9pm; 🐾) – which is actually housed in the old Wheatsheaf pub – is a tapas restaurant with dishes from £3.25 to £5.95.

Opposite, *St John's Place* (☎ 07855-783799, 🖥 stjohnsplacehay.tumblr.com; Fri & Sat from 6pm) is a superior eaterie with a small and ever-changing menu that usually includes about three – exquisite – main course options; exotic ingredients, including monkfish and lamb's tongue, regularly grace the diners' plates. Possibly the finest dining experience on the trail – and certainly a refreshing change from the usual trekkers' pub-grub diets! Note that credit/debit cards are not accepted here.

Nearby, an option with less limited opening hours (daily 10am-4pm) is *Oscar's Bistro* (☎ 01497-821193); specials are £7.80, their homemade meat meals are £11 and their vegetarian options £10.

The Globe (☎ 01497-821762, 🖥 globe athay.org) has food (Wed-Sun noon-2.30pm, Tue & Thur-Sat 7-9pm booking advisable) and also exhibitions and a variety of entertainment.

For fast food there's a **chippy**, *Hay Takeaway* (Tue-Sat noon-2pm & 5-9pm) on Broad St and a **Chinese takeaway**, *Chop Suey* (☎ 01497-820116; Mon & Wed-Sat 5-10.30pm, Sun 5.30-10.30pm) on Lion St. *Red Indigo Indian Restaurant* (☎ 01497-821999, 🖥 redindigo.co.uk; daily 5.30-11.30pm, also Fri-Sun noon-2pm) does the usual Indian dishes (£7.50-16 for a main course).

Just one more thing: since Hay is definitely a place for a spot of indulgence, do try the home-made sheep's milk ice-cream at *Shepherds Parlour* (Mon-Fri 9am-5.30pm, Sat 9.30am-6pm, Sun 10am-5.30pm); it's a real treat. They also sell very good coffee and lunches; the outdoor seating sits below the castle.

ROUTE GUIDE & MAPS

❏ **Where to stay: the details**
In the descriptions of accommodation in this book: 🛏 means at least one room has a bath; Ⓛ means a packed lunch can be prepared if arranged in advance; 🐾 signifies that dogs are welcome in at least one room but also subject to prior arrangement, an additional charge may also be payable; WI-FI means wi-fi is available. See also p84.

CLYRO   off Map 27a, p133

Along the B4351, just 1½ miles north-west from Hay-on-Wye – and thus from the trail – lies the village of Clyro, where the diarist Francis Kilvert (see box below) was curate of St Michael's Church during the mid-19th century.

While Clyro is not on the path, its proximity to Hay and its connection with the diarist make it an appealing prospect for those with literary interests – particularly as it boasts a couple of hotels, some dormitory accommodation and two campsites.

The Baskerville Arms (☎ 01497-820670, 🖳 baskervillearms.co.uk; 1S/7D/4T/1Tr, all en suite; 🛥; WI-FI in public areas mainly; 🐾) – known as The Swan in Kilvert's day – is right opposite the church, with **B&B** at £39.50-42.50pp (sgl/sgl occ £60-65; three sharing from £120). Two night minimum stay on Fri/Sat nights. Standard pub **food** (daily noon-2pm, 6-9pm) is also served.

Just down the road, at the decidedly grand-looking *Baskerville Hall Hotel* (☎ 01497-820033, 🖳 baskervillehall.co.uk; 6S/4T/10D/7Tr/4Qd, all en suite, 🛥; WI-FI; well-behaved 🐾), which was the original setting for Conan Doyle's *Hound of the Baskervilles*, you can choose from **B&B** (£38-60pp, sgl/sgl occ £48-70, four sharing a room £34pp) or a **dormitory room** (two 16-bed dorms, three 8-bed and one quad; separate shower facilities; towels not provided) for £25pp inc breakfast, or **camping** at £6pp (🐾, breakfast £8). Not bad as there's also an indoor swimming pool and sauna – though as hen and stag dos are welcome here, peace and quiet may not be guaranteed. **Food** is served in the restaurant and at the bar (daily 7-10pm).

Dedicated (and more peaceful) **camping** is available about a quarter of a mile (500m) from the church on the Painscastle Rd at *Borders Hideaway* (☎ 01497-820156, 🖳 bhhhp.co.uk; WI-FI; 🐾; mid Mar-mid Oct); a pitch large-enough for a two-man tent costs from £17 including use of shower facilities.

❏ Francis Kilvert (1840-79)

Francis Kilvert was curate of the parish of Clyro for seven years (1865-72). The diaries that he kept during that time were never intended for publication and large parts were destroyed by his wife, whom he married five weeks before his sudden death from peritonitis. The remainder was published in 1938 and achieved immediate notice. Kilvert's simple, honest description of life in the villages around Hay-on-Wye, his evident love of the countryside and – rather more contentiously in this age of political correctness – his eye for pretty young girls have endeared him to the reading public ever since. Kilvert records with close attention to detail the landscape which he loved and through which he constantly walked. Many of the places he describes are much the same today as they were in the Victorian era.

Kilvert left Clyro to become vicar of Chippenham in Wiltshire but returned to what was then Radnorshire to become vicar of Bredwardine for the last year of his life. He is buried there and on his tombstone are the words 'He being dead, yet speaketh'. Judging by this diary entry from 5 April 1870, he would not have welcomed Offa's Dyke walkers:

'What was our horror to see two tourists with staves and shoulder belts all complete postured among the ruins in an attitude of admiration, one of them discoursing learnedly to his gaping companion and pointing out objects of interest with his stick. If there is one thing more hateful than another it is being told what to admire and having objects pointed out to one with a stick. Of all noxious animals too the most noxious is a tourist. And of all tourists the most vulgar, illbred, offensive and loathsome is the British tourist.'

S ▼ FROM PRESTATYN HAY-ON-WYE TO PANDY   MAPS 27-18

[*Route section begins on Map 27, p131*] This **17½-mile (28km, 8¾-10hrs)**
stretch takes in the long spine of **Hatterrall Ridge** (Maps 24-22) and the highest point on Offa's Dyke Path, at 703m (2306ft). It is one of the most demanding days on the entire walk, but is also without doubt one of the most scenic –
on a good day. While it can be enormously rewarding, it can equally be something of an endurance test so needs some thought before it is tackled. Food, drink
(essential en route) and clothing must be adequate for the terrain: wild, open
moorland at a continuous altitude of around 600m (2000ft) with hardly any shelter and relatively few options for escaping to the valleys to the east and west.

The sometimes steep climb up to **Hay Bluff** (Map 25) runs through several fields before finally reaching the ridge. From here, the going underfoot is
good, aided in many places by heavy mill flagstones laid end to end as part of
an erosion-control programme by Brecon Beacons National Park Authority.
These don't please everybody since they introduce a man-made element to
what are natural surroundings, but they do help to address the steadily worsening erosion caused by both walkers and animals.

Most walkers will undertake the section between Hay-on-Wye and Pandy as
a challenge for a single day and it is probably best treated as such rather than
divided by an overnight stop. However, if the idea is too daunting, or the weather particularly bad, the crossing can be broken by staying at **Capel-y-ffin** (off
Map 22) or **Llanthony** (Map 21) in the Vale of Ewyas to the west, or at
Longtown (off Map 20) to the east. The descent off the ridge in either direction
presents no problem, but the climb back is a stiff test for your legs first thing the
following morning. If planning on descending from the ridge you may wish to
have an OS map (see p43) so you can keep a close eye on your route.

Another way to Capel-y-ffin and Llanthony is to follow the valley road
over Gospel Pass (see Maps 25, 22 & 21) rather than ascending Hay Bluff and
walking along Hatterrall Ridge. It's around four miles (6km) along this quiet
lane to the accommodation in Capel-y-ffin, but a rather soul-destroying eight
miles (13km) if you wanted to tread tarmac all the way to Llanthony Abbey.

Coming off **Hatterrall Hill** (Map 19) there are some fine views as you
descend before you catch sight of the main road at Pandy. All the same, it will
be another hour before you find yourself in front of a cup of tea, or a pint in
the Old Pandy Inn, **Pandy (Map 18, p118)**. The last two miles (3km) along
lanes and through fields lead finally across the railway line and over the river
to return to 'civilisation'.   [*Next route overview p119*]

N ▲ FROM CHEPSTOW HAY-ON-WYE TO KINGTON   MAPS 27-34

[*Route section begins on Map 27, p131*] This **14½-mile (23km, 7¼hrs-8hrs
25mins)** walk includes another candidate for the best section of the entire trail:
the route over **Hergest Ridge** (Map 33), an open common grazed by sheep and
wild ponies. From the ridge there are lovely views of the Shropshire Hills, and
of Hay Bluff and the Black Mountains as they slowly disappear behind you: yesterday's challenge completed.   (*cont'd on p140*)

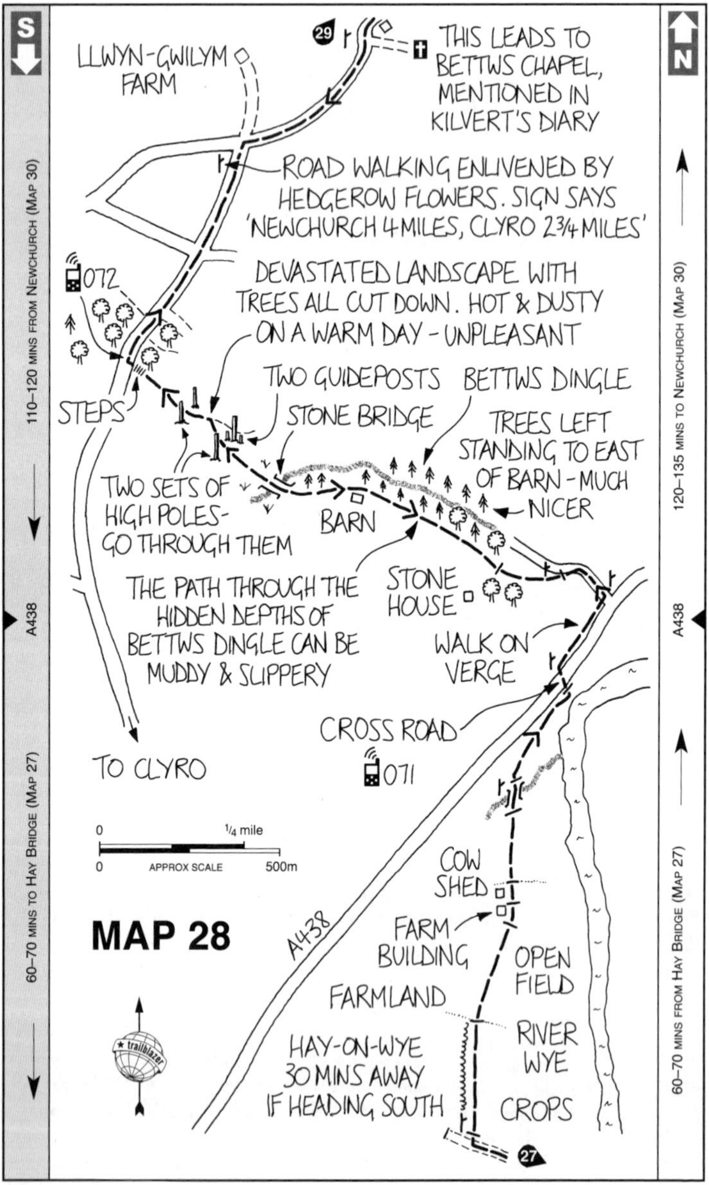

S ⬇

⬆ N

29 🚶 ✝ THIS LEADS TO BETTWS CHAPEL, MENTIONED IN KILVERT'S DIARY

LLWYN-GWILYM FARM

ROAD WALKING ENLIVENED BY HEDGEROW FLOWERS. SIGN SAYS 'NEWCHURCH 4 MILES, CLYRO 2¾ MILES'

📱072

DEVASTATED LANDSCAPE WITH TREES ALL CUT DOWN. HOT & DUSTY ON A WARM DAY - UNPLEASANT

TWO GUIDEPOSTS BETTWS DINGLE

STONE BRIDGE

TREES LEFT STANDING TO EAST OF BARN - MUCH NICER

STEPS

TWO SETS OF HIGH POLES - GO THROUGH THEM

BARN

THE PATH THROUGH THE HIDDEN DEPTHS OF BETTWS DINGLE CAN BE MUDDY & SLIPPERY

STONE HOUSE

WALK ON VERGE

CROSS ROAD

📱071

TO CLYRO

0   ¼ mile

0   APPROX SCALE   500m

MAP 28

COW SHED

FARM BUILDING

OPEN FIELD

FARMLAND

RIVER WYE

HAY-ON-WYE 30 MINS AWAY IF HEADING SOUTH

CROPS

A438

27 ▲

110-120 MINS FROM NEWCHURCH (MAP 30)

A438

60-70 MINS TO HAY BRIDGE (MAP 27)

ROUTE GUIDE & MAPS

120-135 MINS TO NEWCHURCH (MAP 30)

A438

60-70 MINS FROM HAY BRIDGE (MAP 27)

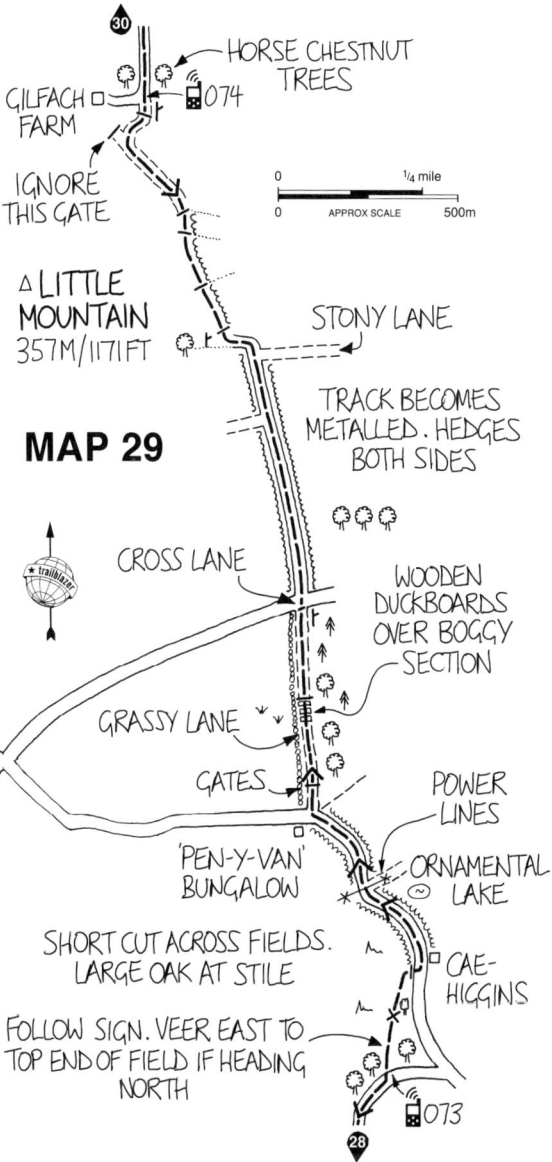

110–120 MINS TO A438 (MAP 28) FROM NEWCHURCH (MAP 30)

120–135 MINS FROM A438 (MAP 28) TO NEWCHURCH (MAP 30)

MAP 29

HORSE CHESTNUT TREES

GILFACH FARM

074

IGNORE THIS GATE

0   ¼ mile

0   APPROX SCALE   500m

△ LITTLE MOUNTAIN
357M/1171FT

STONY LANE

TRACK BECOMES METALLED. HEDGES BOTH SIDES

CROSS LANE

WOODEN DUCKBOARDS OVER BOGGY SECTION

GRASSY LANE

GATES

POWER LINES

'PEN-Y-VAN' BUNGALOW

ORNAMENTAL LAKE

SHORT CUT ACROSS FIELDS. LARGE OAK AT STILE

CAE-HIGGINS

FOLLOW SIGN. VEER EAST TO TOP END OF FIELD IF HEADING NORTH

073

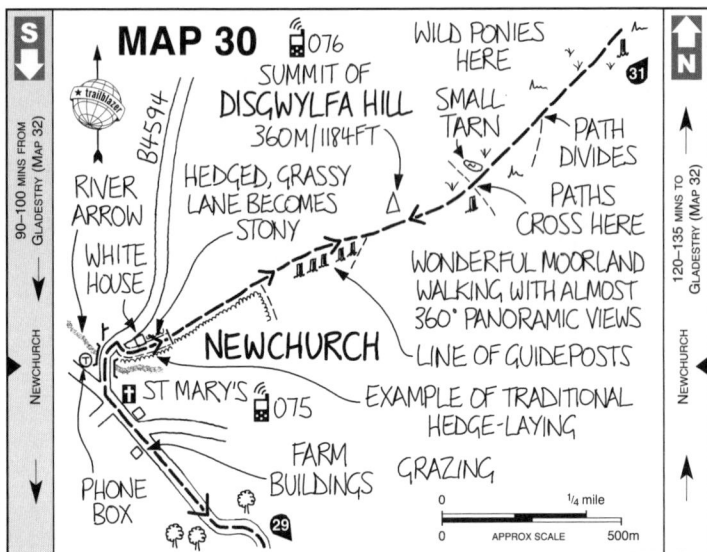

MAP 30

SUMMIT OF DISGWYLFA HILL 360M/1184FT

WILD PONIES HERE

SMALL TARN

PATH DIVIDES

PATHS CROSS HERE

RIVER ARROW

WHITE HOUSE

HEDGED, GRASSY LANE BECOMES STONY

WONDERFUL MOORLAND WALKING WITH ALMOST 360° PANORAMIC VIEWS

NEWCHURCH

LINE OF GUIDEPOSTS

ST MARY'S

EXAMPLE OF TRADITIONAL HEDGE-LAYING

FARM BUILDINGS

GRAZING

PHONE BOX

90–100 MINS FROM GLADESTRY (MAP 32)

NEWCHURCH

120–135 MINS TO GLADESTRY (MAP 32)

NEWCHURCH

0   1/4 mile

0   APPROX SCALE   500m

(cont'd from p137) The going is delightfully easy on springy turf, cropped by sheep for centuries and indeed raced on in the past. Farmers cut the bracken on the ridge and bale it like they do grass elsewhere, but not for fodder – it's poisonous. Instead, it is used as bedding for their animals. Once the bracken has been cut, the grass can grow through more freely, thus improving the grazing.

Before you reach the ridge though, and finally Kington, you have ten miles to the tiny village of Gladestry to entice you along. Yet again waving adieu to the River Wye you leave Hay-on-Wye and its multitudinous volumes behind and travel through **Bettws Dingle** (Map 28), a dark and shaded glen sadly blighted, at least in the latter half, by some indiscriminate tree felling. An uneventful spell of road-walking leads you to **Newchurch** (Map 30) and on over **Disgwyfla Hill** (Map 30), from which there are fantastic panoramic (almost!) views, before more open country is crossed and you arrive at **Gladestry** (Map 32), the southern gateway to the ridge, and ultimately to **Kington (Map 34, p145)**. Take your time; enjoy the crossing, admire the views – there are arduous days ahead. [Next route overview p148]

NEWCHURCH   Map 30

There are no facilities here at all except a **telephone** kiosk and the wonderful **St Mary's Church**, which has become something of a meeting point for walkers thanks largely to its *refreshment table*. Sitting at the back of church, the table has squash, coffee, several varieties of tea and even biscuits and the occasional currant bun. Donations are asked for in return – please give generously, if only to encourage the parishioners to maintain this essential service. And besides, the church itself is not without interest (see box p143).

S

N

0 ___ ¼ mile
0 ___ APPROX SCALE ___ 500m

32

NARROW TARMAC
LANE BETWEEN
HEDGES

📱078

DUTCH BARN

OLD QUARRY

STILE & GATE
CLOSE TOGETHER

FOLLOW
ACORN
POSTS

PATH ENCLOSED BY
FENCES - STRAIT-
JACKETED EVEN

FARMLAND

'FAIRFIELDS'

METAL GATE

★ trailblazer

FARMLAND

GROVE FARM

MAP 31

📱077

WATER TAP
HERE - FREE!

LONE ROWAN TREE

COMMON LAND

GATE GIVES
ACCESS TO OPEN
LAND - DO READ
THE POEM ON
THE GATE

IF COMING FROM THE SOUTH
MAKE SURE YOU DON'T
MISS THIS LEFT TURN

30

LISTEN FOR LARKS

90–100 MINS TO NEWCHURCH (MAP 30) FROM GLADESTRY (MAP 32)

120–135 MINS FROM NEWCHURCH (MAP 30) TO GLADESTRY (MAP 32)

ROUTE GUIDE & MAPS

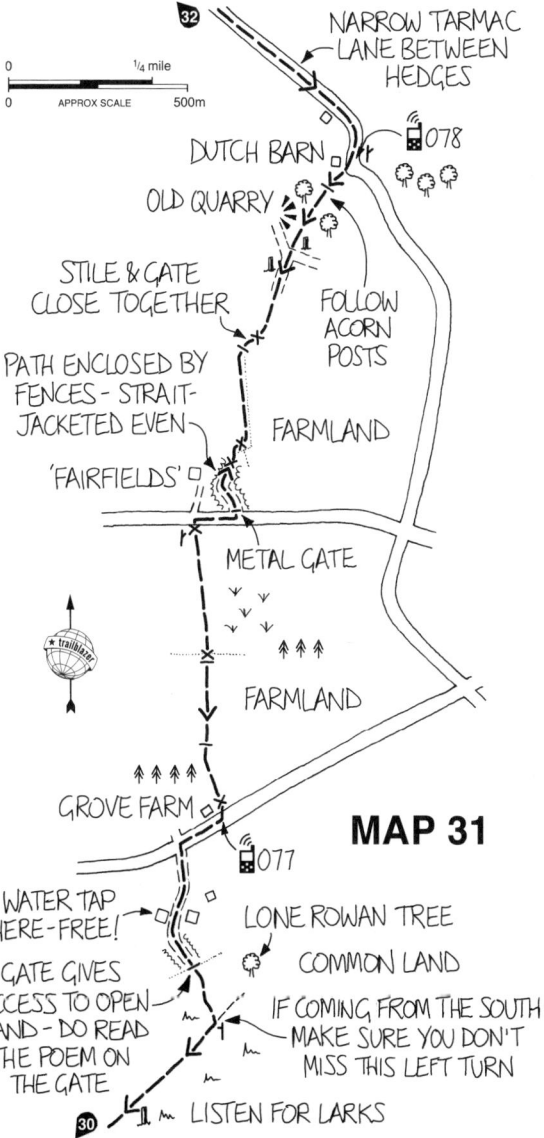

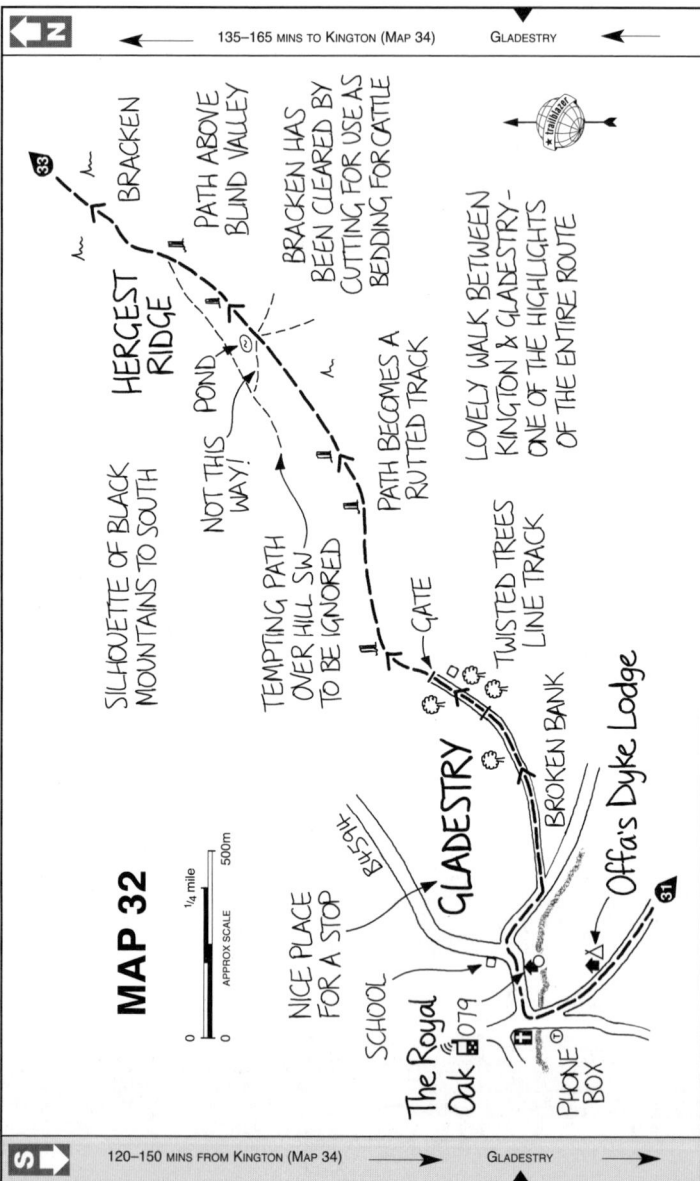

MAP 32

¼ mile   500m
APPROX SCALE

SILHOUETTE OF BLACK MOUNTAINS TO SOUTH

BRACKEN

PATH ABOVE BLIND VALLEY

BRACKEN HAS BEEN CLEARED BY CUTTING FOR USE AS BEDDING FOR CATTLE

HERCEST RIDGE

POND

NOT THIS WAY!

TEMPTING PATH OVER HILL SW TO BE IGNORED

PATH BECOMES A RUTTED TRACK

LOVELY WALK BETWEEN KINGTON & GLADESTRY - ONE OF THE HIGHLIGHTS OF THE ENTIRE ROUTE

GATE

TWISTED TREES LINE TRACK

BROKEN BANK

GLADESTRY

NICE PLACE FOR A STOP

SCHOOL

The Royal Oak

B4594

PHONE BOX

Offa's Dyke Lodge

ROUTE GUIDE & MAPS

❏ **St Mary's Church and Churchyard, Newchurch**   Map 30, p140

Newchurch's St Mary's Church occupies an ancient sacred site, probably of pre-Christian origin. Graves are grouped on the south side, the north side by local custom being the Devil's side. To the right of the steps leading up from the road lies the grave of the Vaughan family. The Rev David Vaughan was curate of the parish for 17 years and then vicar for 33 years until his death, aged 83 in 1903. Under the granite cross lies his daughter, Emmeline, who died aged 14. Her sad figure haunts a passage in *Kilvert's Diary* of 14 March 1873: 'As I stooped over the green grave by the church-yard gate, placing the primrose bunches in a cross upon the turf, large flakes of snow still fell thickly upon us but melted as they fell, and the great yew tree bent weeping upon the grave.' The yew tree fell in a great storm in January 1991, narrowly missing the church. It had stood for 1100 years.

Within the church these lines by RS Thomas are inscribed: 'In cities that have outgrown their promise, people are becoming pilgrims again if not to this place then to the re-creation of it in their own spirits.'

GLADESTRY   Map 32

Gladestry is a more peaceful place to stop than its two busier neighbours.

Its main claim to fame is *The Royal Oak* (☎ 01544-370669, 🖳 royaloak gladestry.co.uk; Wed-Sat 7-10.30pm, Sat & Sun noon-3pm; 1T en suite/3D private facilities; WI-FI; 🐾; ⒧), a proper village pub that serves a good pint and home-made **food** (food served noon-2pm on the days they are open but every evening for guests 7-8.30pm) that's a cut above the rest. **B&B**

here will cost £40pp (sgl occ £60). Baggage transfer is available; contact them for details.

B&B and **camping** (£7 including shower) is also available at *Offa's Dyke Lodge* (☎ 01544-370464, 🖳 offas-dyke-lodge-retreat-at-gladestry.com; 1T private facilities, 2D en suite; ➿; WI-FI; ⒧; £37.50-40pp, sgl occ £65). Evening meals are on offer (two courses £15) and there's even a swimming pool to soak your hard-walked feet in.

KINGTON   Map 34a, p147

You almost expect to find a candlestick-maker in this most traditional of towns – English, despite lying on the western side of the Dyke. Narrow streets, lined with as-yet ungentrified houses, are interspersed with more than their fair share of pubs, but the trappings of the 21st century seem so far to have passed by.

Kington Museum (☎ 01544-231748, 🖳 kingtonmuseum.org.uk; Tue-Thur 10.30am-4pm, Sat 10.30am-1pm; free but donations welcome) is worth a look to learn a little about the local history including artefacts that date back to the Neolithic period and even information on the afore-mentioned 19th-century candlestickmaker.

St Mary's Church is worth a visit, a fine building started in the 12th century and added to later, especially in the reign of

Queen Victoria. In a side chapel is the effi-gy of Sir Thomas Vaughan and his wife, Ellen the Terrible, named, rumour has it, for her cooking.

On the way out of town is **Hergest Croft Gardens** (Map 34; ☎ 01544-230160, 🖳 hergest.co.uk; Mar Sat & Sun noon-5.30pm, Apr-Oct daily noon-5.30pm) where you can visit the gardens (£6.50, free for RHS members), which have over 5000 rare trees and shrubs, and stop for tea and a scone in their tearoom.

Transport

[See pp49-53] Sargeants' **buses** Nos 461 & 462 call here en route between Hereford and Llandrindod Wells and their No 41 goes to Knighton. Buses pick up and drop off by the car park.

ROUTE GUIDE & MAPS

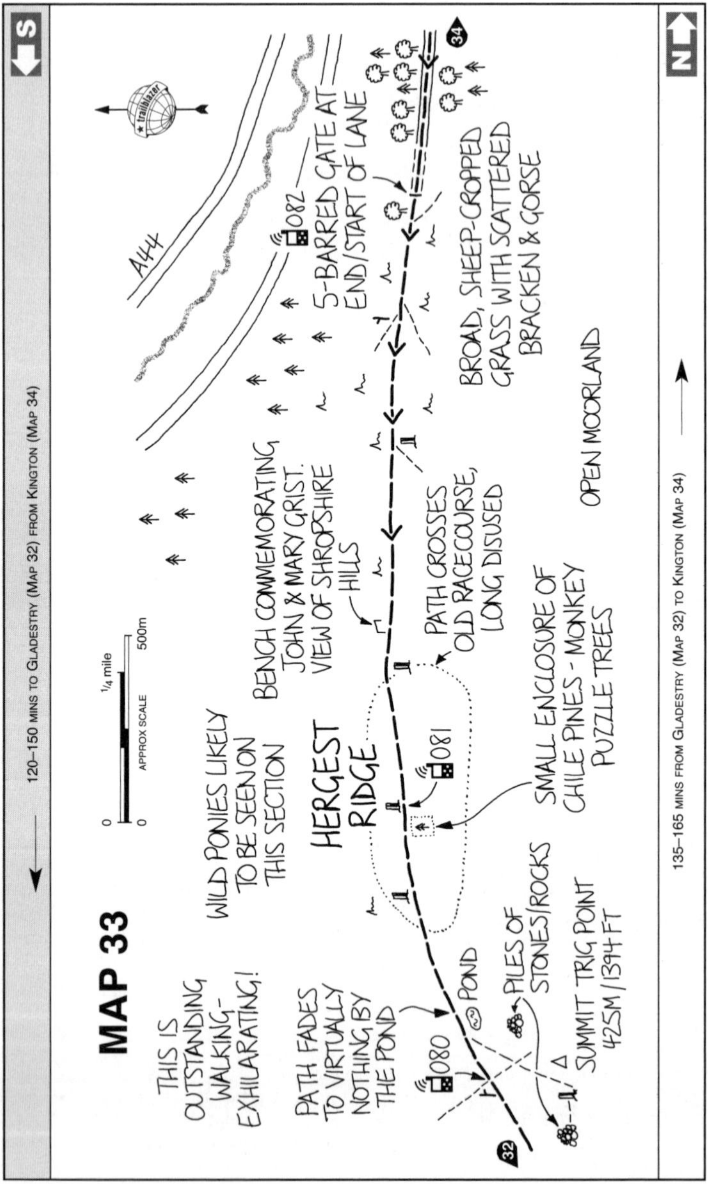

ROUTE GUIDE & MAPS

MAP 33

← 120–150 MINS TO GLADESTRY (MAP 32) FROM KINGTON (MAP 34)

135–165 MINS FROM GLADESTRY (MAP 32) TO KINGTON (MAP 34) →

THIS IS OUTSTANDING WALKING – EXHILARATING!

WILD PONIES LIKELY TO BE SEEN ON THIS SECTION

APPROX SCALE
0 — ¼ mile
0 — 500m

PATH FADES TO VIRTUALLY NOTHING BY THE POND

🏠 080

POND

PILES OF STONES/ROCKS

SUMMIT TRIG POINT 425M /1394 FT

32

BENCH COMMEMORATING JOHN & MARY GRIST. VIEW OF SHROPSHIRE HILLS

HERGEST RIDGE

🏠 081

SMALL ENCLOSURE OF CHILE PINES - MONKEY PUZZLE TREES

PATH CROSSES OLD RACECOURSE, LONG DISUSED

OPEN MOORLAND

A44

🏠 082

5-BARRED GATE AT END/START OF LANE

BROAD, SHEEP-CROPPED GRASS WITH SCATTERED BRACKEN & GORSE

34

N ↑
S ↓

MAP 34

KINGTON SEE TOWN PLAN 34a

Taxis are available from Julie's Cabs (☎ 07899-846592).

Services

As with so many towns along the Dyke, Kington has all the essentials that the walker might need.

The **tourist information centre** (☎ 01544-230778, ☐ kingtontourist.info; Easter-Sep Mon-Sat 10am-4.30pm, Oct Mon-Sat 10am-4pm) is on Church St. The volunteer staff are very helpful and they have plenty of leaflets and suggested walks.

The High St has **cashpoints**, as does the large Co-op **supermarket** (Mon-Sat 7am-11pm, Sun 10am-4pm) off Mill St. There's a second supermarket, Nisa (Mon-Sat 8am-8pm, Sun 9am-6pm), on High St, and a third, Spar (Mon-Sat 7am-11pm, Sun 8am-11pm), on Church St.

There's a **pharmacy**, Rowlands (Mon-Fri 9am-1pm & 1.30-6.30pm, Sat to 5pm only) on High St and there is a **launderette** (Mon-Sun 7.30am-9pm) near the **post office** on Bridge St.

For **walking/camping gear** including maps, The Walking Hub is opposite the clock tower; contact Ali there (☎ 07756-172160) regarding what hours the shop is open. The shop is quite limited stock-wise so if there's something particular that you need you may need to check with Ali that she stocks it.

Market day is Tuesday and **early closing day** for many independent shops is Wednesday – and, believe me, when they say 'early' closing they mean it. Many of these shops shut on Saturday afternoon, too, though the main supermarkets stay open.

Where to stay

YHA Kington (bookings ☎ 0800-019 1700 or ☎ 01629-592700 or online, general ☎ 0345-371 9053, ☐ yha.org.uk/hostel/yha-kington; 28 beds – 1 x 2-, 1 x 3-, 4 x 4-beds,

2 x 5 beds, some rooms have double beds and some are en suite), on Victoria Rd, is the nearest hostel to the path and only a short walk off route. It's housed in a renovated cottage hospital on the edge of town but is self-catering only. There are laundry facilities and a drying room. Beds cost from £15pp (private rooms from £25). Credit/debit cards are accepted.

Camping is available at *Fleece Meadow Campsite* (☎ 01544-231235; Apr to end Oct), Mill St, on the River Arrow. It's owned by Sargeants Buses and is next to their depot; it's an efficient site with toilet & shower facilities and they charge £8pp.

B&B-wise, our favourite is the delightful *Old House* (☎ 01544-239127, 💻 theoldhousebandb.wordpress.com; 1D/1T each with their own private facilities; 📶; WI-FI; 🐾), a lovely place where guests have their own lounge, there's a terrific veranda overlooking the pleasant garden and the neighbouring cattle market – and the breakfasts are great. B&B costs from £35pp (£40 sgl occ) and it is highly recommended.

The elegant *Church House* (☎ 01544-230534, 💻 churchhousekington.co.uk, Church Rd; 1T/1D, shared bathroom; 📶; WI-FI; 🐾; ℚ) is right on the route, only a short walk from the centre of town and costs from £40pp (sgl occ £50-55).

By the River Arrow is the appropriately named *Arrowbank Lodge* (☎ 01544-231115, 💻 arrowbanklodge.co.uk; 2D en suite/1T private facilities; 📶; WI-FI; Apr-Oct), down a track (Tanyard Lane) off the bridge over the river. A little way from the path, nevertheless they are used to catering for walkers and have the full complement of facilities. B&B costs £37.50-42.50pp (sgl occ £50).

'Eco-friendly' B&B can be found at *Castle Hill House* (☎ 01544-209066, 💻 castlehillhousekington.co.uk; 1T/2D/1Tr, en suite; 📶; ℚ; WI-FI; from £40pp, sgl occ £70); the owners here can organise massages should your muscles feel in need of rejuvenation (30 mins £35, 60 mins £55, 90 mins £80), although note that there is generally a two-night minimum stay policy at the weekend. They also offer luggage transfer.

The Walking Hub (☎ 07756-172160, 💻 kingtonwalkinghub.com; 2D/1T bunk-beds, shared facilities; 📶; WI-FI; ℚ; 🐾; Apr-Dec), opposite the clocktower, is a great option for walkers and has been set up specifically to cater to their requirements. Rates (from £38pp, sgl occ £65) include a self-service continental breakfast.

On the path as it makes its way through town is *The Swan Hotel* (☎ 01544-239433, 💻 theswanonthesquare.co.uk; 3S/2T, all en suite; WI-FI; 🐾; from £35pp, sgl £50). A pub with rooms worth considering is *The Oxford Arms* (☎ 01544-230322, 💻 the-oxford-arms.co.uk; 3T/3D, mix en suite & private facilities; 📶; WI-FI; 🐾; £35-37.50pp, sgl occ £50-55).

Where to eat and drink

Kington has a declining array of eateries but you won't go hungry.

Café-wise, centrally, *Border Bean* (☎ 01544-231625; Mon-Sat 9am-5pm; WI-FI) has friendly staff and a small but tasty menu including, unusually but delightfully, Marmite on toast (£1.50). Almost opposite is *Regency Café* (☎ 01544-231344; Tue-Fri 7am-5pm, Sat 7am-4pm), High St, which opens early.

A similar service is offered by *Sally's Pantry* (☎ 01544-239000; summer Mon-Sat 8am-5pm, winter Mon-Sat 9am-4pm), a really lovely place with great sandwiches and fresh coffee served in the tearoom; the only disadvantage with this place is its location, on Bridge St outside the town centre. You could also try *Grumpie Grampies Café & Takeaway* (sandwiches, paninis, hot rolls; from 10am), Bridge St, if the others are full.

Evening dining in Kington is not likely to be an experience to remember but there are three pubs worth considering.

The Swan (see Where to stay; food Wed-Mon noon-2pm, Wed-Sat 6-9pm) is reasonably priced and has a pleasant atmosphere (mains: daytime £5.95-9.95, evening £8.95-£15.95). They also serve a lunchtime menu including sandwiches (£4.50).

At the other end of the town centre, *Oxford Arms* (see Where to stay) is a

Where to stay
1 Church House
2 Castle Hill House
3 Fleece Meadow
  Campsite
4 The Swan
6 The Walking Hub
14 Oxford Arms
15 Old House
16 YHA Kington
17 Arrowbank Lodge

Where to eat and drink
4 The Swan
5 Bamboo Garden
6 The Walking Hub
7 Border Bean
8 Kington Fish & Chips
9 Burton Hotel
10 Regency Café
11 Angel Fish Bar
12 Taj Mahal
13 Grumpie Grampies
  Takeaway
14 Oxford Arms
18 Sally's Pantry

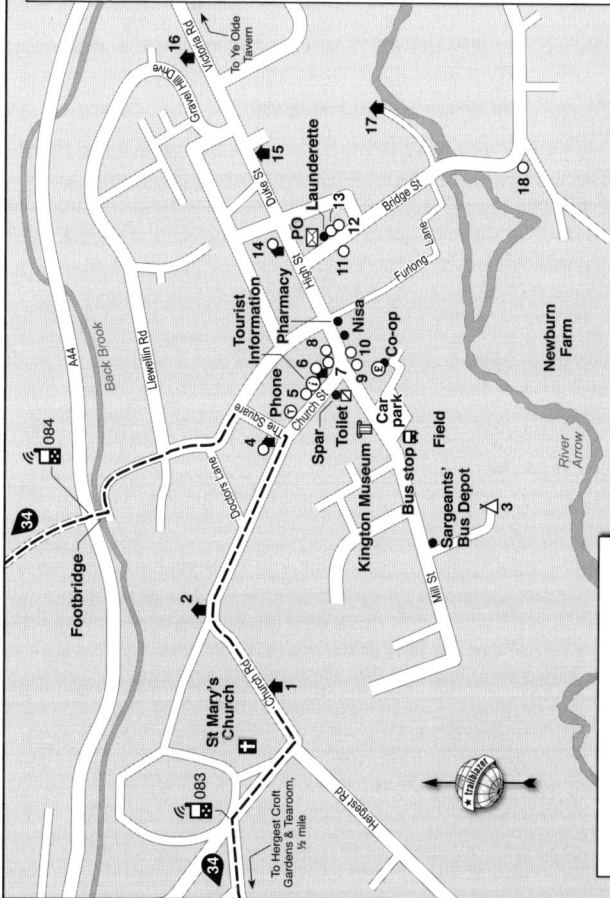

Kington MAP 34a

St Mary's
Church

To Hergest Croft
Gardens & Tearoom, ½ mile

Footbridge

Back Brook

A44

Llewellin Rd

Doctors Lane

Church Rd

Hergest Rd

The Square

Church St

Phone

Tourist
Information

Pharmacy

Spar
Toilet

Kington Museum

Car
park

Bus stop

Sargeants'
Bus Depot

Field

Nisa

Co-op

High St

Duke St

PO

Launderette

Furlong Lane

Bridge St

Newburn
Farm

River
Arrow

Mill St

Gravel St

Hill Drive

Victoria Rd

To Ye Olde
Tavern

0   100   200m

ROUTE GUIDE & MAPS

friendly, locals' place which serves simple pub grub (food daily noon-2.30pm & 6-9pm) with main meals for around a tenner, real ale, and a good selection of vegetarian options.

Ye Olde Tavern (off Map 34a; ☎ 01544-231945; bar Mon-Thur 6.30pm-midnight, to 10.30pm on Mon in winter, Fri 3.30pm-midnight, Sat & Sun noon to midnight), near the bypass on Victoria Rd, is a proper olde worlde pub serving Wye Valley (see box p24), Hobsons, Ludlow and a guest beer, the food is popular, however the hours are more limited (Thur-Mon 6.30-8.30pm) than some of your other options.

The Burton Hotel (☎ 01544-230323, 🖥 hotelherefordshire.co.uk; food daily noon-9.30pm; WI-FI) is highly thought of, with mains in the restaurant for £11.95-21.25. Food is available all day but there is a reduced menu 2-6pm.

There's fast food, with a reliable chippy, *Angel Fish Bar*, on Bridge St, and *Kington Fish & Chips*, on the High St, to choose from.

For Chinese try *Bamboo Garden* (☎ 01544-231089; Tue-Thur & Sun 5-10pm, Fri & Sat to 10.45pm) on Church St; and for Indian, *Taj Mahal* (☎ 01544-231999; Wed-Mon 6.30-10.30/11pm). Both do takeaway.

S ⬇ FROM PRESTATYN — KINGTON TO HAY-ON-WYE — MAPS 34-27

ROUTE GUIDE & MAPS

[*Route section begins on Map 34, p145*] This **14½-mile (23km, 6hrs 20mins -7hrs 20mins)** walk includes possibly the best part of the entire trail, the route over **Hergest Ridge** (Map 33), an open common grazed by sheep and wild ponies. From the ridge there are lovely views of the Shropshire Hills and ahead to Hay Bluff and the Black Mountains, the next day's challenge.

The going is delightfully easy on springy turf, cropped by sheep for centuries and indeed raced on in the past. Farmers cut the bracken on the ridge and bale it like they do grass elsewhere, but not for fodder – it's poisonous. Instead, it is used as bedding for their animals. Once the bracken has been cut, the grass can grow through more freely, thus improving the grazing.

Beyond the tiny village of **Gladestry** (Map 32), more open country follows as the trail crosses the much smaller expanse of the **Disgwylfa Hill** (Map 30), before descending to **Newchurch** (Map 30).

Towards the latter stages of the day is **Bettws Dingle** (Map 28), a dark and shaded glen sadly blighted, at least on the first half, by some indiscriminate tree felling. When you emerge on to the A438 you have to walk along the verge, but fortunately it's not long before you cross over to meet the languorous **River Wye**. Instead of a riverside walk, there follows a series of fields before the trail returns to the river on the edge of the book town of **Hay-on-Wye** (Map 27, p131). After a longish day, it's likely to be time to head straight for your accommodation, leaving a browse among the dusty volumes until later.

[*Next route overview p137*]

❑ **Important note – walking times**
Unless otherwise specified, **all times in this book refer only to the time spent walking.** You will need to add 20-30% to allow for rests, photography, checking the map, drinking water etc. When planning the day's hike count on 5-7 hours' actual walking.

N ↑ FROM CHEPSTOW **KINGTON TO KNIGHTON** **MAPS 34-40**

[*Route section begins on Map 34, p145*] This **13½-mile (22km, 6hrs-6hrs 55mins)** section fits conveniently into a day's walking, inconveniently book-ended by two golf courses. Fortunately, the miles trod between them, away from the purr of golf buggies and the whizz of golf balls, include some marvellous walking, minimal habitation, and plenty of time spent with only the Dyke for company. There are several stretches of the Dyke on view, in places high and formidable and with a well-defined ditch.

Leaving Kington, open hilltops beckon, but first you must negotiate your way to the east of Kington Golf Course: the highest 18-hole course in England. The clubhouse (☎ 01544-230340, 🖥 kingtongolf.co.uk) is surprisingly welcoming to walkers; you can pop in for a bacon roll for £3 (food is available throughout the day from 11am); they have a shop selling waterproof clothing and hats and are also happy for walkers to play a round of golf if they want.

Over **Rushock Hill** (Map 35) you encounter extraordinary scenery, bracken and gorse, heathland and wooded country, that is full of variety, with nothing but the wind and soaring buzzards (with possibly the odd red kite too) for company. More switchbacks follow and more agricultural perambulations with plenty of walking on top of the Dyke. **Dolley Green** (Map 37) is little more than a point on the map but it is close to the attractive little town of **Presteigne** (see p156), worth a detour in its own right if time isn't tight.

Two hills are crossed, **Furrow Hill** and **Hawthorn Hill** (Map 38), fine open airy walking that will raise your spirits and put a spring in your step, before the route becomes agricultural with more of the all-too-familiar stiles to add to your tally and you arrive to the west of the day's second golf course following which a stiff descent leads you into **Knighton (Map 40, p155)**.

[*Next route overview p160*]

ROUTE GUIDE & MAPS

❏ **The Marches**
The Marches refers to the border country between England and Wales. Contested and fought over for centuries, the area has now become a kind of peaceable middle ground, partly Welsh, partly English, characterised by its rounded hills, wooded river valleys and secluded fields and lanes.

The term 'March' derives from the Anglo-Saxon word *mearc* meaning simply 'a boundary'. It was William the Conqueror who resolved to sort out the lawless Welsh once and for all by granting Marcher lordships to his followers. These were virtually independent fiefdoms with the authority to act as they saw fit, owing only their final allegiance to the king. They could impose the force of law on the country, raise taxes and build castles, many of which remain in places such as Chepstow, Monmouth, White and Chirk, all milestones along Offa's Dyke Path. The Marcher lords were a significant factor in the control of England and names such as Roger Mortimer, William Fitzosbern and Gilbert de Clare remind us of turbulent times.

Today, with a population described as Anglo-Welsh, the Marches has a unique identity, with the border towns of Oswestry, Montgomery, Knighton, Kington, Presteigne and Hay-on-Wye all ports of call along the Dyke.

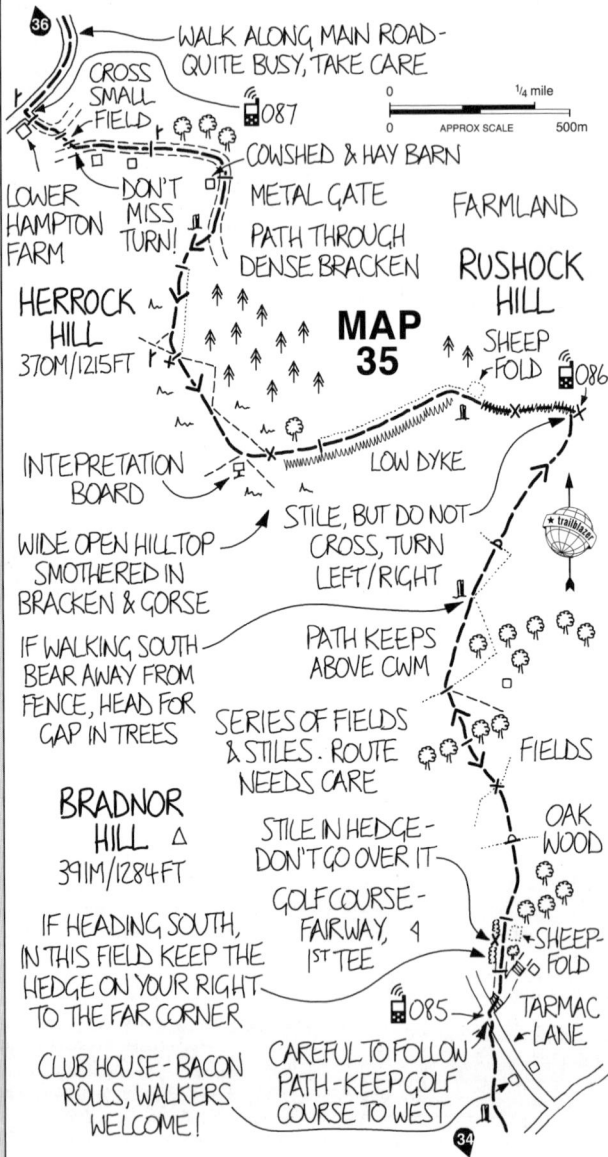

S ⬇

36

WALK ALONG MAIN ROAD-
QUITE BUSY, TAKE CARE

CROSS
SMALL
FIELD

087

0 ─────── ¼ mile
0 ─────── 500m
APPROX SCALE

COWSHED & HAY BARN

LOWER
HAMPTON
FARM

DON'T
MISS
TURN!

METAL GATE

PATH THROUGH
DENSE BRACKEN

FARMLAND

RUSHOCK
HILL

HERROCK
HILL
370M/1215FT

SHEEP
FOLD

086

MAP
35

INTEPRETATION
BOARD

LOW DYKE

WIDE OPEN HILLTOP
SMOTHERED IN
BRACKEN & GORSE

STILE, BUT DO NOT
CROSS, TURN
LEFT/RIGHT

★ trailblazer

IF WALKING SOUTH
BEAR AWAY FROM
FENCE, HEAD FOR
GAP IN TREES

PATH KEEPS
ABOVE CWM

BRADNOR
HILL △
391M/1284FT

SERIES OF FIELDS
& STILES. ROUTE
NEEDS CARE

FIELDS

STILE IN HEDGE-
DON'T GO OVER IT

OAK
WOOD

IF HEADING SOUTH,
IN THIS FIELD KEEP THE
HEDGE ON YOUR RIGHT
TO THE FAR CORNER

GOLF COURSE-
FAIRWAY, ◁
1ST TEE

SHEEP-
FOLD

085

TARMAC
LANE

CLUB HOUSE- BACON
ROLLS, WALKERS
WELCOME!

CAREFUL TO FOLLOW
PATH-KEEP GOLF
COURSE TO WEST

34

N ⬆

ROUTE GUIDE & MAPS

120–130 MINS FROM DITCHYELD BRIDGE (MAP 36) TO KINGTON (MAP 34)

120–135 MINS TO DITCHYELD BRIDGE (MAP 36) FROM KINGTON (MAP 34)

S

N

HILLS TO THE EAST RESEMBLE A PERSON LYING DOWN

HAY BARN

OLD QUARRY

★ trailblazer

GRANNER WOOD

FORESTRY TRACK

MAP 36

EVENJOBB

LOVELY UNDULATING WALK THROUGH THE TREES

STEPS

📱 089

CROPS

SIGN: 'GRANNER WOOD'

STEPS

MAST

PATH MOSTLY ON TOP OF WOODED DYKE ON THIS STRETCH

CROPS

PATCHWORK FIELD

STEPS

STEPS (SOME BROKEN)

'OLD BURFA' HALF-TIMBERED FARM HOUSE

RUINED SHEDS

SHADED PATH

📱 088

DITCHYELD BRIDGE

KNOBBLEY BROOK

OLD BRIDGE NEXT TO ROAD BRIDGE - GOOD FOR POOHSTICKS

ON ROAD FOR ABOUT ¼ MILE

B4362

35

0   ¼ mile

0   APPROX SCALE   500m

120–135 MINS FROM DOLLEY GREEN (MAP 37)

120–135 MINS TO DOLLEY GREEN (MAP 37)

ROUTE GUIDE & MAPS

DITCHYELD BRIDGE

DITCHYELD BRIDGE

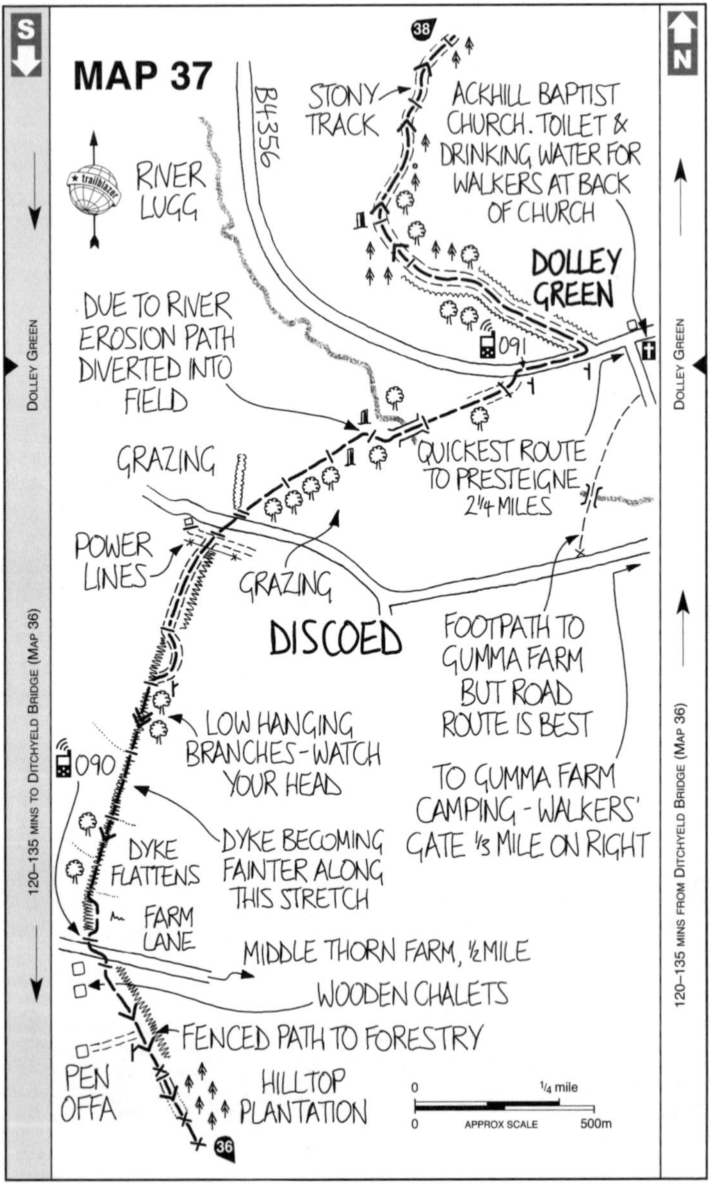

S ⬇

MAP 37

N ⬆

RIVER
LUGG

B4356

38

STONY
TRACK

ACKHILL BAPTIST
CHURCH. TOILET &
DRINKING WATER FOR
WALKERS AT BACK
OF CHURCH

**DOLLEY
GREEN**

DUE TO RIVER
EROSION PATH
DIVERTED INTO
FIELD

📵 091

GRAZING

QUICKEST ROUTE
TO PRESTEIGNE
2¼ MILES

POWER
LINES

GRAZING

DISCOED

FOOTPATH TO
GUMMA FARM
BUT ROAD
ROUTE IS BEST

TO GUMMA FARM
CAMPING - WALKERS'
GATE ⅓ MILE ON RIGHT

📵 090

LOW HANGING
BRANCHES - WATCH
YOUR HEAD

DYKE
FLATTENS

DYKE BECOMING
FAINTER ALONG
THIS STRETCH

FARM
LANE

MIDDLE THORN FARM, ½ MILE

WOODEN CHALETS

FENCED PATH TO FORESTRY

**PEN
OFFA**

HILLTOP
PLANTATION

36

0   ¼ mile
0   APPROX SCALE   500m

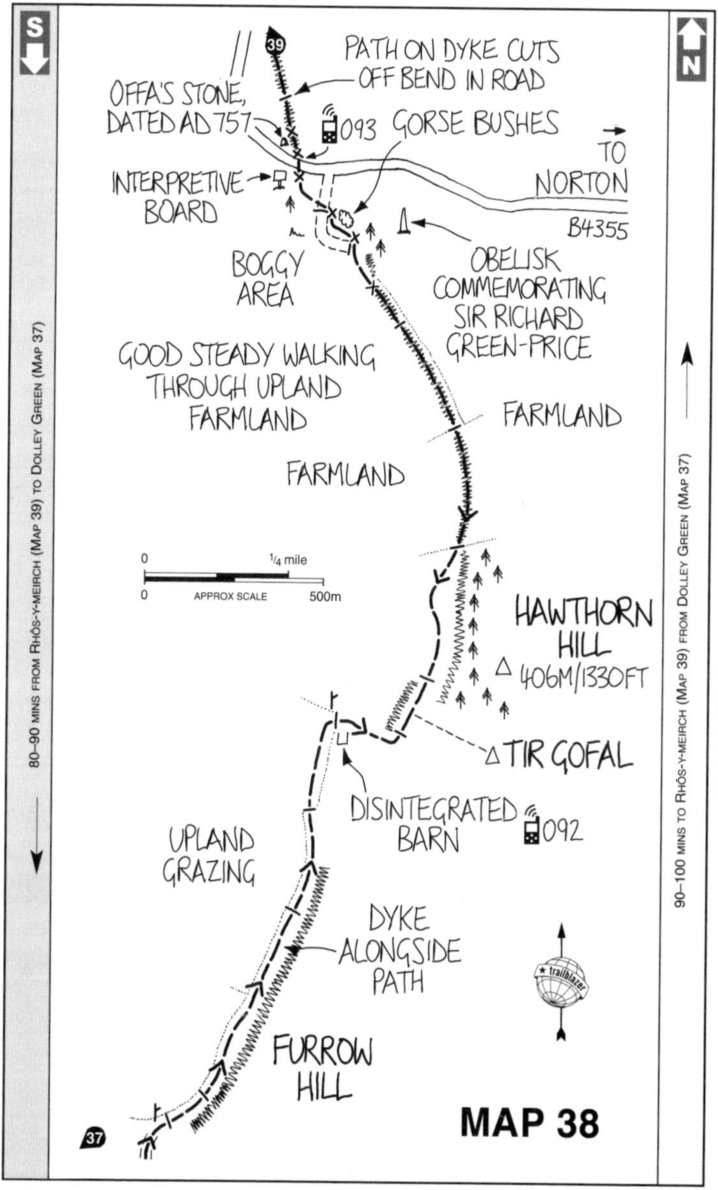

S

N

PATH ON DYKE CUTS
OFF BEND IN ROAD

39

OFFA'S STONE,
DATED AD 757

📱093 GORSE BUSHES

→
TO
NORTON
B4355

INTERPRETIVE
BOARD

BOGGY
AREA

OBELISK
COMMEMORATING
SIR RICHARD
GREEN-PRICE

GOOD STEADY WALKING
THROUGH UPLAND
FARMLAND

FARMLAND

FARMLAND

0   1/4 mile
0   APPROX SCALE   500m

HAWTHORN
HILL
△ 406M/1330FT

△ TIR GOFAL

DISINTEGRATED
BARN

📱092

UPLAND
GRAZING

DYKE
ALONGSIDE
PATH

trailblazer

FURROW
HILL

37

MAP 38

ROUTE GUIDE & MAPS

DISCOED   Map 37, p152

The best way to reach *Gumma Farm* (☎ 01547-560243; ✹) is to walk along the road to Discoed and continue through the hamlet until you come to a gate with a sign on the right saying 'Gumma walkers'; walk straight up from the gate and Gumma is in front of you. However, they recommend you call in advance so they know you are coming. There are toilet facilities as well as a cold and hot water tap for **campers** (£5pp). You can walk the 1¼ miles (2km) into Presteigne – it's quite a fast road, so take a torch for the return – for supplies or an evening meal.

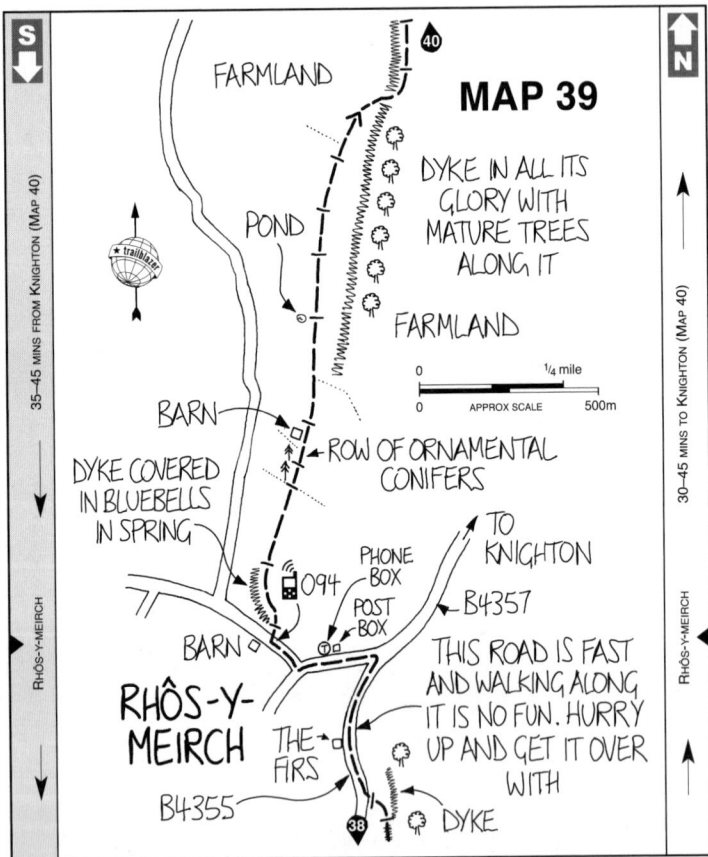

MAP 39

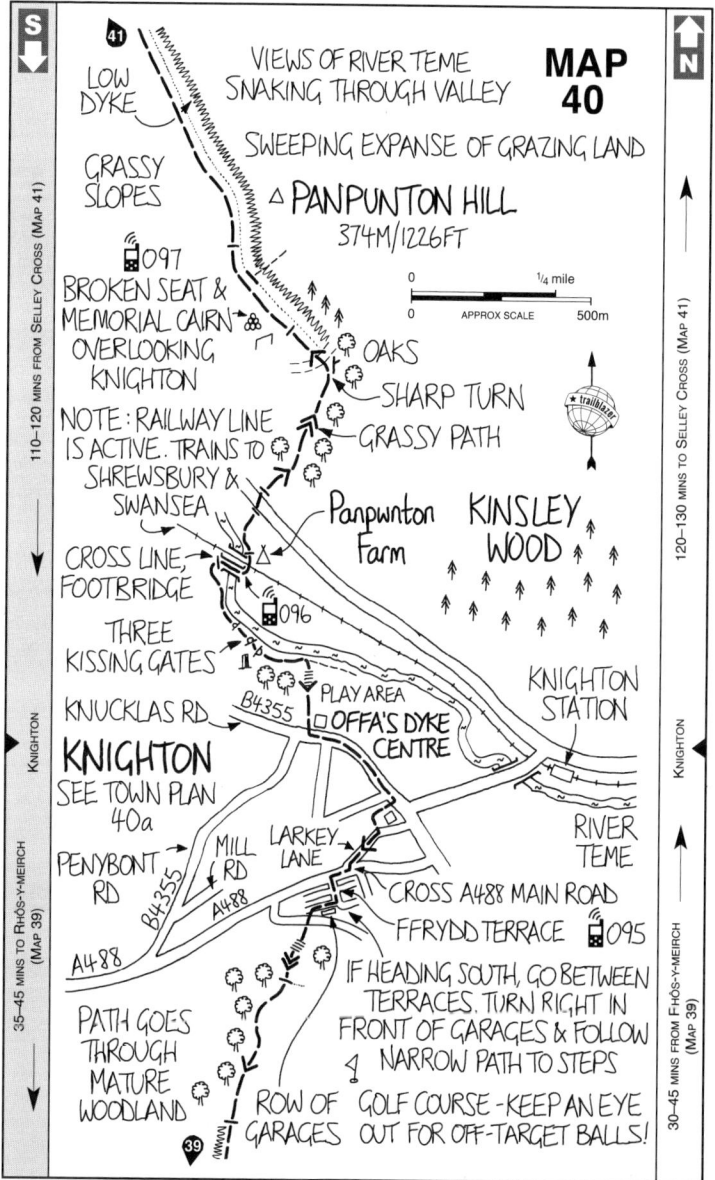

S

N

110–120 MINS FROM SELLEY CROSS (MAP 41)

120–130 MINS TO SELLEY CROSS (MAP 41)

ROUTE GUIDE & MAPS

41

LOW DYKE

VIEWS OF RIVER TEME SNAKING THROUGH VALLEY

MAP 40

GRASSY SLOPES

SWEEPING EXPANSE OF GRAZING LAND

△ PANPUNTON HILL
374M/1226FT

📱097

0   ¼ mile

BROKEN SEAT & MEMORIAL CAIRN OVERLOOKING KNIGHTON

0   APPROX SCALE   500m

OAKS

SHARP TURN

NOTE: RAILWAY LINE IS ACTIVE. TRAINS TO SHREWSBURY & SWANSEA

GRASSY PATH

★ trailblazer

Panpunton Farm

KINSLEY WOOD

CROSS LINE, FOOTBRIDGE

📱096

THREE KISSING GATES

KNUCKLAS RD
B4355

PLAY AREA

□ OFFA'S DYKE CENTRE

KNIGHTON STATION

KNIGHTON
SEE TOWN PLAN 40a

PENYBONT RD
B4355

MILL RD
A488

LARKEY LANE

RIVER TEME

CROSS A488 MAIN ROAD

A488

FFRYDD TERRACE 📱095

IF HEADING SOUTH, GO BETWEEN TERRACES. TURN RIGHT IN FRONT OF GARAGES & FOLLOW NARROW PATH TO STEPS

PATH GOES THROUGH MATURE WOODLAND

ROW OF GARAGES

GOLF COURSE - KEEP AN EYE OUT FOR OFF-TARGET BALLS!

39

KNIGHTON

35–45 MINS TO RHÔS-Y-MEIRCH (MAP 39)

KNIGHTON

30–45 MINS FROM RHÔS-Y-MEIRCH (MAP 39)

PRESTEIGNE (LLANANDRAS)
off Map 37, p152

Only 2¼ miles (4km) from Offa's Dyke Path at Dolley Green, Presteigne is a gem of a small town with narrow streets, striking period architecture and an excellent museum. You can find **supermarkets** (including Premier; ☎ 01544-267702; daily 7am-10pm, which also houses the **post office**), and **cashpoints** in town.

Judge's Lodging (☎ 01544-260650, 🖳 judgeslodging.org.uk; Mar-Oct Tue-Sun 10am-5pm, Nov Wed-Sun 10am-4pm, 1-22 Dec Sat & Sun 10am-4pm; admission £7.95) is a winner of Britain's Local Museum of the Year Award. The restored judges' apartments with servants' quarters below give a fascinating insight into the upstairs-downstairs world of the Victorian era. It also houses the **tourist information centre** which is open the same days and hours as the Lodging. For further information visit 🖳 presteigne.org.uk.

Presteigne Festival (see box p27) is held here in late August.

Sargeants No 41 **bus** stops here en route between Kington and Knighton; see public transport map and table, pp49-53.

Presteigne Taxi Service (☎ 07572 112757, ☎ 01544-267143) will pick up from Dolley Green; expect to pay about £10.

No 1 The Byre (☎ 01544-260544, 🖳 j.tomlinson39@btinternet.com; 1T private bathroom; WI-FI; ⓛ) is one mile from Presteigne and three from the path but if arranged in advance the proprietor will pick up from Dolley Green. B&B costs from £30pp (also for sgl occ). Evening meals are not available so guests need to walk into Presteigne for a meal, or get a taxi.

In **Norton** (off Map 38), north of Presteigne, B&B is available at *Corte Cottage* (☎ 01544-267749, 🖳 cortecottage.co.uk; 1D/1T private bathroom; ▬; WI-FI; ⓛ; 🐾). They offer free pick up and drop off for guests. B&B costs from £35pp. Also evening meals (from £14) if arranged in advance. They also have a sauna and Jacuzzi.

For lunches in Presteigne you have plenty of options, with *Lorna's Sandwich Shop* (☎ 01544-262727; Mon-Fri 8am-3pm, Sat 8am-1pm) a good spot for a takeaway sarnie. If you'd prefer to make your own, *Deli Tinto* (☎ 01544-260534, 🖳 delitinto.com; Mon 9am-4pm, Tue-Fri 9am-5.30pm, Sat 9am-5pm) has a good range of ingredients.

For an evening meal try the cosy bistro-style *Hat Shop* (☎ 01544-260017, 🖳 thehatshoprestaurant.co.uk; Mon-Sat 10am-3pm & Wed-Sat 6-9pm; WI-FI), on the High St; it offers an imaginative choice of food.

Also on the High St is *Victoria Fish Bar* (☎ 01544-260565; daily noon-2pm & 5-9.30pm), which serves fish & chips (from £4.10) to take away.

KNIGHTON (TREF Y CLAWDD)
Map 40a

The Welsh name for Knighton means 'the town on the Dyke', which is literally true: the town actually bestrides the Dyke, as opposed to places such as Llangollen and Welshpool that just miss it. It is also regarded as the halfway point on Offa's Dyke Path, though if you're travelling from Prestatyn it's over halfway, so this could be the excuse for a minor celebration.

Apart from Offa's Dyke Centre (see Services p158), Knighton's attractions amount to a few **antique shops**, most lining the High St, the cobbled lane that climbs up from the clock tower and leads into The Narrows.

Knighton Show (see box p27) is held here on the last Saturday in August.

Transport

[See pp49-53] Knighton is a stop on the Shrewsbury to Swansea **railway** line; services are operated by Transport for Wales. Arriva's No 740 **bus** goes to Ludlow and Sargeant's No 41 goes to Kington via Presteigne. The local **taxi** firm is Knighton Taxis (☎ 01547-528165).

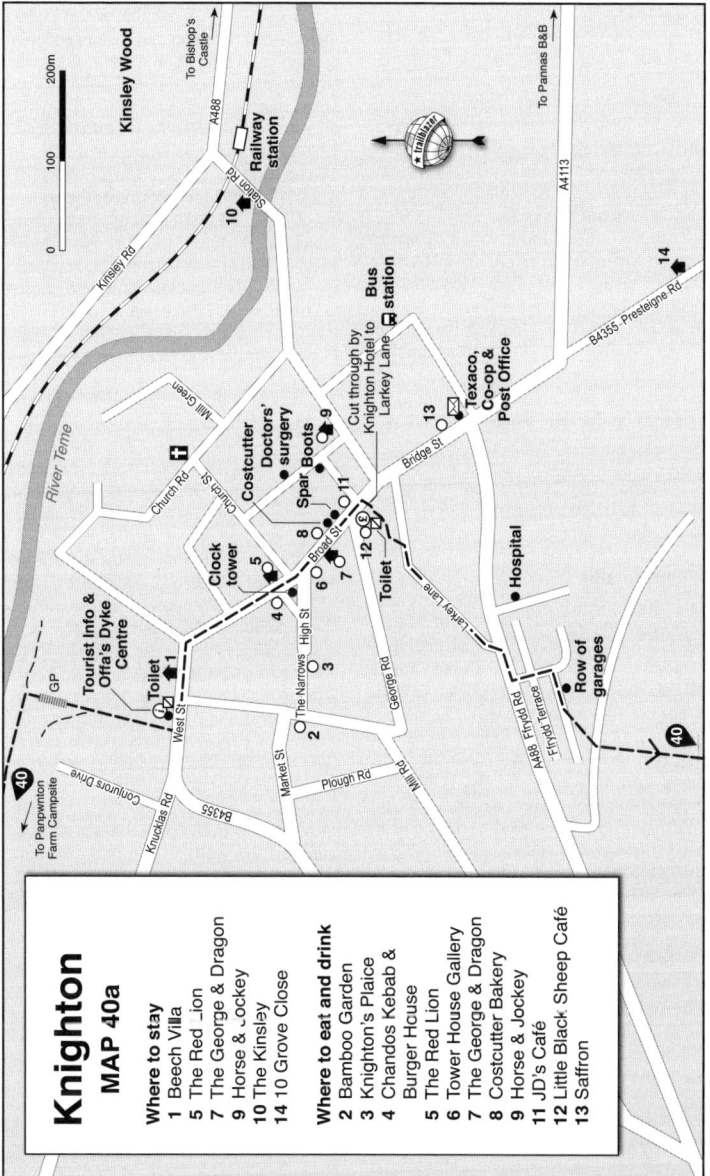

Kinsley Wood

Kinsley Rd

River Teme

Mill Green

Church Rd

Church St

Clock tower

Costcutter

Doctors' surgery

Spar, Boots

Tourist Info & Offa's Dyke Centre

Toilet

GP

The Narrows

High St

West St

Broad St

Toilet

Larkey Lane

George Rd

Market St

Mill Rd

Plough Rd

Knucklas Rd

Conlurns Drive

To Panpwnton Farm Campsite

To Bishop's Castle

A488

Railway station

Station Rd

Bus station

Cut through by Knighton Hotel to Larkey Lane

Texaco, Co-op & Post Office

Bridge St

B4355 Presteigne Rd

To Pannas B&B

A4113

Hospital

A488

Ffrydd Rd

Ffrydd Terrace

Row of garages

40

0   100   200m

★ trailblazer

Knighton
MAP 40a

Where to stay
1 Beech Villa
5 The Red Lion
7 The George & Dragon
9 Horse & Jockey
10 The Kinsley
14 10 Grove Close

Where to eat and drink
2 Bamboo Garden
3 Knighton's Plaice
4 Chandos Kebab & Burger House
5 The Red Lion
6 Tower House Gallery
7 The George & Dragon
8 Costcutter Bakery
9 Horse & Jockey
11 JD's Café
12 Little Black Sheep Café
13 Saffron

Services

The **tourist information centre**, on West St, is also home to **Offa's Dyke Centre** (☎ 01547-528753, 🖥 offasdyke.demon.co .uk; Apr/Easter to end Oct daily 10am-5pm, Nov to Easter/Apr Mon-Sat 10am-4pm; they close for lunch for half an hour around 1pm). Cold drinks and ice-creams are on sale and **toilets** are located just outside. See also 🖥 visitknighton.co.uk.

Barclays has a **bank** with a cashpoint here on Broad St and two of the shops have ATMs. There is a **post office** (Mon-Fri 8am-6pm, Sat 8am-2pm) in the Co-op (Mon-Sat 7am-8pm, Sun 10am-4pm) at Texaco. On Broad St there's a Spar **supermarket** (Mon-Sat 5.45am-9pm, Sun 6.30am-7pm) as well as a Costcutter (daily 7am-8pm). There is a **doctors' surgery** (☎ 01547-528523, 🖥 wylcwmstreetsurgery.co.uk) on Wylcwm St, which runs parallel to Broad St.

Market day is Thursday and **early closing day** is Wednesday, although most shops remain open.

Where to stay

The closest place to **camp** around Knighton is at *Panpwnton Farm* (Map 40; ☎ 01547-528112 or ☎ 01544-260199; all enquiries Lower Panpwnton Farm next door; Easter to end Oct), where you can pitch a tent for £5pp; the rate includes use of the shower facilities. If you happen to have a car that will cost an extra £1. Note that they will never turn walkers away but sometimes they have school groups staying so if you don't want to be disturbed by kids call to check in advance. Also note that signs sometimes say 'Panpwncton'. Compared to many sites on the trail, with their designated pitches, rules, regulations, and extra charges for showers and electricity, this one is a breath of fresh air.

Three of Knighton's **pubs** have rooms. *The George and Dragon Inn* (☎ 01547-528532, 🖥 thegeorgeknighton.co.uk; 3T/ 2D, all en suite; WI-FI in pub only; (L); 🐾) has converted the stables at the back to create rooms with real character. **B&B** costs £37.50pp (sgl occ £40). Perhaps slightly better, *The Horse and Jockey* (☎ 01547-520062, 🖥 thehorseandjockeyinn.co.uk;

1D/5T or D/1Qd, all en suite; 🍺; WI-FI; 🐾) offers smart and pleasant accommodation upstairs from the pub in what was once the hayloft. B&B costs from £37.50pp (sgl occ £60); room only is possible too, contact them for details. *Red Lion Inn* (☎ 01547-428080, 🖥 redlionknighton.co.uk; 1T/2D/ 1Tr, en suite, WI-FI, 🐾; from £42.50pp, sgl occ £55), West St, is your other option.

Classic B&B rather than a room above a pub can be found on West St at *Beech Villa* (☎ 01547-428142, ☎ 07375-320239, 🖥 beechvilla-knighton.com; 2D shared facilities; 🍺; £32.50pp, sgl occ £35; No 9).

Other B&Bs to consider include: *Pannas* (☎ 01547-528937, 🖥 staypannas knighton.co.uk; 1D en suite in an apartment, 🐾; WI-FI; room rate £25pp, £35 sgl occ; continental breakfast is £5pp), 15 The Dingle; and *10 Grove Close* (☎ 01547-528777, ☎ 07970-550195; 3D en suite, shared facilities; from £35pp, sgl occ £40; 🍺; WI-FI). Both are a 10- to 15-minute stroll from the trail.

On the edge of town by the River Teme is *The Kinsley* (☎ 01547-520753, ☎ 07506-172659, 🖥 johnnyows@hotmail.co.uk; 2D/2T en suite; (L); £30pp, sgl occ £35).

Where to eat and drink

While Knighton cannot be described as the gastronomic capital of the Borders the choice has improved in recent years. *JD's Café* (☎ 01547-528218; Mon-Sat 9am-3pm, Sun 10am-3pm; winter hours depend on demand) is a continental-style restaurant with wrought-iron chairs and arts & crafts adorning the walls – a lovely place for home-cooked food. A more traditional café is the comfy, *Little Black Sheep Café* (☎ 01547-529333; Mon-Sat 8am-5pm; 🐾). Up the hill, *Tower House Gallery* (☎ 01547-529530, 🖥 galleryknighton.co.uk; Wed-Fri 10am-5pm, Sat 10am-4.30pm; Sun 11am-4pm; 🐾) is said to do the best coffee in town and you can also get cake and light lunches. As a social enterprise they support numerous local community-based organisations and as such are certainly worthy of the walking community's support.

If you're just rambling through, pop in at the **bakery** (Mon-Sat 7am-4.45pm, Sun

9am-3pm) on Broad St, an annex of the Costcutters shop; it sells excellent hot pies, including *oggies* (£3.85), the Welsh equivalent of the Cornish pasty. In fact, fast food is in plentiful supply, with a **fish & chip shop**, *Knighton's Plaice* (Mon-Wed noon-2pm & 4.30-10pm, Thur-Sat 11.30am-2pm & 4.30-10pm), which can be highly recommended, on The Narrows – the pedestrianised section leading up from the High St. There's also *Chandos Kebab & Burger House* (Sun-Thur 2-11.30pm, Fri & Sat noon-midnight) on Broad St, and an Indian restaurant, *Saffron* (☎ 01547-528510; Tue-Sun 6-11pm) on Bridge St. For Chinese, at the top of The Narrows is *Bamboo Garden* (☎ 01547-520010; Sun-Thur 5-10.30pm, Fri & Sat 5-11pm).

For something more substantial, three pubs stand out. *The George and Dragon* (see Where to stay; food served Tue-Sun noon-2pm, daily 6.30-9pm) does standard pub grub such as beef & mushroom stroganoff for £13.95, as does *The Horse and Jockey* (see Where to stay; food Mon-Sat noon-2pm & 6-9pm, Sun 12.30-9pm) which is our favourite spot for dinner, with some sizeable dishes at reasonable prices including a chicken & bacon enchilada for £9.50.

The Red Lion (see Where to stay; food Tue & Wed 6.30-9pm, Thur-Sat noon-2pm & 6.30-9pm) has a good menu too (from a veggie-burger £11.50 to ribeye steak £18.50).

[*Route section begins on Map 40, p155*] This **13½-mile (22km, 5hrs 55mins-6hrs 40mins)** section fits conveniently into a day's walking. Knighton is left behind with a stiff climb up to the golf links, then the route becomes agricultural with more of the all-too-familiar stiles to add to your tally. There are several stretches of the Dyke on view, in places high and formidable with a well-defined ditch.

Two hills are crossed, **Hawthorn Hill** (Map 38) and **Furrow Hill**, fine open airy walking that will raise your spirits and put a spring in your step.

Dolley Green (Map 37) is little more than a point on the map but it is close to the attractive little town of **Presteigne** (see p156), worth a detour in its own right if time isn't tight.

More switchbacks follow and more agricultural perambulations with plenty of walking on top of the Dyke. Over **Rushock Hill** (Map 35) you encounter extraordinary scenery, bracken and gorse, heathland and wooded country, that is full of variety, followed by a summit ridge with nothing but the wind and soaring buzzards (with possibly the odd red kite too) for company.

The long descent towards Kington ensnares you in a succession of fields until the sight of a manicured green tells you that you are on course – another golf course, to be exact, the highest 18-hole course in England. The clubhouse (☎ 01544-230340, 🖥 kingtongolf.co.uk) is surprisingly welcoming to walkers; you can pop in for a bacon roll for £3 (food is available throughout the day from 11am); they have a shop selling waterproof clothing and hats and are also happy for walkers to play a round of golf if they want.

From here it's a final mile into **Kington (Map 34, p145)** itself, which is approached by the back door, over a fast by-pass and a footbridge leading to neat bungalows and into The Square.   [*Next route overview p148*]

ROUTE GUIDE & MAPS

KNIGHTON TO BROMPTON CROSSROADS
MAPS 40-47

N ↑ FROM CHEPSTOW

[*Route section begins on Map 40, p155*] This **14½-mile (23km)** section will take about **8-9¼ hours** and includes a series of undulations known as **The Switchbacks**, a series of steep ascents and descents, some with almost no break in between – be prepared.

It begins by following the River Teme before a sharp but short ascent of **Panpunton Hill** (Map 40), where a cairn has been placed in honour of early Offa's Dyke pioneers, so you can reflect for a moment on those who made it all possible, and from the top of which there are views back over Knighton.

There are superior views from the next hill, **Cwm-Sanaham** (Map 41) and the trail offers lovely walking across **Llanfair Hill** (Map 42), which at 432m (1417ft) is the highest point on the Dyke (although not the highest point on the trail – that is in the Black Mountains). Don't miss the Dragon on the Dyke statue.

Campers, carrying their own supplies, could pitch up at *Springhill Farm Campsite* (Map 43; ☎ 01588-640337; £7.50), where there are showers, a kettle, and a toaster, but nothing else, and so you'd need to walk into **Newcastle-on-Clun** (Map 43; approx 30 mins), for the nearest pub, the Crown Inn, for food.

A possible distraction is the secluded Shropshire town of **Clun** (Map 43a), which is a little gem, although as it's three miles (5km) off the route few walkers make the detour. Actually on the path, and at the foot of one of the descents, set in a beautiful and secluded valley, the tiny chapel of St John the Baptist at **Churchtown** (Map 45), with its exquisite biblical wall texts, provides a welcome interlude and the opportunity for a moment of quiet reflection before ascending, descending, ascending again. The trail crosses the east–west track of the **Kerry Ridgeway** (Map 46; see box p166), some 4 miles (6km) west of the captivating small town of **Bishop's Castle**. From the ridgeway the trail strides atop the Dyke itself to **Brompton Crossroads (Map 47, p170)**, an opportunity to walk in the footsteps of those who worked, willingly or unwillingly, to realise the vision of King Offa.   [*Next route overview p172*]

❏ **Glyndwr's Way**

Many a walker tackling Offa's Dyke Path is sufficiently captivated by the area to think of returning to mid Wales. Such enthusiasts could well seek out Glyndwr's Way, which was designated a national trail in 2000. The trail visits many sites associated with the 15th-century Welsh hero Owain Glyndwr, who 700 years ago pulled off a famous victory over the English at Knighton. It can either be walked independently or linked to Offa's Dyke Path; the two meet at Knighton and come close near Welshpool.

The 135-mile (217km) route describes a near-complete circle starting in Knighton. Clockwise, the trail goes west through the Radnorshire hills to Machynlleth then crosses the Cambrian Mountains to touch Lake Vyrnwy before wandering east to finish at Welshpool, by Montgomery Canal. At this point, the trail is just three miles or so from Offa's Dyke Path that leads south to Knighton through the rolling Shropshire Hills; completing the loop in this way adds a further 30 miles (48km) to the walk. Glyndwr's Way is a splendid route through a variety of marvellous terrain that would otherwise be overlooked. If you have time, go for it without hesitation. If not, plan to return another day. See 🖳 nationaltrail.co.uk/GlyndwrsWay.

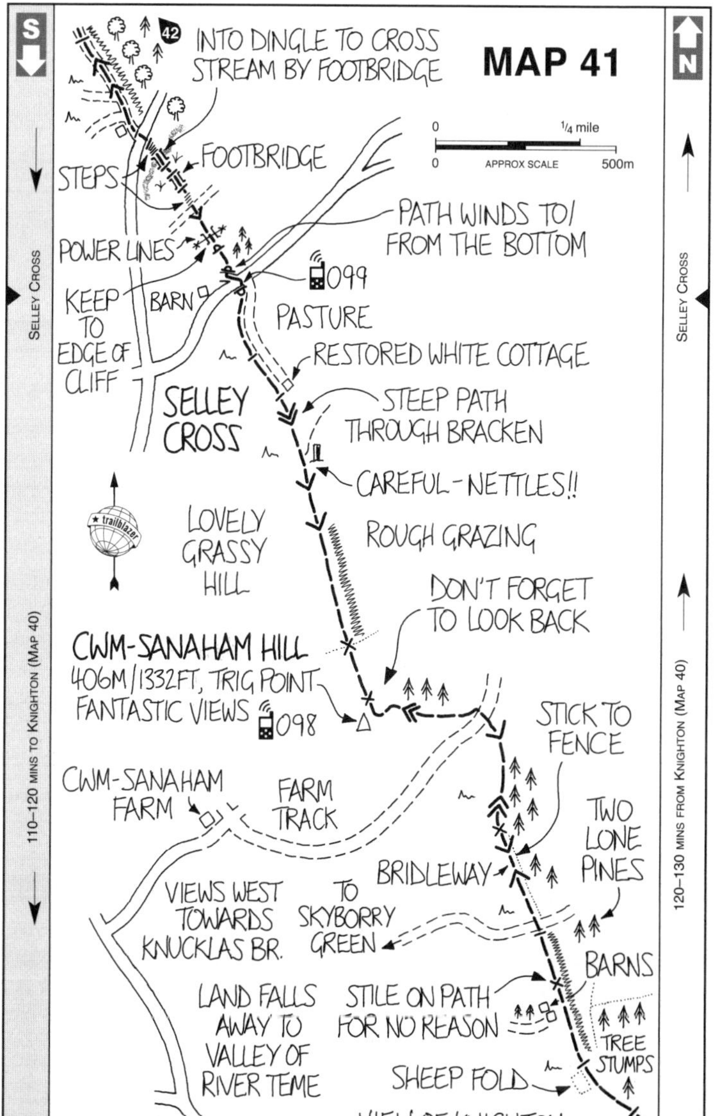

MAP 41

S

N

SELLEY CROSS

SELLEY CROSS

110–120 MINS TO KNIGHTON (MAP 40)

120–130 MINS FROM KNIGHTON (MAP 40)

ROUTE GUIDE & MAPS

0   ¼ mile

0   APPROX SCALE   500m

42

INTO DINGLE TO CROSS STREAM BY FOOTBRIDGE

FOOTBRIDGE

STEPS

POWER LINES

KEEP TO EDGE OF CLIFF

BARN

099

PASTURE

PATH WINDS TO/ FROM THE BOTTOM

RESTORED WHITE COTTAGE

SELLEY CROSS

STEEP PATH THROUGH BRACKEN

CAREFUL – NETTLES!!

LOVELY GRASSY HILL

ROUGH GRAZING

DON'T FORGET TO LOOK BACK

★ trailblazer

CWM-SANAHAM HILL
406M/1332FT, TRIG POINT
FANTASTIC VIEWS 098

STICK TO FENCE

CWM-SANAHAM FARM

FARM TRACK

TWO LONE PINES

VIEWS WEST TOWARDS KNUCKLAS BR.

BRIDLEWAY

TO SKYBORRY GREEN

BARNS

LAND FALLS AWAY TO VALLEY OF RIVER TEME

STILE ON PATH FOR NO REASON

TREE STUMPS

SHEEP FOLD

SKYBORRY GREEN

VIEW OF KNIGHTON TO SOUTH EAST

40

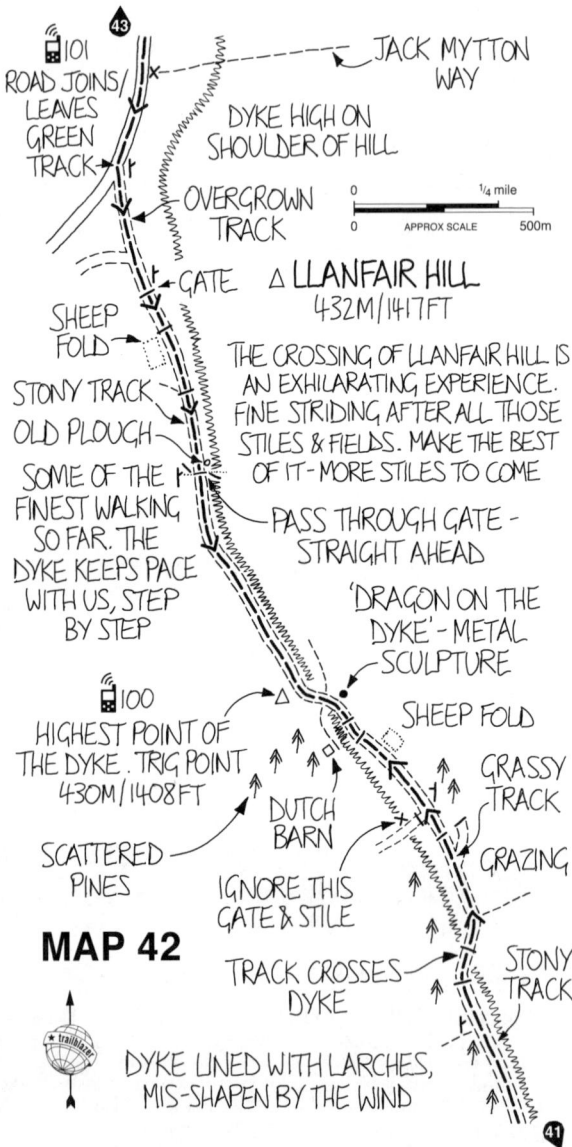

S

N

90–105 MINS FROM NEWCASTLE-ON-CLUN (MAP 43)

TRIG. POINT

45–50 MINS TO SELLEY CROSS (MAP 41)

90–105 MINS TO NEWCASTLE-ON-CLUN (MAP 43)

TRIG. POINT

80–90 MINS FROM SELLEY CROSS (MAP 41)

ROUTE GUIDE & MAPS

43

📱101
ROAD JOINS/
LEAVES
GREEN
TRACK

JACK MYTTON
WAY

DYKE HIGH ON
SHOULDER OF HILL

OVERGROWN
TRACK

0   ¼ mile
0   APPROX SCALE   500m

GATE

△ LLANFAIR HILL
432M/1417FT

SHEEP
FOLD

THE CROSSING OF LLANFAIR HILL IS
AN EXHILARATING EXPERIENCE.
FINE STRIDING AFTER ALL THOSE
STILES & FIELDS. MAKE THE BEST
OF IT - MORE STILES TO COME

STONY TRACK

OLD PLOUGH

SOME OF THE
FINEST WALKING
SO FAR. THE
DYKE KEEPS PACE
WITH US, STEP
BY STEP

PASS THROUGH GATE -
STRAIGHT AHEAD

'DRAGON ON THE
DYKE' - METAL
SCULPTURE

SHEEP FOLD

📱100
HIGHEST POINT OF
THE DYKE . TRIG POINT
430M/1408FT

DUTCH
BARN

GRASSY
TRACK

GRAZING

SCATTERED
PINES

IGNORE THIS
GATE & STILE

MAP 42

TRACK CROSSES
DYKE

STONY
TRACK

★ trailblazer

DYKE LINED WITH LARCHES,
MIS-SHAPEN BY THE WIND

41

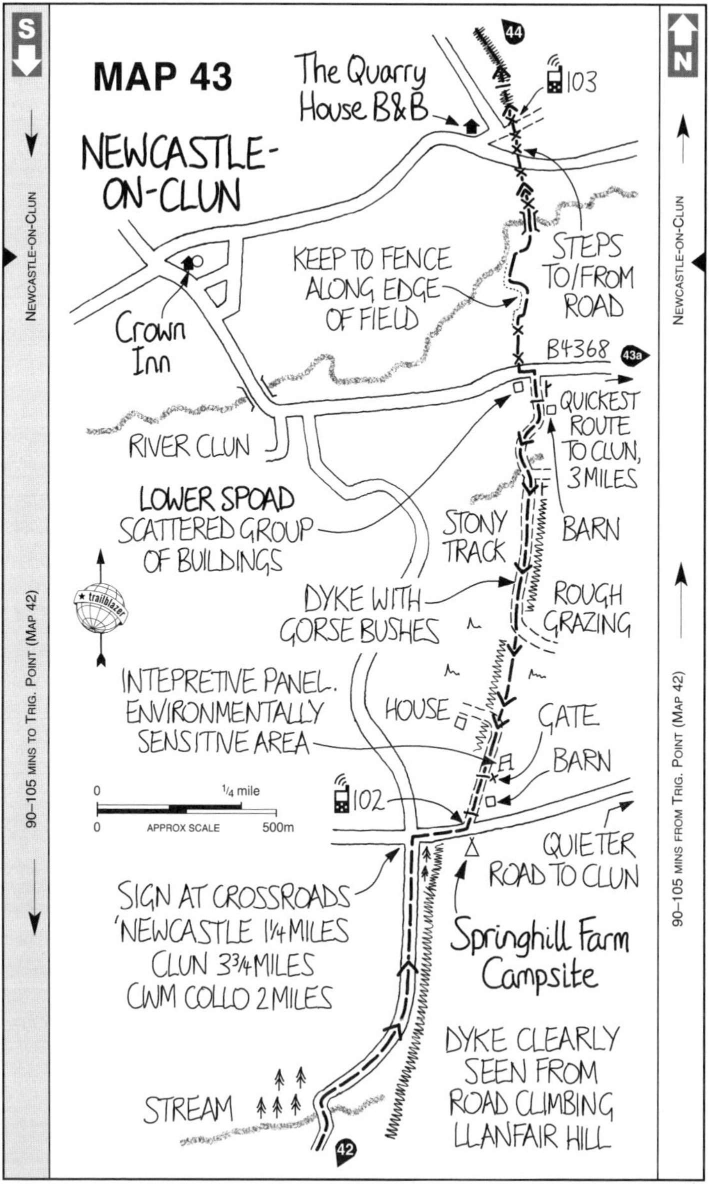

MAP 43

NEWCASTLE-ON-CLUN

The Quarry House B&B

📱 103

KEEP TO FENCE ALONG EDGE OF FIELD

STEPS TO/FROM ROAD

Crown Inn

B4368 43a

RIVER CLUN

QUICKEST ROUTE TO CLUN, 3 MILES

LOWER SPOAD
SCATTERED GROUP OF BUILDINGS

STONY TRACK

BARN

DYKE WITH GORSE BUSHES

ROUGH GRAZING

INTERPRETIVE PANEL.
ENVIRONMENTALLY SENSITIVE AREA

HOUSE

GATE

BARN

📱 102

0   ¼ mile
0   APPROX SCALE   500m

QUIETER ROAD TO CLUN

SIGN AT CROSSROADS
'NEWCASTLE 1¼ MILES
CLUN 3¾ MILES
CWM COLLO 2 MILES

Springhill Farm Campsite

DYKE CLEARLY SEEN FROM ROAD CLIMBING LLANFAIR HILL

STREAM

42

NEWCASTLE-ON-CLUN

90–105 MINS TO TRIG. POINT (MAP 42)

NEWCASTLE-ON-CLUN

90–105 MINS FROM TRIG. POINT (MAP 42)

ROUTE GUIDE & MAPS

NEWCASTLE-ON-CLUN
Map 43, p163

This tidy village clusters round *The Crown Inn* (☎ 01588-640271, 🖳 crowninnrestaurant@gmail.com; 3T/2D, all en suite; WI-FI; 🐾 bar only; (Ⓛ)) where **B&B** costs from £42.50pp (sgl occ £65) and there is some great food on offer. The opening hours have been somewhat sporadic of late and as your only food option locally you'd be advised to phone ahead. *The Quarry House* (☎ 01588-640774, 🖳 quarry-house .com; 1D/1T/1Tr, mix of en suite and private facilites; 🍷; WI-FI; 🐾; (Ⓛ)), on Church Rd, charges from £37.50pp (sgl occ £50; rates for three sharing on request) for **B&B**. Evening meals are available if requested in advance; expect to pay about £15.

CLUN
Map 43a

You could choose to ignore Newcastle-on-Clun and settle for the rather wider choice of accommodation offered in Clun, 3 miles (5km, 1¼-1½hrs) east of the main path, which AE Housman (see box opposite) described as one of the 'quietest places under the sun'. The quickest route to the village is from Lower Spoad down the busy B4368. The walk will take just over an hour and is enlivened in the latter stages by the view of the ruins of the romantic-looking **castle** on its mound close to the road. The site is managed by English Heritage and it is free to wander around the ruins.

The village has **cafés** (*Maltings*; 🖳 themaltingscafeclun.co.uk; next to The Sun Inn and open daily 10am-4pm, is our favourite), pubs and a Spar **shop** (Mon-Sat 7am-8pm, Sun 8am-8pm). There's also a **Visitor Information Point** in the florist's by the bridge.

YHA Clun Mill (bookings ☎ 0800-019 1700, general ☎ 0845-371 9112, 🖳 yha.org .uk/hostel/clun; 23 beds – 2 x 4-, 1 x 7-, 1 x 8-beds, most en suite; Apr-Aug), on the edge of the town, is one of the very few hostels along the length of the path. A dorm bed costs from £23.50pp (private rooms from £99, sleeps 4); it's self-catering only but has laundry & drying facilities. There is space for 20 people to **camp** (from £12pp). Credit/debit cards are accepted.

For B&B, *The Sun Inn* (☎ 01588-640559, 🖳 thesunatclun.co.uk; 1T/3D, all en suite; 🐾; WI-FI) has **B&B** for £40-50pp (sgl occ rates on request), some in a con-

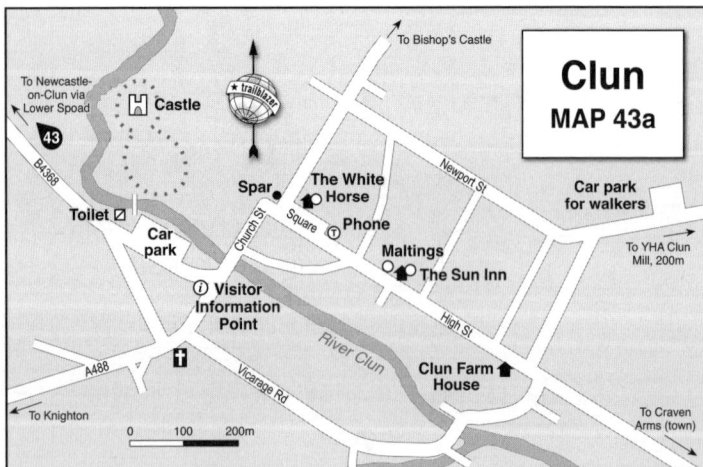

Clun
MAP 43a

To Bishop's Castle

To Newcastle-on-Clun via Lower Spoad

43

B4368

🏰 Castle

⊕ trailblazer

Toilet ☒

Car park

Church St

Spar ●

● The White Horse

Square

Phone ⓘ

Newport St

Car park for walkers

To YHA Clun Mill, 200m

Maltings ○
● The Sun Inn

High St

ⓘ Visitor Information Point

A488

Vicarage Rd

River Clun

Clun Farm House 🏠

To Knighton

0   100   200m

To Craven Arms (town)

verted stable block and also a double with its own sitting area in the granary. There's a good selection of meals in the cosy bar (**food** summer Tue-Sat noon-2.30pm & 6-8.30pm, Sun noon-2.30pm; winter Tue & Thur-Sat 6-9.30pm, Fri-Sun noon-2.30pm).

Just down the road, *Clun Farm House* (☎ 01588-640432, 🖳 clunfarmhouse.co.uk; 2S shared bathroom. 1D or T/1Tr, both en suite; 🍽; WI-FI; 🐾; (Ⓛ) has quiet and comfortable accommodation at £45pp (sgl £50). Luggage transfer and pick up from the Dyke are available. The other pub in the village, *The White Horse* (☎ 01588-418125, 🖳 whi-clun.co.uk; 1D/3Tr, all en suite; 🐾; WI-FI; (Ⓛ), also provides accommodation, charging from £32.50pp (sgl occ £45), though the landlord is keen to point out that it is a lively pub and thus may not, on occasion, be the quietest place to lay your head, especially if you have the room at the front. Both pubs also serve food, with The White Horse boasting the better menu (**food** served Mon-Sat noon-2pm, Sun 12.30-2.30pm, daily 6.30-8.30pm).

A useful website is 🖳 visitshropshire hills.co.uk/towns/clun.

❏ **AE Housman**

Almost every visitor to Shropshire is likely to come across its connection with the lyric poet AE Housman, who died in 1936. Although he knew the area hardly at all, it became for him the ideal setting for his poems of loss – lost innocence, lost love, lost ideals – that provide the basis for much of his work.

'Up, lad, up, 'tis late for lying
Hear the drums of morning play;
Hark the empty highways crying
Who'll beyond the hills away?'
AE Housman,
Ludlow from the North-West

Best known for *A Shropshire Lad*, a collection of 63 nostalgic poems that appeared in 1896, Housman seems to catch the spirit of the place, the 'blue remembered hills' of childhood, like nobody else. Housman's poems are inhabited by young men doomed to die before the flush of youth is off them, as soldiers who march away, or murderers condemned to hang; by girls to be forsaken and lovers betrayed. They are conceived in hope and end in death, the bourn from which no traveller returns.

BISHOP'S CASTLE off Map 46, p169

Four miles (6km) off route, Bishop's Castle is a good centre for those walking the trail in separate chunks rather than continuously.

Minsterley Motors **bus** Nos 552 and 553 go to Shrewsbury; see public transport map and table, pp49-53.

Parking in the town is free but **taxis** are not easy to obtain, although you may be able to arrange for one to come out from Knighton. Otherwise allow at least an hour to walk up Kerry Ridgeway to Offa's Dyke Path. Better still, stay at one of the town's B&Bs and they may run you up to the path and indeed collect you if necessary.

The High St is an interesting collection of half-timbered houses, many of them now shops selling second-hand books and antiques. The town has a **post office** (which shares the same building as the Boar's Head), **banks** with ATMs, a **launderette**, cafés aplenty, pubs, **takeaways** (Indian and Thai) and a couple of small **grocery stores**, including a Co-op with late opening hours (daily 6am-10pm).

The **tourist information centre** (☎ 01588-630023, 🖳 bishopscastletownhall .co.uk; Easter-Sep Mon-Sat 10am-4pm, Oct Thur-Tue 10.30am-3pm; Jan to Easter Thur-Sat 10.30am-3pm; at half-terms they are open Mon-Sat), in the Town Hall, can point you in the right direction to most things.

See also 🖳 bishopscastle.co.uk.

Where to stay, eat and drink

Bishop's Castle also has a good choice of accommodation. Note that most of the places listed have a minimum two-night stay for Friday and Saturday nights and a three-night minimum over bank holiday weekends.

The three **wooden pods** at *The King's Head* (☎ 01588-630770, 🖳 glampinginshropshire.com; 🐾; WI-FI in pub) make for a pleasant compromise between camping and B&B. These simple huts (£35 per pod for up to two people, £5 for each extra person) sleep up to three people though you need to bring your own sleeping mat and bedding; in addition they have a railway carriage with 2D. There are electricity sockets and a small heater and toilet & shower facilities are available. The pub has a **bar** (Mon 5-11pm, Tue-Sun noon-11pm) but they don't serve food. Alternatively, *Old Time* (☎ 01588-638467, 🖳 oldtime.co.uk, 29 High St; 1T/2D, all en suite; 🛁; 🐾; WI-FI; Ⓛ) charges £30-35pp (sgl occ £45) for **B&B**.

Both accommodation and a good choice of bar meals can be had at *The Boars Head* (☎ 01588-638521, 🖳 boarsheadhotel.co.uk; bar summer Sun-Tue

11.30am-11pm, Wed & Thur 11am-11pm, Fri & Sat 11am-midnight; winter Mon-Thur to 10.30pm, weekends same as summer), a 17th-century pub where Royalist soldiers in the Civil War left off sacking the town to slake their thirst. A **room** (3D or T/1Tr, all en suite; 🛁; WI-FI) costs from £50pp (sgl occ £60; three sharing a room from £85) including a continental breakfast; a cooked breakfast costs £6.99-8.99pp. At certain times they have a minimum two-night stay policy at weekends. The menu (**food** served daily noon-9pm, but to 8pm on Sun in winter) is enticing.

Finally, no visit would be complete without sampling the beer, such as 1642 and Cleric's Cure (see box p24), brewed on the premises of *The Three Tuns* (☎ 01588-638797, 🖳 thethreetunsinn.co.uk; bar Mon-Sat noon-11pm, Sun to 10.30pm), a genuine curiosity dating back to 1642. They serve **meals**, too (Mon-Sat noon-2.30pm & 6.30-9pm, Sun noon-3pm), including some decent steaks and burgers.

❏ Where to stay: the details

In the descriptions of accommodation in this book: 🛁 means at least one room has a bath; Ⓛ means a packed lunch can be prepared if arranged in advance; 🐾 signifies that dogs are welcome in at least one room but also subject to prior arrangement, an additional charge may also be payable; WI-FI means wi-fi is available. See also p84.

❏ Kerry Ridgeway

Kerry Ridgeway (see Map 46) is an ancient trackway that, of all the drovers' roads and green lanes that criss-cross the Welsh Marches, has survived more or less intact. Nearby Bronze Age and Iron Age burial sites and stone circles are evidence that the trackway had a symbolic purpose in ancient times as well as a practical use as a line of communication.

The route is gently undulating and traffic-free, an ideal day's expedition through 15 miles of unspoilt countryside. It's used by mountain bikers and horseriders, as well as walkers. The starting point is just north of Cider House Farm, once a drovers' inn on the B4355 road between Newtown and Knighton, and it finishes at Bishop's Castle. If you've time to spare and would like to walk the whole track there's a car park at Cider House Farm; however, you'll need to arrange a lift to get you back to the starting point.

MAP 44

0 — 1/4 mile
APPROX SCALE
0 — 500m

45

SYCAMORES

STEPS →

PASTURE

SHROPSHIRE WAY TO CLUN

105

FOLLOW THE LINE OF THE DYKE

SHED WITH CORRU-GATED IRON ROOF

SMALL BRIDGE OVER STREAM

△ HERGAN 408M/1340FT

FOLLOW LINE OF TREES & WORN PATH

FLIGHT OF 122 STEPS INFILLED WITH LIMESTONE

FINE WALKING ALONG DYKE LONG ADOPTED AS A GREEN ROAD

LOVELY WOODED WALK

GRASSY TRACK

104

'LOWER MOUNT' COTTAGE

STREAM

BRIDGE FARM →

FOOTBRIDGE

POND

LINE OF ORNAMENTAL CONIFERS - RATHER SUBURBAN

trailblazer

GRAIG HILL △ 369M/1210FT

VERY STEEP!

POOR WAYMARKING ALONG HERE

PATH ON DYKE OVERGROWN IN PLACES

CRAB APPLE TREES

43

DYKE LINED BY OLD LARCHES MUCH BLOWN BY THE WIND

90–105 MINS TO NEWCASTLE-ON-CLUN (MAP 43) FROM CHURCHTOWN (MAP 45)

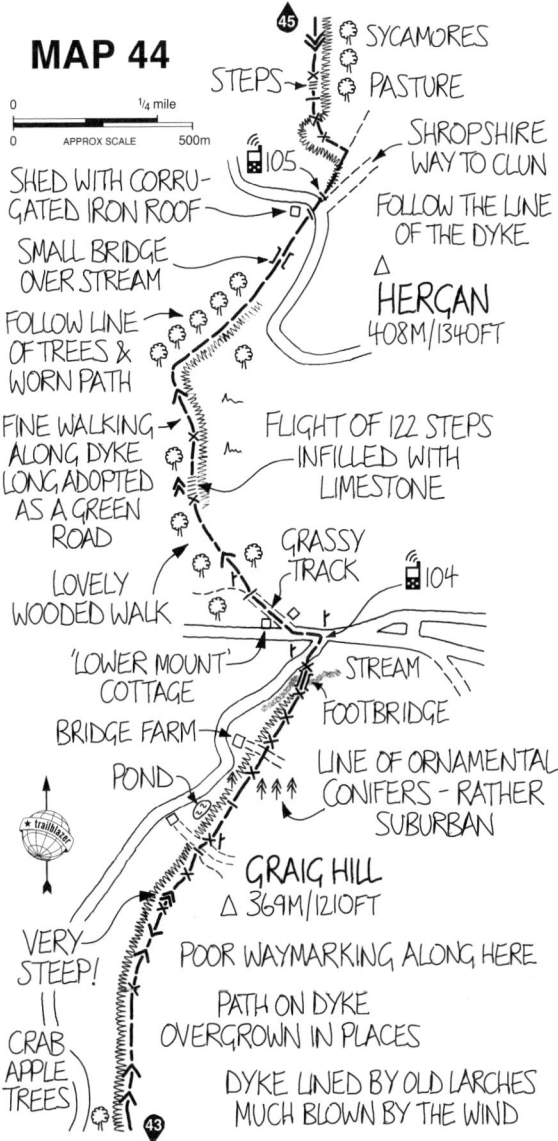

90–105 MINS FROM NEWCASTLE-ON-CLUN (MAP 43) TO CHURCHTOWN (MAP 45)

ROUTE GUIDE & MAPS

S

N

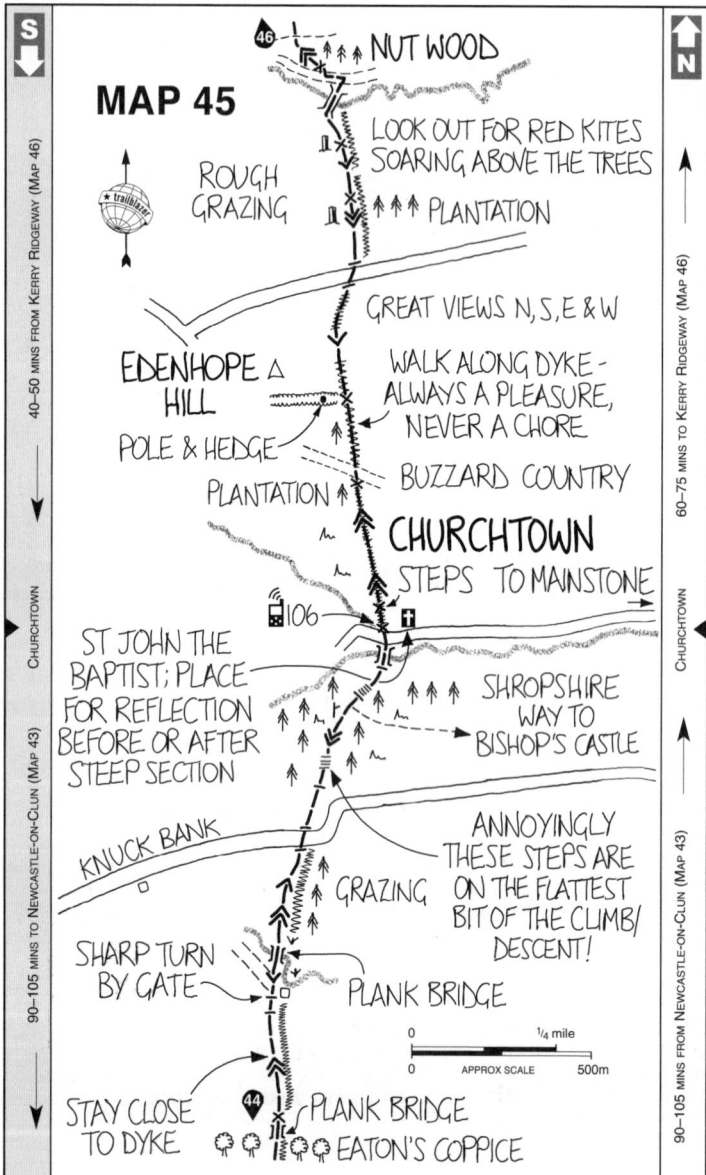

40–50 MINS FROM KERRY RIDGEWAY (MAP 46)

ROUTE GUIDE & MAPS

CHURCHTOWN

90–105 MINS TO NEWCASTLE-ON-CLUN (MAP 43)

60–75 MINS TO KERRY RIDGEWAY (MAP 46)

CHURCHTOWN

90–105 MINS FROM NEWCASTLE-ON-CLUN (MAP 43)

46

NUT WOOD

MAP 45

★ trailblazer

ROUGH
GRAZING

LOOK OUT FOR RED KITES
SOARING ABOVE THE TREES

PLANTATION

GREAT VIEWS N, S, E & W

EDENHOPE △
HILL

WALK ALONG DYKE -
ALWAYS A PLEASURE,
NEVER A CHORE

POLE & HEDGE

BUZZARD COUNTRY

PLANTATION

CHURCHTOWN

STEPS TO MAINSTONE

📱106

✝

ST JOHN THE
BAPTIST; PLACE
FOR REFLECTION
BEFORE OR AFTER
STEEP SECTION

SHROPSHIRE
WAY TO
BISHOP'S CASTLE

KNUCK BANK

ANNOYINGLY
THESE STEPS ARE
ON THE FLATTEST
BIT OF THE CLIMB/
DESCENT!

GRAZING

SHARP TURN
BY GATE

PLANK BRIDGE

0   ¼ mile
0   APPROX SCALE   500m

STAY CLOSE
TO DYKE

44

PLANK BRIDGE

EATON'S COPPICE

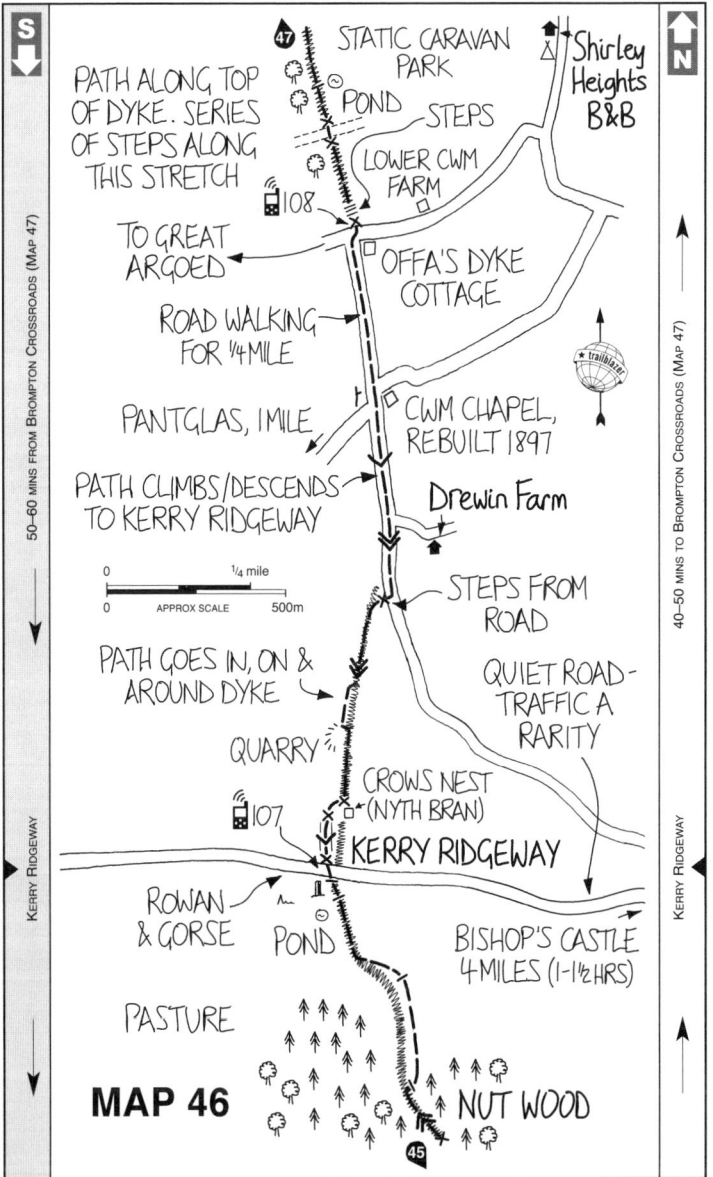

S

N

50–60 MINS FROM BROMPTON CROSSROADS (MAP 47)

40–50 MINS TO BROMPTON CROSSROADS (MAP 47)

ROUTE GUIDE & MAPS

KERRY RIDGEWAY

KERRY RIDGEWAY

47

STATIC CARAVAN PARK

Shirley Heights B&B

POND

STEPS

LOWER CWM FARM

PATH ALONG TOP OF DYKE. SERIES OF STEPS ALONG THIS STRETCH

108

TO GREAT ARGOED

OFFA'S DYKE COTTAGE

ROAD WALKING FOR ¼ MILE

CWM CHAPEL, REBUILT 1897

PANTGLAS, 1 MILE

PATH CLIMBS/DESCENDS TO KERRY RIDGEWAY

Drewin Farm

STEPS FROM ROAD

QUIET ROAD - TRAFFIC A RARITY

| 0 | ¼ mile |
| 0 | APPROX SCALE 500m |

PATH GOES IN, ON & AROUND DYKE

QUARRY

CROWS NEST (NYTH BRAN)

107

KERRY RIDGEWAY

ROWAN & GORSE

POND

BISHOP'S CASTLE 4 MILES (1-1½ HRS)

PASTURE

MAP 46

NUT WOOD

45

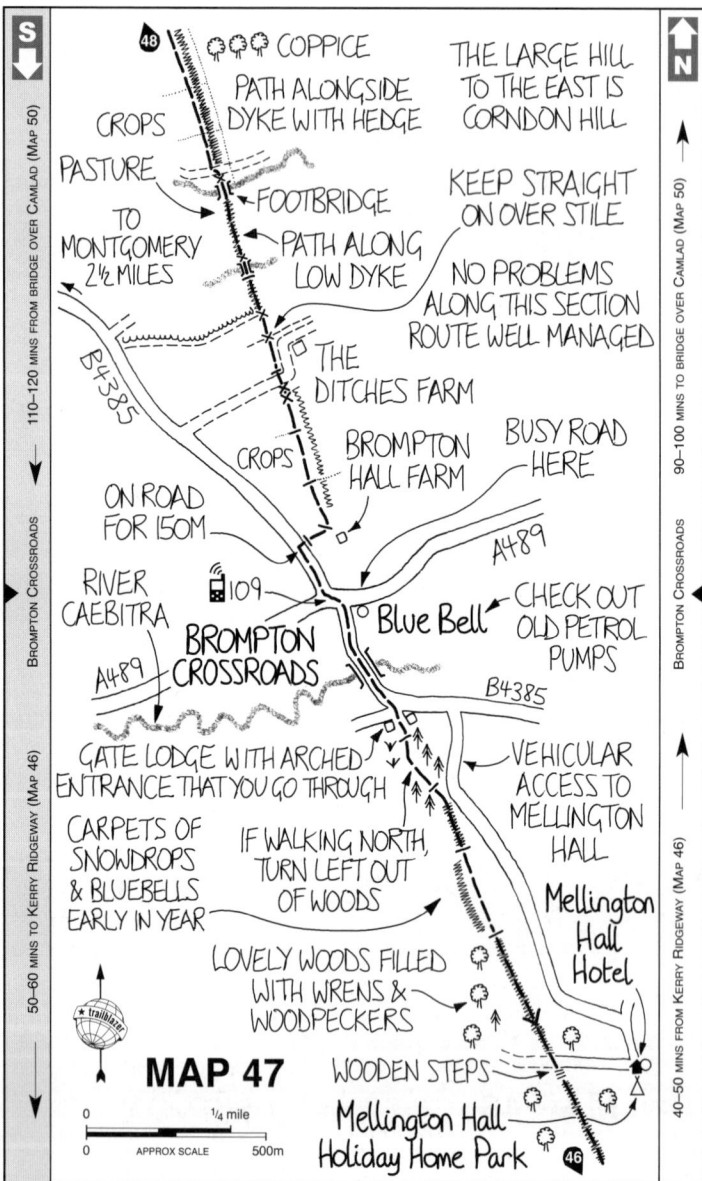

ROUTE GUIDE & MAPS

S

48

COPPICE

THE LARGE HILL
TO THE EAST IS
CORNDON HILL

PATH ALONGSIDE
DYKE WITH HEDGE

CROPS

PASTURE

FOOTBRIDGE

KEEP STRAIGHT
ON OVER STILE

TO
MONTGOMERY
2½ MILES

PATH ALONG
LOW DYKE

NO PROBLEMS
ALONG THIS SECTION
ROUTE WELL MANAGED

B4385

THE
DITCHES FARM

CROPS

BROMPTON
HALL FARM

BUSY ROAD
HERE

ON ROAD
FOR 150M

A489

RIVER
CAEBITRA

109

Blue Bell

CHECK OUT
OLD PETROL
PUMPS

A489

BROMPTON
CROSSROADS

B4385

GATE LODGE WITH ARCHED
ENTRANCE THAT YOU GO THROUGH

VEHICULAR
ACCESS TO
MELLINGTON
HALL

CARPETS OF
SNOWDROPS
& BLUEBELLS
EARLY IN YEAR

IF WALKING NORTH,
TURN LEFT OUT
OF WOODS

Mellington
Hall
Hotel

LOVELY WOODS FILLED
WITH WRENS &
WOODPECKERS

★ trailblazer

MAP 47

WOODEN STEPS

Mellington Hall
Holiday Home Park

46

0   ¼ mile
0   APPROX SCALE   500m

N

110–120 MINS FROM BRIDGE OVER CAMLAD (MAP 50)

BROMPTON CROSSROADS

50–60 MINS TO KERRY RIDGEWAY (MAP 46)

90–100 MINS TO BRIDGE OVER CAMLAD (MAP 50)

BROMPTON CROSSROADS

40–50 MINS FROM KERRY RIDGEWAY (MAP 46)

BROMPTON CROSSROADS & MELLINGTON   Map 47

The Blue Bell (☎ 01588-620231; Mon-Fri 5.30-11pm, Sat 11am-11pm, Sun 11.30am-2.30pm & 7-10.30pm) has remained immune to the changing fashions of the brewing industry; no one has decided to theme it or turn it into an Irish tavern and I hope they never do. The rusting petrol pump outside is just that, a rusting petrol pump, not a furnishing accessory. It's well worth a visit and should be open the days and hours quoted above but these can change.

A mile south of The Blue Bell and set in beautiful grounds among bluebell woods is *Mellington Hall Hotel* (☎ 01588-620056, 🖳 mellingtonhall.co.uk; 9D, most can be T, 2Tr, all en suite; ☻; 🐾; WI-FI; Ⓛ), a gothic pile where B&B will cost from £60pp (sgl occ from £75). You can stop for breakfast (reasonably priced considering the location) afternoon tea (Mon-Sat 2-4.30pm; around £13/19 for one/two people) or dinner (daily 6-9pm). A main course in one of their restaurants costs around £16-20 and in the bar from £7.95.

At the separately run *Mellington Hall Holiday Home Park* (☎ 01588-620011, 🖳 mellingtonhallcaravanpark.co.uk; 🐾; open all year) there's a small campground where you can pitch a **tent** for £7.50pp including use of shower/toilet facilities.

Continuing southwards, you come to *Drewin Farm* (Map 46; ☎ 01588-620325, 🖳 drewinfarm@hotmail.com; 1T/1Tr, both en suite; WI-FI; Ⓛ; Mar/Apr-Oct), a working farm with a view where B&B costs from £40pp (sgl occ £50).

There's a lovely B&B bordering the caravan park, which is easiest to reach from the road junction (see Map 46). The pleasant hosts are at the modern and very comfortable *Shirley Heights* (☎ 07802-596900, 🖳 sheilaesttu@aol.com; 2Tr shared bathroom/one en suite room sleeping up to five people; ☻; WI-FI; 🐾; Ⓛ) know what walkers want, with a fridge full of beer, luggage transfer and evening meals (£20) available. B&B costs from £40pp (sgl occ £50). They also offer **camping** (£5pp).

BROMPTON CROSSROADS TO KNIGHTON
MAPS 47-40

[S ▼ FROM PRESTATYN]

[*Route section begins on Map 47, opposite*] This **14½-mile (23km)** stage will take about **7-8¼ hours**. From **Brompton Crossroads (Map 47)**, early on the trail crosses the east–west track of the **Kerry Ridgeway** (Map 46; see box p166), some 4 miles (6km) west of the captivating small town of **Bishop's Castle**, before embarking on a series of steep undulations known as **The Switchbacks**. The path follows the Dyke through rolling, wooded farmland, much of the time atop the Dyke itself, an opportunity to walk in the footsteps of those who worked, willingly or unwillingly, to realise the vision of King Offa.

There are many fields to be crossed but of far greater note is a series of steep ascents and descents, some with almost no break in between. At the foot of one of these, set in a beautiful and secluded valley, the tiny chapel of St John the Baptist at **Churchtown** (Map 45, p168), with its exquisite biblical wall texts, provides a welcome interlude and the opportunity for a moment of quiet reflection.

Other distractions include the secluded Shropshire town of **Clun** (Map 43a, p164) which is a little gem, although as it's three miles (5km) off the route few walkers make the detour.

Campers, who aren't carrying supplies may wish to divert (10-15 mins) to **Newcastle-on-Clun** (Map 43, p163), where the nearest pub is for food, before continuing to **Springhill Farm Campsite** (Map 43; ☎ 01588-640337; £7.50), where there are showers, a kettle and a toaster to use, but nothing else. T h e trail offers lovely walking across **Llanfair Hill** (Map 42, p162), which at 432m (1417ft) is the highest point on the Dyke (although not the highest point on the trail – that honour is reserved for the section across the Black Mountains). All the same, better views are to be had from the next hill, **Cwm-Sanaham** (Map 41, p161).

At **Panpunton Hill** (Map 40), a cairn has been placed in honour of early Offa's Dyke pioneers so you can reflect for a moment on those who made it all possible. The character of **Knighton (Map 40, p155)** viewed from here is rather spoiled by the modern housing on its outskirts: this is no Bishop's Castle, nor Montgomery. But fear not, Knighton is the path's **halfway mark** and offers plenty of opportunity for rest and relaxation to refresh you for part two of the walk. *[Next route overview p159]*

N ↑ FROM CHEPSTOW

BROMPTON CROSSROADS TO BUTTINGTON (FOR WELSHPOOL) MAPS 47-55

[Route section begins on Map 47, p170] This **12½-mile (20km, 4hrs 55mins to 5hrs 40mins)** stretch stays true to the Dyke, crossing the **Plain of Montgomery**, before climbing to the summit of **Beacon Ring** (Map 53; see box p178), site of an Iron Age hill-fort but now planted with beech trees and transmitter masts rather than affording the views that you might expect. In older times, beacon fires would have been lit here, hence the name, a common-enough one to anyone familiar with maps of England and Wales.

En route, you have the option of a detour to the town of **Montgomery** (Maps 49 and 49a), well worth a visit if you can include it in your schedule; although you could settle for the views of the town's castle ruins, and stay with the path and Dyke, on which after yesterday's exertions the walking, as it traces the hidden hedgerows and copses of the secretive country of the **River Camlad** (Map 50), is straightforward and un-strenuous. The low-lying meadows through which the Camlad flows are typical of much of this section. The views to all sides are good and the walking undemanding and rather uneventful.

You pass through the villages of **Forden** and **Kingswood** (Map 51) before a forested ramble follows through **Leighton Estate** (Map 52) with its Chile pines (monkey puzzle trees), and you ascend to Beacon Ring, from which a long descent sees you through more fields and pasture to **Buttington (Map 55, p184)**. *[Next route overview p186]*

❏ **Important note – walking times**
Unless otherwise specified, **all times in this book refer only to the time spent walking.** You will need to add 20-30% to allow for rests, photography, checking the map, drinking water etc. When planning the day's hike count on 5-7 hours' actual walking.

Map 48 & Map 49 173

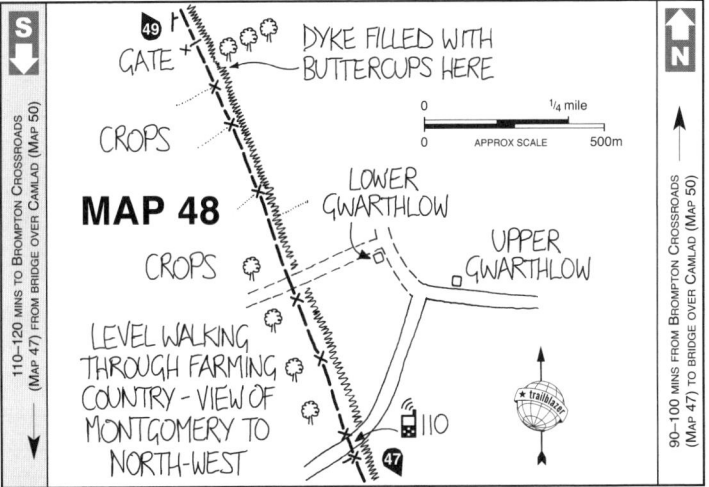

MAP 48

DYKE FILLED WITH BUTTERCUPS HERE

GATE

CROPS

CROPS

LOWER GWARTHLOW

UPPER GWARTHLOW

LEVEL WALKING THROUGH FARMING COUNTRY - VIEW OF MONTGOMERY TO NORTH-WEST

110

110-120 MINS TO BROMPTON CROSSROADS (MAP 47) FROM BRIDGE OVER CAMLAD (MAP 50)

90-100 MINS FROM BROMPTON CROSSROADS (MAP 47) TO BRIDGE OVER CAMLAD (MAP 50)

ROUTE GUIDE & MAPS

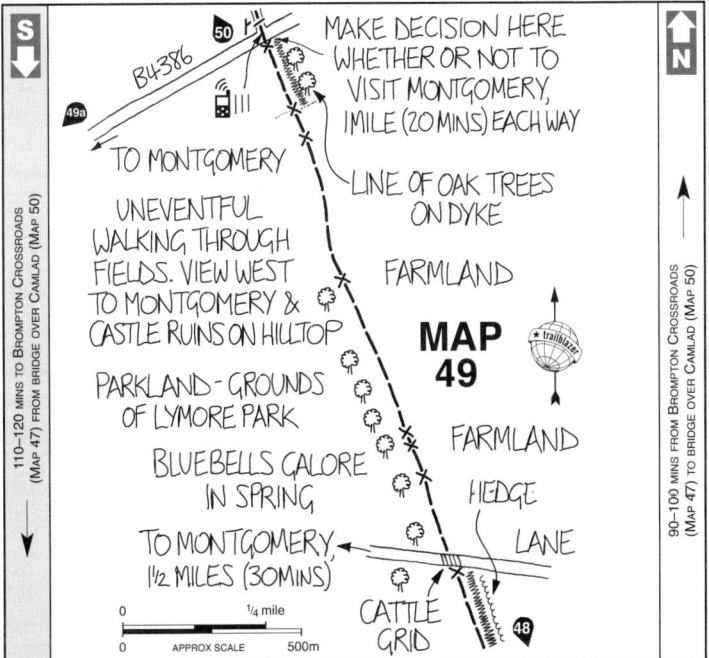

MAP 49

B4386

MAKE DECISION HERE WHETHER OR NOT TO VISIT MONTGOMERY, 1 MILE (20 MINS) EACH WAY

TO MONTGOMERY

LINE OF OAK TREES ON DYKE

UNEVENTFUL WALKING THROUGH FIELDS. VIEW WEST TO MONTGOMERY & CASTLE RUINS ON HILLTOP

FARMLAND

PARKLAND - GROUNDS OF LYMORE PARK

BLUEBELLS GALORE IN SPRING

TO MONTGOMERY, 1½ MILES (30MINS)

FARMLAND

HEDGE

LANE

CATTLE GRID

MONTGOMERY (TREFALDWYN)
Map 49a

The path passes to the east of the small Georgian town of Montgomery, missing it by a mile, but it's well worth a diversion to check out its attractions. At its centre, the Georgian **Town Hall** lies at the end of Broad St, which is lined with elegant townhouses. A short walk from here takes you to the **castle ruins**, which can be seen clearly by walkers on Offa's Dyke Path.

The parish **church of St Nicholas** contains a fine open oak ceiling with arched beams and a beautiful east window, depicting the crucifixion and the ascension in bright primary colours. In the south transept are the Herbert tomb and two effigies, one of which is of Edmund Mortimer, son-in-law to Owen Glendower, of interest to those familiar with Shakespeare's *Henry IV Part 1*.

In the churchyard is the whimsical Robber's Grave, helpfully indicated by a sign. The story goes that Robert Newton, condemned to death in 1821 for robbery, swore his innocence and maintained that the proof would be known by nothing growing on his grave for a hundred years. Somewhat ironically, a rose bush marks the spot.

Services

With cafés, a **shop** (Mon-Sat 7am-8pm, Sat 8am-8pm, Sun 9am-6pm) and a **post office** (Mon-Fri 9am-5.30pm, Sat & Sun 9am-5pm), Montgomery has all the essentials for the tourist, if not the long-stay visitor. A couple of **banks** have cashpoints, and there are **public toilets** behind the town hall.

Montgomery is on Tanat Valley's and Lloyds Coaches shared T12 (Machynlleth to Wrexham) **bus** route as well as Tanat Valley's No 558 to Shrewsbury. See the public transport map and table, pp49-53, for details.

Where to stay

The town's longstanding favourite is *The Dragon Hotel* (☎ 01686-668359, ☐ dragon hotel.com, Market Sq; 2S/4T/12D/4Tr/2Qd, all en suite; ●; ☆ by arrangement; WI-FI; ⓛ), an imposing half-timbered prop-

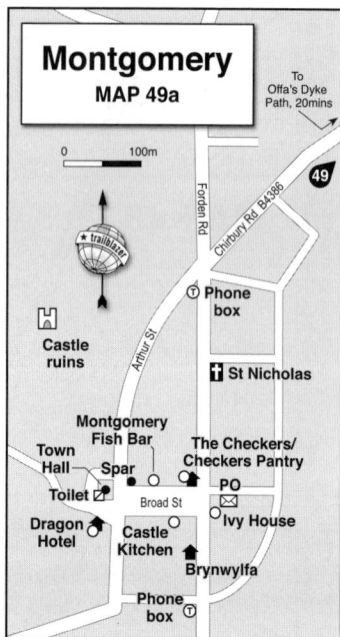

erty where the great and the good of the town can often be seen. If you count yourself among them, expect to pay from £72pp (sgl/sgl occ £65-115) for B&B – but you do get an indoor heated pool and sauna for your money.

The Dragon's position as the top place in town is challenged by *The Checkers* (☎ 01686-669822, ☐ checkerswales.co.uk; 4D/1D or T, all en suite; ●; WI-FI), a restaurant (see Where to eat) but with luxurious rooms attached. B&B costs from £45pp (sgl occ from £75).

Brynwylfa (☎ 01686-668555, ☐ hmd jones@btinternet.com; 1T/1D or T, both en suite; ●; WI-FI; ⓛ) charges from £40pp (sgl occ £50) for B&B; they will collect you from the path if arranged in advance.

Where to eat and drink

There's a great little café on Broad St, *Castle Kitchen* (☎ 01686-668795; Mon-Sat

9.30am-4.30pm, Sun 11.30am-4.30pm; lunches served noon-2pm). With a strong emphasis on healthy eating, it features plenty of locally sourced produce with home-made soups, baked potatoes, savoury bakes and sandwiches made to order, and some fantastic specials (around £8). Running it close is *Ivy House Café* (daily 9am-5.30pm), with a lovely line in sandwiches and other light bites, a fair ice-cream selection and a decent view down the square to the town hall.

Checkers Pantry (see Where to stay; Tue-Sat 9am-4:30pm), Broad St, offers breakfasts until 11.30am, light lunches from noon-2.45pm and coffee and cakes all day.

For evenings, head to *The Dragon Hotel* (see Where to stay; daily noon-2.30pm & 6-9pm).

As a **takeaway**, *Montgomery Fish Bar* (☎ 01686-668911; daily noon-11pm) offers a somewhat cheaper alternative.

> ❏ **George Herbert**
> Montgomery was the birthplace of the poet George Herbert (1593-1632), whom many may have first encountered if they studied the *Oxford Book of Verse* at school:
>
> *Sweet day, so cool, so calm, so bright!*
> *The dew shall weep thy fall tonight;*
> *The bridle of the earth and sky –*
> *For thou must die.* (From *Virtue*)
>
> Herbert's association with Montgomery included acting as MP for the town for two years. He was later ordained and settled in Bemerton, near Salisbury.

KINGSWOOD & FORDEN
Map 51, p177

Although Kingswood and Forden are in theory two entirely separate communities, the road sign at the entrance to Kingswood states 'Forden'; presumably a reflection of the new housing that has threatened to engulf the small community.

Both Tanat Valley Coaches and Lloyds Coaches operate the T12 **bus** service (see public transport map and table pp49-53); in Kingswood the buses stop by Cock Hotel and in Forden by the Village Hall.

Despite the rather grand name, *Cock Hotel* (☎ 01938-580226; WI-FI; 🐾) in **Kingswood** is just a pub (daily 5-11pm). When they are open they do standard pub **food** (daily 6-8.30pm). You can also **camp** in the beer garden (£5); there's no shower block but you can use the pub's facilities.

Almost opposite the pub is *Heath Cottage* (☎ 01938-580453, 🖃 heathcottage wales@tiscali.co.uk; 1S/2D/1T, all en suite; 🐾; 🐾 in the stable only; WI-FI; ⓛ), where you can expect a quintessential English welcome from the owner, with tea and home-made cake. B&B in large, tradition-

ally furnished rooms costs from £40pp a night (£60 sgl occ), and guests have a comfy lounge to themselves. **Camping** is also available at £7.50pp, including access to a shower and toilet. The path actually runs through the fields that are owned by them, so there's easy access back to the trail.

Meadow Rise (☎ 01938-580243; 🐾; Apr-Oct), in **Forden**, is right on the trail and offers **camping** (£7pp inc shower) and a **bunkhouse** (£12pp), which sleeps two people. The bunkhouse has its own bathroom but bedding is not provided.

Half-a-mile from the path (off Map 51) is *The Railway Inn* (☎ 01938-580661, 🖃 therailwayinnforden.com; 1S/3D/2T; WI-FI; ⓛ), where **food** (daily noon-9pm; meals from £8.95) and **B&B** (from £37.50pp, sgl occ £50) are available for hikers.

ROUTE GUIDE & MAPS

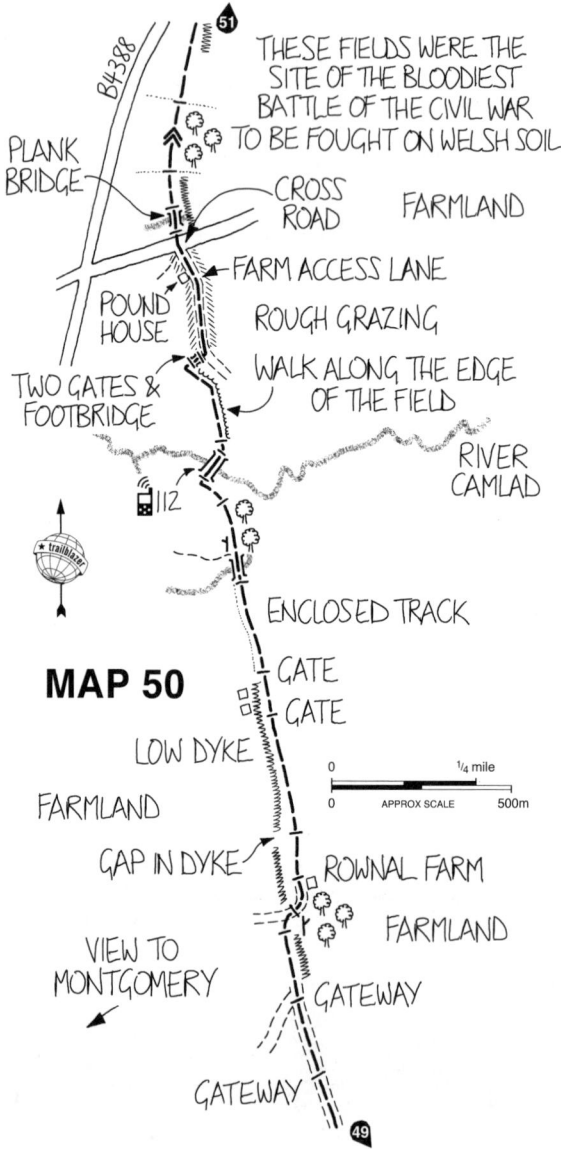

S

N

70–80 MINS FROM FORDEN
T-JUNCTION (MAP 51)

70–75 MINS TO FORDEN
T-JUNCTION (MAP 51)

BRIDGE OVER CAMLAD

BRIDGE OVER CAMLAD

110–120 MINS TO BROMPTON CROSSROADS (MAP 47)

90–100 MINS FROM BROMPTON CROSSROADS (MAP 47)

B4388

51

THESE FIELDS WERE THE
SITE OF THE BLOODIEST
BATTLE OF THE CIVIL WAR
TO BE FOUGHT ON WELSH SOIL

PLANK
BRIDGE

CROSS
ROAD

FARMLAND

FARM ACCESS LANE

POUND
HOUSE

ROUGH GRAZING

TWO GATES &
FOOTBRIDGE

WALK ALONG THE EDGE
OF THE FIELD

112

RIVER
CAMLAD

★ trailblazer

ENCLOSED TRACK

MAP 50

GATE
GATE

LOW DYKE

0   ¼ mile

FARMLAND

0   APPROX SCALE   500m

GAP IN DYKE

ROWNAL FARM

FARMLAND

VIEW TO
MONTGOMERY

GATEWAY

GATEWAY

49

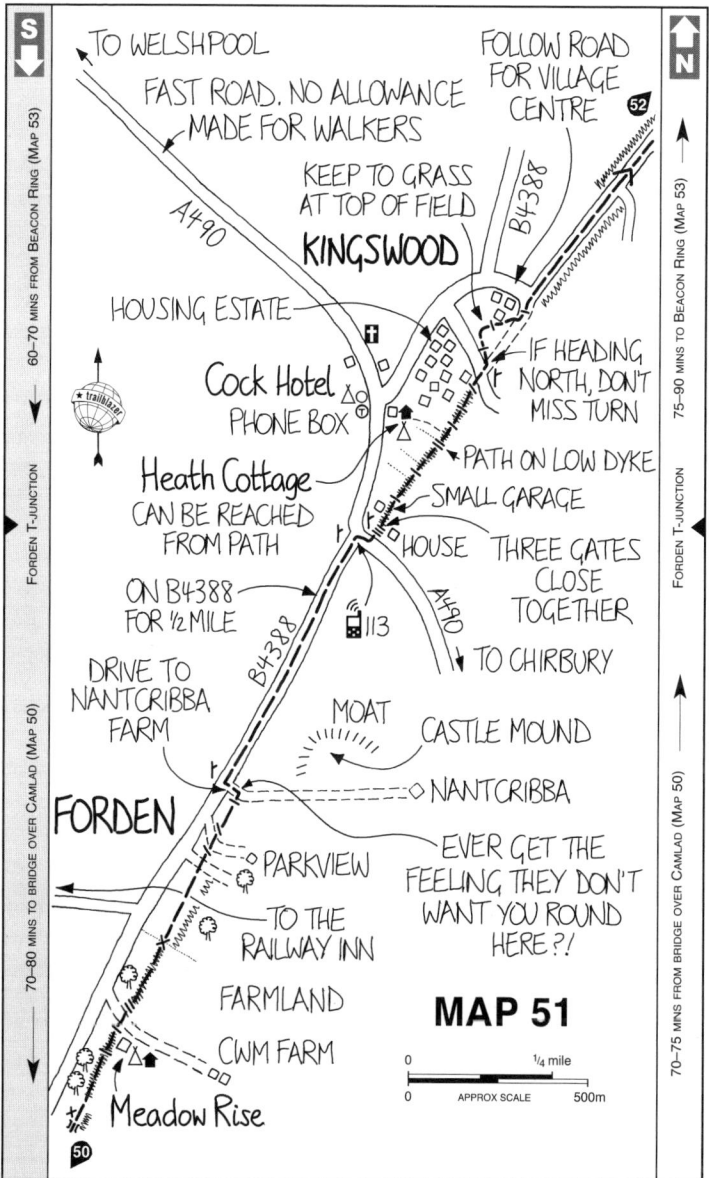

S ↓

N ↑

TO WELSHPOOL

FAST ROAD. NO ALLOWANCE MADE FOR WALKERS

FOLLOW ROAD FOR VILLAGE CENTRE

52

KEEP TO GRASS AT TOP OF FIELD

B4388

A490

KINGSWOOD

HOUSING ESTATE

60–70 MINS FROM BEACON RING (MAP 53)

75–90 MINS TO BEACON RING (MAP 53)

★ trailblazer

Cock Hotel

PHONE BOX

IF HEADING NORTH, DON'T MISS TURN

PATH ON LOW DYKE

Heath Cottage

CAN BE REACHED FROM PATH

SMALL GARAGE

FORDEN T-JUNCTION

FORDEN T-JUNCTION

HOUSE

THREE GATES CLOSE TOGETHER

ON B4388 FOR ½ MILE

B4388

A490

113

TO CHIRBURY

DRIVE TO NANTCRIBBA FARM

MOAT

CASTLE MOUND

FORDEN

NANTCRIBBA

70–80 MINS TO BRIDGE OVER CAMLAD (MAP 50)

70–75 MINS FROM BRIDGE OVER CAMLAD (MAP 50)

PARKVIEW

EVER GET THE FEELING THEY DON'T WANT YOU ROUND HERE?!

TO THE RAILWAY INN

FARMLAND

MAP 51

CWM FARM

0   ¼ mile

0   APPROX SCALE   500m

Meadow Rise

50

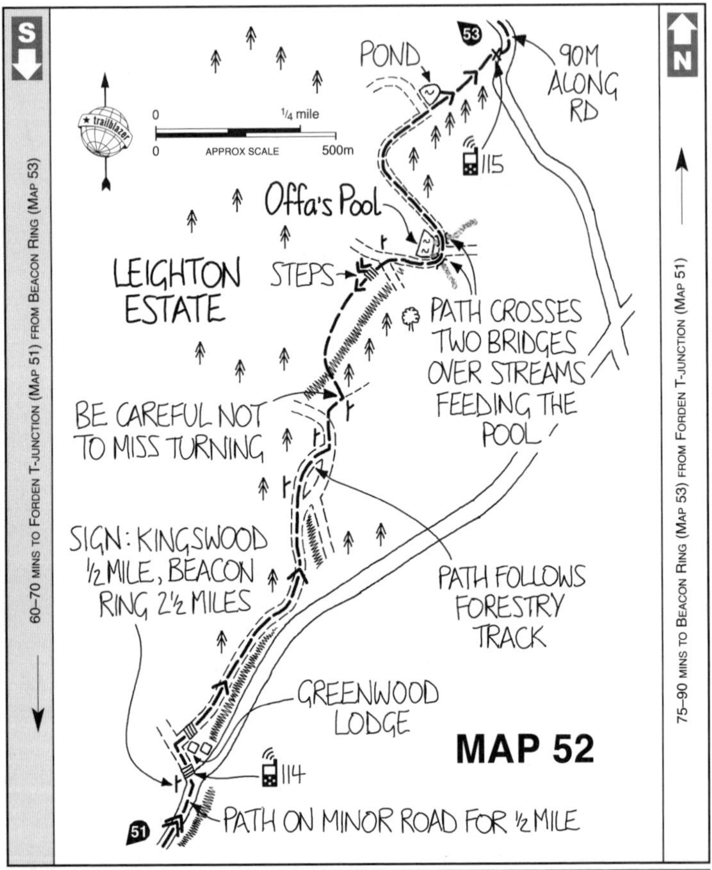

60–70 MINS TO FORDEN T-JUNCTION (MAP 51) FROM BEACON RING (MAP 53)

75–90 MINS TO BEACON RING (MAP 53) FROM FORDEN T-JUNCTION (MAP 51)

S

N

53

POND

90M ALONG RD

📱 115

Offa's Pool

LEIGHTON ESTATE

STEPS

PATH CROSSES TWO BRIDGES OVER STREAMS FEEDING THE POOL

BE CAREFUL NOT TO MISS TURNING

SIGN: KINGSWOOD ½ MILE, BEACON RING 2½ MILES

PATH FOLLOWS FORESTRY TRACK

GREENWOOD LODGE

MAP 52

📱 114

51

PATH ON MINOR ROAD FOR ½ MILE

trailblazer
0 — ¼ mile
0 — APPROX SCALE — 500m

❑ **Beacon Ring Hill Fort** *(Caer Digoll)*   **Map 53, p179**
Dating from the Iron Age, the fortifications at Beacon Ring housed a small village
where the inhabitants eked out a perilous existence hunting and farming. The circular
embankment and ditch would have been supplemented by a palisade made from tree
trunks with an opening on the south side for a gateway. The site also contained a
much-older long barrow or burial mound, suggesting that it would have had a sacred
significance for its inhabitants.

A plantation of beech trees was established in 1953 to mark the coronation of
Her Majesty Queen Elizabeth II but the commemorative stone has become defaced.
To be frank, the trees spoil the site and rob it of any sense of place or space. As if the
trees were not bad enough, two ugly transmitter masts with their accompanying
buildings add to the lack of harmony.

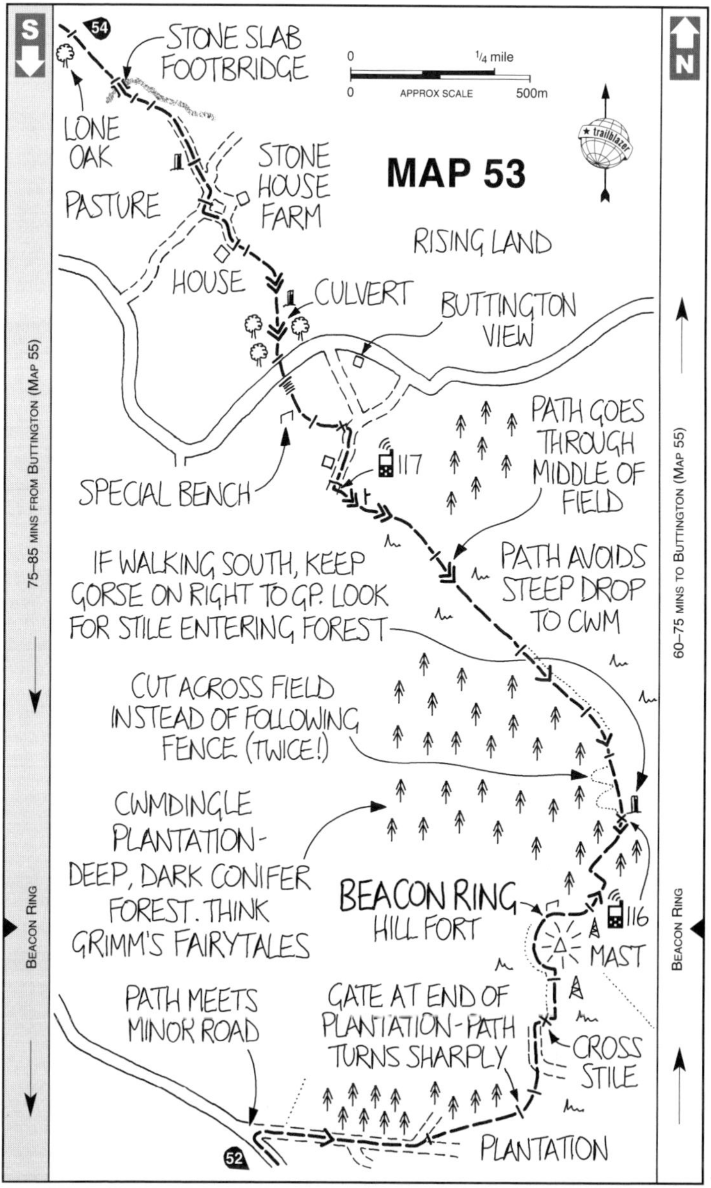

S ⬇

54

STONE SLAB
FOOTBRIDGE

0   ¼ mile
0   APPROX SCALE   500m

N ⬆

⭐ trailblazer

LONE
OAK

PASTURE

STONE
HOUSE
FARM

MAP 53

RISING LAND

HOUSE

CULVERT

BUTTINGTON
VIEW

SPECIAL BENCH

117

PATH GOES
THROUGH
MIDDLE OF
FIELD

PATH AVOIDS
STEEP DROP
TO CWM

IF WALKING SOUTH, KEEP
GORSE ON RIGHT TO G.P. LOOK
FOR STILE ENTERING FOREST

CUT ACROSS FIELD
INSTEAD OF FOLLOWING
FENCE (TWICE!)

CWMDINGLE
PLANTATION-
DEEP, DARK CONIFER
FOREST. THINK
GRIMM'S FAIRYTALES

BEACON RING
HILL FORT

116

MAST

PATH MEETS
MINOR ROAD

GATE AT END OF
PLANTATION-PATH
TURNS SHARPLY

CROSS
STILE

52

PLANTATION

75–85 MINS FROM BUTTINGTON (MAP 55)

BEACON RING

60–75 MINS TO BUTTINGTON (MAP 55)

BEACON RING

ROUTE GUIDE & MAPS

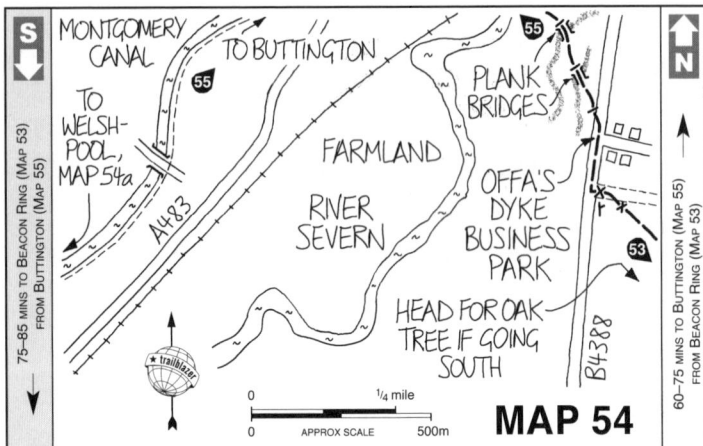

WELSHPOOL (Y TRALLWNG)
Map 54a, p182

Welshpool is only 1½ miles (2km) south of the trail, along the towpath. Due to the relatively limited accommodation in the vicinity of Buttington, walkers sometimes choose to stay in the town, but even here there aren't that many places to stay and what there is gets booked up in peak periods.

The town used to be known as Pool but confusion with Poole, Dorset, led to the council attaching 'Welsh' as a prefix, and it has been Welshpool ever since. And this is very much a traditional Welsh town, with a conservative feel about it. If you had any doubt, road signs, bus and railway timetables, public notices and tourist information are shown in both English and Welsh – the clearest reminder for the visitor that you have crossed the boundary into Wales.

A highlight of a visit to Welshpool is **Powis Castle & Garden** (see box opposite). The **motte and bailey castle** north of the railway station, also known as Domen Gastell, dates from Norman times and is now the site of a bowling green. Just off Broad St, is the old **Cockpit**, a beautifully restored red-brick building that takes its name from the days when cock-fighting was popular. **Powysland Museum and Canal Centre** (☎ 01938-554656, 🖳 customer.powys.gov.uk/article/1698/Powysland-Museum; June-Aug Mon-Fri 10.30am-1pm & 2-5pm, Sat 10.30am-3pm, September to May Mon, Tue, Thur, Fri 11am-1pm & 2-5pm, Sat 11am-2pm; free entry) is an intriguing local museum concentrating on items relevant to the old county of Montgomeryshire.

❑ Site of Strata Marcella Abbey   Map 55, p184
Founded in 1170 by a grant from Owain Cyfeiliog, a prince of Powys, the abbey was colonised by the Cistercian 'white monks' from Whitland, near Carmarthen. They were called white monks because they chose to use undyed cloth for their habits. Owain himself became a monk and was buried here. At the time of the dissolution of the monasteries only three monks lived there. Since then the site has been plundered for stone for local building and today not one stone remains visible. Some finds are on display at Powysland Museum (see above) in Welshpool.

❏ Powis Castle & Garden

Less than a mile south of the centre of Welshpool, Powis Castle & Garden (☎ 01938-551944, 🖥 nationaltrust.org.uk/powis; late Mar-Sep castle and museum daily 11am-5pm, garden 10am-6pm; Mar & Oct-Dec castle and museum 11am-4pm, garden 10am-4pm, Jan-Feb all weekends only noon-4pm; castle & garden £14.30/13; higher price includes giftaid; NT members free) was originally built in the early 13th century. Constructed of startling pink sandstone, the castle has connections with Clive of India and contains a collection of memorabilia relevant to his career as a soldier and statesman.

It takes a pleasant half-hour to walk from the town through the deer park, notable for its giant redwood trees, to reach the castle entrance; the park gates are opened at dawn and close an hour after sunset. Visitors pass a small plaque marking the spot where an arrow landed, shot by Sir Ralph from the castle bowling green in 1910, though it does not record if it hit anyone. There's a magnificent herd of red deer in the park and peacocks provide an ornamental diversion, especially in the display season.

Transport

[See pp49-53] Welshpool is a stop on Transport for Wales's **train** service to Birmingham, Aberystwyth and Shrewsbury.

National Express's NX409 **coach** service operates a similar route but starts in London.

Celtic Travel's X75 **bus** service plies the route between Shrewsbury and Llanidloes. Tanat Valley's T12, which is shared with Lloyds Coaches, also calls here.

For a **taxi** call Amber Cabs (☎ 01938-556611).

Services

The **tourist information centre** (☎ 01938-552043; Mon-Sat 9.30am-4.15pm, Sun 10am-3.45pm) is by the large public car park by St Mary's Church. They offer accommodation booking and are also happy to book accommodation for the entire Offa's Dyke Path; they charge £2 per booking plus 10% deposit. Another source of information is 🖥 welshpool.com.

There is a **post office** as well as two **banks** with cash machines on Broad St, a **launderette** on the High St and a Boots **pharmacy** on Broad St, useful for such essentials as blister plasters.

Food stocks can be replenished at any of three **supermarkets** here: Sainsbury's

(Mon-Thur 7.30am-9pm, Sat 8am-9.30pm, Sun 11am-5pm) on Brook St; a large Morrisons (Mon-Sat 7am-10pm, Sun 10am-4pm) on Berriew St; and Tesco (Mon to Sat 6am-midnight, Sun 10am-4pm), on Smithfield Rd.

Alexanders of Welshpool (☎ 01938-552329, 29 Broad St; Mon-Sat 8am-5.30pm) is the only **camping shop** and is good for gas cylinders and any vital items of clothing or equipment. The **hospital** can be contacted on ☎ 01938-553133.

Where to stay

On Salop Rd, *The Westwood Park* (☎ 01938-553474, 🖥 westwoodparkhotel.co .uk; 1S/4T/2D, most en suite, some share facilities; WI-FI; 🐾; Ⓛ), which despite its name is a pub which offers B&B; they charge around £30-35pp (sgl/sgl occ £30-45). The bar (Mon-Thur 4.30-11pm, Fri, Sat & Sun noon-midnight) serves real ales.

On Brookfield Rd, the modern *Tresi-Aur* (☎ 01938-552430; 1S/1T/1Tr, shared bathroom; ▼; WI-FI; Ⓛ) provides B&B from £30pp (sgl/sgl occ from £35).

The most central option is *Stone House* (☎ 01938-691039, 🖥 welshpool .com/stonehouse.html, 🖥 thestonehousebb @gmail.com; 1D/1Tr, both en suite; WI-FI), a simple place with rooms for £40-47.50pp (sgl occ from £55).

Welshpool
MAP 54a

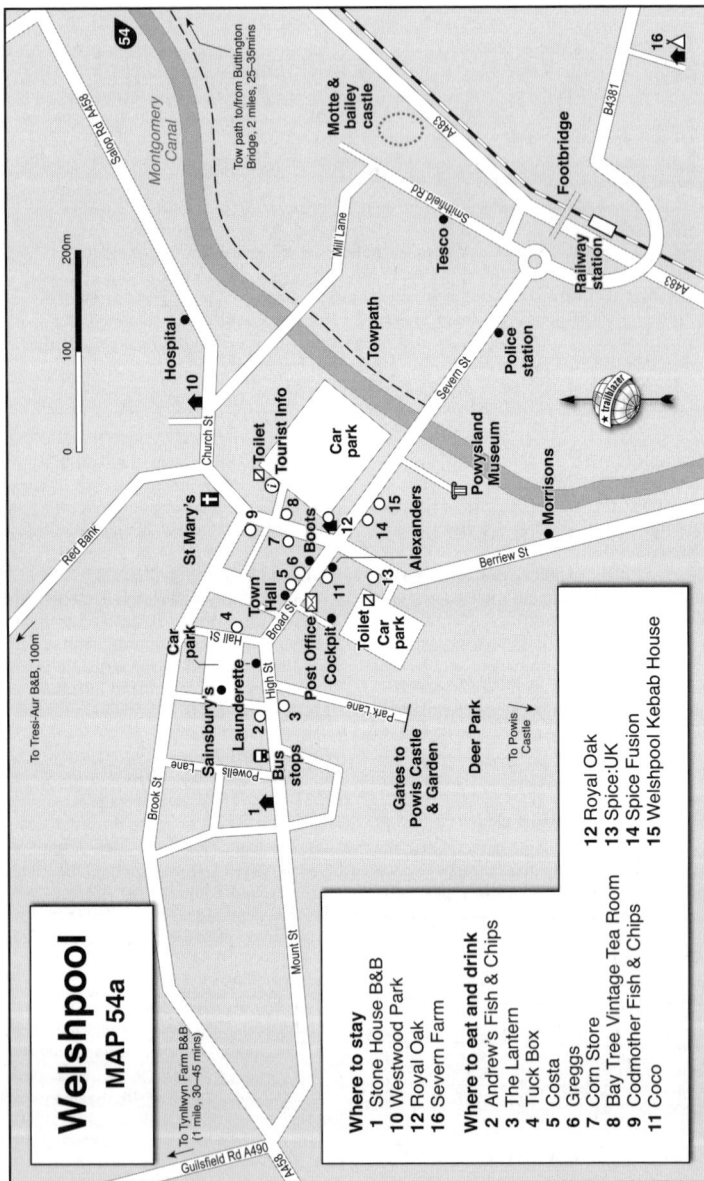

To Tyrllwyn Farm B&B
(1 mile, 30-45 mins)

To Guillsfield Rd A490

To Tresi-Aur B&B, 100m

ROUTE GUIDE & MAPS

Montgomery Canal

Salop Rd A458

Tow path to/from Buttington Bridge, 2 miles, 25-35mins

Motte & bailey castle

Footbridge

B4381

16

54

Hospital
10

Church St

Red Bank

Mill Lane

Smithfield Rd

A483

Tesco

Towpath

Railway station

A483

Police station

Severn St

Toilet
Tourist Info

Car park

Powysland Museum

Morrisons

St Mary's

9
8
7
6 5
12
14 15

Boots

Berriew St

Alexanders

Town Hall

Post Office
Cockpit

Brook St

Broad St

11
13

Toilet
Car park

Hall St

Car park

4

Launderette

Sainsbury's

High St

Powells Lane

2
3

Bus stops

1

Park Lane

Deer Park

Gates to Powis Castle & Garden

To Powis Castle

Mount St

200m
100
0

Where to stay
1 Stone House B&B
10 Westwood Park
12 Royal Oak
16 Severn Farm

Where to eat and drink
2 Andrew's Fish & Chips
3 The Lantern
4 Tuck Box
5 Costa
6 Greggs
7 Corn Store
8 Bay Tree Vintage Tea Room
9 Codmother Fish & Chips
11 Coco

12 Royal Oak
13 Spice:UK
14 Spice Fusion
15 Welshpool Kebab House

If you fancy splashing out, you could try *The Royal Oak* (☎ 01938-552217, 🖥 royaloakwelshpool.co.uk; 5S/4T/14D, all en suite; ✆; WI-FI; Ⓛ), a former coaching inn at the main crossroads where B&B is from around £55pp (sgl from £59).

East of the railway station is Mrs Joyce Jones's *Severn Farm* (☎ 01938-555999, ☎ 07736-180811; 2T/1D/2Tr, shared bathrooms; ✆; WI-FI; Ⓛ) where guests have their own traditionally furnished lounge and dining room. **B&B** costs from £34pp (sgl occ £34) and **camping** £7pp plus £1 for a shower or bath; campers have access to basic cooking facilities. There is also a small annexe (1S/1T; £17.50pp without breakfast) which shares the camping facilities.

About a mile north of town on the A490, set up high on the side of the hill, is *Tynllwyn Farm* (☎ 01938-553175, 🖥 tyn llwynfarm.co.uk; 1T/3D/1Tr, all en suite; WI-FI; Ⓛ). A working farm, it offers comfortable rooms from £40pp (sgl occ £60) and has drying facilities. A three-course evening meal costs from £22 but should be requested in advance. They also have some holiday cottages (🐾; three have ✆) and if available these can be used for B&B. They also offer pick up and luggage transfer. Contact them for details.

It's pleasant walking along the canal to the bridge over Severn St, but if at the end of a hard day this is a bridge too far, it's easy enough to arrange to be picked up (£3-5) from Buttington Bridge.

Where to eat and drink
Welshpool is not blessed with eateries. There is a *Costa* (Mon-Fri 7am-6.30pm, Sat 8am-6.30pm, Sun 9am-6pm) and a *Greggs*

bakery (Mon-Sat 7am-6pm, Sun 9am-6pm) on Broad St. For a takeaway sandwich try *Tuck Box* (8am-2.30pm; baps from £3.20).

There is also *Coco Coffee House* (☎ 01938-552366; Mon-Fri 6.30am-5pm, Sat 8am-5pm, Sun 8am-4pm).

Corn Store (☎ 01938-554614; Tue-Sat noon-2pm & 6-9pm, Sun noon-4pm) is set in unpretentious surroundings on Church St. Steaks and grills loom large on the menu, but with a fresh take, and the menu includes vegetarian and gluten-free options.

Currently, the most popular place in Welshpool is *Bay Tree Vintage Tearoom* (☎ 01938-555456; Mon 9am-5pm, Tue-Thur 9am-10.30pm, Fri & Sat 9am-late, Sun 9am-5pm), where you can get burgers, steaks, and cocktails.

The Royal Oak (see Where to stay) has a good **restaurant** (daily noon-9pm).

Welshpool has two Indian restaurants: *Spice:UK* (☎ 01938-553431; Sun-Thur 5-11pm, Fri & Sat 5pm-midnight) and *Spice Fusion* (☎ 01938-556669; Sun-Thur 5-11.30pm, Fri & Sat 5pm to 1am).

Next door to the latter is *Welshpool Kebab House* (☎ 01938-556215, 🖥 welsh poolkebab.co.uk; Sun-Wed 3pm-midnight, Thur 4pm-midnight, Fri & Sat noon-2am). Further takeaway options are provided by the **chippies**, the best being either *The Codmother* (Mon-Thur noon-2pm & 5-10pm, Sat noon-10pm, Sun 5-10pm) or *Andrew's* (Mon-Thur 11am-2.30pm, Fri & Sat 11am-3pm, Mon-Sat 4.30-10pm).

For Chinese try *The Lantern* (☎ 01938-553252; Tue-Thur 5-10pm, Fri & Sat 5-10.30pm, Sun 5-9pm).

❏ Buttington Wharf   Map 55, p184
The Montgomery Canal links Pool Quay and Buttington Wharf, at one time an important site for limestone burning. When the Severn burst its banks in the winter of 2000, Offa's Dyke Path was diverted along the towpath to the wharf.

The lime kilns still remain more or less intact, if rather overgrown. A surviving accounts book tells us that in 1830, 2000 tons of limestone were burnt here, most of it destined for the fields east of the Severn: it fed the soil with the minerals needed for decent crops. The trade in limestone along the canal was short-lived due to the coming of the railways which offered quicker, cheaper transportation.

S

MAP 55

0   ¼ mile
APPROX SCALE
0   500m

N

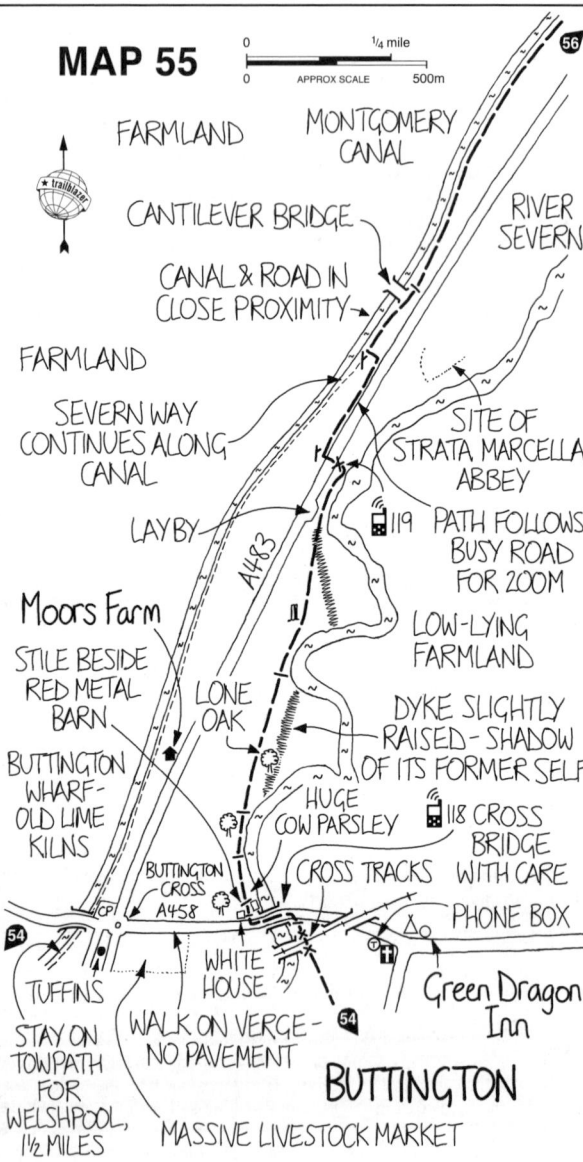

ROUTE GUIDE & MAPS

45–60 MINS FROM POOL QUAY (MAP 56)

BUTTINGTON

45–60 MINS TO POOL QUAY (MAP 56)

BUTTINGTON

★ trailblazer

FARMLAND

MONTGOMERY CANAL

RIVER SEVERN

CANTILEVER BRIDGE

CANAL & ROAD IN CLOSE PROXIMITY →

FARMLAND

SEVERN WAY CONTINUES ALONG CANAL

SITE OF STRATA MARCELLA ABBEY

LAYBY

119 PATH FOLLOWS BUSY ROAD FOR 200M

A483

LOW-LYING FARMLAND

Moors Farm

STILE BESIDE RED METAL BARN

LONE OAK

DYKE SLIGHTLY RAISED – SHADOW OF ITS FORMER SELF

BUTTINGTON WHARF – OLD LIME KILNS

HUGE COW PARSLEY

118 CROSS BRIDGE WITH CARE

CROSS TRACKS

BUTTINGTON CROSS A458

PHONE BOX

54

WHITE HOUSE

Green Dragon Inn

TUFFINS

STAY ON TOWPATH FOR WELSHPOOL, 1½ MILES

WALK ON VERGE – NO PAVEMENT

54

BUTTINGTON

MASSIVE LIVESTOCK MARKET

BUTTINGTON   Map 55

Although Buttington itself has few ameni-
ties, it has a decidedly wide spread of
accommodation styles. There is, however,
Tuffins **supermarket** (daily 5am-11pm) at
Buttington Cross.

You can **camp** (🐾; Mar-Oct depending on the weather; shower & toilet facilities available; £7.50pp) at the local pub,
Green Dragon Inn (☎ 01938-553076 or
07443652718, 🖥 greendragonbuttington
.com; bar Mon-Fri noon-2.30pm & 6.30-
11pm, Sat & Sun noon-11pm; **food** served
daily noon-2.30pm & 6.30-9pm). The food
is great but it's worth calling them to check
their food hours.

You can get to *Moors Farm* (☎ 01938-
553395, 🖥 moors-farm.com; 2T or D/4D,
all en suite; 🛀; WI-FI) via the towpath
alongside the canal rather than along the
main road. Once the main farmhouse for
Powis Castle, it is still a working farm.
B&B costs £42.50-45pp (sgl occ from
£70). There's also a **self-catering barn**
(5D/1T, all en suite; 🛀; 🐾; WI-FI) with a
kitchen but is really only for groups though
if it is not already booked it can be used by
people (dogs, too). Phone for more information.

The **bus** stop is served by Celtic
Travel's X75 (Llanidloes to Shrewsbury);
see pp49-53.

S ⬇ FROM PRESTATYN   BUTTINGTON TO BROMPTON CROSSROADS
MAPS 55-47

[*Route section begins on Map 55, opposite*] This **12½-mile (20km, 5¼hrs-
5hrs 55mins)** stretch leaves **Buttington** and the River Severn and climbs
steeply for an hour to the summit of **Beacon Ring** (Map 53; see box p178), site
of an Iron Age hill-fort but now planted with beech trees and transmitter masts
rather than affording the views that you might expect. In older times, beacon
fires would have been lit here, hence the name, a common-enough one to anyone familiar with maps of England and Wales.

A largely forested ramble follows through **Leighton Estate** (Map 52) with
its Chile pines (monkey puzzle trees) to the villages of **Kingswood** (Map 51)
and **Forden**, then a lengthy crossing of the **Plain of Montgomery** with the
Dyke in evidence throughout. The walking is relatively easy as it traces the
hidden hedgerows and copses of the secretive country of the **River Camlad**
(Map 50). The low-lying meadows through which the Camlad flows are typical
of much of this section. The views to all sides are good and the walking undemanding and rather uneventful.

Near **Montgomery** the landscape of **Lymore Park** (Map 49) shows the
distant town and its castle to good effect and the woods are the haunt of numerous pheasants. To the south the skyline is dominated by the Kerry Ridgeway
and to the west the wooded mound of Corndon Hill is clearly seen. The Dyke
is the border along here, although this doesn't worry the buzzards who pursue
their hunting with their characteristic diligence, their cries a trademark of the
deep country of the Dyke. You eventually reach **Brompton Crossroads (Map
47, p170).**   [*Next route overview p171*]

BUTTINGTON (FOR WELSHPOOL)
TO LLANYMYNECH   MAPS 55-59 (MAPS 54-54a)

[*Route section begins on Map 55, p184*] This stretch of **10½ miles (17km, 4hrs-4hrs 40mins** plus a 20- to 30-minute walk each way to/from Welshpool) is dead flat and straightforward – without a doubt, the easiest section along the entire path. That said, it does begin with a hazard: **Buttington Bridge**. Take care as you cross the bridge – this has the potential to be the hairiest piece of road-walking on the entire trail. You follow fields bordering the **River Severn** before crossing the busy A483 and arriving at a **cantilever bridge**, from which the **Montgomery Canal**, abandoned in 1944, is followed as far as **Pool Quay**. The river was at one time navigable as far as Pool Quay and in the early 19th century vessels of up to 30 tons were used to ship goods to Worcester and Gloucester. The weir that made the river navigable was destroyed by floods in 1881.

ROUTE GUIDE & MAPS

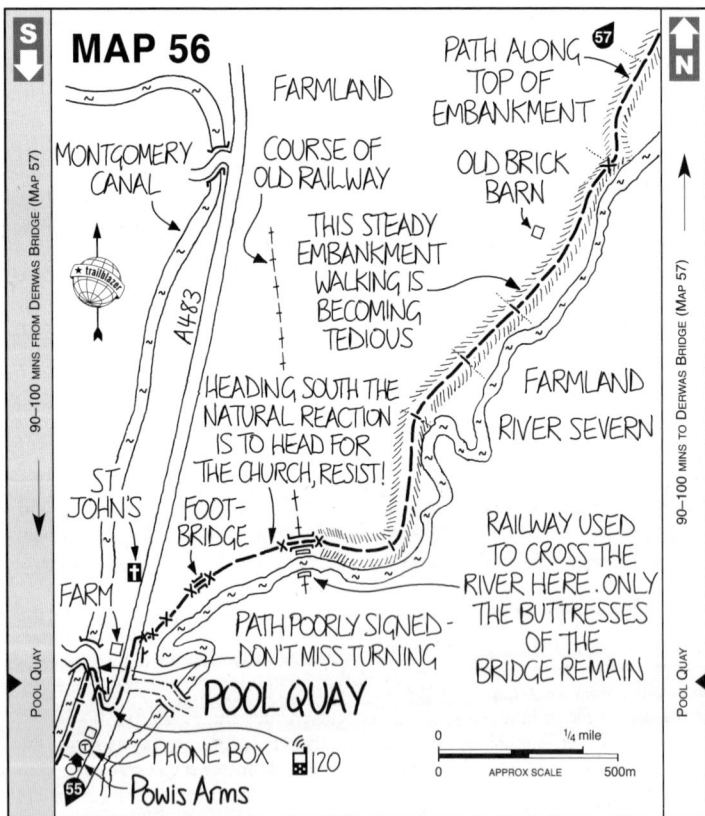

MAP 56

S ↓

↑ N

57

PATH ALONG TOP OF EMBANKMENT

FARMLAND

MONTGOMERY CANAL

COURSE OF OLD RAILWAY

OLD BRICK BARN

★ trailbleezer

A483

THIS STEADY EMBANKMENT WALKING IS BECOMING TEDIOUS

FARMLAND

RIVER SEVERN

HEADING SOUTH THE NATURAL REACTION IS TO HEAD FOR THE CHURCH, RESIST!

ST JOHN'S FOOT-BRIDGE

RAILWAY USED TO CROSS THE RIVER HERE. ONLY THE BUTTRESSES OF THE BRIDGE REMAIN

FARM

PATH POORLY SIGNED - DON'T MISS TURNING

POOL QUAY

90–100 MINS FROM DERWAS BRIDGE (MAP 57)

90–100 MINS TO DERWAS BRIDGE (MAP 57)

POOL QUAY

POOL QUAY

PHONE BOX 📱120

Powis Arms

55

0   ¼ mile

0   APPROX SCALE   500m

You swap canal for river again and are back in the company of the Severn as the path goes along the top of **Tir-y-mynach Embankment** (Map 57) for four miles (6km). Look out for the house offering cake and possibly tea. The walking is across farmland, fairly ordinary but you can take pleasure from the swirling eddies of the Severn as it twists and turns its way to the sea. The river flows northwards at this stage, towards Shrewsbury, before changing course to start on its journey back towards Chepstow. Occasionally the river floods and the fields are left strewn with driftwood as the waters recede. Each fence has its pile of debris – everything from twigs to whole tree trunks. When you come to the course of the old railway line (Map 56, p186) between Oswestry and Welshpool, now long abandoned, keep a look out for the remains of a bridge over the river. The going is enlivened by views of the tree-covered **Breidden Hills** (see box below) to the east and the birdlife along the river. Listen out for the cry of curlews across the fields.

As the Severn meanders its way north, you go your way and remain in line with the Dyke following it as far as **Four Crosses** (Map 58), from where you pass under the A483 and re-join the canal. An air of neglect may pervade, but swan nests and the attractively restored **Carreghofa Locks** (Map 59) make for a pleasant sight. From there it isn't far to **Llanymynech (Map 59, p191)**. Take your time over today's easy walk and enjoy the horizontal ramble alongside river and canal – tomorrow the path returns to its vertical nature.

[Next route overview p192]

POOL QUAY   Map 56

Powis Arms (☎ 01938-590255; 🐾 in bar only; WI-FI; bar summer generally open daily all day, winter generally Mon-Fri 5-11pm, all day Sat & Sun but hours depend on demand) is a few steps down the road from the path and is worth the short detour for the **food** (an evening meal is always available for B&B guests and usually at other times but check in advance) and real ales. **B&B** (2T/1F, both en suite) costs from £35pp (sgl occ £45).

At **St John's Church** there is a *tea room* and toilets (Thur-Sat 10am-3pm).

❏ Breidden Hills   Map 57, p188

Between Pool Quay and Four Crosses the path follows the River Severn as it meanders its way through the Severn Plain, an area of no outstanding beauty but characterised by the spectacular view of a compact range of hills to the east sprouting radio masts and transmitters and disfigured in part by quarrying. These are the Breidden Hills, a volcanic outcrop of dolerite rock rising to 365m (1198ft) above sea level that was used by Caractacus against the Romans in AD43. Cefn-y-castell, on Middletown Hill, is one of the many places where he is said to have fought his last battle. The site is a clearing in an otherwise heavily wooded area; the forest was planted 300 years ago for use by the shipyards at Chatham. The monument (**Rodney's Pillar**) on top of Breidden Hill commemorates Admiral Rodney who won a sea battle at Dominica in 1782.

Caractacus, also known in Welsh as Caradoc, held out against the Romans for nine years before an expedition sent by Claudius defeated him in AD51. He was taken to Rome in chains but his bearing and demeanour so impressed his judges that he was pardoned and spent the rest of his life a free man, although unable to return home to gaze once more across the Severn Plain.

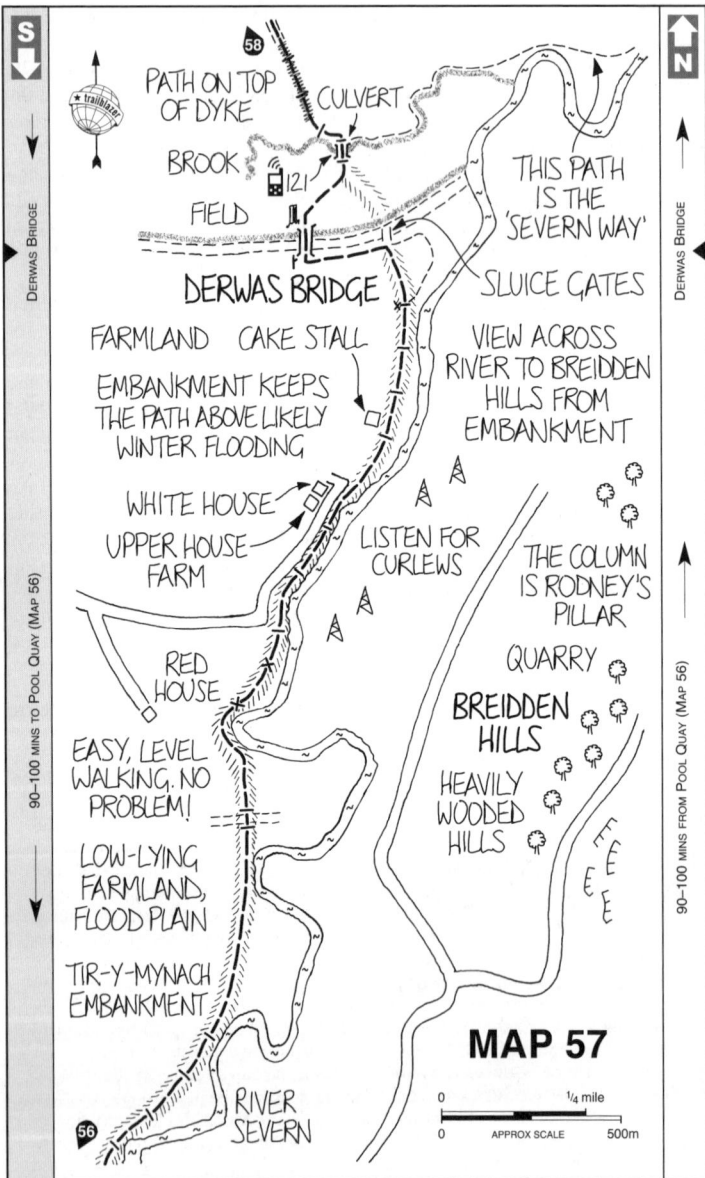

S

N

58

PATH ON TOP OF DYKE

CULVERT

BROOK

121

FIELD

THIS PATH IS THE 'SEVERN WAY'

DERWAS BRIDGE

DERWAS BRIDGE

DERWAS BRIDGE

SLUICE GATES

FARMLAND   CAKE STALL

VIEW ACROSS RIVER TO BREIDDEN HILLS FROM EMBANKMENT

EMBANKMENT KEEPS THE PATH ABOVE LIKELY WINTER FLOODING

WHITE HOUSE

UPPER HOUSE FARM

LISTEN FOR CURLEWS

THE COLUMN IS RODNEY'S PILLAR

QUARRY

RED HOUSE

BREIDDEN HILLS

EASY, LEVEL WALKING. NO PROBLEM!

HEAVILY WOODED HILLS

LOW-LYING FARMLAND, FLOOD PLAIN

TIR-Y-MYNACH EMBANKMENT

MAP 57

56

RIVER SEVERN

0 .... 1/4 mile

0 .... 500m

APPROX SCALE

ROUTE GUIDE & MAPS

90–100 MINS to POOL QUAY (MAP 56)

90–100 MINS from POOL QUAY (MAP 56)

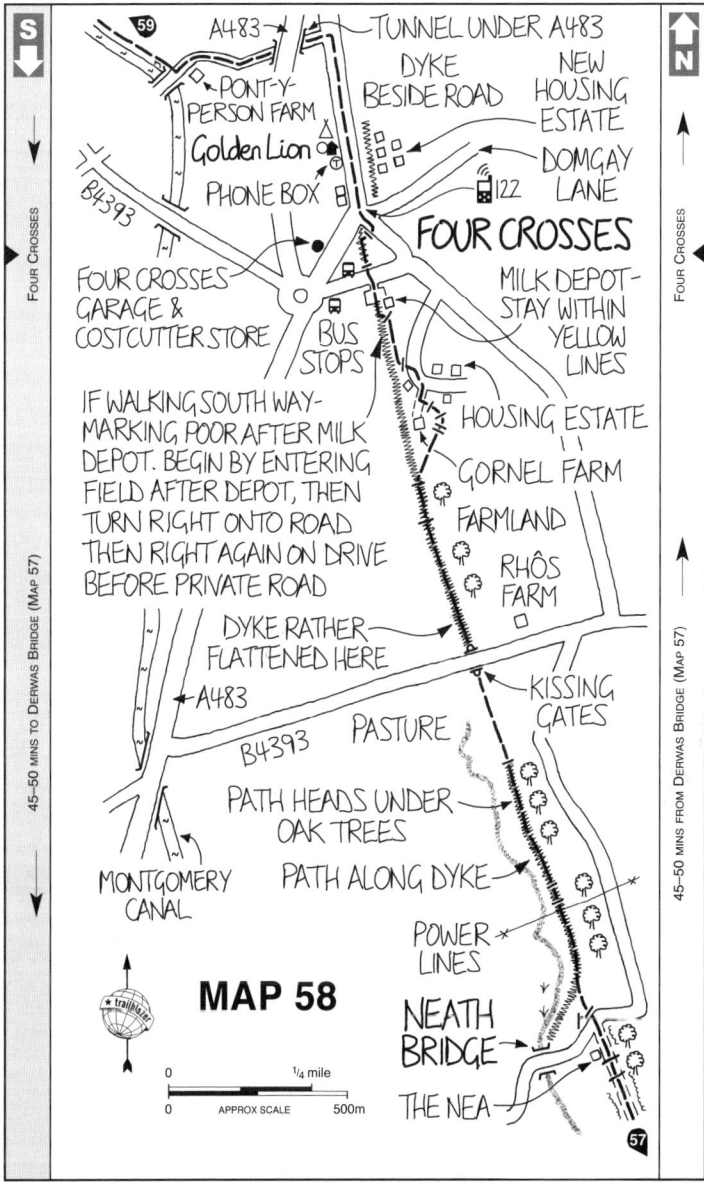

MAP 58

FOUR CROSSES   Map 58, p189

Costcutter **supermarket** (daily 7.30am-10pm) is in Four Crosses Garage.

The village is a stop on Tanat Valley's No 74 **bus** route. It is also on their T12 service (Machynlleth to Wrexham), which is shared with Lloyds Coaches; see the public transport map and table, pp49-53.

The path briefly follows the quiet road right outside the door of *The Golden Lion* (☎ 01691-830295, 🖥 goldenlion.org.uk;

bar Mon-Sat 6.30-10pm, Sun 7-10pm). **B&B** (5T/3D/1Tr, all en suite; WI-FI) costs from £37.50pp (£52 sgl occ; three sharing £115) and you can **camp** for £6pp (there are toilet/shower facilities). The welcome is friendly and **pub meals** (Mon-Sat 7-8pm, Sun 7-8pm) are available in the bar. The pub is a Grade II listed building and over 250 years old. Luggage transfers are available; contact them for details.

LLANYMYNECH   Map 59

The small town of Llanymynech is no beauty spot and has traffic thundering through day and night. Despite this, many walkers break their journey here: it's a convenient place to call a halt, though Four Crosses (see above) could be a better choice.

Tanat Valley Coaches run several **buses** through the town: the T12 service (which is shared with Lloyds Coaches) stops here en route between Machynlleth and Wrexham. Tanat Valley's No 72 (Oswestry to Llanfyllin) and their No 74 (Llanfyllin to Shrewsbury) also call here. For details see the public transport map and table, pp49-53.

Llanymynech Village Shop (Mon-Fri 7am-9pm, Sat 8am-9pm, Sun 8am-4pm) incorporates the **post office**.

There are several pubs to choose from but the best is *Bradford Arms Hotel* (☎ 01691-830582, 🖥 bradfordarmshotel.co.uk; bar daily 11.30am-3pm & 5-11pm, occasionally open all day at the weekend), where **B&B** (1T/3D/one suite with 3D sleeping up to six people, all en suite; ☞; 🐾; WI-FI; Ⓛ) in modern but warmly decorated rooms costs £35-40pp (sgl occ from £40, £90 for the suite room). In the bar or dining room a comprehensive menu, including that pub favourite steak & kidney pudding (£8.95), is on offer (**food** served daily 11.30am-2pm & 5.30-9pm); they also do takeaway meals. Luggage transfer is available if requested in advance.

There's accommodation at the traditional *Cross Keys Hotel* (☎ 01691-831585, 🖥 crosskeyshotel.info; 2T share facilities/ 2D/2T, all en suite; WI-FI; 🐾), too, from £35pp (sgl occ £40-60). The **food** (daily noon-2pm & 5-8pm) is great value (mains all £8.95). Pool and darts can be played in the bar (open daily noon-11pm, 10pm on Sunday).

The third pub in the village, *The Dolphin* (☎ 01691-839672, 🖥 phininn.co.uk; 1T/1D/1Tr, all en suite; ☞; WI-FI; Ⓛ) charges from £35pp (sgl occ £40). Once again food is served (Tue-Sat 6-8.30pm, Thur-Sat noon-2pm), but not on a Sunday or Monday.

A mile or so south of the village on the A483 towards Four Crosses is *Ty-coch* (☎ 01691-830361; 1T/1D, both en suite; WI-FI; Ⓛ), pronounced 'Tee Coe', a modern bungalow charging from £35pp (sgl occ from £40). They also offer a lift to the pub for an evening meal.

In addition to the pubs above, there is a café, *The Village Pantry* (Mon-Fri 8am-2pm, Sat 9am-2pm), opposite The Dolphin, and a curry house, *Bengal Spices* (☎ 01691-830170; daily 5-11pm), next door to the village store, where standard Indian fare is available, including takeaways.

There is also a Chinese takeaway, *Golden Valley* (☎ 01691-830426; Wed-Mon 5-11pm), and *Sam's Kebab & Pizza* (☎ 01691-830242; Sun-Thur 4-11pm, Fri & Sat 4pm-midnight).

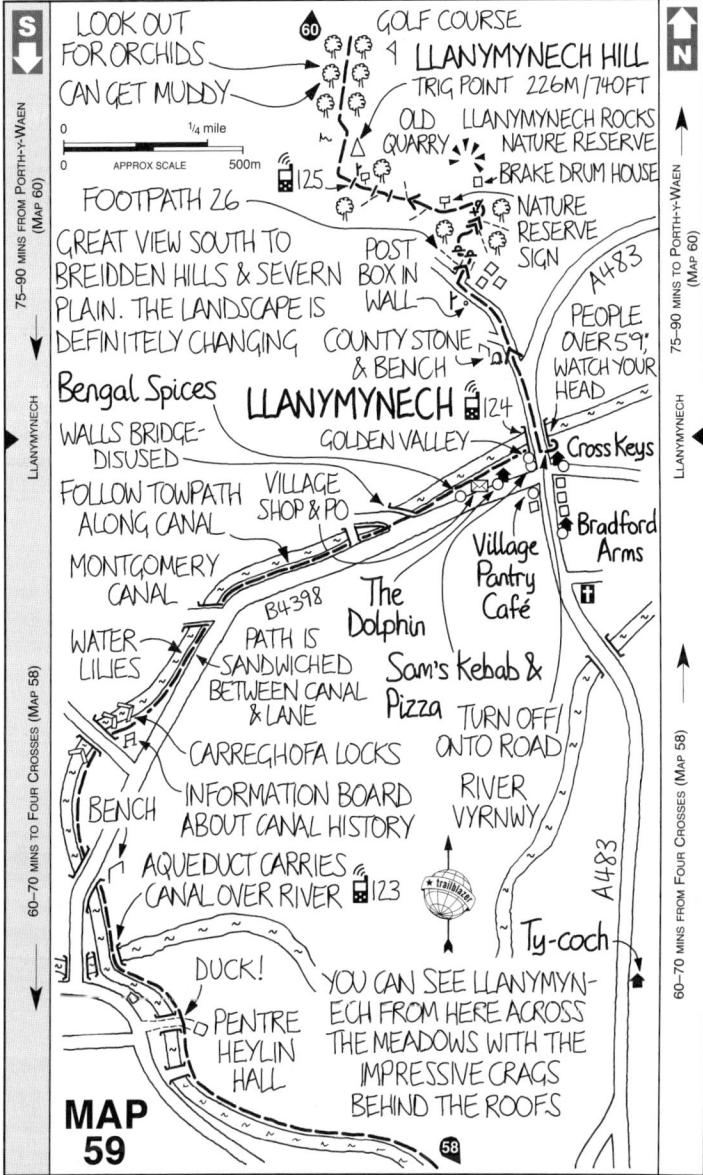

S ↓

N ↑

LLANYMYNECH ▶

LLANYMYNECH

ROUTE GUIDE & MAPS

LOOK OUT FOR ORCHIDS

CAN GET MUDDY

GOLF COURSE

60

LLANYMYNECH HILL

TRIG POINT 226M/740FT

OLD QUARRY

LLANYMYNECH ROCKS NATURE RESERVE

BRAKE DRUM HOUSE

125

NATURE RESERVE SIGN

FOOTPATH 26

GREAT VIEW SOUTH TO BREIDDEN HILLS & SEVERN PLAIN. THE LANDSCAPE IS DEFINITELY CHANGING

POST BOX IN WALL

COUNTY STONE & BENCH

A483

PEOPLE OVER 59, WATCH YOUR HEAD

Bengal Spices

LLANYMYNECH 124

GOLDEN VALLEY

Cross Keys

WALLS BRIDGE- DISUSED

FOLLOW TOWPATH ALONG CANAL

VILLAGE SHOP & PO

Bradford Arms

MONTGOMERY CANAL

B4398

The Dolphin

Village Pantry Café

WATER LILIES

PATH IS SANDWICHED BETWEEN CANAL & LANE

Sam's Kebab & Pizza

TURN OFF ONTO ROAD

CARREGHOFA LOCKS

RIVER VYRNWY

A483

BENCH

INFORMATION BOARD ABOUT CANAL HISTORY

AQUEDUCT CARRIES CANAL OVER RIVER 123

★ trailblazer

Ty-coch

DUCK!

PENTRE HEYLIN HALL

YOU CAN SEE LLANYMYN- ECH FROM HERE ACROSS THE MEADOWS WITH THE IMPRESSIVE CRAGS BEHIND THE ROOFS

MAP 59

58

0   ¼ mile
0   APPROX SCALE   500m

S ⬇ FROM PRESTATYN **LLANYMYNECH TO BUTTINGTON (FOR WELSHPOOL) MAPS 59-55 (MAPS 54-54a)**

[Route section begins on Map 59, p191] This stretch of **10½ miles** (**17km**, **4hrs-4hrs 40mins** plus a 20-30-minute walk each way to/from Welshpool) is dead flat and straightforward, starting along the towpath of **Montgomery Canal**, abandoned in 1944. An air of neglect pervades the early stages, before the attractively restored **Carreghofa Locks**, but the lack of human intervention has its upside, for swans nest along this stretch. The path leaves the canal and passes through the underpass beneath the A483 to enter **Four Crosses** (Map 58).

After Four Crosses the trail takes to the fields. From **Gornel Farm** you will again find yourself keeping company with the Dyke, which in this area doubles as a flood-defence system to prevent damage from errant streams.

The path then goes along the top of the **Tir-y-mynach Embankment** (Map 57) for four miles (6km), following the course of the River Severn to Pool Quay. Look out for the house offering cake and possibly tea. The walking is across farmland, fairly ordinary but you can take pleasure from the swirling eddies of the Severn as it twists and turns its way to the sea. The river flows northwards at this stage, towards Shrewsbury, before changing course to start on its journey back towards Chepstow, where you'll meet it again at the end of the trail. Occasionally the river floods and the fields are left strewn with driftwood as the waters recede. Each fence has its pile of debris – everything from twigs to whole tree trunks. The going is enlivened by views of the tree-covered **Breidden Hills** (see box p187) to the east and· the birdlife along the river. Listen out for the cry of curlews across the fields.

When you come to the course of the old railway line (Map 56, p186) between Oswestry and Welshpool, now long abandoned, keep a look out for the remains of a bridge over the Severn. The river was at one time navigable as far as Pool Quay and in the early 19th century vessels of up to 30 tons were used to ship goods to Worcester and Gloucester. The weir that made the river navigable was destroyed by floods in 1881.

The trail rejoins the towpath after Pool Quay and you can stay on it as far as **Welshpool** if you intend using the services there or if you are staying at Moors Farm (see p185) in Buttington. If not, the main Offa's Dyke Path leaves the canal after the **cantilever bridge** and follows the busy A483 for a mercifully short distance before crossing into the fields that border the **River Severn**.

From here, the path and the river converge at **Buttington Bridge**. Take care as you cross the bridge – perhaps the hairiest piece of road-walking on the entire trail. *[Next route overview p185]*

N ⬆ FROM CHEPSTOW **LLANYMYNECH TO RACECOURSE COMMON MAPS 59-63**

[Route section begins on Map 59, p191] This **8½-mile** (**14km**) section takes about 4¾ to 5½ hours.

Leaving the canal, you follow the road out of Llanymynech, turning left after the county stone (Map 59) and ascending through woodland to the landmark limestone crags and quarries that give **Llanymynech Rocks** nature reserve its name. The area is notable for butterflies in summer, and for superb views over the Severn Plain to the Breidden Hills at any time. You arrive on the plateau-like summit of **Llanymynech Hill** before a lovely sylvan stroll beside a golf course leads you down to the neat bungalows of **Porth-y-waen** (Map 60). From here you follow the road to **Nant-Mawr**, slowly climb **Moelydd**, from where there are views west to Snowdonia, before descending to **Trefonen** (Map 61): home to Offa's Dyke brewery (see box p24).

Back in the company of the Dyke the stage sees you pass through the **Morda Valle**, pretty **Ty'n-y-Coed**, over the common and through **Racecourse Wood**, and on to a fine leisurely end to the stage at **Racecourse Common (Map 63, p197)**. Don't worry that you might arrive on race day; the course closed in Victorian times and the turf resounds to the thud of horses' hooves no more.   *[Next route overview p198]*

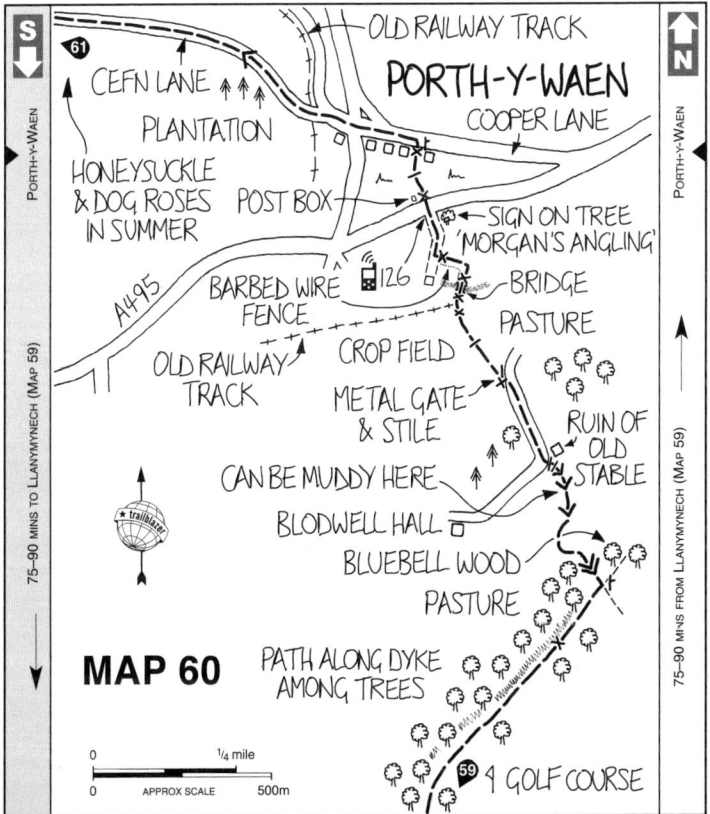

MAP 60

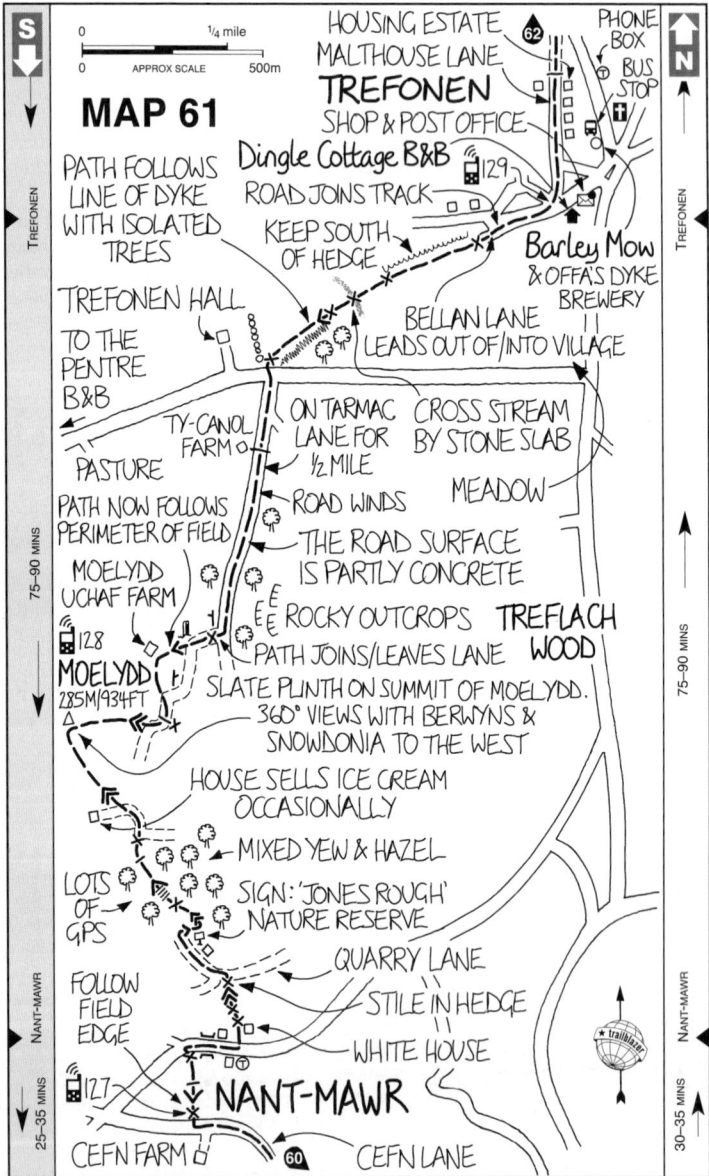

S ↓

0 ¼ mile
APPROX SCALE
0 500m

N ↑

MAP 61

HOUSING ESTATE
MALTHOUSE LANE
TREFONEN
SHOP & POST OFFICE
62
PHONE BOX
BUS STOP

PATH FOLLOWS LINE OF DYKE WITH ISOLATED TREES

Dingle Cottage B&B 📱129
ROAD JOINS TRACK
KEEP SOUTH OF HEDGE

Barley Mow
& OFFA'S DYKE BREWERY

TREFONEN HALL

BELLAN LANE
LEADS OUT OF/INTO VILLAGE

TO THE PENTRE B&B

PASTURE

TY-CANOL FARM

ON TARMAC LANE FOR ½ MILE

CROSS STREAM BY STONE SLAB

MEADOW

PATH NOW FOLLOWS PERIMETER OF FIELD

ROAD WINDS

THE ROAD SURFACE IS PARTLY CONCRETE

MOELYDD UCHAF FARM

📱128

ROCKY OUTCROPS

TREFLACH WOOD

MOELYDD
285M/934FT

PATH JOINS/LEAVES LANE

SLATE PLINTH ON SUMMIT OF MOELYDD. 360° VIEWS WITH BERWYNS & SNOWDONIA TO THE WEST

HOUSE SELLS ICE CREAM OCCASIONALLY

MIXED YEW & HAZEL

LOTS OF GPS

SIGN: 'JONES ROUGH' NATURE RESERVE

QUARRY LANE

STILE IN HEDGE

FOLLOW FIELD EDGE

WHITE HOUSE

📱127

NANT-MAWR

CEFN FARM

60

CEFN LANE

★ trailblazer

□ **The Dyke or not the Dyke?**
Whatever was thought in the past, all who have studied the Dyke in recent years would agree that it was built by a Mercian king (almost certainly Offa) in the 8th century AD as a defensive wall along the 60 miles or so of the border between Mercia and the Welsh kingdom of Powys.

It is also generally agreed now that any other defensive earthworks, whether dykes or hill forts, near the border but not on the direct line of Offa's Dyke, were separate fortifications built in the Dark Ages but not at the same time as the Dyke. For instance, all agree that Wat's Dyke, the earthwork nearest in length and scale to Offa's Dyke and running a few miles to the east of it along the northern stretch of the border, was built rather earlier in the 8th century. In the past, however, Wat's Dyke was usually seen as the continuation of Offa's Dyke, even though as long ago as 1730 Welshman William Williams had argued that the two dykes were distinctly separate fortifications built at different times. **Colin Vickerman**

TREFONEN   Map 61
This neat little settlement has a **shop** (Mon-Fri 8am-7pm, Sat 8.30am-7pm, Sun 9am-2pm), which incorporates the **post office**.

Tanat Valley's No 79A **bus** service stops here (see public transport map and table pp49-53). Arriva's No 54 bus service also calls here but it only operates 1/day in each direction during term-time.

The only pub is *Barley Mow Inn* ☎ 01691-656889; **food** served Tue-Fri 5-9pm, Sat noon-3pm & 5-9pm, Sun noon-3pm), which is right next door to **Offa's Dyke Brewery** (see box p24) and serves several of their beers including the light Barley Gold and the Grim Reaper porter. The food is great too; overall, one of the nicer places near the path.

B&B-wise, on the path is *Dingle Cottage* (☎ 01691-658032, 🖳 dinglecot

tage.co.uk; 1D or T, en suite; ①; WI-FI; £40pp, sgl occ £50), Bellan Lane, where, should the pub not be serving food, an evening meal can be provided (£17 for two courses).

Half a mile west from the path is *The Pentre* (☎ 01691-653952, 🖳 thepentre.com; 1T/1D/1Tr, all en suite; ➥; WI-FI; 🐾 but see note below), a lovely old farmhouse where **B&B** costs from £40pp (sgl occ £50). The twin room is self-contained and has its own basic kitchen which is the only place where visiting dogs are allowed to stay. At weekends in the summer bookings must be for a minimum of two nights. Evening meals are available (two/three courses £22/25) if booked at least 48 hours in advance. Also if arranged in advance they are happy to pick walkers up from the path.

S ⬇ FROM PRESTATYN RACECOURSE COMMON TO LLANYMYNECH
MAPS 63-59

[*Route section begins on Map 63, p197*] This **8½-mile (14km)** section takes about **4½hrs-5hrs 25mins**. The Old Racecourse may inspire you to set off like a thoroughbred, and indeed the walking over the common and through **Racecourse Wood** to **Morda Valley** and **Ty'n-y-Coed** is a fine start to this stage. The Dyke is much in evidence with opportunities for walking on the very top of the earthwork in places until you come to **Trefonen** (Map 61) and **Nant-Mawr**, small but expanding villages offering little in the way of interest.

There is more than enough road walking before the stiff climb from the neat bungalows of **Porth-y-waen** (Map 60) onto the plateau-like summit of

(cont'd on p198)

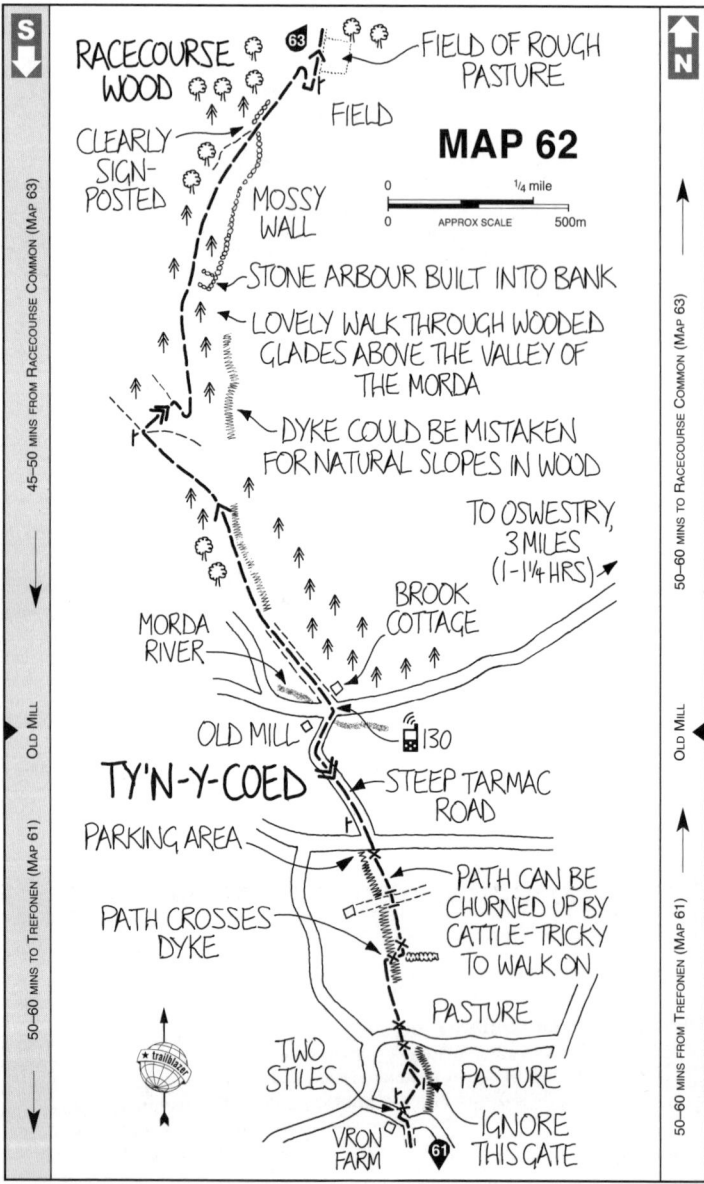

ROUTE GUIDE & MAPS

45–50 MINS FROM RACECOURSE COMMON (MAP 63)

OLD MILL

50–60 MINS TO TREFONEN (MAP 61)

50–60 MINS TO RACECOURSE COMMON (MAP 63)

OLD MILL

50–60 MINS FROM TREFONEN (MAP 61)

S

N

RACECOURSE WOOD

FIELD OF ROUGH PASTURE

63

FIELD

CLEARLY SIGN-POSTED

MAP 62

0 — 1/4 mile
0 — APPROX SCALE — 500m

MOSSY WALL

STONE ARBOUR BUILT INTO BANK

LOVELY WALK THROUGH WOODED GLADES ABOVE THE VALLEY OF THE MORDA

DYKE COULD BE MISTAKEN FOR NATURAL SLOPES IN WOOD

TO OSWESTRY, 3 MILES (1–1¼ HRS)

BROOK COTTAGE

MORDA RIVER

OLD MILL

130

TY'N-Y-COED

STEEP TARMAC ROAD

PARKING AREA

PATH CAN BE CHURNED UP BY CATTLE-TRICKY TO WALK ON

PATH CROSSES DYKE

PASTURE

PASTURE

TWO STILES

IGNORE THIS GATE

VRON FARM

61

trailblazer

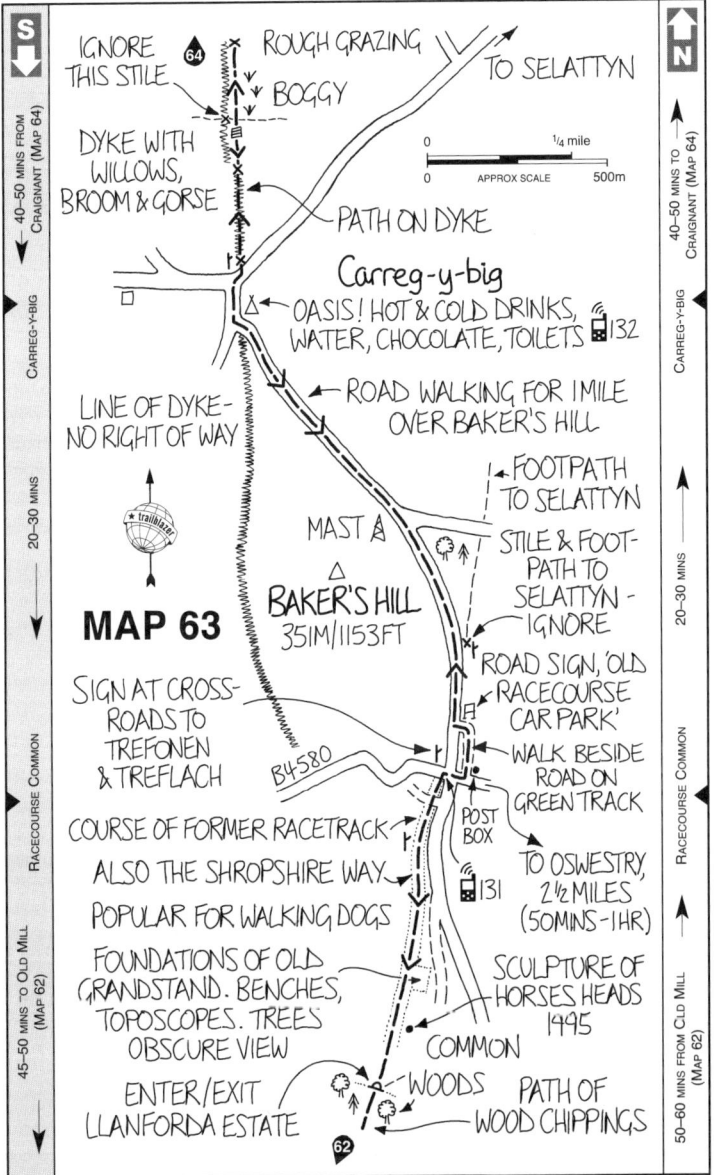

IGNORE THIS STILE

ROUGH GRAZING

TO SELATTYN

BOGGY

DYKE WITH WILLOWS, BROOM & GORSE

PATH ON DYKE

Carreg-y-big

OASIS! HOT & COLD DRINKS, WATER, CHOCOLATE, TOILETS 📶132

ROAD WALKING FOR 1 MILE OVER BAKER'S HILL

LINE OF DYKE - NO RIGHT OF WAY

FOOTPATH TO SELATTYN

MAST

STILE & FOOT- PATH TO SELATTYN - IGNORE

BAKER'S HILL 351M/1153FT

MAP 63

ROAD SIGN, 'OLD RACECOURSE CAR PARK'

SIGN AT CROSS- ROADS TO TREFONEN & TREFLACH

WALK BESIDE ROAD ON GREEN TRACK

B4580

POST BOX

COURSE OF FORMER RACETRACK

ALSO THE SHROPSHIRE WAY.

POPULAR FOR WALKING DOGS

📶131

TO OSWESTRY, 2½ MILES (50MINS-1HR)

FOUNDATIONS OF OLD GRANDSTAND. BENCHES, TOPOSCOPES. TREES OBSCURE VIEW

SCULPTURE OF HORSES HEADS 1995

COMMON

WOODS

PATH OF WOOD CHIPPINGS

ENTER/EXIT LLANFORDA ESTATE

0 ¼ mile
0 APPROX SCALE 500m

S

N

40-50 MINS FROM CRAIGNANT (MAP 64)

CARREG-Y-BIG

20-30 MINS

RACECOURSE COMMON

45-50 MINS TO OLD MILL (MAP 62)

40-50 MINS TO CRAIGNANT (MAP 64)

CARREG-Y-BIG

20-30 MINS

RACECOURSE COMMON

50-60 MINS FROM OLD MILL (MAP 62)

ROUTE GUIDE & MAPS

(*cont'd from p195*) **Llanymynech Hill** (Map 59) but it brings its own rewards. A lovely sylvan stroll beside the golf course precedes the leafy glades of **Llanymynech Rocks** nature reserve, which descends through woodland to the landmark limestone crags and quarries that give the reserve its name. The area is notable for butterflies in summer, and for superb views over the Severn Plain to the Breidden Hills at any time. Here, you are on the very border between England and Wales. This stage ends in **Llanymynech (Map 59, p191)**.

[*Next route overview p192*]

[*Next route overview p192*]

N↑ FROM CHEPSTOW **RACECOURSE COMMON TO CASTLE MILL**
MAPS 63-65

[*Route section begins on Map 63, p197*] This **4½-mile (7km, 1hr 50mins-2hrs 20mins)** stage is your last with the Dyke for company.

The path initially follows the road over **Baker's Hill** (Map 63), before climbing over the shoulder of **Selattyn Hill**, and descending to **Craignant** (Map 64), a secretive little settlement in the depths of the countryside. From here the path follows the line of **Offa's Dyke** one last time, sometimes beside it, sometimes on the very top itself, descending steeply to Castle Mill. As it does so you are treated to spectacular views of **Chirk Castle** (Map 65; see box p201), and the knowledge that you have walked the length of this once great rampart, if not yet the length of the path which bears its name.

[*Next route overview p201*]

[*Next route overview p201*]

AROUND BAKER'S HILL
Map 63, p197

North of Baker's Hill and right on the trail is the relaxed equestrian centre of *Carreg-y-big* (☎ 01691-654754, 🖳 carreg-y-big-farm.co.uk) where you can **camp** for £8pp.

Breakfast (£6) for campers is available if requested in advance. They also have a **facility centre** with vending machines (hot and cold drinks, crisps, chocolate), a sitting area and toilets.

OSWESTRY
off Map 63, p197

Since accommodation near the path in the Baker's Hill area is now rather limited, you may need to venture 2½ miles east to the market town of Oswestry; if that sounds too far to walk contact Oswestry Taxis (☎ 01691-658658) for a lift.

For general information on Oswestry see 🖳 oswestry-welshborders.org.uk.

B&B at *Chilton House* (☎ 01691-656616, ☎ 07813-149741, 🖳 chiltonhouse oswestry.co; 1D/2D or T, all en suite; ☞; WI-FI; Ⓛ) costs £42.50-50pp (sgl occ £65-85). If arranged in advance they are happy to do an evening meal (from £20) and will also pick up and drop off. Another option on Ferrers Rd is *Laurels Guest House* (☎ 01691-655395, 🖳 laurelsguesthouseoswes try.co.uk; 1T/2D, all en suite; WI-FI; Ⓛ). They charge from £44pp (sgl occ £66) and are happy for guests to bring food in for supper and eat it in their dining room.

There is a wide range of eating options in central Oswestry but for craft beers, gins, locally made pork pies and scotch eggs (from £2.80), ploughman's lunches and cheeseboards (£3-7) – as well as a big welcome for dogs – go to *The Bailey Head* (☎ 01691-570418, 🖳 baileyhead.co.uk; food served daily noon till 9pm; WI-FI; 🐾).

For upmarket dining there's *Sebastians* (☎ 01691-655444, 🖳 sebas-tians-hotel.com). It's open Wed-Sat 6.30-9pm and reservations are required; expect to pay £47.50 for five courses.

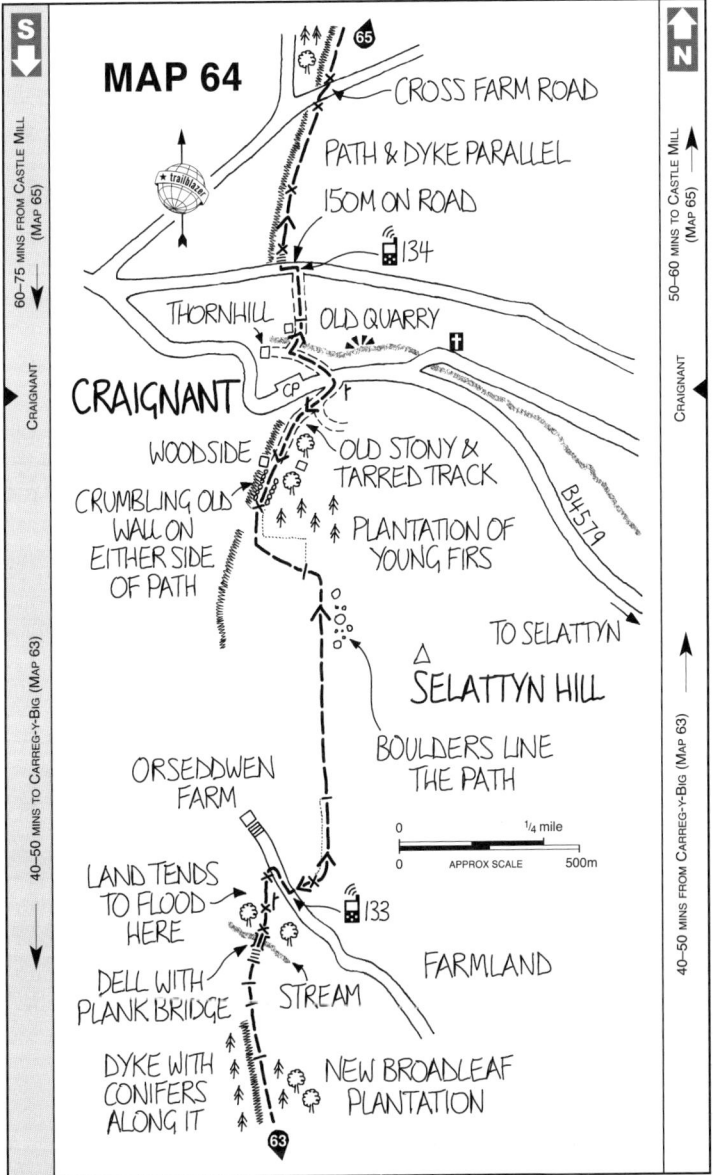

MAP 64

60–75 MINS FROM CASTLE MILL (MAP 65)

CRAIGNANT

40–50 MINS TO CARREG-Y-BIG (MAP 63)

50–60 MINS TO CASTLE MILL (MAP 65)

CRAIGNANT

40–50 MINS FROM CARREG-Y-BIG (MAP 63)

ROUTE GUIDE & MAPS

trailblazer

65

CROSS FARM ROAD

PATH & DYKE PARALLEL

150M ON ROAD

134

THORNHILL   OLD QUARRY

CRAIGNANT   CP

WOODSIDE   OLD STONY &
                TARRED TRACK

CRUMBLING OLD
WALL ON
EITHER SIDE
OF PATH

PLANTATION OF
YOUNG FIRS

B4579

TO SELATTYN

SELATTYN HILL

BOULDERS LINE
THE PATH

ORSEDDWEN
FARM

0   ¼ mile

0   APPROX SCALE   500m

LAND TENDS
TO FLOOD
HERE

133

DELL WITH
PLANK BRIDGE   STREAM

FARMLAND

DYKE WITH
CONIFERS
ALONG IT

NEW BROADLEAF
PLANTATION

63

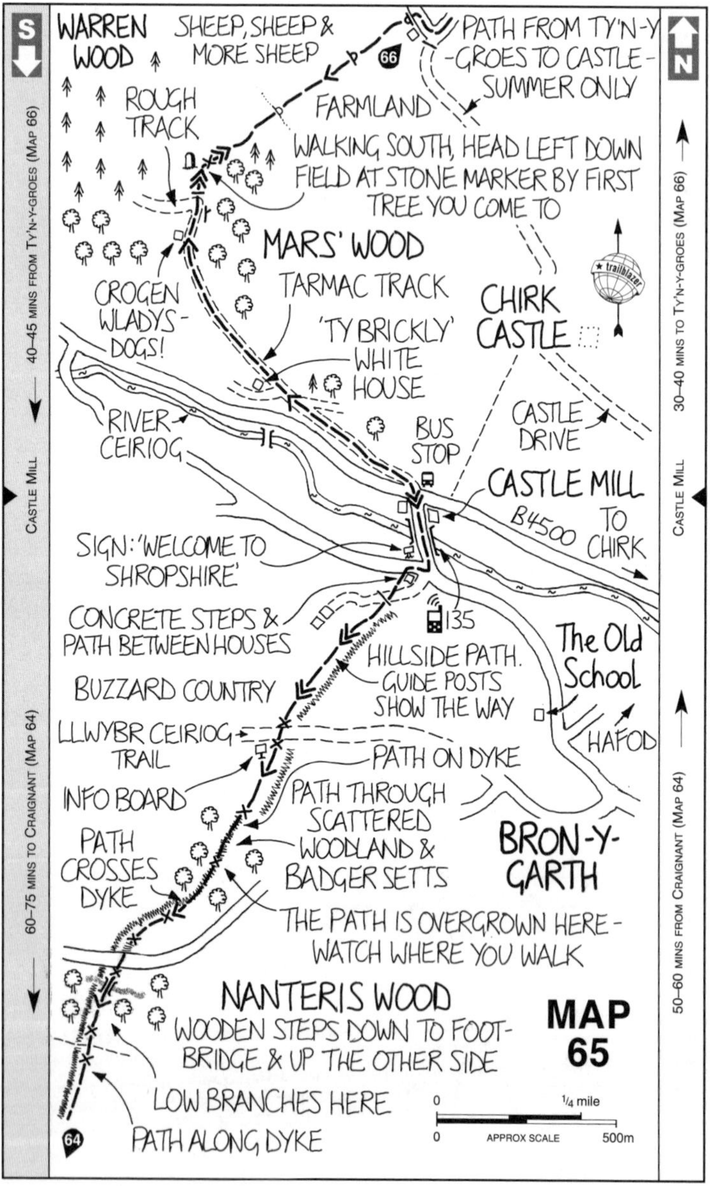

ROUTE GUIDE & MAPS

40–45 MINS FROM TY'N-Y-GROES (MAP 66)

CASTLE MILL

60–75 MINS TO CRAIGNANT (MAP 64)

30–40 MINS TO TY'N-Y-GROES (MAP 66)

CASTLE MILL

50–60 MINS FROM CRAIGNANT (MAP 64)

S

N

WARREN WOOD

SHEEP, SHEEP & MORE SHEEP

PATH FROM TY'N-Y -GROES TO CASTLE- SUMMER ONLY

66

ROUGH TRACK

FARMLAND

WALKING SOUTH, HEAD LEFT DOWN FIELD AT STONE MARKER BY FIRST TREE YOU COME TO

MARS' WOOD

TARMAC TRACK

CHIRK CASTLE

★ trailblazer

CROGEN WLADYS- DOGS!

'TY BRICKLY' WHITE HOUSE

RIVER CEIRIOG

BUS STOP

CASTLE DRIVE

CASTLE MILL

B4500 TO CHIRK

SIGN: 'WELCOME TO SHROPSHIRE'

135

The Old School

CONCRETE STEPS & PATH BETWEEN HOUSES

HILLSIDE PATH. GUIDE POSTS SHOW THE WAY

BUZZARD COUNTRY

HAFOD

LLWYBR CEIRIOG TRAIL

PATH ON DYKE

INFO BOARD

PATH THROUGH SCATTERED WOODLAND & BADGER SETTS

BRON-Y- GARTH

PATH CROSSES DYKE

THE PATH IS OVERGROWN HERE – WATCH WHERE YOU WALK

NANTERIS WOOD

WOODEN STEPS DOWN TO FOOT- BRIDGE & UP THE OTHER SIDE

LOW BRANCHES HERE

PATH ALONG DYKE

64

MAP 65

0   1/4 mile
0   APPROX SCALE   500m

BRON-Y-GARTH   Map 65, p200

Currently still open, there's **camping** at *The Old School* (☎ 01691-772546), some 20 minutes' walk south-east of the village of **Castle Mill**, for £4pp plus £1 for the use of the shower or bath. Booking is requested and you'll need to have food with you. Note that after September 2019 they may close.

Follow the lane almost opposite the Old School (see Map 65) to reach *Wren Cottage at Hafod* (☎ 01691-778750, 🖥 sueefoster@googlemail.com; 1T en suite; WI-FI; ⓛ; Apr-end Oct). B&B costs from £36pp). If requested in advance an evening meal (£15) is also available.

S ▼ FROM PRESTATYN CASTLE MILL TO RACECOURSE COMMON
MAPS 65-63

[*Route section begins on Map 65, p200*] For most of the next **4½ miles (7km, 2hrs-2hrs 35mins)** you follow the line of **Offa's Dyke** for the first time, sometimes beside it, sometimes on the very top itself, as it climbs steeply away from Castle Mill. The path drops down to **Craignant** (Map 64), a secretive little settlement in the depths of the countryside, and then climbs over the shoulder of **Selattyn Hill**. At the foot of **Baker's Hill** (Map 63) the Dyke leaves you and you are forced to follow the tarmac, a tedious plod, to the crossroads at **Racecourse Common (Map 63, 197)**. Don't worry that you might arrive on race day; the course closed in Victorian times and the turf resounds to the thud of horses' hooves no more.   [*Next route overview p195*]

N ▲ FROM CHEPSTOW CASTLE MILL TO DINAS BRAN (& LLANGOLLEN)
MAPS 65-69

[*Route section begins on Map 65, p200*] This **8½-mile (14km)** section takes about **3hrs 50mins-4½ hrs**. The stage begins by leaving the delightful River Ceiriog, climbing up away from the valley through mixed woodland and farmland and passing the 'garden gate' of **Chirk Castle** (see box below); which allows summertime access to the grounds (Apr-Sep). You join the road here at **Ty'n-y-groes** (Map 66) and although you may no longer be able to walk on the Dyke it remains a companion, skulking amongst a line of trees to your east; until you reach the A5 that is, when the Dyke finally disappears for good.

At **Irish Bridge** (Map 67; presumably built by Irish navvies), where the B5605 crosses the canal, you join the **Llangollen Canal**, which is followed to

---

❏ **Chirk Castle**   Map 65, p200

Chirk Castle (☎ 01691-777701, 🖥 nationaltrust.org.uk/chirk; Mar-Oct castle approx 10am-6pm, estate approx 7am-7pm; visit website for winter opening times; entry £12.60, National Trust members free) was built around 1300 by Roger Mortimer and has been lived in by the Myddleton family since 1595. The medieval tower and dungeon stand alongside state rooms dating from the 18th century and a servants' hall where the tables were so arranged that the most important servants sat nearest to the fire. There is also a bedroom in which King Charles I was said to have slept when visiting the castle in 1645. The gardens are delightful with their topiary hedges and views to the surrounding countryside.

the village of **Froncysyllte** (Map 67). Offa's Dyke Path officially follows the road to the old bridge over the River Dee and heads (briefly) towards the village of **Trevor**. Far more rewarding, though, is the alternative route across Telford's extraordinary achievement, **Pontcysyllte Aqueduct** (Map 68; see box p204), one of the highlights of the entire walk – though it's not for anyone who suffers from vertigo.

The two paths meet again on the canal towpath before ascending together through **Trevor Hall Wood** (Map 68), a damp, dark domain where you imagine there must be dragons or at least hobbits, and from the darkness of which you arrive on **Panorama Walk**.

Prospect Garden Tea Room (☎ 01978-821602; Wed-Fri noon-5pm, Sat, Sun & bank holidays 10.30am-5.30pm), is about half a mile from Offa's Dyke Path and is an option for a stop should you not wish to visit Llangollen.

Continuing on, the road keeps company with limestone crags and screes; **Castell Dinas Bran** (Map 69, p206; see box p212) and **Trefor Rocks** offering magnificent views ahead until you arrive at the footpath to the castle and have the option of a descent to **Llangollen (Map 69, p206)**.

ROUTE GUIDE & MAPS

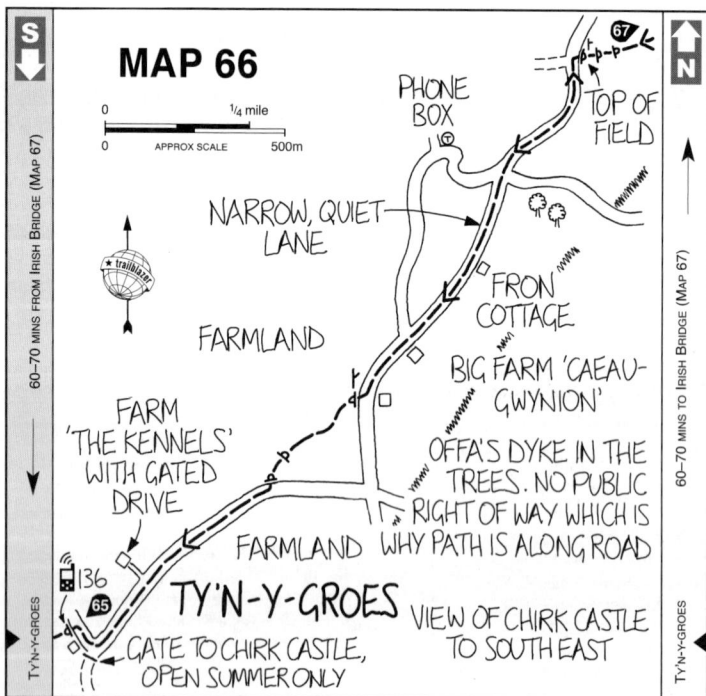

MAP 66

0 .... 1/4 mile
0 ...... APPROX SCALE 500m

★ trailblazer

60–70 MINS FROM IRISH BRIDGE (MAP 67)

PHONE BOX

TOP OF FIELD

67

NARROW, QUIET LANE

FRON COTTAGE

FARMLAND

BIG FARM 'CAEAU-GWYNION'

OFFA'S DYKE IN THE TREES. NO PUBLIC RIGHT OF WAY WHICH IS WHY PATH IS ALONG ROAD

FARM 'THE KENNELS' WITH GATED DRIVE

FARMLAND

136

65

TY'N-Y-GROES

VIEW OF CHIRK CASTLE TO SOUTH EAST

GATE TO CHIRK CASTLE, OPEN SUMMER ONLY

60–70 MINS TO IRISH BRIDGE (MAP 67)

TY'N-Y-GROES

TY'N-Y-GROES

Campers, not wishing to leave the trail, can pitch a tent a little further on at *Tan Y Castell Farm* (Map 69; ☎ 01978-861780; 🦮 ; £4); there's a toilet and fresh water for campers but no shower facilities and if you're not carrying food, you'll still need to descend to Llangollen. *[Next route overview p213]*

CHIRK off Map 65, p200

The small town of Chirk, 2 miles (3km) east from Castle Mill along the B4500, has a **railway** station that is on Transport for Wales's Birmingham to Holyhead and Cardiff to Holyhead lines (see box p49).

The Spar (daily 7am-11pm) convenience store, 16 Church St, is also home to the **post office** and an **ATM**.

For Chirk Castle see p201.

Arriva's 2/2A **bus** services call here en route between Wrexham and Oswestry. Chirk is also a stop on Lloyds Coaches/ Tanat Valley's shared T12 service.

Tanat Valley's No 64 (Llangollen to Llanarmon Dyffryn Ceiriog) also passes

through; see public transport map and table, pp49-53.

Castle Bistro Tea Room (☎ 01691-239133, 🖥 castlebistro.co.uk; daily 9am-9pm; WI-FI; 🐕 in courtyard only), 6 Courtyard Terrace, Church St, has food suitable for any time of the day from breakfast (cooked breakfast from £6.95) through to sandwiches and panini (from £5.95), cakes and scones at tea time, and mains from £11.95 including Persian-style chicken curry for £12.95.

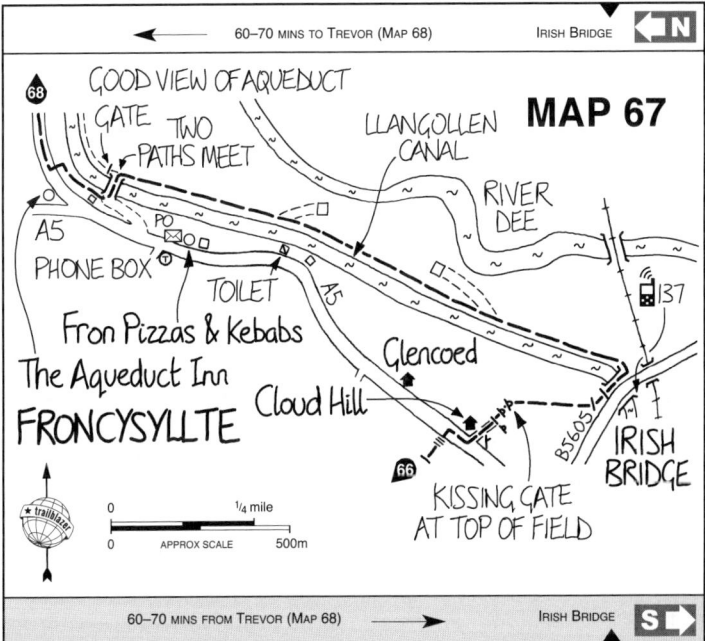

ROUTE GUIDE & MAPS

AROUND IRISH BRIDGE   Map 67

Cloud Hill (☎ 01691-773359, 🖳 chirk .com/cloud.html; 1D/2T, en suite; intermittent WI-FI; Ⓛ) is an architecturally unique **B&B** dating from the 1960s. The property is on the A5 but Offa's Dyke Path forms one of its boundaries. The rate is from £35pp (sgl occ £40); an evening meal (£18) can be arranged if booked in advance. About 200m to the west, just off the A5, *Glencoed* (☎ 01691-778148, 🖳 glen coed.co.uk; 1D/1T, shared facilities and 1D/1S in Canal Cottage with lounge; WI-FI; Ⓛ) is an 18th-century Welsh cottage. B&B costs £35-40pp (sgl occ rates on request).

FRONCYSYLLTE   Map 67, p203

Situated astride the main A5 trunk road, Froncysyllte itself is no place for walkers. Your best bet would be to pass it by on the far side of the canal. On the positive side it does have a rudimentary **shop/post office** (Mon-Thur 9am-1pm & 2-5.30pm, Fri 9am-1pm, Sat 9am-12.30pm), although rudimentary is being kind; provisions-wise, you'll be lucky to get much more than crisps and a chocolate bar. There is a takeaway (*Fron Pizzas & Kebabs* ☎ 01691-777111), and a **pub**, *The Aqueduct Inn* (☎ 01691-777118; 🐾, food daily noon-9pm, earlier on a Sunday) that peers down over the canal and serves real ale, but you'd be better off carrying on along the tow/path to Trevor.

Tanat Valley's No 64 **bus service** between Llangollen and Llanarmon Dyffryn Ceiriog calls here; see pp49-53.

TREVOR   Map 68

You can hire **narrowboats** at Trevor marina (see box below). It takes 1½-2 hours to walk back along the towpath to Llangollen, a lovely circular trail full of variety.

Lloyds Coaches T3 (Wrexham to Barmouth) **bus** service calls here; see public transport map and table, pp49-53.

There's a **toilet** at the marina, and a small **shop** selling snacks and hot and cold drinks. Note that the car park closes at 5pm.

For **food**, there's *Telford Inn* (☎ 01978-820469, 🖳 thetelford.com; WI-FI; 🐾; bar Mon-Fri 11am-10pm, Sat & Sun 11am to late) which caters for folk off the narrowboats who tie up at the marina in preparation for the crossing of the aqueduct. From April to October they generally serve food daily noon-9pm but for the rest of the year daily noon-3pm & 6-9pm.

❏ **Pontcysyllte Aqueduct** (pronounced *Pont-keselty*)   **Map 68**

Built to carry the canal over the River Dee, this is one of the wonders of the walk. Thomas Telford, among the finest engineers of the Industrial Revolution, came up with the idea of containing the water in an iron tank supported by brick arches high above the river. Canal narrowboats are perfectly safe crossing, even though there is nothing between them and a 126ft drop on the opposite side to the towpath. Walkers take the securely fenced towpath, but don't look down if you have a fear of heights! The first stone was laid on 25 July 1795 and the aqueduct took ten years to complete. It's 1007ft long with 18 piers built of local sandstone, expertly cut and dressed by Telford's masons who used a mortar consisting of lime, ox blood and water. The cost of the operation was £47,000 and Telford took pride in knowing that only one life was lost during the construction. Water for the canal is supplied from the River Dee at Berwyn, Telford having constructed the Horseshoe Falls to provide the necessary 12 million gallons needed daily.

If you want to **cross the aqueduct by boat**, Jones the Boats (☎ 01978-824166, 🖳 canaltrip.co.uk) offers a 45-minute trip (Apr-Oct daily 11am, noon, 1pm, 2pm and 3pm) from £7.50pp; booking is advisable if you want to do the trip on a particular day, especially as the boats can sometimes be fully booked by a group.

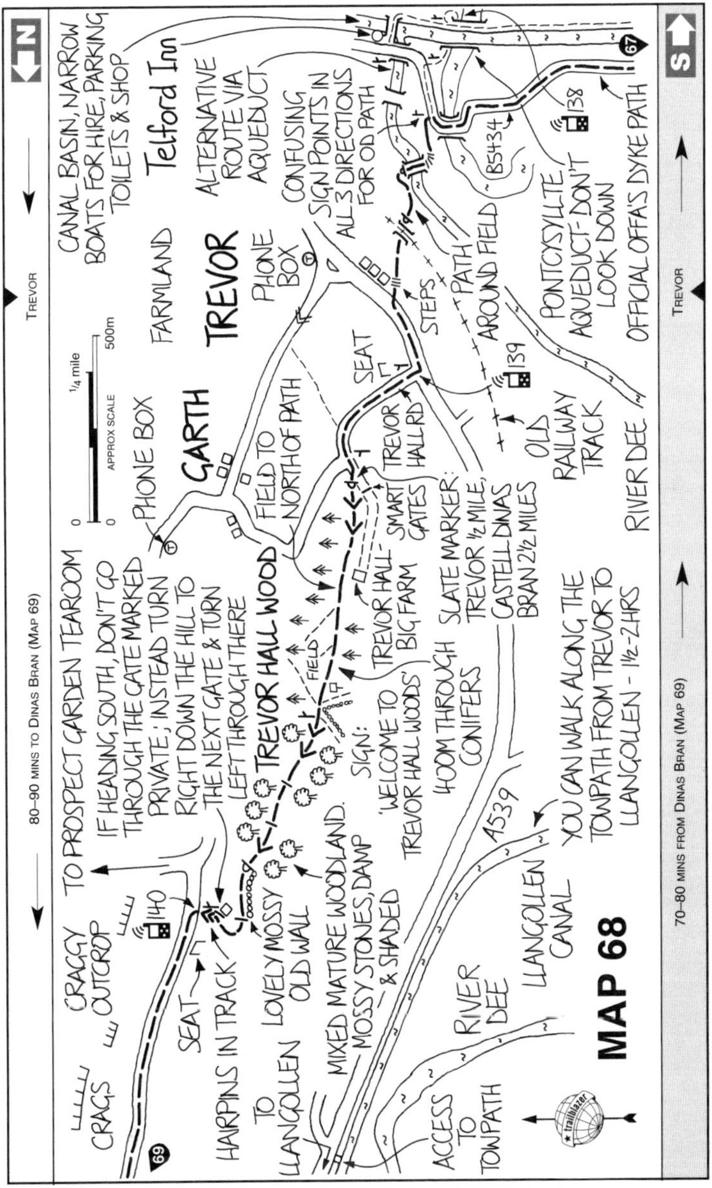
MAP 68
TREVOR
80–90 MINS TO DINAS BRAN (MAP 69)
70–80 MINS FROM DINAS BRAN (MAP 69)
TREVOR
N
S
69
67
CANAL BASIN, NARROW BOATS FOR HIRE, PARKING TOILETS & SHOP
Telford Inn
ALTERNATIVE ROUTE VIA AQUEDUCT
CONFUSING SIGN POINTS IN ALL 3 DIRECTIONS FOR OD PATH
B5434
138
PONTCYSYLLTE AQUEDUCT- DON'T LOOK DOWN
OFFICIAL OFFA'S DYKE PATH
FARMLAND
TREVOR
PHONE BOX
STEPS
PATH AROUND FIELD
SEAT
139
APPROX SCALE
1/4 mile
500m
GARTH
PHONE BOX
FIELD TO NORTH OF PATH
TREVOR HALL RD
SMART GATES
SLATE MARKER: TREVOR ½ MILE, CASTELL DINAS BRAN 2½ MILES
OLD RAILWAY TRACK
RIVER DEE
TO PROSPECT GARDEN TEAROOM
IF HEADING SOUTH, DON'T GO THROUGH THE GATE MARKED PRIVATE; INSTEAD TURN RIGHT DOWN THE HILL TO THE NEXT GATE & TURN LEFT THROUGH THERE
TREVOR HALL WOOD
FIELD
TREVOR HALL BIG FARM
SIGN: 'WELCOME TO TREVOR HALL WOODS'
400M THROUGH CONIFERS
A539
YOU CAN WALK ALONG THE TOWPATH FROM TREVOR TO LLANGOLLEN - 1½-2HRS
CRAGGY OUTCROP
140
SEAT
HAIRPINS IN TRACK
LOVELY MOSSY OLD WALL
MIXED MATURE WOODLAND. MOSSY STONES, DAMP & SHADED
TO LLANGOLLEN
CRAGS
LLANGOLLEN CANAL
RIVER DEE
ACCESS TO TOWPATH
trailblazer

ROUTE GUIDE & MAPS

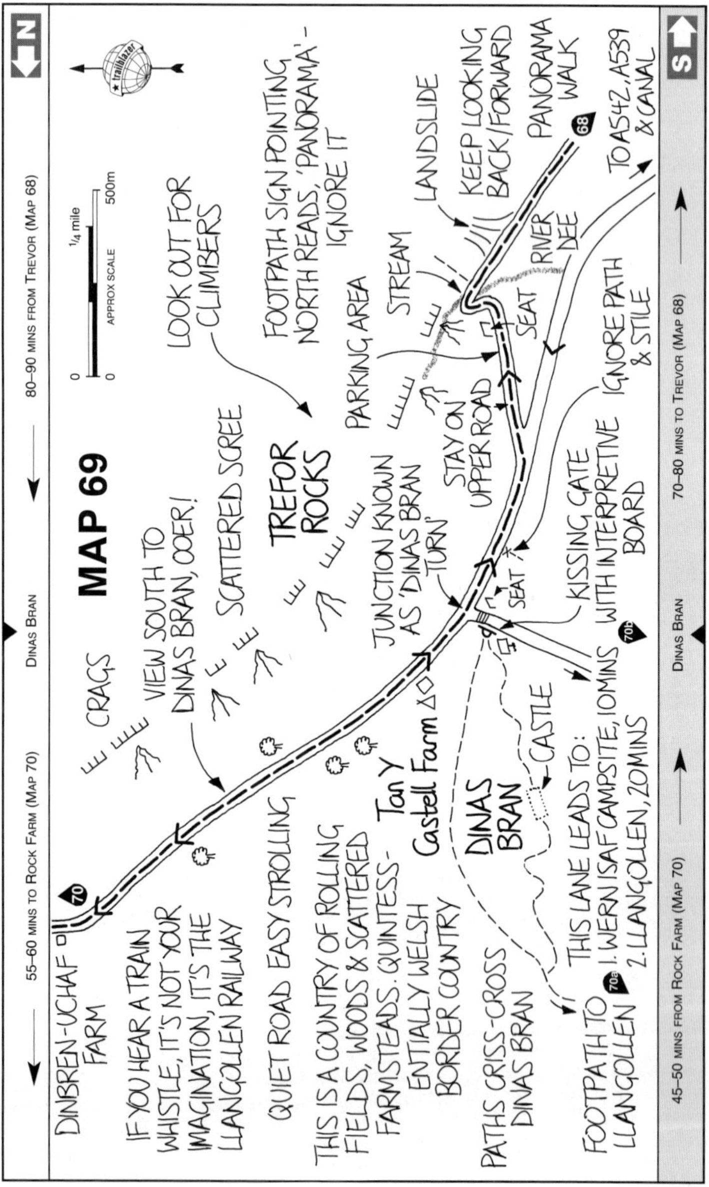

ROUTE GUIDE & MAPS

N

S

80–90 MINS FROM TREVOR (MAP 68)

DINAS BRAN

MAP 69

0   ¼ mile
0   APPROX SCALE   500m

LOOK OUT FOR CLIMBERS

FOOTPATH SIGN POINTING NORTH READS, 'PANORAMA' - IGNORE IT

LANDSLIDE

KEEP LOOKING BACK/FORWARD

PANORAMA WALK

TO A542, A539 & CANAL

STREAM

PARKING AREA

RIVER DEE

SEAT

STAY ON UPPER ROAD

E CRAGS

VIEW SOUTH TO DINAS BRAN, OER!

E SCATTERED SCREE

TREFOR ROCKS

JUNCTION KNOWN AS 'DINAS BRAN TURN'

SEAT

IGNORE PATH & STILE

KISSING GATE

IGNORE PATH & STILE

KISSING GATE WITH INTERPRETIVE BOARD

55–60 MINS TO ROCK FARM (MAP 70)

DINBREN-UCHAF FARM

IF YOU HEAR A TRAIN WHISTLE, IT'S NOT YOUR IMAGINATION, IT'S THE LLANGOLLEN RAILWAY

QUIET ROAD EASY STROLLING

THIS IS A COUNTRY OF ROLLING FIELDS, WOODS & SCATTERED FARMSTEADS. QUINTESS-ENTIALLY WELSH BORDER COUNTRY

PATHS CRISS-CROSS DINAS BRAN

FOOTPATH TO LLANGOLLEN

Tan Y Castell Farm △◇

DINAS BRAN

CASTLE

THIS LANE LEADS TO:
1. WERN ISAF CAMPSITE, 10MINS
2. LLANGOLLEN, 20MINS

70

70a

70b

68

45–50 MINS FROM ROCK FARM (MAP 70)

DINAS BRAN

70–80 MINS TO TREVOR (MAP 68)

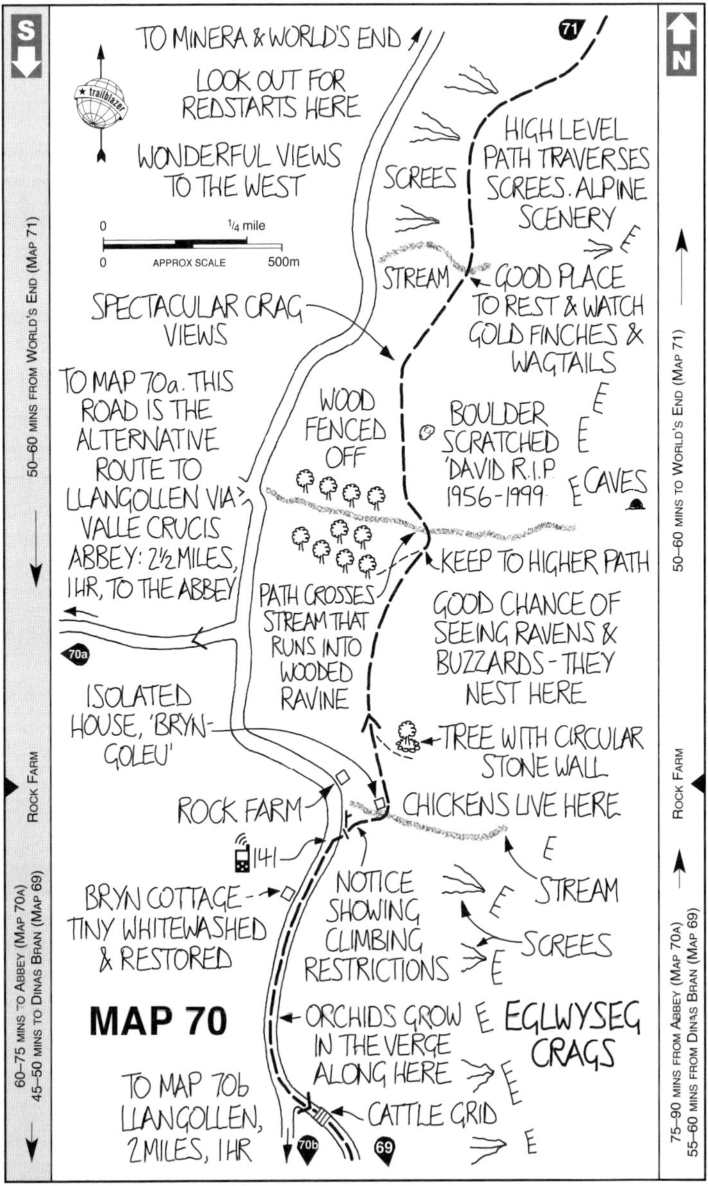

S ↓

★ trailblazer

TO MINERA & WORLD'S END ↗

LOOK OUT FOR REDSTARTS HERE

WONDERFUL VIEWS TO THE WEST

0 — ¼ mile
0 — APPROX SCALE — 500m

SPECTACULAR CRAG VIEWS

TO MAP 70a. THIS ROAD IS THE ALTERNATIVE ROUTE TO LLANGOLLEN VIA VALLE CRUCIS ABBEY: 2½ MILES, 1HR, TO THE ABBEY

70a

ISOLATED HOUSE, 'BRYN-GOLEU'

ROCK FARM

BRYN COTTAGE - TINY WHITEWASHED & RESTORED

MAP 70

TO MAP 70b LLANGOLLEN, 2 MILES, 1HR

71

N ↑

SCREES

HIGH LEVEL PATH TRAVERSES SCREES. ALPINE SCENERY

STREAM

GOOD PLACE TO REST & WATCH GOLD FINCHES & WAGTAILS

WOOD FENCED OFF

BOULDER SCRATCHED 'DAVID R.I.P. 1956-1999'

CAVES

KEEP TO HIGHER PATH

GOOD CHANCE OF SEEING RAVENS & BUZZARDS - THEY NEST HERE

PATH CROSSES STREAM THAT RUNS INTO WOODED RAVINE

TREE WITH CIRCULAR STONE WALL

CHICKENS LIVE HERE

141

NOTICE SHOWING CLIMBING RESTRICTIONS

STREAM

SCREES

ORCHIDS GROW IN THE VERGE ALONG HERE

EGLWYSEG CRAGS

CATTLE GRID

70b   **69**

50-60 MINS FROM WORLD'S END (MAP 71)

ROCK FARM

60-75 MINS TO ABBEY (MAP 70A)
45-50 MINS TO DINAS BRAN (MAP 69)

50-60 MINS TO WORLD'S END (MAP 71)

ROCK FARM

75-90 MINS FROM ABBEY (MAP 70A)
55-60 MINS FROM DINAS BRAN (MAP 69)

ROUTE GUIDE & MAPS

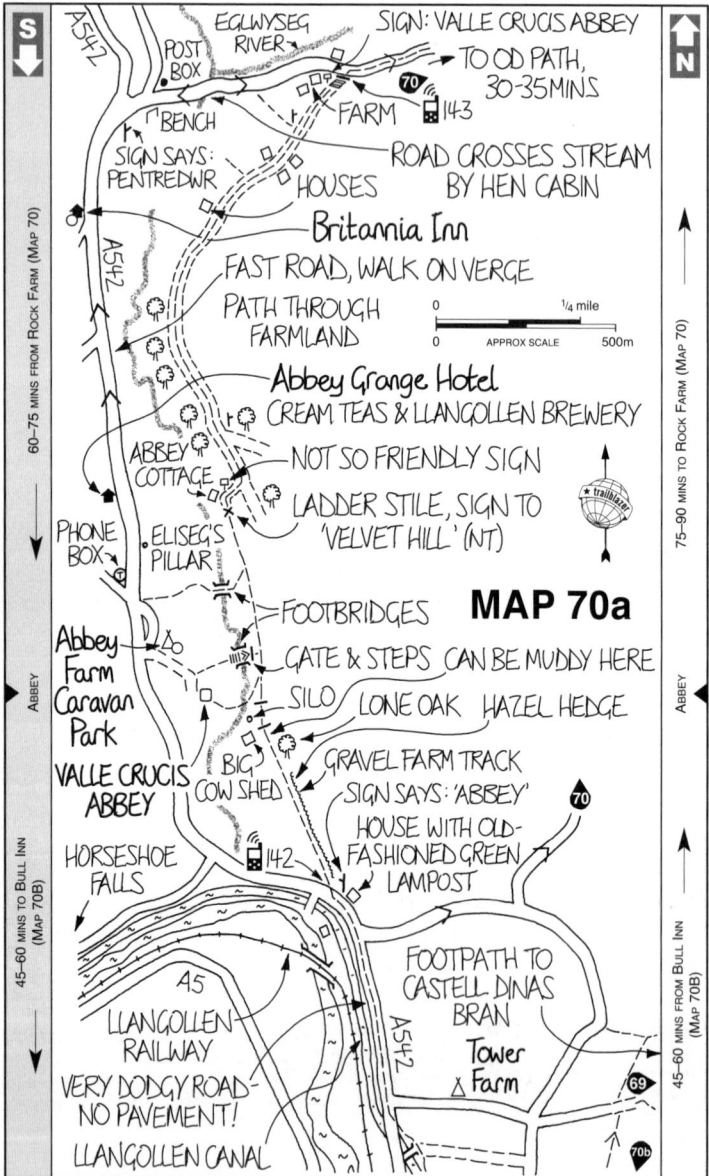

S

N

A542

EGLWYSEG RIVER

POST BOX

SIGN: VALLE CRUCIS ABBEY

TO OD PATH, 30-35 MINS.

70 📱143

FARM

BENCH

SIGN SAYS: PENTREDWR

A542

HOUSES

ROAD CROSSES STREAM BY HEN CABIN

Britannia Inn

FAST ROAD, WALK ON VERGE

PATH THROUGH FARMLAND

0   ¼ mile

0   APPROX SCALE   500m

Abbey Grange Hotel

CREAM TEAS & LLANGOLLEN BREWERY

ABBEY COTTAGE

NOT SO FRIENDLY SIGN

LADDER STILE, SIGN TO 'VELVET HILL' (NT)

trailblazer

PHONE BOX

ELISEG'S PILLAR

FOOTBRIDGES

MAP 70a

Abbey Farm Caravan Park

GATE & STEPS CAN BE MUDDY HERE

SILO   LONE OAK   HAZEL HEDGE

VALLE CRUCIS ABBEY

BIG COW SHED

GRAVEL FARM TRACK

SIGN SAYS: 'ABBEY' 70

HORSESHOE FALLS

📱142

HOUSE WITH OLD-FASHIONED GREEN LAMPOST

A5

LLANGOLLEN RAILWAY

VERY DODGY ROAD - NO PAVEMENT!

LLANGOLLEN CANAL

A542

FOOTPATH TO CASTELL DINAS BRAN

Tower △ Farm

69

70b

60-75 MINS FROM ROCK FARM (MAP 70)

ABBEY

45-60 MINS TO BULL INN (MAP 70B)

75-90 MINS TO ROCK FARM (MAP 70)

ABBEY

45-60 MINS FROM BULL INN (MAP 70B)

LLANGOLLEN   Map 70b, p210
The path does not actually pass through Llangollen (pronounced 'clan-goth-len') but if there is time in your schedule it is well worth the mile detour.

It is a charming small town with a unique character which attracts an element of the alternative society who have found a haven here. In summer it also attracts the holiday hordes with plenty of things for them to do from a sedate steam railway (Llangollen Railway; see Transport) and canal-barge trip to adrenalin-pumping white-water rafting down the River Dee. If these appeal a rest day might be in order especially as there are also a number of interesting historical monuments within easy reach.

Llangollen Museum (☎ 01978-862862, ☐ llangollenmuseum.org.uk; summer daily 10am-5pm, winter 10am-4pm; free entry but donation appreciated), on Parade St, is worth a peek, with over 350 artefacts from the local area dating back to the Bronze Age.

Plas Newydd (☎ 01978-861314; house Apr-Sep daily 10.30am-5pm, grounds open daily all day; admission to the house £6), home of the 'Ladies of Llangollen' (see Recommended reading, p46) from 1780 to 1829, is decorated in an eclectic mix of Tudor and Gothic styles and is well worth visiting. It lies off Hill St, south of the main part of town.

For details of other places to visit in the area see the box on p212.

If you are planning to walk in July be warned that for seven days during the first or second week of the month Llangollen is the venue for the massive **International Musical Eisteddfod** (see box p27) which fills the Royal International Pavilion with musicians, singers and dancers from all over the world.

Transport
[See pp49-53]   There are frequent **bus services** to Wrexham (Arriva's No 5 & 5E and Lloyds Coaches' T3). Tanat Valley's No 64 runs to Llanarmon Dyffryn Ceiriog via Chirk & Froncysyllte. All the bus/coach services go to the bus station on Parade St.

The nearest **railway stations** are at Chirk and Ruabon; Llangollen's railway (☎ 01978-860979; ☐ llangollen-railway.co .uk; daily Apr-Sep; weekends occasionally in winter, contact them for details; £16 return, 🐾 £1) operates services along the scenic River Dee; the line is now 10 miles since being extended from Carrog to Corwen.

For a **taxi** contact Premier Cars (☎ 01978-861999) near Dee Bridge.

Services
The excellent **tourist information centre** (☎ 01978-860828, ☐ llangollen@nwtic .com; Mon-Sat 9.30am-5pm, Sun 9.30am-4pm) is in Y Capel on Castle St, the same building as the library though they are separate. They provide accommodation booking (see box p44). A useful website is ☐ llangollen.org.uk.

There are three **banks** in town, Barclays and NatWest on Castle St and HSBC on Bridge St, all with cash machines.

Tuesday is **market day**, worth catching if you are in town as the centre comes alive.

The best place to stock up with food is at the Spar **supermarket** (daily 7am-11pm) on Castle St, or the larger Co-op (Mon-Sat 6am-10pm, Sun 10am-4pm) on Regent St. Regent St is also home to the **launderette**.

There is a **post office** in the Nisa Local on Berwyn St.

For any **outdoor equipment** try Pro Adventure on Castle St.

Where to stay
Owing to its prominence as a tourist destination there are many excellent B&Bs in Llangollen. As long as you avoid the time of the Eisteddfod (see box p27) you shouldn't have any problems finding somewhere to stay.

Those **camping** have a good choice within relatively easy reach of the town, though some distance from the trail. **Wern Isaf** (off Map 69; ☎ 01978-860632, ☐ wernisaf.co.uk; 🐾; Easter to end Oct), Wern Rd, is a quiet working farm east of town, just three-quarters of a mile off the

ROUTE GUIDE & MAPS

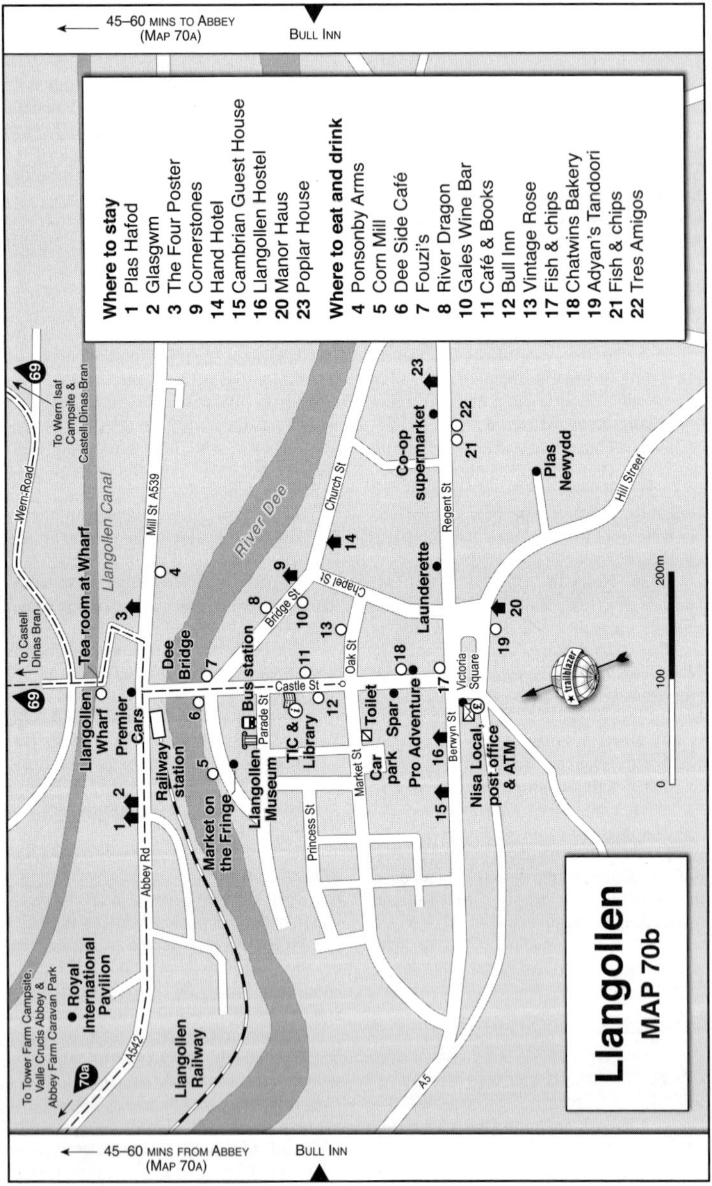

← 45–60 MINS TO ABBEY
(MAP 70A)

BULL INN

Where to stay
1 Plas Hafod
2 Glasgwm
3 The Four Poster
9 Cornerstones
14 Hand Hotel
15 Cambrian Guest House
16 Llangollen Hostel
20 Manor Haus
23 Poplar House

Where to eat and drink
4 Ponsonby Arms
5 Corn Mill
6 Dee Side Café
7 Fouzi's
8 River Dragon
10 Gales Wine Bar
11 Café & Books
12 Bull Inn
13 Vintage Rose
17 Fish & chips
18 Chatwins Bakery
19 Adyan's Tandoori
21 Fish & chips
22 Tres Amigos

To Wern Isaf
Campsite &
Castell Dinas Bran

Wern Road

Llangollen Canal

Mill St A539

River Dee

Tea room at Wharf

To Castell
Dinas Bran

Llangollen
Wharf

Premier
Cars

Dee
Bridge

Bus station

Church St

Co-op
supermarket

Regent St

Plas
Newydd

Hill Street

Bridge St

Chapel St

Launderette

Railway
station

Abbey Rd

Market on
the Fringe

Parade St

Castle St

Llangollen
Museum

TIC &
Library

Oak St

Car
park

Toilet

Spar

Pro Adventure

Market St

Princess St

Victoria
Square

Berwyn St

Nisa Local,
post office
& ATM

trailblazer

To Tower Farm Campsite,
Valle Crucis Abbey &
Abbey Farm Caravan Park

Royal
International
Pavilion

A542

Llangollen
Railway

A5

Llangollen
MAP 70b

0   100   200m

← 45–60 MINS FROM ABBEY
(MAP 70A)

BULL INN

route. Camping costs £9pp for a hiker with a small tent; a shower costs 20p.

The independent *Llangollen Hostel* (☎ 01978-861773, 🖳 llangollenhostel.co.uk; 32 beds – rooms sleep 2-6 people; some en suite; WI-FI) charges £20pp for a bed in a 4- to 6-bed dorm; £22.50-25pp for a twin/double based on two sharing, and £20pp for three/four sharing a room. The rate generally includes a self-service continental breakfast. There is a kitchen as well as laundry facilities and a drying room. Reservations are recommended in the main season especially because the hostel may be fully booked by a group.

There is a glut of **B&Bs** on the north side of the river including, on Abbey Rd, the Edwardian townhouses of *Plas Hafod* (☎ 01978-869225, 🖳 plas-hafod.co.uk; 3D en suite/1Tr with private bathroom; ▼; WI-FI; Ⓛ), charging £37.50-42.50pp (sgl occ from £50), and the excellent-value *Glasgwm* (☎ 01978-861975, 🖳 glasgwm-llangollen.co.uk; 1S/1T/2D, all en suite, ▼; WI-FI; Ⓛ), which charges £35-40pp (sgl £42.50-65). The hosts are friendly and knowledgeable and are happy to do evening meals if arranged in advance.

The Four Poster B&B (☎ 01978-861062, 🖳 thefourposter.co.uk; 3D/1Tr, all en suite; ▼; 🐾; WI-FI), on Mill St, charges £40-45pp (sgl occ from £60) and £130 for three people sharing a room.

Not short of a bed or two is *Hand Hotel* (☎ 01978-860303, 🖳 hand-hotel-llangollen.com; 58 en suite rooms; ▼; 🐾; Ⓛ), on Church St, with B&B from £48.75pp (sgl/sgl occ from £57.50).

Right on the River Dee, *Cornerstones* (☎ 01978-861569, 🖳 cornerstones-guest house.co.uk; 2D/1D or T, all en suite, ▼; WI-FI; Ⓛ), 15 Bridge St, charges £60-72.50pp (sgl occ Mon-Thur £90, room rate at weekends). Lifts to and from the path are offered subject to prior arrangement.

Perhaps the smartest place in the town centre is *Manor Haus* (☎ 01978-860775, 🖳 manorhaus.com; 6S/4D/4D or T, all en suite' ▼; WI-FI; 🐾); it offers sophisticated accommodation – with iPod-docking stations in the rooms and a hot tub on the roof (free during the day; evenings £15 per hour

inc a bottle of Prosecco) – and rooms of muted monochromatic tones. The room rate is £70-100 and breakfast costs £10; discounts available online.

Also conveniently central is *Cambrian Guest House* (☎ 01978-861418, 🖳 camb rianhouse.co.uk; 2S/3T/3D/2Qd, all en suite; WI-FI; Ⓛ) which charges from £35pp (sgl/sgl occ from £44/50) for B&B.

On Regent St the friendly *Poplar House* (☎ 01978-861772, ☎ 07731-572989; 2Tr in house with private bathrooms, 1Qd in self-contained cottage; ▼; WI-FI; 🐾 in cottage only, free or £5 depending on cleaning required; Ⓛ) charges £35-50pp (sgl occ from £50). There is a hot tub (£5pp) outside. An evening meal (£10-15) is available if requested in advance. The cottage, behind the house and converted from the former stables, is self-contained and has a kitchen where guests can make their own evening meal but they are asked to tidy up and leave it as they found it. There is also a healing room should you wish/need to have a sports massage, spiritual reading or any other type of healing treatment (from £30). Enquire directly by contacting the proprietor.

Where to eat and drink

There are several cafés and cheap eateries in town. The best of the lot – and a fine place for afternoon teas and lunches – is *Vintage Rose* (Tue-Sat 10am-4pm), a lovely café on Oak St, with polka-dot tablecloths and smiley staff. For pies and filled rolls there's *Chatwins Bakery*, on Castle St, where you can sit in or take away. *Dee Side Café* (daily 9am-9pm) by the bridge does all-day breakfasts. Before you cross the Dee, there is a lovely little – if unsurprisingly, very busy – **tea room** at Llangollen Wharf.

Café and Books (☎ 01978-860334, 🖳 booksllangollen.co.uk; summer daily 8am-8pm, winter Mon-Sat 9am-5pm, Sun from 10am year-round), on Castle St, is a bit of an institution: a former cinema where you can get a decent bacon sandwich, to eat in or takeaway, or a full fry-up while perusing over 100,000 second-hand volumes.

For the best coffee head to *Fouzi's* (☎ 01978-861399, 🖳 fouzis.com; Sun-Thur

9am-9pm, Fri-Sat to 10pm) by the bridge; it also does pizzas (from £8.95) and breakfasts.

For a good local pub, try **Bull Inn** on Castle St; it's an 18th-century coaching inn that has a good choice of beers and bar meals. Many locals will also tell you that **Ponsonby Arms**, on Mill St, is the best place for real ale.

For a gastronomic treat head for **Corn Mill** (☎ 01978-869555, 🖳 brunningand price.co.uk/cornmill; bar daily 11am-11pm, food Mon-Sat noon-9.30pm, Sun noon-9pm), perched in an enviable location by the river. The daily menu (mains £8.95-17.45) caters for all tastes, budgets and appetites and the establishment was recently picked out by *The Guardian* newspaper as being one of the UK's ten best waterside pubs.

Gales Wine Bar (☎ 01978-860089, 🖳 galesofllangollen.co.uk; food daily noon-2pm, Mon-Sat 6-9.30pm) is of the same ilk but you'll probably want to forsake your outdoor clothing for your city clothes if you don't want to stand out like a pauper at a posh function. The menu covers everything from Welsh black ribeye (£18.95) to burgers (£9.95).

Mexican meals can be found at the recently opened **Tres Amigos** (☎ 01978-861877; daily 9am-9pm) on Regent St.

If you're hankering after an Indian meal try **Adyan's Tandoori** on Victoria Sq; for Chinese, there's **River Dragon** on Bridge St. In fact, there are numerous places on Bridge St that offer value for money without exciting the craving for original cooking.

If you're just after a good bag of **fish & chips** you'll find two chippies on Regent St.

❏ Historic monuments around Llangollen

● **Castell Dinas Bran** The sight of the ruins of the medieval Castell Dinas Bran (Map 69, p206) looming over the trail is one of the highlights of the walk. The castle's historical origins are somewhat obscured in the mists of Celtic legend, its brooding presence striking a chill, especially on misty evenings when nothing can be heard but the call of the ravens. The conical hill on which the ruins stand seems an ideal stronghold but was perhaps too exposed to have been of much use defensively. For a closer look, there's a steep path up to the top, affording great views and the opportunity for moody photographs.

● **Valle Crucis Abbey** (Map 70a, p208; Apr-Oct daily 10am-4/5pm; £4) was founded by Cistercian monks in the 12th century. Now a ruin, but with much of its original beauty surviving, it is exquisitely situated beside the River Eglwyseg, a tributary of the Dee. When the white-robed monks first came to this valley to build their monastery they chose it for its remote and wild location where prayer and work could go on with minimal distractions and intrusions from the outside world. The ruins today give you a good idea, with a little imagination, of the once-glorious abbey building with its rose window and carved doorway. The fishpond remains, as does the Chapter House with its rib-vaulted roof, but perhaps the most striking impression will be left by its dramatic position below the wooded crags: a truly magical place. In the winter months the only access is via a side gate; entry is free but it isn't possible to see the whole site.

● **Eliseg's Pillar** (daily 10am-4pm; free) This is the surviving stump of a much higher pillar set up in memory of King Eliseg who drove out the Anglo-Saxon invaders in about AD750. It was originally surmounted by a carved stone cross from which Valle Crucis, the Valley of the Cross, takes its name. Eliseg's Pillar (Map 70a, p208) stands in a field to the right of the A542 road between Llangollen and Ruthin (the Horseshoe Pass). Perhaps not meriting a detour on its own, it can be taken in when you're visiting the abbey ruins.

S ▼ FROM PRESTATYN **DINAS BRAN (& LLANGOLLEN) TO CASTLE MILL**
MAPS 69-65

[*Route section begins on Map 69, p206*] This **8½-mile (14km)** section takes about **3hrs 50mins-4hrs 25mins**.

Along the so-called **Panorama Walk** the road keeps company with the limestone crags and screes until the path leaves it before it reaches the turning to *Prospect Garden Tea Room* (Wed-Fri noon-5pm, Sat, Sun & bank holidays 10.30am-5.30pm), which is about half a mile from Offa's Dyke Path. From here the path ventures down into **Trevor Hall Wood** (Map 68), a damp, dark domain where you imagine there must be dragons or at least hobbits, eventually exiting into fields that lead to **Llangollen Canal**.

Offa's Dyke Path officially follows the road to the old bridge over the River Dee and on through the village of **Froncysyllte** (Map 67) before taking a track across the canal to the towpath by the cantilever bridge.

Far more rewarding, though, is the alternative route across Telford's extraordinary achievement, **Pontcysyllte Aqueduct** (Map 68; see box p204), one of the highlights of the entire walk – though it's not for anyone who suffers from vertigo. Where the two paths reunite you keep to the canal towpath as far as **Irish Bridge** (Map 67; presumably built by Irish navvies), where the B5605 crosses the canal; just beyond this the trail brings you to the A5 where you meet the Dyke for the first time, skulking amongst a line of trees.

You cannot join it yet, but keep pace with it along by-roads to **Ty'n-y-groes** (Map 66) where the 'garden gate' of **Chirk Castle** (Map 65; see box p201) allows summertime access to the grounds (Apr-Sep) and an alternative route to Castle Mill. A field path over farmland takes you up over a hill to descend through mixed woodland to the valley of the delightful River Ceiriog which you cross at **Castle Mill (Map 65, p200)**.   [*Next route overview p201*]

ROUTE GUIDE & MAPS

N ▲ FROM CHEPSTOW **DINAS BRAN (& LLANGOLLEN) TO LLANDEGLA**
MAPS 69-73

[*Route section begins on Map 69, p206*] This **8-mile (13km)** section takes about **4-4½ hours**, with an additional 15 minutes each way to/from Llangollen. (See p214 for the alternative route from Llangollen, which takes 4½-5½hrs).

From **Castell Dinas Bran** (Map 69, p206; see box opposite) you traverse the screes below **Eglwyseg Crags** (Map 70), a haunt for hawks and ravens, and a popular spot for climbers. You arrive at **World's End** (Map 71), no more than a dot on the map, before ascending the unfenced road to **Minera.** Turning off the road, **Llandegla Forest** looms on the horizon and you cross open moorland; thankfully railway sleepers aid the walking across the most boggy areas.

From the stillness of the forest, with its dank, mossy undergrowth and criss-crossing bridleways, the path descends, emerging in agricultural land and shortly after, **Llandegla (Map 73, p217).**   [*Next route overview p219*]

Alternative route from/to Llangollen via Valle Crucis Abbey
Map 70, p207 & Map 70a, p208

For those with the time or a thirst for ruins, there is another way down to Llangollen that takes in both Valle Crucis Abbey and Eliseg's Pillar whilst also providing a choice of two places offering B&B and a campsite.

If heading north, ignore the turn off the lane and continue straight on, past Rock Farm. If heading south, when the path meets the lane turn right onto the lane and follow it past Rock Farm. For both see Map 17, WPT 141.

From here, follow the quiet by-roads north and then west to meet the busy A542 (Map 70a). Stay on the road for Britannia Inn (see below) and Abbey Grange Hotel but stick to the path for Abbey Farm Caravan Park and Llangollen.

The tidily upgraded 15th-century *Britannia Inn* (☎ 01978-860144, 🖳 britinn.com; bar daily summer 11.30am till close, winter Mon-Fri 11.30am-3pm & 6pm till close, Sat & Sun 11.30am till close) offers **B&B** (5D/1Tr, all en suite; ☛; WI-FI; Ⓛ) at £37.50pp (sgl occ £55), or dinner, bed & breakfast for £56pp (sgl occ £73.50). The **restaurant** is open daily (Sun-Thur 11.30am-8.30pm, Fri & Sat to 9pm) in summer; winter hours depend on demand. The whole place is closed for 2-3 weeks in January.

Further down the valley is the more affordable *Abbey Grange Hotel* (☎ 01978-860753, 🖳 abbey-grange-hotel.co.uk; 4T/2D/2Tr, all en suite; ☛; WI-FI; 🐾), where Steven Evans has held sway for over 40 years. **B&B** costs from £40pp (£60pp for a room with a four-poster bed; sgl occ £50). He will collect guests at Rock Farm if requested in advance; if not, you can walk from there in about an hour. **Food** is also available (summer daily noon-9.30pm, winter 5-9.30pm). **Llangollen Brewery** is also here in the old farm shop and cream teas are available.

Almost opposite is the ancient **Eliseg's Pillar** (see box p212) and a few metres further down (or accessed from the path) you'll come to *Abbey Farm Caravan Park* (☎ 01978-861297, 🖳 theabbeyfarm.co.uk; 🐾 on lead but phone first to check; Feb-Dec), where campers can pitch a tent for £14-18pp (per pitch and two adults) close to the lofty ruins of **Valle Crucis Abbey** (see box p212), which stands serene and proud above the nearby static caravans. Note that there is a two-night minimum stay policy at the weekends over summer. If you are walking with others you might like to try the **wooden camping pods**: from £40-120 for a pod sleeping 2-6 people. There is a shower/toilet block (for everyone) and a *tea room* and *bistro* (food Mon & Tue 10am-4pm, Wed 10am-9pm, Thur-Sat 9am-9pm, Sun 9am-8pm); booking is advisable in the summer.

A path from here follows the river through farmland to the A542, passing the turn to *Tower Farm* (☎ 01978-860029, 🖳 towerfarmholidays.co.uk; 🐾) where the rate for campers (from £6pp) includes use of the shower/toilet facilities. Booking is preferred especially in the summer months.

The towpath continues to Llangollen Wharf, past the **Royal International Pavilion**, a futuristic structure put up for the International Musical Eisteddfod.

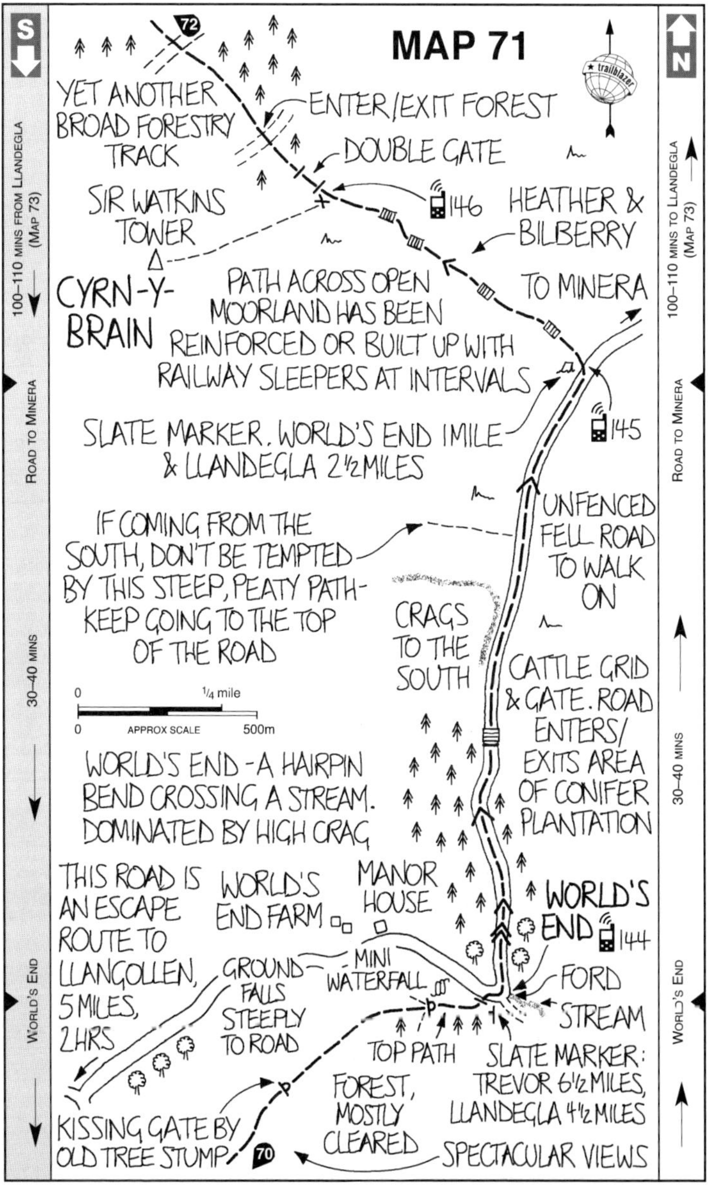

MAP 71

S

N

100–110 MINS FROM LLANDEGLA (MAP 73)

100–110 MINS TO LLANDEGLA (MAP 73)

ROAD TO MINERA

ROAD TO MINERA

30–40 MINS

30–40 MINS

WORLD'S END

WORLD'S END

ROUTE GUIDE & MAPS

YET ANOTHER BROAD FORESTRY TRACK

ENTER/EXIT FOREST

DOUBLE GATE

📱146

SIR WATKINS TOWER

HEATHER & BILBERRY

CYRN-Y-BRAIN

PATH ACROSS OPEN MOORLAND HAS BEEN REINFORCED OR BUILT UP WITH RAILWAY SLEEPERS AT INTERVALS

TO MINERA

SLATE MARKER. WORLD'S END 1 MILE & LLANDEGLA 2½ MILES

📱145

IF COMING FROM THE SOUTH, DON'T BE TEMPTED BY THIS STEEP, PEATY PATH- KEEP GOING TO THE TOP OF THE ROAD

UNFENCED FELL ROAD TO WALK ON

CRAGS TO THE SOUTH

CATTLE GRID & GATE. ROAD ENTERS/ EXITS AREA OF CONIFER PLANTATION

0   ¼ mile

0   500m
APPROX SCALE

WORLD'S END - A HAIRPIN BEND CROSSING A STREAM. DOMINATED BY HIGH CRAG

THIS ROAD IS AN ESCAPE ROUTE TO LLANGOLLEN, 5 MILES, 2 HRS

WORLD'S END FARM

MANOR HOUSE

WORLD'S END 📱144

GROUND FALLS STEEPLY TO ROAD

MINI WATERFALL

FORD STREAM

KISSING GATE BY OLD TREE STUMP 70

TOP PATH FOREST, MOSTLY CLEARED

SLATE MARKER: TREVOR 6½ MILES, LLANDEGLA 4½ MILES

SPECTACULAR VIEWS

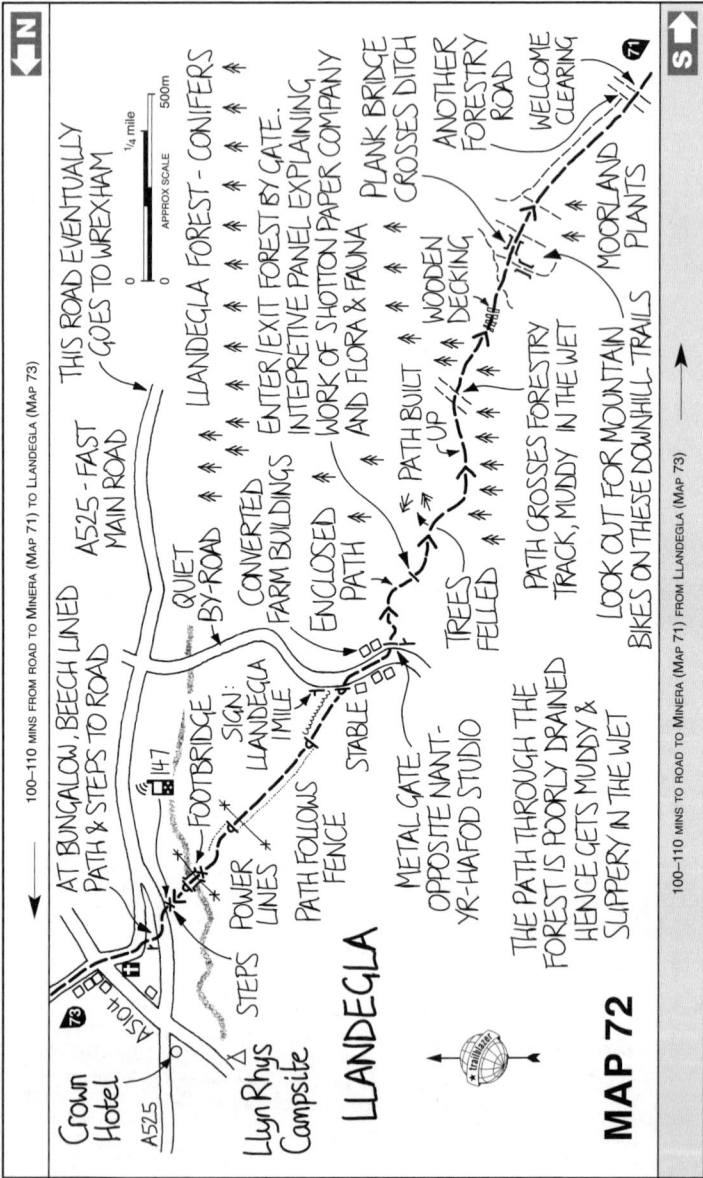

ROUTE GUIDE & MAPS

100–110 MINS FROM ROAD TO MINERA (MAP 71) TO LLANDEGLA (MAP 73)

N

THIS ROAD EVENTUALLY GOES TO WREXHAM

A525 - FAST MAIN ROAD

APPROX SCALE
0   ¼ mile
0   500m

LLANDEGLA FOREST - CONIFERS

ENTER/EXIT FOREST BY GATE. INTERPRETIVE PANEL EXPLAINING WORK OF SHOTTON PAPER COMPANY AND FLORA & FAUNA

PLANK BRIDGE CROSSES DITCH

ANOTHER FORESTRY ROAD

WELCOME CLEARING

71

S

QUIET BY-ROAD

CONVERTED FARM BUILDINGS

ENCLOSED PATH

PATH BUILT UP

WOODEN DECKING

MOORLAND PLANTS

TREES FELLED

PATH CROSSES FORESTRY TRACK, MUDDY IN THE WET

LOOK OUT FOR MOUNTAIN BIKES ON THESE DOWNHILL TRAILS

AT BUNGALOW, BEECH LINED PATH & STEPS TO ROAD

FOOTBRIDGE

SIGN: LLANDEGLA 1 MILE

STABLE

POWER LINES

PATH FOLLOWS FENCE

METAL GATE OPPOSITE NANT-YR-HAFOD STUDIO

THE PATH THROUGH THE FOREST IS POORLY DRAINED HENCE GETS MUDDY & SLIPPERY IN THE WET

STEPS

Crown Hotel

A525

Llyn Rhys Campsite

A5104

73

LLANDEGLA

MAP 72

100–110 MINS TO ROAD TO MINERA (MAP 71) FROM LLANDEGLA (MAP 73)

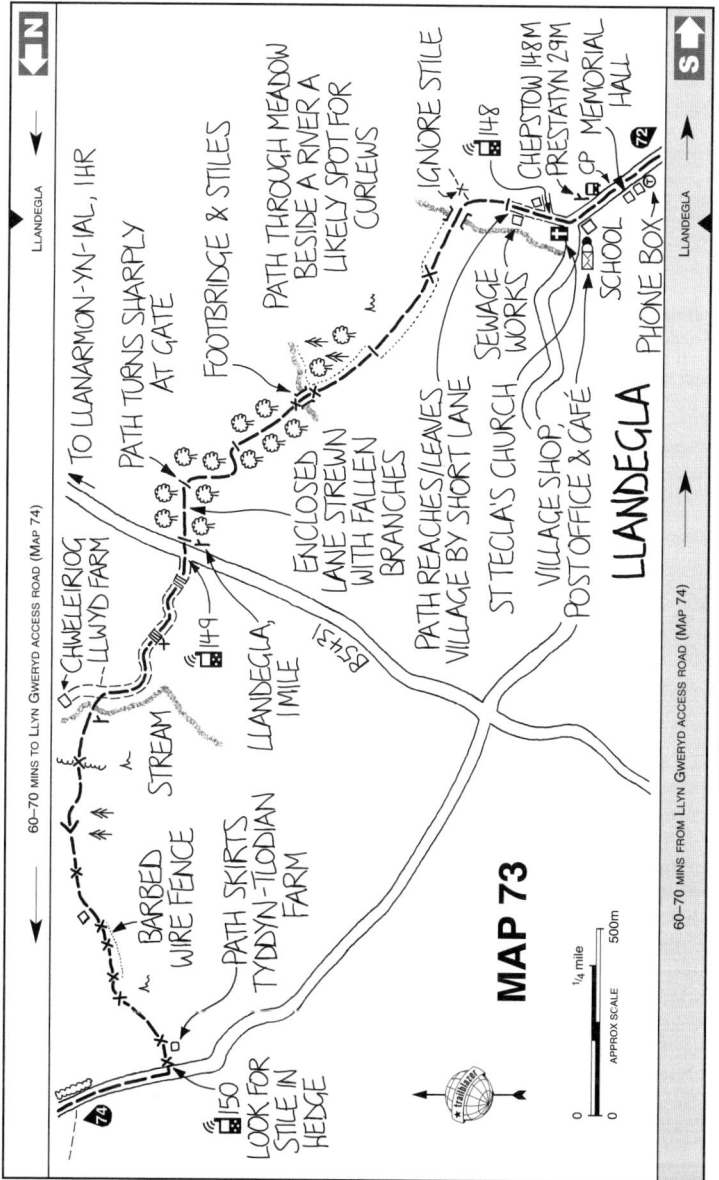

ROUTE GUIDE & MAPS

MAP 73

N

S

60–70 MINS TO LLYN GWERYD ACCESS ROAD (MAP 74)

60–70 MINS FROM LLYN GWERYD ACCESS ROAD (MAP 74)

LLANDEGLA

TO LLANARMON-YN-IAL, 1HR

CHWELERIOG-LLWYD FARM

PATH TURNS SHARPLY AT GATE

FOOTBRIDGE & STILES

PATH THROUGH MEADOW BESIDE A RIVER A LIKELY SPOT FOR CURLEWS

IGNORE STILE

148

CHEPSTOW 148M
PRESTATYN 29M

CP MEMORIAL HALL

72

149

LLANDEGLA, 1 MILE

STREAM

B5431

ENCLOSED LANE STREWN WITH FALLEN BRANCHES

PATH REACHES/LEAVES VILLAGE BY SHORT LANE

ST TECLA'S CHURCH

VILLAGE SHOP, POST OFFICE & CAFÉ

SEWAGE WORKS

SCHOOL

PHONE BOX

LLANDEGLA

BARBED WIRE FENCE

PATH SKIRTS TYDDYN-TLODIAN FARM

150

LOOK FOR STILE IN HEDGE

74

¼ mile

500m

0

0

APPROX SCALE

LLANDEGLA
Map 72, p216 & Map 73, p217

At 255m (835ft) the highest settlement you visit along the way, the well-kept village of Llandegla is on Arriva's X51 **bus** route between Denbigh and Wrexham; see public transport map and table, pp49-53.

Llandegla Community Village Shop and Café (☎ 01978-790604, 🖥 llandegla shop.com; Mon-Sat 8am-6.30pm, Sun 8am-4pm; WI-FI) feels like the beating heart of this small community; multi-tasking since the old shop closed here – even **post office** services (Thur 9.15-11.15am) are incorporated. The shop is well-stocked, the staff couldn't be friendlier or more helpful and the café is worthy of a stop whatever time of day you pass through; the breakfasts (around £5-6.50) are smashing. This really is the sort of place walkers need to use and support as more and more small villages lose their services.

Campers will find *Llyn Rhys Campsite* (Map 72; ☎ 01978-790627, 🖥 llynrhyscampsite.co.uk; 🐾; Mar-Oct) a short walk off the path. The rate (£8pp) includes use of the showers and there are also facilities where you can wash and dry clothes. Booking is recommended at the weekends in summer.

For **food** in the evening, the choice is limited to the dog-friendly *Crown Hotel* (☎ 01978-790714; 🐾; bar Mon-Thur 5pm-midnight, Fri 4pm-midnight, Sat noon to midnight, Sun noon-11pm) on the A525. They dish up large portions of very tasty food (Wed & Thur 5-9pm, Fri 4-9pm, Sat noon-9pm, Sun noon-7pm); mains costing £9.95-19.95. There was talk of opening on Monday and Tuesday evenings here too and serving pizza so it may be worth giving them a call to check if these plans have been realised. Despite the name they don't provide accommodation.

Finally, **St Tecla's Church** offers 'help-yourself' refreshments to walkers.

S ⬇ FROM PRESTATYN LLANDEGLA TO DINAS BRAN (& LLANGOLLEN)
MAPS 73-69

[*Route section begins on Map 73, p217*] This **8-mile (13km)** section takes about **3¾hrs-4hrs 20mins**, with an additional 15 mins each way to Llangollen. (See p214 for the alternative route to Llangollen, which takes 4½-5½hrs). Leaving Llandegla, you are soon in the dense **Llandegla Forest**.

From the stillness of the forest, with its dank, mossy undergrowth and criss-crossing bridleways, the path emerges on to open moorland, where railway sleepers aid the walking across the most boggy areas. It continues along the unfenced road from **Minera**, with fine views ahead before descending to **World's End** (Map 71), no more than a dot on the map. From here, you begin the fine traverse of the screes below **Eglwyseg Crags** (Map 70), a haunt for hawks and ravens, and a popular spot for climbers.

Ahead, the forbidding outline of **Castell Dinas Bran** (Map 69, p206; see box p212) looms into view and you will soon be within reach of the comfortable borough of **Llangollen** nestling in the valley; worth the short detour as it's a haven for travellers with its many services and attractions.

Campers, wishing to remain up high, can pitch a tent below Dinas Bran at *Tan Y Castell Farm* (Map 69; ☎ 01978-861780; 🐾; £4); there's a toilet and fresh water for campers but no shower facilities and if you're not carrying food, you'll still need to descend to **Llangollen** (**Map 69, p206**).

[*Next route overview p213*]

LLANDEGLA TO CLWYD GATE (FOR LLANFERRES)

FROM CHEPSTOW

MAPS 73-75

[*Route section begins on Map 73, p217*] This **6-mile (10km, 2hrs 50mins-3hrs 20mins)** stage sees you arrive amongst the southernmost peaks of the Clwydian Hills (see box p228).

You exit the attractive village of **Llandegla** (Map 73), beside the church dedicated to St Tegla after whom the village is named, before wandering through water meadows alongside the **River Alun**. You follow paths through fields and the road briefly before the hills begin. You follow a track and then path to the west of the summit of **Moel y Plâs** (Map 74; 440m/1443ft), before arriving at a road which leads to the peaceful village of **Llanarmon-yn-Ial** (Map 74a). From here you contour round the broad shoulders of **Moel Llanfair** (Map 74; 447m/ 1466ft) and **Moel Gyw** (Map 75; 467m/1531ft), before descending through fields to **Clwyd Gate (Map 75, p222)**.   [*Next route overview p223*]

❏ **Hill-forts**
As many as 30 hill-forts have been identified in the county of Clwyd and some of the best are on the path. These fortified settlements date from the Iron Age, 800-600 years before the Roman invasion of Britain in AD43. They were inhabited by tribes who lived by hunting and farming but who tried to guarantee their security by fortifying hilltops for their protection. There was usually a double rampart and ditch; the inner rampart would carry a timber stockade from which attackers could be repulsed. The coming of the Romans meant that the superior discipline and power of the fighting troops was able to overwhelm them and they were abandoned. Although viewed to best effect from the air, the ring of former ramparts can be made out on the ground, but for the most part you'll need to use your imagination to conjure up an idea of their significance.

LLANARMON-YN-IAL
Map 74 p220 & Map 74a, p221

The village is 20 minutes east of the path and has a small community-run **shop** (☎ 01824-780509; Mon-Fri 8am-5.30pm, Sat 8am-4pm & Sun 9am-2pm) as well as a community-run **pub** (☎ 01824-780833, 🖥 raveninn.co.uk; bar Tue-Thur 5-10.30pm, Fri 5-11pm, Sat noon-11pm, Sun noon-9pm; they are closed on Mondays apart from Bank Hol Mons). **Food** is served: on Thursdays (5.30-8pm) specials night; fish & chips on Fridays (5.30-8pm); light lunches, steaks and pies on Saturdays (noon-2.30pm) and a full menu in the evening (5.30-8pm) and traditional roast dinners on Sundays (12.30-3pm). It's a lovely, friendly place.

They also have three self-contained **apartments**, each with a double or twin bed and en suite facilities, which can be booked on a nightly basis (£27.50-30pp, contact direct regarding sgl occ rates); booking is possible through their website.

Tyn y Groesffordd (☎ 01824-780259, 🖥 dorothygent@yahoo.co.uk; 1S/1T/1D, private facilities; 🐾; WI-FI; Ⓛ) is by the junction of two roads but even so you can expect a peaceful night here. **B&B** costs from £25pp; evening meals (£7.50-10) are available if requested in advance. They will also pick you up from near Moel y Plâs if requested in advance.

Only 500m or so from the path is *Gweryd Lakes* (☎ 01824-780230, 🖥 gweryd lakes.co.uk), which offers fishing but makes a good spot for walkers too. **Campers** can pitch here for £10pp and there is a toilet/ shower block.

M&H Coaches No 1/X1/2 Ruthin–Mold **bus services** call here (see public transport map and table, pp49-53).

ROUTE GUIDE & MAPS

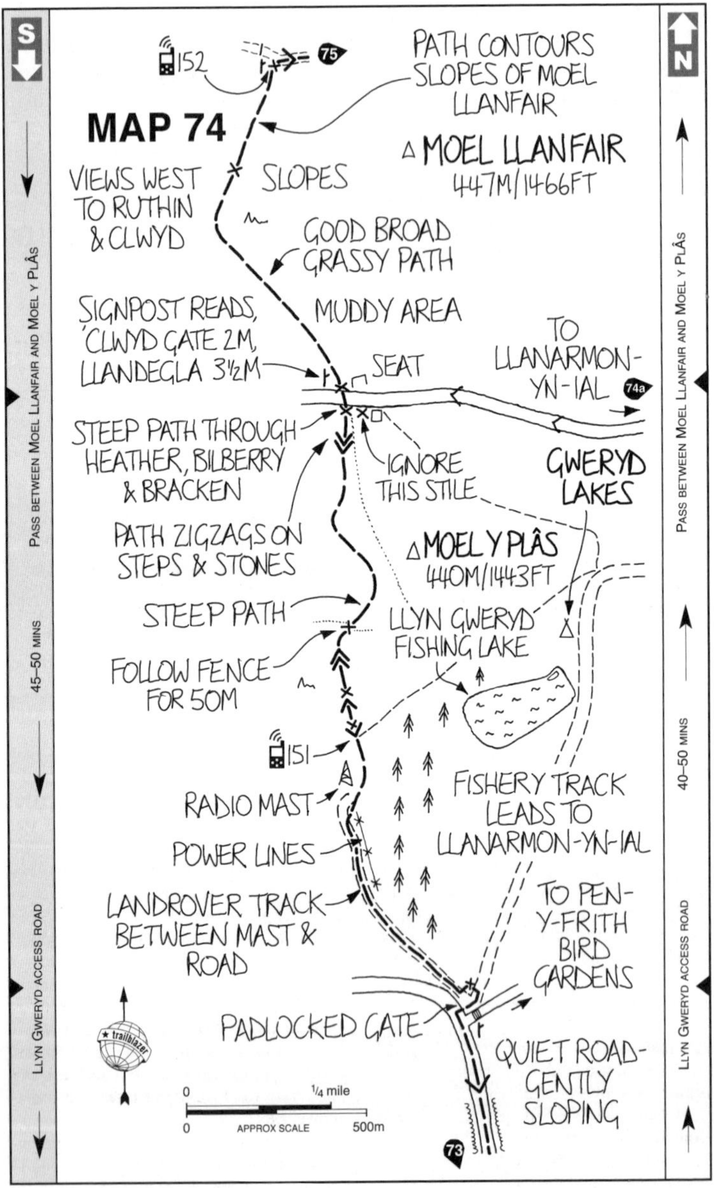

📱152

75

PATH CONTOURS
SLOPES OF MOEL
LLANFAIR

MAP 74

△ MOEL LLANFAIR
447M/1466FT

SLOPES

VIEWS WEST
TO RUTHIN
& CLWYD

GOOD BROAD
GRASSY PATH

MUDDY AREA

SIGNPOST READS,
'CLWYD GATE 2M,
LLANDEGLA 3½M'

SEAT

TO
LLANARMON-
YN-IAL

74a

STEEP PATH THROUGH
HEATHER, BILBERRY
& BRACKEN

IGNORE
THIS STILE

GWERYD
LAKES

PATH ZIGZAGS ON
STEPS & STONES

△ MOEL Y PLÂS
440M/1443FT

STEEP PATH

LLYN GWERYD
FISHING LAKE

FOLLOW FENCE
FOR 50M

📱151

FISHERY TRACK
LEADS TO
LLANARMON-YN-IAL

RADIO MAST

POWER LINES

LANDROVER TRACK
BETWEEN MAST &
ROAD

TO PEN-
Y-FRITH
BIRD
GARDENS

★ trailblazer

PADLOCKED GATE

QUIET ROAD-
GENTLY
SLOPING

0   ¼ mile
0   APPROX SCALE   500m

73

ROUTE GUIDE & MAPS

PASS BETWEEN MOEL LLANFAIR AND MOEL Y PLÂS

45-50 MINS

LLYN GWERYD ACCESS ROAD

PASS BETWEEN MOEL LLANFAIR AND MOEL Y PLÂS

40-50 MINS

LLYN GWERYD ACCESS ROAD

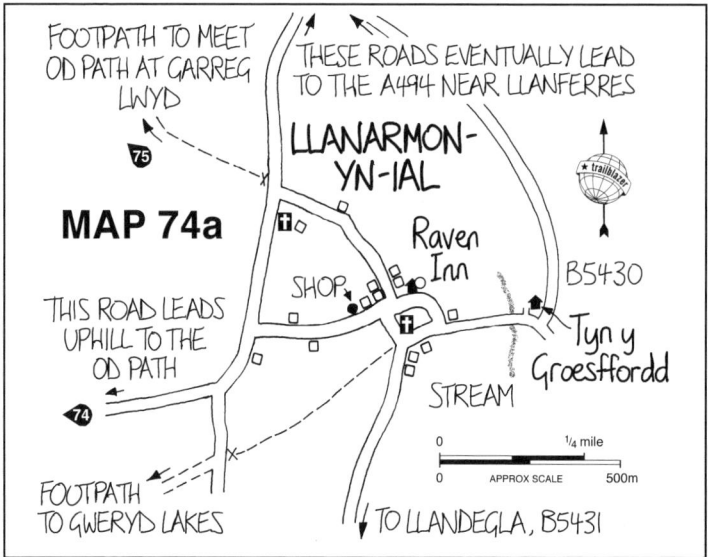

FOOTPATH TO MEET OD PATH AT GARREG LWYD

75

MAP 74a

THIS ROAD LEADS UPHILL TO THE OD PATH

74

FOOTPATH TO GWERYD LAKES

THESE ROADS EVENTUALLY LEAD TO THE A494 NEAR LLANFERRES

LLANARMON-YN-IAL

Raven Inn

SHOP

B5430

Tyn y Groesffordd

STREAM

trailblazer

0   1/4 mile
0   APPROX SCALE   500m

TO LLANDEGLA, B5431

ROUTE GUIDE & MAPS

❏ Was it really the Romans who built Offa's Dyke?

In *The Keys To Avalon*, Steve Blake and Scott Lloyd (Element, 2000) argue that, over centuries, a key Roman text has been misinterpreted so that a reference to the Roman emperor Severus building a wall to keep out the Welsh has been applied to him reinforcing the Roman Wall to keep out the Picts. It is difficult to reconcile this claim with accounts of his arrival in Britain in 208AD to go directly to set up his base in York and then proceed north to repair and reinforce the Roman Wall, which had been over-run by the northern tribesmen. He then pushed on into the Scottish central lowlands and even across the long-abandoned Antonine Wall of earlier Roman incursions which had been built from the Clyde to the Forth. Eventually, severe weather and his own illness forced him to return to York, where he died in 211AD. There seems to be no record of him showing any interest in the frontier with Wales.

The argument about Roman walls is put forward in an intriguing work which boldly attempts to locate on modern maps events associated with the legendary King Arthur, even events which are patently supernatural or even mythical. This has been done through the painstaking analysis of medieval manuscripts – primarily a Welsh work of about 1200AD which was itself a compendium of older Welsh annals and folklore.

Using the same sources, the writers also assert that the hordes of Germanic raiders and settlers who made enormous inroads to become the dominant racial element in England were no more than a single expedition of three boats, which sailed (and presumably must have had to row) all along the south coast of England and then round into the Bristol Channel to attack finally a corner of south-east Wales.

Such arguments, based more or less exclusively on the reinterpretation of a particular group of ancient texts, must be treated with caution at least. **Colin Vickerman**

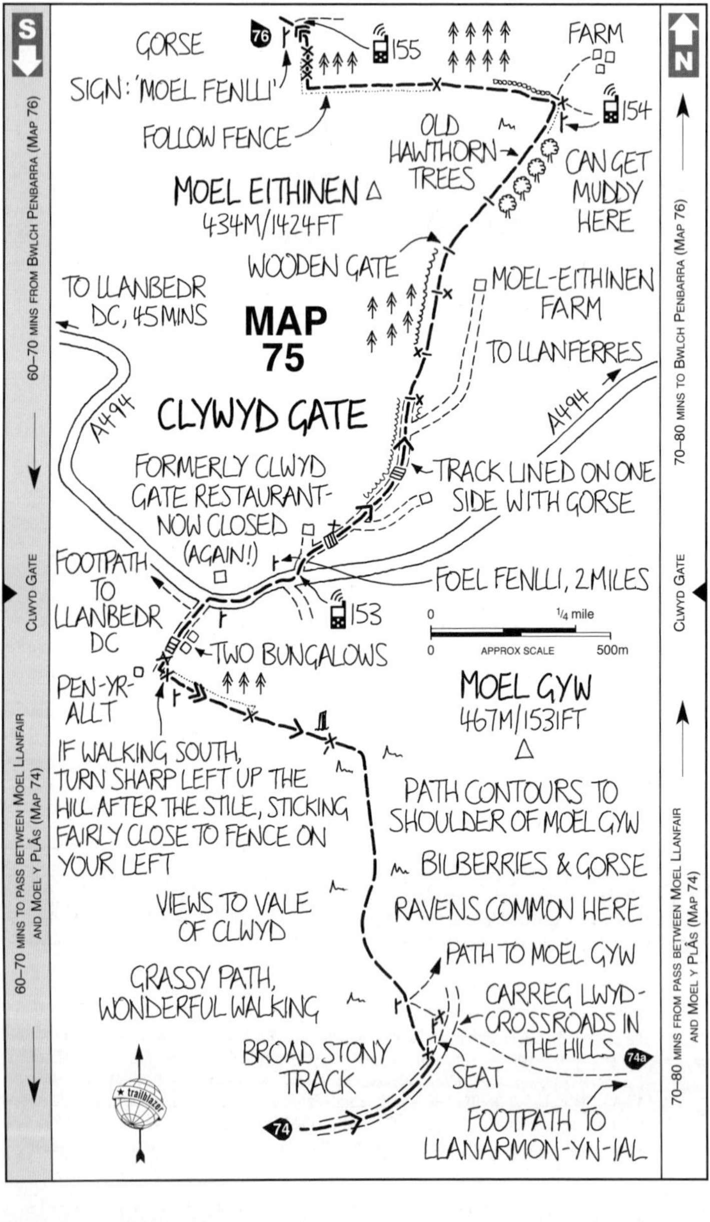

S ↓

N ↑

GORSE

76

📱155

FARM

SIGN: 'MOEL FENLLI'

FOLLOW FENCE

📱154

OLD HAWTHORN TREES

CAN GET MUDDY HERE

MOEL EITHINEN △
434M/1424FT

WOODEN GATE

MOEL-EITHINEN FARM

TO LLANBEDR DC, 45 MINS

MAP 75

TO LLANFERRES

A494

CLWYD GATE

A494

FORMERLY CLWYD GATE RESTAURANT – NOW CLOSED (AGAIN!)

TRACK LINED ON ONE SIDE WITH GORSE

FOOTPATH TO LLANBEDR DC

FOEL FENLLI, 2 MILES

📱153

0 ————— ¼ mile
0 ————— 500m
APPROX SCALE

TWO BUNGALOWS

PEN-YR-ALLT

MOEL GYW
467M/1531FT
△

IF WALKING SOUTH, TURN SHARP LEFT UP THE HILL AFTER THE STILE, STICKING FAIRLY CLOSE TO FENCE ON YOUR LEFT

PATH CONTOURS TO SHOULDER OF MOEL GYW

BILBERRIES & GORSE

RAVENS COMMON HERE

VIEWS TO VALE OF CLWYD

PATH TO MOEL GYW

CARREG LWYD-CROSSROADS IN THE HILLS **74a**

GRASSY PATH, WONDERFUL WALKING

BROAD STONY TRACK

SEAT

74

FOOTPATH TO LLANARMON-YN-IAL

trailblazer

S ⬇ FROM PRESTATYN CLWYD GATE (FOR LLANFERRES) TO LLANDEGLA   MAPS 75-73

[*Route section begins on Map 75, p222*] From **Clwyd Gate** (Map 75), for the next **6 miles (10km, 2¾hrs-3hrs 10mins)** the route continues through the southernmost peaks in the **Clwydian Hills** (see box p228), with a final climb to contour round the broad shoulders of **Moel Gyw** (467m/1531ft), and from **Moel Llanfair** (Map 74; 447m/1466ft) to the col between it and **Moel y Plâs** (440m/1443ft), where the road comes up from the peaceful village of **Llanarmon-yn-Ial** (Map 74a). From Moel y Plâs the hills peter out in the valley of the River Alun and Llandegla.

Leaving the hills behind, you follow field paths with some road walking until, at the **River Alun**, you find yourself among water meadows on the approach to the attractive village of **Llandegla (Map 73, p217)**, arriving beside the church dedicated to St Tegla after whom the village is named.

[*Next route overview p218*]

N ⬆ FROM CHEPSTOW CLWYD GATE (FOR LLANFERRES) TO BODFARI   MAPS 75-81

[*Route section begins on Map 75, p222*] This is a challenging **11-mile (18km, 5½hrs-6hrs 20mins)** stage which involves crossing the northern ranges of the **Clwydian Hills** (see box p228). Traversing the spine of the hills there are several escape routes should you wish to retreat to the safety of a village pub or a warm B&B if the weather closes in.

Leaving the A494, you skirt to the east of **Moel Eithinen** (Map 75; 434m/1424ft) and have the option of ascending a footpath to the summit of **Foel Fenlli** (Map 76; 511m/1676ft), as the path contours its western shoulder. You descend to **Bwlch Penbarra** where there is a **seasonal café** (Maps 76 & 77; *The Hut*; summer 10am-4pm; hours may differ over winter) with hot and cold drinks and ice cream available. You can opt to walk to **Llanferres** (Map 76; see p224; 2 miles; 40-50 mins) from here where bus services (see pp49-53) and a pub can be accessed.

Choosing to continue, you climb **Moel Famau** (Map 77; 555m/1820ft). 'The mother mountain', is the highest point of the range and is protected as an AONB (see p60). Its summit is crowned with the squat blockhouse of Jubilee Tower, built in 1810 to mark the jubilee of George III but rebuilt many times since, being no match for the fierce winds (but a welcome shelter for passing walkers). Although you may have been teased with the odd glimpse of the Irish Sea prior to this day, the wind turbines which line Prestatyn's seafront are in full view from here and you get the sense that the end edges ever closer.

Descending from the tower, the challenges keep on coming, and you pass **Moel Dywyll** (Map 78; 472m/1550ft) and **Moel Llŷs-y-coed** (465m/1524ft).

A dramatic loss in height on each side of **Moel Arthur** (Map 78; 456m/1496ft), a striking, conical hill surmounted by another hill-fort that you'll miss unless you divert from the path to visit the summit, follows before you top out on the next hill, **Pen-y-Cloddiau** (Map 79; 440m/1442ft), the site of an Iron

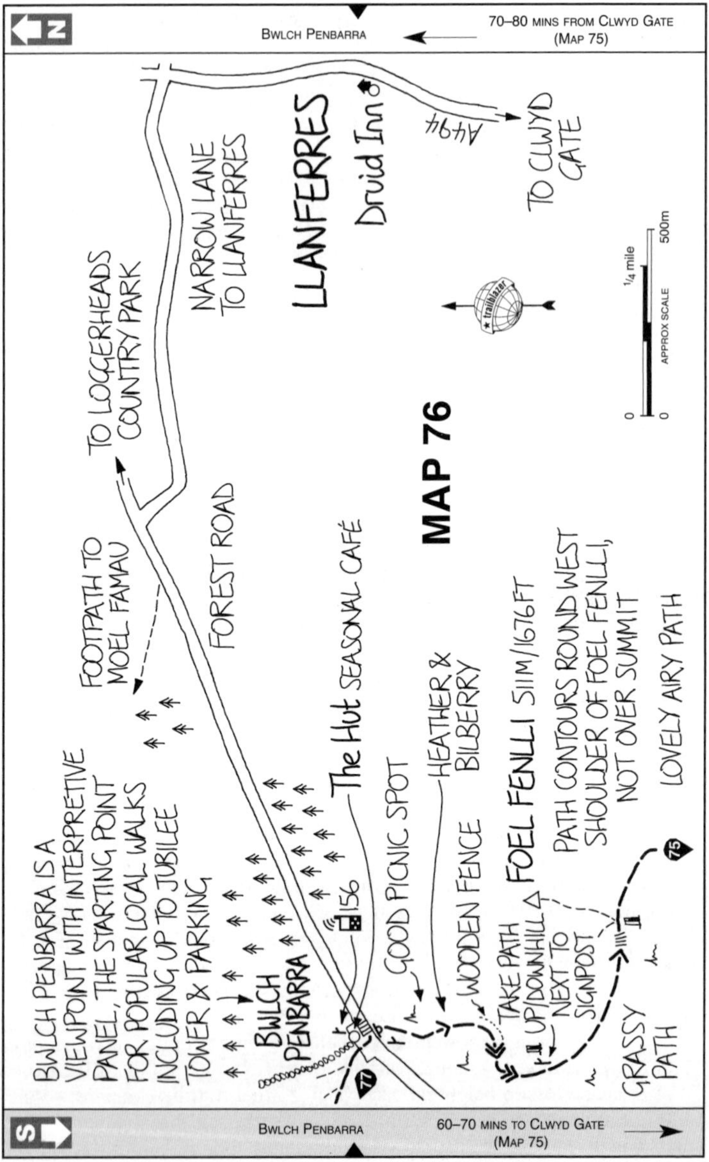

MAP 76

BWLCH PENBARRA

70–80 MINS FROM CLWYD GATE
(MAP 75)

LLANFERRES

Druid Inn

A494

TO CLWYD GATE

NARROW LANE
TO LLANFERRES

TO LOGGERHEADS
COUNTRY PARK

FOOTPATH TO
MOEL FAMAU

FOREST ROAD

¼ mile   500m
APPROX SCALE
0   0

The Hut SEASONAL CAFÉ

BWLCH PENBARRA IS A
VIEWPOINT WITH INTERPRETIVE
PANEL, THE STARTING POINT
FOR POPULAR LOCAL WALKS
INCLUDING UP TO JUBILEE
TOWER & PARKING

HEATHER &
BILBERRY

FOEL FENLLI 511M/1676FT

PATH CONTOURS ROUND WEST
SHOULDER OF FOEL FENLLI,
NOT OVER SUMMIT

LOVELY AIRY PATH

1156

GOOD PICNIC SPOT

WOODEN FENCE

BWLCH PENBARRA

TAKE PATH
UP/DOWNHILL
NEXT TO
SIGNPOST

GRASSY PATH

75

77

BWLCH PENBARRA

60–70 MINS TO CLWYD GATE
(MAP 75)

ROUTE GUIDE & MAPS

Age hill-fort, with a flat top surrounded by the vestiges of earthwork defences and the last of the hill-forts which you will come across on this stage.

The last hill of the day, **Moel-y-Parc** (Map 80; 398m/1306ft), is the hill with the radio mast on top that has been in sight throughout most of this section, although your route takes you over the shoulder without visiting the summit. After this stage's exertions you'll be glad to see the A541 as you pop out of the wilderness at **Bodfari (Map 81, p231)**. [*Next route overview p232*]

LLANFERRES   Map 76

If you head east (about 2 miles/3km) down the lane at **Bwlch Penbarra** you'll reach *The Druid Inn* (☎ 01352-810225, 🖥 druid-inn.co.uk; bar Mon-Thur noon-3pm & 5.30-11pm, Fri, Sat & bank hols noon to midnight, Sun noon-10.30pm) which does **B&B** (1S/2T/2D, all en suite; 🛁; WI-FI; 🐕) from £42.50pp (sgl £60, sgl occ £72), and **food**, with main meals (Mon-Thur noon-2pm & 6-9pm, Fri-Sun noon-9pm) from £10.95. They also offer pick up and luggage transfer.

M&H Coaches 1/X1 **bus** services call here (see pp49-53 for details).

CILCAIN
off Map 78, p227, or off Map 77, p226

There are footpaths to here from the road with the cattle grid (Map 78) and also from the summit of Moel Famau (Map 77).

From Moel Dywyll another path descends east via the reservoir to Cilcain, 2 miles (3km, 45-60 mins) away. The *White Horse* (☎ 01352-740142; bar Mon-Fri noon-3pm & 6-11pm, Sat noon-11pm, Sun noon-10.30pm) serves **food** (Tue-Sun noon-2.15pm, daily 6.30-9pm).

LLANGYNHAFAL   off Map 78, p227

From the cattle grid on the road crossed between Moel Arthur and Moel Llŷs-y-coed you could walk west then south down the lane towards Llangynhafal, 2½ miles away (4km, 1-1¼hrs). Llangynhafal can also be reached from the summit of Moel Dywyll where there is a path descending west to the village, 1¼ miles away (2km, 30-40 mins).

The cosy *Golden Lion* (☎ 01824-790451, 🖥 info@thegoldenlioninn.co.uk; bar Tue-Sun noon-10.30pm; 🐕 in bar only) in the village has rooms (2T/1Qd, both en suite; 🛁; WI-FI; Ⓛ) from £32.50pp (sgl occ from £58). They serve **pub meals** (Tue-Sun noon-3pm & 6-9pm). Evening meals for B&B guests are available if booked in advance.

You can **camp** round the back for £10pp. Campers can use the toilet in the pub and have breakfast (about £6) if requested in advance.

The pub is closed on Monday year-round apart from bank holiday Mondays.

❏ **Where to stay: the details**
In the descriptions of accommodation in this book: 🛁 means at least one room has a bath; Ⓛ means a packed lunch can be prepared if arranged in advance; 🐕 signifies that dogs are welcome in at least one room but also subject to prior arrangement, an additional charge may also be payable; WI-FI means wi-fi is available. See also p84.

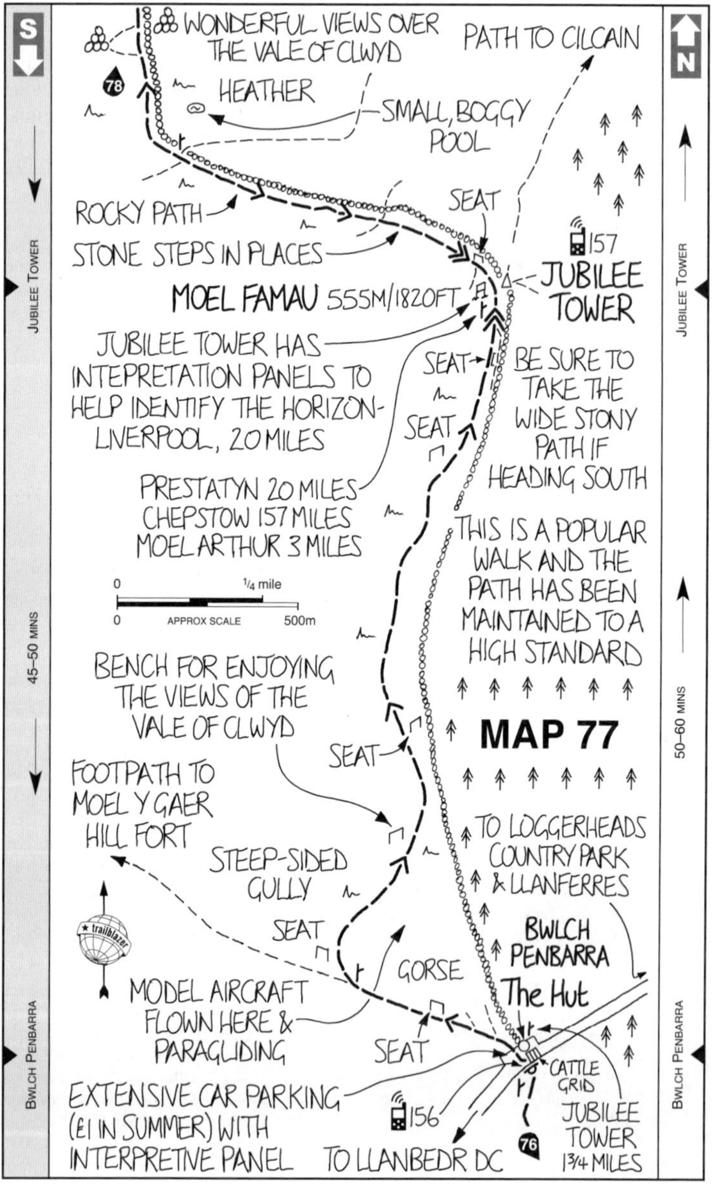

S ⬇

N ⬆

JUBILEE TOWER

45–50 MINS

ROUTE GUIDE & MAPS

BWLCH PENBARRA

JUBILEE TOWER

50–60 MINS

BWLCH PENBARRA

WONDERFUL VIEWS OVER THE VALE OF CLWYD

PATH TO CILCAIN

78

HEATHER

SMALL, BOGGY POOL

SEAT

ROCKY PATH

STONE STEPS IN PLACES

📱157

JUBILEE TOWER

MOEL FAMAU 555M/1820FT

JUBILEE TOWER HAS INTEPRETATION PANELS TO HELP IDENTIFY THE HORIZON- LIVERPOOL, 20 MILES

SEAT

SEAT

BE SURE TO TAKE THE WIDE STONY PATH IF HEADING SOUTH

PRESTATYN 20 MILES
CHEPSTOW 157 MILES
MOEL ARTHUR 3 MILES

THIS IS A POPULAR WALK AND THE PATH HAS BEEN MAINTAINED TO A HIGH STANDARD

0 ¼ mile
0 APPROX SCALE 500m

BENCH FOR ENJOYING THE VIEWS OF THE VALE OF CLWYD

SEAT

MAP 77

FOOTPATH TO MOEL Y GAER HILL FORT

TO LOGGERHEADS COUNTRY PARK & LLANFERRES

STEEP-SIDED GULLY

BWLCH PENBARRA

The Hut

⭐ trailblazer

SEAT

GORSE

MODEL AIRCRAFT FLOWN HERE & PARAGLIDING

SEAT

CATTLE GRID

EXTENSIVE CAR PARKING (£1 IN SUMMER) WITH INTERPRETIVE PANEL

📱156

TO LLANBEDR DC

76

JUBILEE TOWER 1¾ MILES

S ↓

N ↑

VIEW NORTH TO PEN-Y-CLODDIAU & MOEL-Y-PARC

GORSE

79

IF WALKING SOUTH, YOU CAN SEE STEPS LEADING UP THE OPPOSITE SLOPE. THIS DAUNTING ASCENT IS YOUR NEXT DESTINATION

SLATE MARKER △

★ trailblazer

MOEL ARTHUR
456M/1496FT

SEAT

📱159

ESCAPE ROUTE TO LLANGYNHAFAL, 1-1HR 15MINS

CATTLE GRID

LAY-BY WITH BENCH

FOOTPATH TO CILCAIN

MOEL LLYS-Y-COED, ½ MILE

IF WALKING SOUTH, TURN RIGHT ON ROAD THEN GO THROUGH THE GATE BY THE CATTLE GRID - NOT THE STILE

PATH HAS FORMED A RUN OFF FOR WATER FROM HILL

BRACKEN △

MOEL LLYS-Y-COED
465M/1524FT

SHARP TURN IN PATH. VIEWS NORTH TO MOEL ARTHUR & A GLIMPSE OF THE SEA

HEATHER CARPET

MUDDY PATH HERE SOMETIMES

VIEWS WEST TO VALE OF CLWYD. THE LARGE TOWN WEST IS DENBIGH

0   ¼ mile

0   500m
APPROX SCALE

GREAT WALKING. LEVEL, EASY TURF

PATH UNDULATES THROUGHOUT THIS SECTION

MAP 78

CILCAIN, 2 MILES

SIGN: 'MOEL FAMAU COUNTRY PARK

COL

BOTH THESE PATHS LEAD TO CILCAIN, 45MINS-1HR

PATH TO LLANGYNHAFAL, 30-40 MINS

📱158

MOEL DYWYLL
472M/
1550FT

PATH SHOWING EROSION BY BOOTS & TRACKS OF BIKES. SIGNS PROHIBIT CYCLING BUT ARE IGNORED

LAKES

WALL RUINOUS HERE

SPRINGY TURF

JUBILEE TOWER LOOKS A LONG WAY OFF!

77

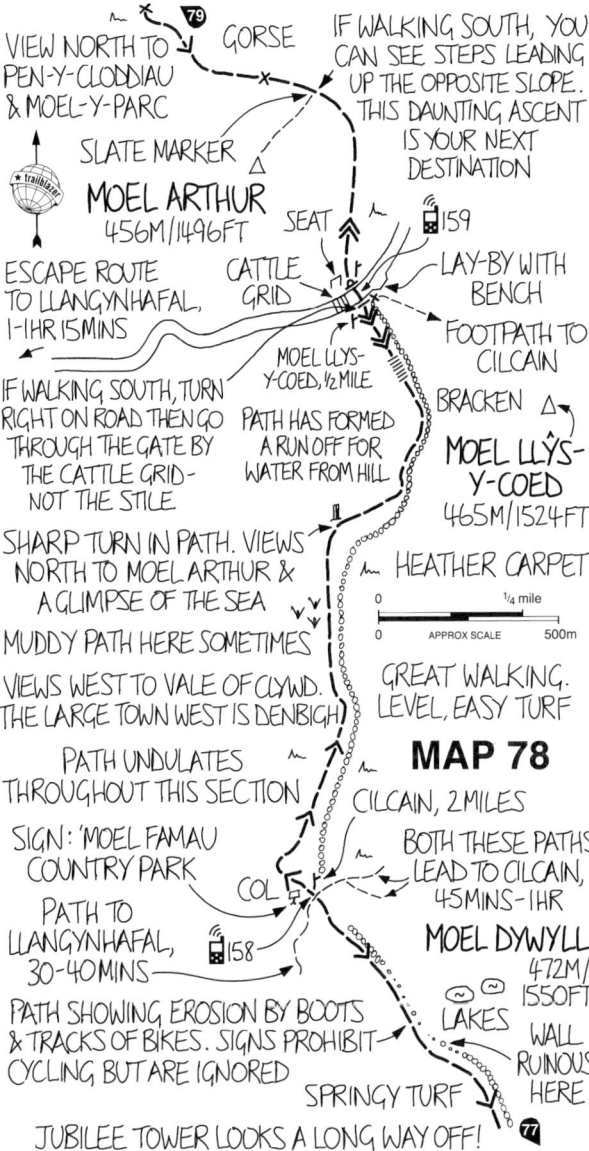

90-100 MINS FROM ROAD (MAP 79) TO JUBILEE TOWER (MAP 77)

80-90 MINS FROM JUBILEE TOWER (MAP 77) TO ROAD (MAP 79)

ROUTE GUIDE & MAPS

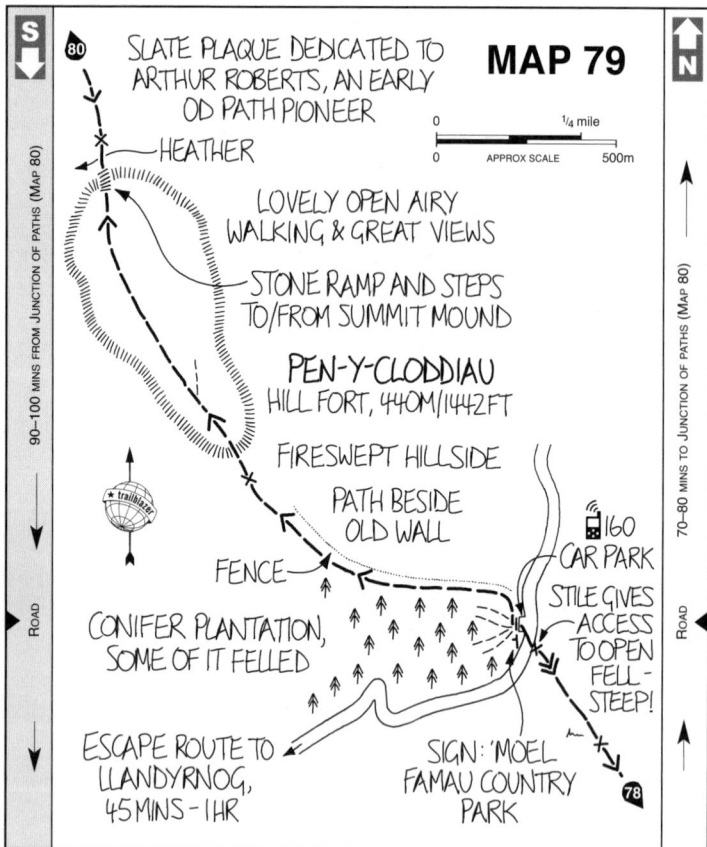

S ⬇
(80)

SLATE PLAQUE DEDICATED TO ARTHUR ROBERTS, AN EARLY OD PATH PIONEER

MAP 79

⬆ **N**

0 — ¼ mile
0 — 500m
APPROX SCALE

HEATHER

90–100 MINS FROM JUNCTION OF PATHS (MAP 80)

ROAD

LOVELY OPEN AIRY WALKING & GREAT VIEWS

STONE RAMP AND STEPS TO/FROM SUMMIT MOUND

PEN-Y-CLODDIAU HILL FORT, 440M/1442FT

FIRESWEPT HILLSIDE

PATH BESIDE OLD WALL

trailblaze

FENCE

CONIFER PLANTATION, SOME OF IT FELLED

ESCAPE ROUTE TO LLANDYRNOG, 45 MINS – 1 HR

SIGN: 'MOEL FAMAU COUNTRY PARK'

160 CAR PARK

STILE GIVES ACCESS TO OPEN FELL – STEEP!

70–80 MINS TO JUNCTION OF PATHS (MAP 80)

ROAD

(78)

ROUTE GUIDE & MAPS

❑ **The Clwydian Hills**

Stretching for 20 miles (32km) in a series of whaleback ridges, the narrow line of the Clwydian Hills marks the boundary between the industrial landscape of Deeside and the gentle Vale of Clwyd, a lush area of trees and fields interspersed with small settlements and a few compact towns such as Ruthin and Denbigh. Springy turf greets the walker across these heather- and bilberry-covered hills, and the views on a good day are splendid.

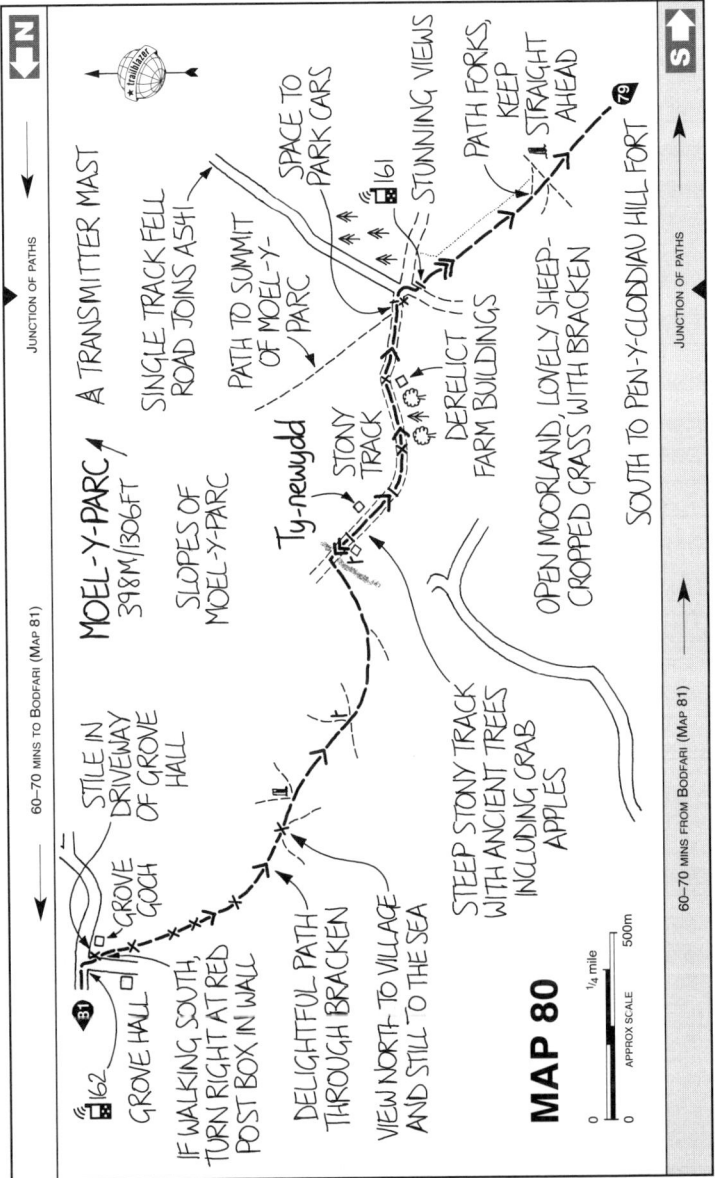

MAP 80

60-70 MINS TO BODFARI (MAP 81)

60-70 MINS FROM BODFARI (MAP 81)

¼ mile

500m

0

0

APPROX SCALE

N

S

JUNCTION OF PATHS

JUNCTION OF PATHS

A TRANSMITTER MAST

MOEL-Y-PARC 398M/1306FT

SLOPES OF MOEL-Y-PARC

SINGLE TRACK FELL ROAD JOINS ASH

PATH TO SUMMIT OF MOEL-Y-PARC

SPACE TO PARK CARS

STUNNING VIEWS

PATH FORKS, KEEP STRAIGHT AHEAD

161

STONY TRACK

Ty-newydd

DERELICT FARM BUILDINGS

OPEN MOORLAND, LOVELY SHEEP-CROPPED GRASS WITH BRACKEN

SOUTH TO PEN-Y-CLODDIAU HILL FORT

79

STILE IN DRIVEWAY OF GROVE HALL

GROVE HALL

162

GROVE COCH

IF WALKING SOUTH, TURN RIGHT AT RED POST BOX IN WALL

DELIGHTFUL PATH THROUGH BRACKEN

VIEW NORTH TO VILLAGE AND STILL TO THE SEA

STEEP STONY TRACK WITH ANCIENT TREES INCLUDING CRAB APPLES

81

ROUTE GUIDE & MAPS

230 Bodfari

BODFARI   Map 81

The village is little more than a staging post on the A541 road. The old shop here has gone the way of many other small businesses on the trail and is no more.

P&O Lloyd's No 14 Denbigh–Mold **bus** stops here (see map and table, pp49-53).

Where to stay, eat and drink

There's **camping** for eight tents at £8pp at *Station House Caravan Park* (☎ 01745-710372, 🖳 stationhousecaravanpark.co.uk; mid Mar to mid Oct; 🐾); booking is advisable particularly for school and bank holiday periods. Showers cost £1.

If you're coming from the south, you're pretty certain to have heard talk of

Dinorben Arms (☎ 01745-775090, 🖳 brunningandprice.co.uk/dinorbenarms; **food** daily noon-9/10pm; WI-FI; 🐾) some distance before you reach Bodfari – it's a popular place. The food is certainly worth the cost (mains £11.45-25.95); the views south to Jubilee Tower from the patios are great, and you may even be treated to a pianist accompanied by a conductor and the whole place bursting into song!

Over a mile from the path but willing to pick hikers up (and drop off/take to the pub) is *Glan Clwyd Isa* (☎ 01745-710557, 🖳 glanclwydisa.co.uk; 2T/ D/2D/1F, mix of en suite and private facilities; 🛏; WI-FI; Ⓛ; 🐾; from £40pp, sgl occ £60).

S ⬇ FROM PRESTATYN — BODFARI TO CLWYD GATE (FOR LLANFERRES) MAPS 81-75

[*Route section begins on Map 81, opposite*] This is a challenging **11-mile (18km, 5¾-6½hrs)** section which involves crossing the first part of the **Clwydian Hills** (see box on p228).

Leaving Bodfari, the first landmark of the day is **Moel-y-Parc** (Map 80; 398m/1306ft), the hill with the radio mast on top that remains in sight throughout this section, although your route takes you over the shoulder without visiting the summit. You do top out on the next hill, **Pen-y-Cloddiau** (Map 79; 440m/1442ft). The site of an Iron Age hill-fort, with a flat top surrounded by the vestiges of earthwork defences, it's the first of several hill-forts which you come across on this stage. The trail crosses one hill after another: there's a dramatic loss in height on each side of **Moel Arthur** (Map 78; 456m/1496ft); it's a striking, conical hill surmounted by another hill-fort that you'll miss unless you divert from the path to visit the summit.

Continuing through the range, you pass **Moel Llŷs-y-coed** (465m/1524ft), **Moel Dywyll** (472m/1550ft) and **Moel Famau** (Map 77; 555m/1820ft). Moel Famau, 'the mother mountain', is the highest point of the range and is protected as an AONB (see p60). Its summit is crowned with the squat blockhouse of **Jubilee Tower**, built in 1810 to mark the jubilee of George III but rebuilt many times since, being no match for the fierce winds (but a welcome shelter for passing walkers). From the tower, you descend to **Bwlch Penbarra** where there is a **seasonal café** (Maps 77 & 76; *The Hut*; summer 10am-4pm; hours may differ over winter) with hot and cold drinks and ice-cream available. You can opt to walk to **Llanferres (Map 76; see p224**; 2 miles; 40-50 mins) from here where bus services (see pp49-53) and a pub can be accessed.

Foel Fenlli (Map 76; 511m/1676ft) and **Moel Eithinen** (Map 75; 434m/1424ft) follow on, before another gap allows the road (the A494 Mold to Ruthin road) at **Clwyd Gate** to cut through the range. This section along the spine of the

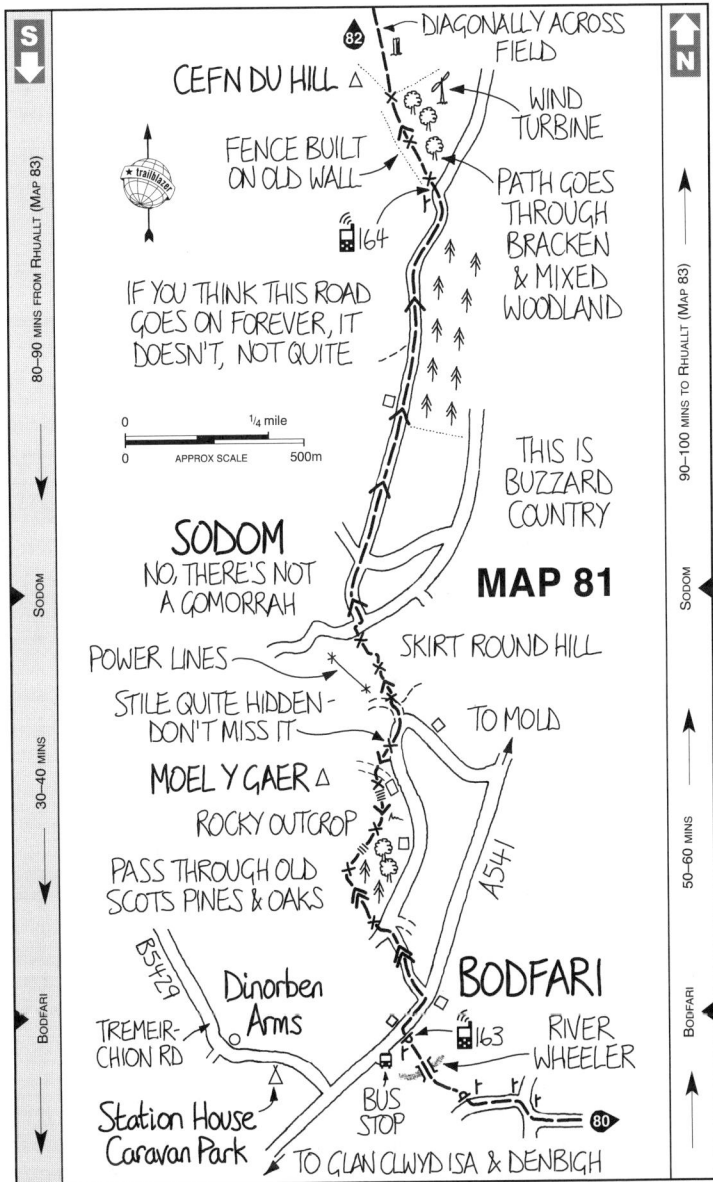

MAP 81

CEFN DU HILL △

DIAGONALLY ACROSS FIELD

WIND TURBINE

PATH GOES THROUGH BRACKEN & MIXED WOODLAND

FENCE BUILT ON OLD WALL

IF YOU THINK THIS ROAD GOES ON FOREVER, IT DOESN'T, NOT QUITE

trailblazer

1/4 mile

0   APPROX SCALE   500m

THIS IS BUZZARD COUNTRY

SODOM
NO, THERE'S NOT A GOMORRAH

POWER LINES

SKIRT ROUND HILL

STILE QUITE HIDDEN — DON'T MISS IT

TO MOLD

MOEL Y GAER △

ROCKY OUTCROP

PASS THROUGH OLD SCOTS PINES & OAKS

A541

BODFARI

RIVER WHEELER

B5429

Dinorben Arms

TREMEIR-CHION RD

Station House Caravan Park

BUS STOP

TO GLAN CLWYD ISA & DENBIGH

80–90 MINS FROM RHUALLT (MAP 83)

SODOM

30–40 MINS

BODFARI

90–100 MINS TO RHUALLT (MAP 83)

SODOM

50–60 MINS

BODFARI

ROUTE GUIDE & MAPS

Clwydian Hills has several escape routes so you can retreat to the safety of a village pub or a warm B&B if the weather closes in. [*Next route overview p223*]

N ↑ FROM CHEPSTOW **BODFARI TO RHUALLT** **MAPS 81-83**

[*Route section begins on Map 81, p231*] Following the last section's strenuous
nature, you may hope for some respite from this short **5-mile (8km, 2hrs
20mins-2hrs 40mins)** stretch, but it includes some tough ascents: you may be
in the 'foothills' of the **Clwydian Range**, but there is still plenty of work to do
before reaching Rhuallt.

Beginning by contouring **Moel y Gaer (Map 81)**, the trail arrives in the
scattered hamlet of **Sodom**; from where a steep but rewarding pull up to the
wind turbine on **Cefn Du** (Map 81) follows. You climb and then descend the
western shoulder of **Moel Marn-Efa** (Map 82; 290m/949ft), arriving on the
road by St Beuno's (see box p234). From here rough grazed fields and the obligatory stiles see you to the footbridge crossing the busy A55, and **Rhuallt (Map
83, opposite)**.   [*Next route overview p235*]

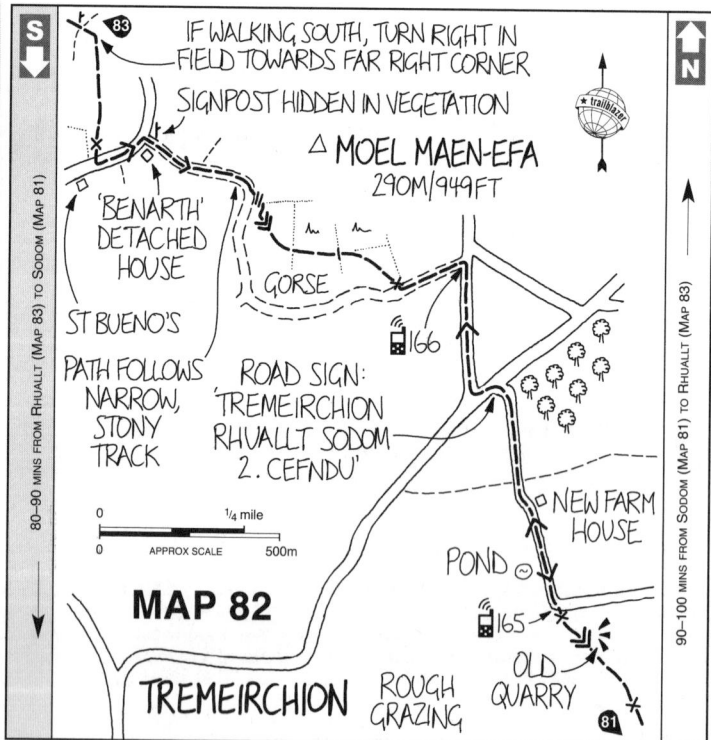

S ↓   **83**   IF WALKING SOUTH, TURN RIGHT IN
FIELD TOWARDS FAR RIGHT CORNER
SIGNPOST HIDDEN IN VEGETATION

△ MOEL MAEN-EFA
290M/949FT

'BENARTH'
DETACHED
HOUSE

GORSE

ST BUENO'S

📱166

PATH FOLLOWS
NARROW,
STONY
TRACK

ROAD SIGN:
'TREMEIRCHION
RHUALLT SODOM
2. CEFNDU'

0   1/4 mile
0   APPROX SCALE   500m

MAP 82

NEW FARM
HOUSE

POND ⊙

📱165

OLD
QUARRY

TREMEIRCHION   ROUGH
GRAZING   **81**

N ↑

ROUTE GUIDE & MAPS

80-90 MINS FROM RHUALLT (MAP 83) TO SODOM (MAP 81)

90-100 MINS FROM SODOM (MAP 81) TO RHUALLT (MAP 83)

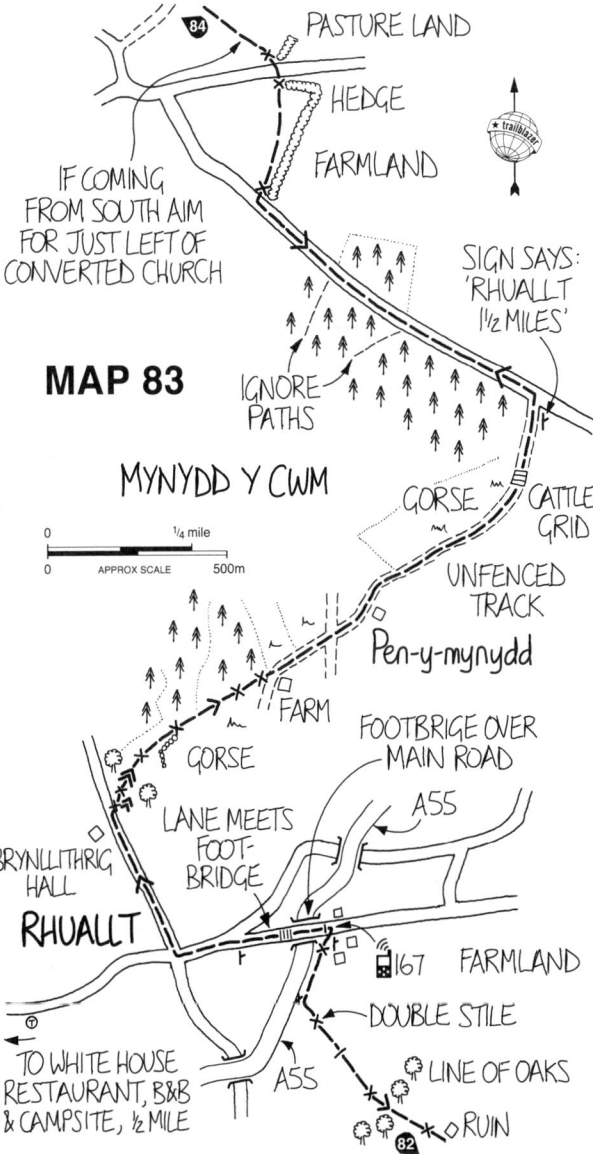

S

N

84

PASTURE LAND

HEDGE

FARMLAND

IF COMING
FROM SOUTH AIM
FOR JUST LEFT OF
CONVERTED CHURCH

SIGN SAYS:
'RHUALLT
1½ MILES'

MAP 83

IGNORE
PATHS

MYNYDD Y CWM

¼ mile

APPROX SCALE 500m

GORSE

CATTLE
GRID

UNFENCED
TRACK

Pen-y-mynydd

FARM

FOOTBRIGE OVER
MAIN ROAD

A55

GORSE

LANE MEETS
FOOT-
BRIDGE

BRYNLLITHRIG
HALL

RHUALLT

167 FARMLAND

DOUBLE STILE

LINE OF OAKS

TO WHITE HOUSE
RESTAURANT, B&B
& CAMPSITE, ½ MILE

A55

RUIN

82

75-90 MINS FROM TAI-MARIAN (MAP 84)

100-110 MINS TO TAI-MARIAN (MAP 84)

RHUALLT

RHUALLT

ROUTE GUIDE & MAPS

❏ **St Beuno's**   Map 82, p232

The best-known student of this theological college, which is now a centre offering spiritual retreat, was the poet and Jesuit priest Gerard Manley Hopkins (1844-89), who studied here as a young man. He loved the natural world and took delight in its infinite variety. It is said that he composed one of his most celebrated poems, *Pied Beauty*, on a walk through open meadows to a nearby chapel, the very surroundings experienced by the Offa's Dyke walker.

You can imagine the poet absorbing the impressions vying for his attention, from sky, clouds, trees and fields to the animals and birds around him. Hopkins learned the Welsh language and drew from its tonal qualities the inspiration for his own innovative 'sprung rhythm', based on the Welsh *cynghanedd*, the 'chiming of consonants'.

Glory be to God for dappled things –
For skies of couple-colour as a brinded cow,
For rose-moles all in stipple upon trout that swim:
Fresh-firecoal chestnut-falls, finches' wings:
Landscape plotted and pieced – fold, fallow and plough;
And all trades, their gear and tackle and trim.
Gerard Manley Hopkins, *Pied Beauty*

RHUALLT   Map 83, p233

With the old Smithy Arms now a private residence, walkers in need of sustenance have to walk half a mile down the road from the crossroads to the swish *White House* (☎ 01745-530000, 💻 whitehouse rhuallt.co.uk; 🐾 bar area only; bar and **food** Mon-Thur noon-3pm & 5-9pm, Fri noon-3pm & 5-9.30pm, Sat noon-9.30pm, Sun noon-7pm). This place is a cut above your average walker's watering hole, but they still allow dogs in the bar area. There are eight rooms (2T/6D; en suite, 🛏; WI-FI), two of which are penthouse suites; **B&B** costs from £40pp (sgl occ room rate) if you book direct. They also have a **campsite** (£7.50 for one person plus tent; contact them for details of rates for additional people). Booking is recommended if you want to eat here on a Saturday evening.

S ⬇ **FROM PRESTATYN** **RHUALLT TO BODFARI**   **MAPS 83-81**

[*Route section begins on Map 83, p233*] From the crossroads in Rhuallt the path for this **5-mile (8km, 1hr 50mins-2hrs 10mins)** stretch starts by crossing the footbridge over the busy A55 and then turning right; for the next hour it climbs through a succession of rough grazed fields, each with its obligatory stiles.

This is farming country and you will almost certainly be walking through stock. Leave any cows and sheep alone and they will ignore you. Look back for glimpses of the sea. When the path reaches the road turn left. To the right is St Beuno's (see box above).

You are entering the foothills of the **Clwydian Range** and have plenty of work to do before reaching

As the road climbs
You will pause for breath and the far sea's
Signal will flash, till you turn again
To the steep track, buttressed with cloud.
RS Thomas *Ninetieth Birthday*

Bodfari, including a steep but rewarding pull up to **Cefn Du** (Map 81) before you descend to the scattered hamlet of **Sodom**. **Bodfari (Map 81, p231)** is 30-40 minutes further on.   [*Next route overview p230*]

Prestatyn 235

RHUALLT TO PRESTATYN — MAPS 83-86

[*Route section begins on Map 83, p233*] And so, the last **8-miles (13km, 3hrs 50mins-4hrs 35mins)** arrive. Field paths, woodland, enclosed lanes, heathland and deep countryside are all encountered as they have been throughout your journey. This last stage, however, is deceptive; you can see Prestatyn and the Irish Sea to the north throughout much of it, but just as you think you'll be making a beeline for the beach the trail leads you to the east of **Mynydd y Cwm** (Map 83) and over the top of **Marian Ffrith** (Map 84; 240m; 787ft), before crossing the **Bryn Prestatyn Hillside** (Map 85), a gorse- and bracken-covered escarpment, with fine views to your destination: the sea, and also Snowdonia.

The descent to **Prestatyn (Map 86, p239)** is a long one and once out of the trees and past the Roman helmet sculpture the trail follows suburbia onto the High St, over the railway bridge and on to the sea; where the sign tells you that Chepstow is 182 miles away, but it's definitely 177 you've completed.

At this point, many choose to take off their boots one last time and refresh their feet in the sea with a celebratory paddle – your journey is over.

PRESTATYN   Map 86, p239

Prestatyn came to prominence in the 19th century with its combined attractions of sea bathing and the supposed abundant sunshine, although what became of the sunshine is anybody's guess. Today it is home, in common with most of the North Wales coastal resorts, to thousands of caravans, which is fine for enthusiasts but rather detrimental to the landscape.

Offa's Dyke Path starts, or ends, on the seafront at Prestatyn, where ranks of wind turbines stand to attention out at sea, saluting the departing walkers or welcoming the new arrivals. A smart signpost boldly proclaims 'Chepstow 182 miles' – despite the official trail length of 177 miles (and the even-shorter distance of 168 miles that is carefully engraved at Sedbury Cliffs!)

Transport

[See pp49-53] Prestatyn is a stop on Virgin Train's London to Holyhead service and also on Transport for Wales's Manchester to Llandudno/Llandudno Junction **train** service.

National Express's NX375 **coach service** calls here and Arriva runs the No 11G/11M (Rhyl to Hollywell) **bus services** as well as the No 35 & 36 to Rhyl. All the bus services go to the bus station. Roberts (☎ 01745-888444) is a reliable local **taxi** firm; it is located on the High St near the railway station.

Services

Unfortunately, Prestatyn is ill-served by any form of tourist information, although there is a **tourist information point** of sorts in the Nova Centre where there is an Offa's Dyke book that you can sign.

Prestatyn's High St contains the major **banks**, all with cashpoints, and a **post office**; this is incorporated within Spar (daily 7am-11pm), one of several **supermarkets**, where you can pick up provisions for the trail. There is a Co-op on Meliden Rd (daily 7am-10pm), with another small post office nearby. Alternatively, there's the all-purpose **General Stores** (daily 7am-7pm) near the beach for the essentials, while east of the High St, on Nant Hall Rd, is a huge, gleaming retail centre including a Tesco supermarket, a Marks & Spencer and a *Costa Coffee* with free WI-FI for customers.

There is a lively **outdoor market** on Tuesday, Friday and Sunday between the bus station and railway station. There is a **launderette** on Meliden Rd.

The **medical centre** (☎ 01745-886444) is on Ffordd Pendyffryn which runs parallel with the High St, while on the High St itself are several **pharmacies**.

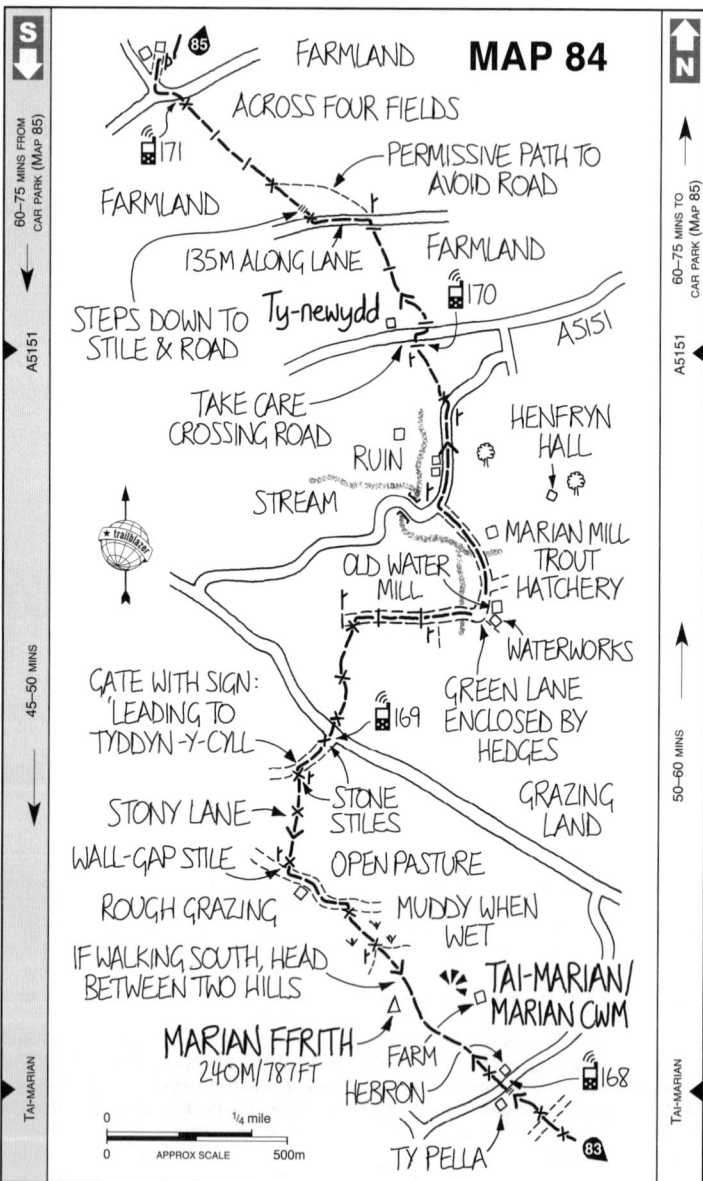

S

N

MAP 84

FARMLAND

ACROSS FOUR FIELDS

85

171

PERMISSIVE PATH TO AVOID ROAD

FARMLAND

135M ALONG LANE

FARMLAND

Ty-newydd

170

A5151

STEPS DOWN TO STILE & ROAD

TAKE CARE CROSSING ROAD

RUIN

HENFRYN HALL

STREAM

MARIAN MILL TROUT HATCHERY

OLD WATER MILL

WATERWORKS

GATE WITH SIGN: 'LEADING TO TYDDYN-Y-CYLL'

169

GREEN LANE ENCLOSED BY HEDGES

STONY LANE

STONE STILES

GRAZING LAND

WALL-GAP STILE

OPEN PASTURE

ROUGH GRAZING

MUDDY WHEN WET

IF WALKING SOUTH, HEAD BETWEEN TWO HILLS

TAI-MARIAN/ MARIAN CWM

MARIAN FFRITH 240M/787FT

FARM HEBRON

168

TY PELLA

83

0   ¼ mile

0   500m
APPROX SCALE

trailblazer

60–75 MINS FROM CAR PARK (MAP 85)

A5151

45–50 MINS

TAI-MARIAN

60–75 MINS TO CAR PARK (MAP 85)

A5151

50–60 MINS

TAI-MARIAN

ROUTE GUIDE & MAPS

Where to stay

Nant Mill Caravan Park (☎ 01745-852360, 🖥 nantmilltouring.co.uk; end Mar to mid Oct; 🐾 by prior arrangement) charges from £12 for a hiker and a tent. However, it is a couple of miles out of town to the east, and you will be tripping over their rules.

Thankfully, the best B&B in town which also allows camping in its back garden, is right on the trail – and your pooch is welcome to camp here too. *Plas Ifan* (☎ 01745-887883, ☎ 07789-992385; 1D/1D or T/1Tr, all en suite; WI-FI; Ⓛ; 🐾 with campers only), 17 Ffordlas, has at times been a chapel and a school but the current owners offer **B&B**, which costs £40-45pp (sgl occ from £70), and **camping** (£10pp; breakfast £5). They have a log cabin for laundry and drying facilities; contact them for details of both their luggage-transfer service and their house in Prestatyn (*Braemar Lodge*) which sleeps up to seven and if available can be booked on a nightly basis. They also have plans in motion to

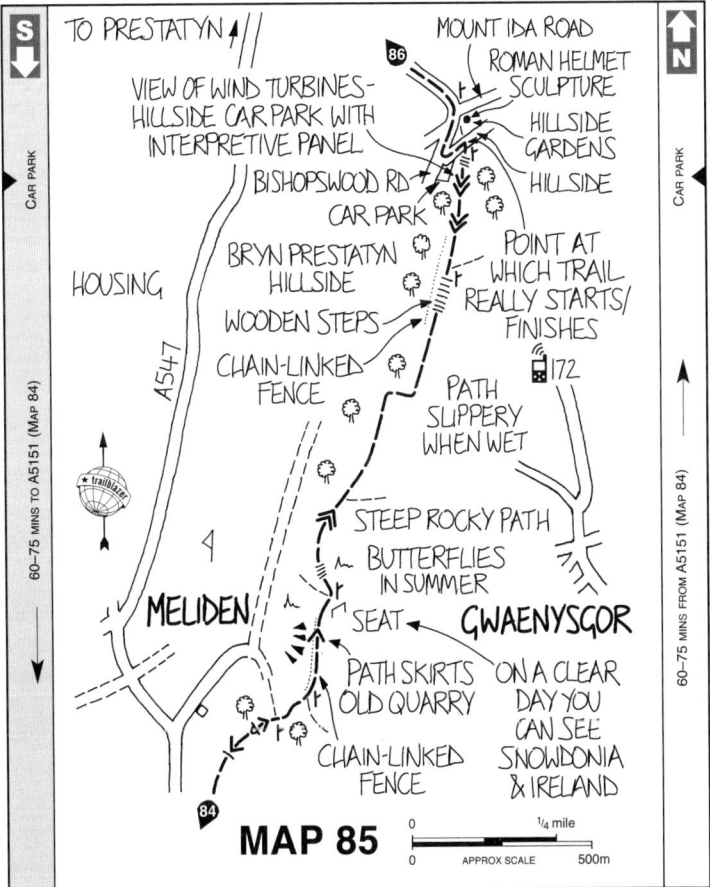

TO PRESTATYN

MOUNT IDA ROAD

ROMAN HELMET SCULPTURE

VIEW OF WIND TURBINES - HILLSIDE CAR PARK WITH INTERPRETIVE PANEL

HILLSIDE GARDENS

HILLSIDE

BISHOPSWOOD RD

CAR PARK

POINT AT WHICH TRAIL REALLY STARTS/ FINISHES

BRYN PRESTATYN HILLSIDE

HOUSING

WOODEN STEPS

CHAIN-LINKED FENCE

PATH SLIPPERY WHEN WET

172

STEEP ROCKY PATH

BUTTERFLIES IN SUMMER

MELIDEN

SEAT

GWAENYSGOR

PATH SKIRTS OLD QUARRY

ON A CLEAR DAY YOU CAN SEE SNOWDONIA & IRELAND

CHAIN-LINKED FENCE

MAP 85

0 ¼ mile

0 APPROX SCALE 500m

CAR PARK

60–75 MINS TO A5151 (MAP 84)

A547

★trailblazer

S

N

CAR PARK

60–75 MINS FROM A5151 (MAP 84)

ROUTE GUIDE & MAPS

open another house for walkers, *Penny Patch Cottage*, in 2019.

Other than Plas Ifan, **B&B** accommodation is pretty thin on the ground in Prestatyn, which is surprising for a seaside town. Gronant Rd is the location of *Halcyon Quest* (☎ 01745-852442, 🖳 halcy onquest-hotel.com; 1S/1T/3D/2Tr, all en suite; ☛; WI-FI), a small hotel where B&B costs £27.50-35pp (sgl from £40, sgl occ £48-60, three in a room £80).

If you fancy something a bit more lively for your first (or last) night, consider *The Beaches Hotel* (☎ 01745-853072, 🖳 the beacheshotel.com; 71 rooms, all en suite, ☛; WI-FI; Ⓛ) where B&B costs from approximately £40pp (sgl from £65; three sharing from £110) but it's always worth checking their website for offers. **Food** is served in their restaurant (Bryn Restaurant; daily 6-9pm; booking essential), or in their bar (Promenade Bar; daily noon-9pm).

Where to eat and drink

Prestatyn has an abundance of small sandwich shops and cafés, either for a quick coffee or to stock up for a packed lunch. Those worth a look include the eccentric *Teddy Bears & Teapots* (Mon-Sat 9am-5pm, Sun 10am-4pm), right by the railway station, where they produce fish-finger sarnies and some great cakes and cones; *Café Cranberry* (Mon-Fri 9am to about 4pm, Sat 10am to about 5pm), halfway down the High St, a dainty place with white wicker chairs and crisp white tablecloths, where you'll get baguettes and fajitas; and, *The Almond Tree Café* (daily 8.30am-3pm), Kings Ave, where friendly service and fry-ups are to be found. By the beach, the **Nova Centre** has a café too.

Recommended by walkers and locals alike and both serving real/cask ale are *Archies* (☎ 01745-855657, 🖳 archiesbar.co .uk; bar Mon 4pm-midnight, Tue-Thur noon-midnight, Fri & Sat noon-10.30pm; **food** Tue Thur noon-2.30pm & 5-8.30pm, Fri & Sat noon-9pm, Sun noon-4pm), which has a Cask Marque from CAMRA to go with its hearty and very reasonably priced menu (Padstow fish pie £9.95), and *Cross Foxes* (☎ 01745-889477; bar Sun-Thur

noon-11pm, Fri & Sat noon-midnight, **food** Sat noon-7pm Sun noon-4pm, which also has a fine reputation for its beer and food.

Next to the railway station and so only a matter of minutes from the North Sea is *Cookhouse Carvery* (☎ 08450-132257, 🖳 cookhousepubandcarvery.co.uk; bar Mon-Thur 9am-11pm, Fri & Sat 9am-midnight, Sun 9am-11pm; **food** 9am-10pm), which acts as a fine stop for those with metres to go, although it may be a little early to celebrate if you're heading south; not to worry – Chepstow has pubs too. It's cheap and cheerful but there's seating outside for you to ponder how long the walk is to the sea, be that to the North or South.

For something more swish but less real ale head towards the beach, where The *Beaches Hotel* (see Where to stay), has a restaurant.

Italian food is best represented by the intimate *La Ricetta* (☎ 01745-856844, 🖳 laricetta.co.uk; Wed-Sat 6-11pm) at the top of High St. As well as pizzas and pastas they do lots of other mouth-watering dishes (mains approx £10-20).

There are several Chinese places, the best being *Chynna Garden* (☎ 01745-855888, 🖳 chynnagarden.co.uk; closed Tue), right in the heart of the High St. You can sit in or takeaway.

Prestatyn's Indian restaurants enjoy a fine reputation and there are several to choose from: *Suhail Tandoori* (☎ 01745-856829, 🖳 thesuhailrestaurant.co.uk), on Bastion Rd, has previously won some regional curry house awards; *Rozi's Tandoori* (☎ 01745-856310; Mon-Fri 5pm-midnight, Sat & Sun noon-midnight), on Meliden Rd, is a long-established eatery with a good reputation; while *Paanshee* (☎ 01745-889196, 🖳 paansheerestaurant.co.uk; daily 5-11pm), is a smart place with seating for over two hundred on two floors.

For fish & chips try *Karl's Fish & Chicken* (🖳 karlsfishandchicken.co.uk), or *Crispy Cod* (☎ 01745-886663), which gets rave reviews. There's a **kebab shop**, *Efes*, on the High St, which does everything from pizzas and burgers to slices of meat, spinning on a metal stick.

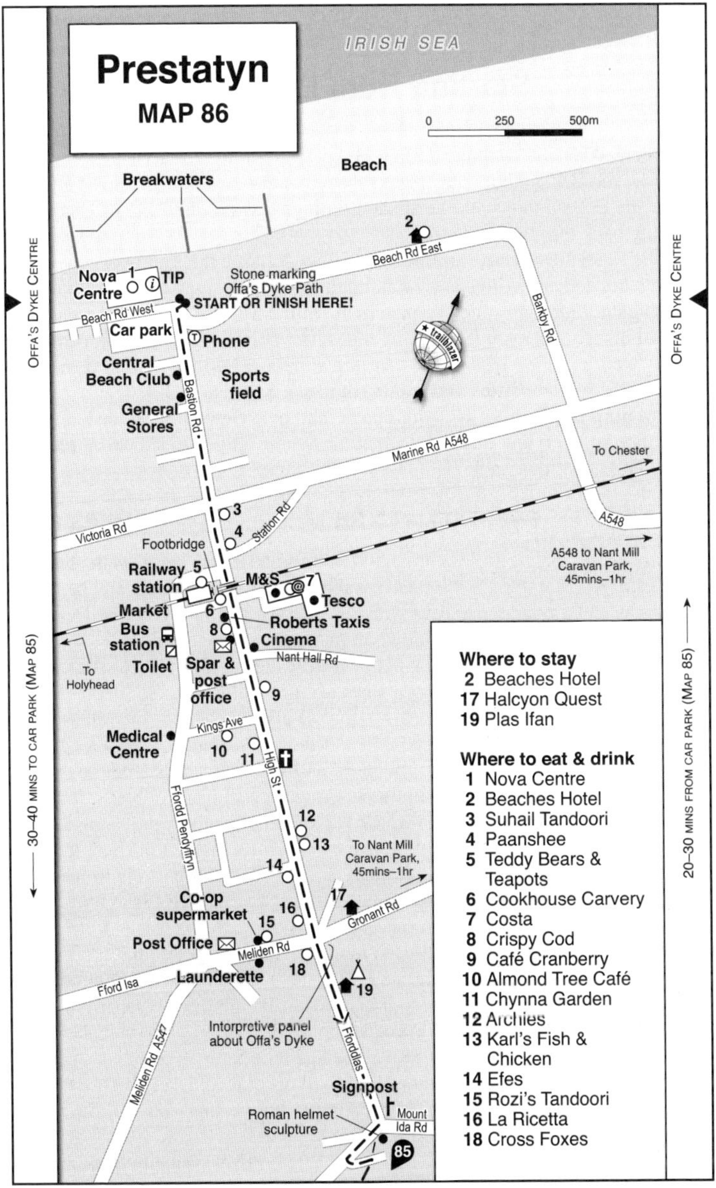

Prestatyn
MAP 86

IRISH SEA

0   250   500m

Beach

Breakwaters

OFFA'S DYKE CENTRE

Nova 1
Centre ⊙ (i) TIP
Beach Rd West
Car park
(i) Phone
Central
Beach Club
General
Stores

Stone marking
Offa's Dyke Path
START OR FINISH HERE!

2
Beach Rd East

Barkby Rd

OFFA'S DYKE CENTRE

Sports
field

Trailblazer

Marine Rd A548

To Chester

Baston Rd.

A548

Victoria Rd

Station Rd

A548 to Nant Mill
Caravan Park,
45mins–1hr

Footbridge

3

4

Railway 5
station
Market
Bus
station
Toilet
Spar &
post
office

M&S 7
6
8
Roberts Taxis
Cinema
Nant Hall Rd
9

Tesco

To
Holyhead

30–40 MINS TO CAR PARK (MAP 85)

Medical
Centre

Kings Ave

10
11

High St.

12

13
To Nant Mill
Caravan Park,
45mins–1hr

14

Co-op
supermarket
15
Post Office ⊠
Meliden Rd
Launderette

16

17

Gronant Rd

Fford Penrhyn

Fford Isa

18

19

Meliden Rd A547

Interpretive panel
about Offa's Dyke

Ffordlas

Signpost

Roman helmet
sculpture

Mount
Ida Rd

85

ROUTE GUIDE & MAPS

20–30 MINS FROM CAR PARK (MAP 85)

Where to stay
2 Beaches Hotel
17 Halcyon Quest
19 Plas Ifan

Where to eat & drink
1 Nova Centre
2 Beaches Hotel
3 Suhail Tandoori
4 Paanshee
5 Teddy Bears &
Teapots
6 Cookhouse Carvery
7 Costa
8 Crispy Cod
9 Café Cranberry
10 Almond Tree Café
11 Chynna Garden
12 Archies
13 Karl's Fish &
Chicken
14 Efes
15 Rozi's Tandoori
16 La Ricetta
18 Cross Foxes

Starting from Prestatyn

Start here if you're walking Offa's Dyke Path from Prestatyn to Chepstow. Look for the **S↓** symbol with shaded shaded overview text (as below) and followed the **S↓** symbol with the shaded timings text on one edge of each map, working back through the book.

The shaded text **route summaries** below describe the trail between significant places and are written as if walking the path from south to north. To enable you to plan your own itinerary **practical information** is presented clearly on the trail maps. This includes walking times, waypoints, places to stay, camp and eat, as well as shops where you can buy supplies. Further service details are given in the text under the entry for each place. See also p83-4.

For **map profiles** see the colour pages and **overview maps** at the end of the book. For an overview of this information see the 'Itineraries' box on p37 and the 'Village facilities' table on pp32-5.

S↓ **FROM PRESTATYN** **PRESTATYN TO RHUALLT** **MAPS 86-83**

[*Route section begins on Map 86, p239*] Offa's Dyke Path starts on the seafront at **Prestatyn** (Map 86). Traditionally walkers remove their boots and paddle in the sea as an introduction to their walk. Since the act is purely symbolic, there's no need to go barefoot: just go down to the water's edge; that'll do!

After ascending out of the town, this **8-mile (13km, 3½-4¼hrs)** stretch gets off to a fine start across the **Bryn Prestatyn Hillside**, a gorse- and bracken-covered escarpment with fine views to the sea and Snowdonia, as well as to the challenging Clwydian Hills ahead. Most of the walk, though, involves navigating a network of fields, tracks and lanes, and with numerous stiles to cross it should not be underestimated. In the wet it will be slippery in places, particularly in the early stages. However, the waymarking is good and route-finding is unlikely to be a problem though take care leaving Prestatyn where the path initially avoids the obvious trail through Hillside Gardens, past the Roman helmet sculpture, preferring instead to head right (west) along Bishopswood Rd and then left up Hillside. Be warned, too, that there are no places for refreshment along the way so you will need to carry your own water and food.

At **Tai-Marian** (Map 84; Marian Cwm) there are some houses but no services – even the phone's been decommissioned (though the box is still there).

This somewhat agricultural introduction to the trail is not untypical of what you are going to meet as you move south. Field paths, woodland, enclosed lanes, heathland and deep countryside are all encountered, relatively easy terrain for the first day but sufficiently taxing to ensure that you will have tired legs by the time you reach **Rhuallt (Map 83, p233)**.

[*Next route overview p234*]

APPENDIX A – MAP KEY

Map key

♠	Where to stay	📖	Library/bookstore	☐	Building
O	Where to eat and drink	@	Internet	●	Other
Δ	Campsite	🏛	Museum/gallery	CP	Car park
⊠	Post Office	✝	Church/cathedral	🚌	Bus station/stop
�€	Bank/ATM	☎	Telephone	▭	Rail line & station
ⓘ	Tourist Information	☒	Public toilet	▭	Park

	Offa's Dyke Path		Cattle grid		Hedge
	Other path		Bridge		Trees/woodland
	4 x 4 track		Stone wall		Rough grassland
	Tarmac road		Water		Finger post
	Steps		Cleft/small valley		Cairn
	Slope/ Steep slope		Crags		Trig point
	Stile and fence		Stream	GP	Guide post
	Gate and fence		River	007	GPS marker
	Kissing gate		Bog or marsh	88	Map continuation

APPENDIX B – GPS WAYPOINTS

Each GPS waypoint below was taken on the route at the reference number marked on the map as below. **Where two instructions are given (eg 'Turn onto/off road'), the first is for walkers travelling from Chepstow north and the second for walkers travelling from Prestatyn south.** This list of GPS waypoints is also available in downloadable form from the Trailblazer website – 🖳 trailblazer-guides.com/gps-waypoints.

MAP	REF	GPS WAYPOINT		DESCRIPTION
1	001	51°38.270'	-02°39.910'	Track joins/leaves path near sewage works
1	002	51°38.677'	-02°39.902'	Road crosses over A48
2	003	51°38.774'	-02°39.988'	Private road/main road junction
2	004	51°38.947'	-02°40.314'	Steps by main road
2	005	51°39.479'	-02°39.717'	Path rejoins main road briefly
2	006	51°39.777'	-02°39.802'	Path crosses main road
2	007	51°39.968'	-02°39.589'	Path leaves/joins Netherhope Lane
3	008	51°40.593'	-02°38.977'	Leave/join the B4228
3	009	51°40.769'	-02°39.238'	Path crosses track
3	010	51°41.229'	-02°39.959'	Bend in path; path leaves/joins track
3	011	51°41.579'	-02°39.819'	Devil's Pulpit
4	012	51°41.815'	-02°40.618'	Ruins of Tintern Abbey
4	013	51°42.221'	-02°39.553'	Guidepost where path crosses track
4	014	51°42.521'	-02°39.506'	Junction of path with stony track
5	015	51°42.642'	-02°39.639'	Cross road
5	016	51°42.963'	-02°40.011'	Turn onto/off lane by signpost
5	017	51°43.436'	-02°40.097'	Path/track junction by stone gate post
5	018	51°43.489'	-02°40.298'	Gate in hedge; path joins/leaves lane
6	019	51°43.821'	-02°40.126'	Lane by St Briavels Common
7	020	51°44.445'	-02°40.082'	Path joins/leaves track after crossing stone bridge
7	021	51°44.867'	-02°39.679'	Interpretive panel near Offa's Mead
8	022	51°45.797'	-02°40.093'	Guidepost near Coxbury Farm
8	023	51°46.390'	-02°40.197'	Path/track junction at kissing gate, Highbury Wood
9	024	51°46.768'	-02°40.098'	Join/leave track after gate
9	025	51°47.040'	-02°40.301'	Path joins/leaves road (steps)
9	026	51°47.528'	-02°40.395'	House on hill, Upper Redbrook
10	027	51°48.047'	-02°40.994'	Gate to track by stables
10	028	51°48.549'	-02°41.193'	The Kymin
10	029	51°48.776'	-02°41.612'	Path joins/leaves road by covered reservoir
10	030	51°48.682'	-02°42.592'	Wye Bridge, Monmouth
10	031	51°48.536'	-02°43.205'	Monnow Bridge, Monmouth
10	032	51°48.713'	-02°43.482'	Minor road/Drybridge St junction
11	033	51°48.832'	-02°44.395'	Path leaves/meets track and Watery Lane
11	034	51°48.751'	-02°45.796'	Bench on top of hill in King's Wood
12	035	51°48.479'	-02°47.165'	Hendre Farm
12	036	51°49.001'	-02°47.999'	Path joins/leaves lane at gate after Abbey Bridge
13	037	51°49.275'	-02°49.419'	Llanvihangel-Ystern-Llewern
13	038	51°49.059'	-02°50.318'	Path joins/leaves road at gate
13	039	51°49.044'	-02°50.941'	Pass The Grange
14	040	51°49.107'	-02°51.505'	Join/leave the B4233 at gate
14	041	51°49.623'	-02°52.476'	Path leaves/joins road by gate
14	042	51°49.820'	-02°52.737'	Cross road in Llantilio-Crossenny
15	043	51°50.087'	-02°54.044'	Track leaves/joins lane

MAP	REF	GPS WAYPOINT		DESCRIPTION
15	044	51°50.700'	-02°54.020'	Turn off track onto road / off road onto track
15	045	51°50.679'	-02°54.363'	Duke's Barn
15	046	51°50.841'	-02°54.745'	Gate after crossing River Trothy
16	047	51°51.127'	-02°55.106'	Join/leave road by gate; Caggle Street
16	048	51°51.955'	-02°55.643'	Gate in hedge by road
17	049	51°52.544'	-02°55.753'	Join/leave road at gate by St Cado's Church in Llangattock-Lingoed
17	050	51°52.889'	-02°56.895'	Gate in hedge by road
17	051	51°52.929'	-02°57.376'	Turn onto/off road from/towards Llanerch Farm
18	052	51°53.417'	-02°58.222'	Cross the A465, Pandy
18	053	51°53.736'	-02°59.306'	Crossroads in lane; turn left
18	054	51°53.955'	-02°58.993'	Stile on edge of open hill and wood
18	055	51°54.092'	-02°59.331'	Path goes between wall and grassbank of old fort
19	056	51°54.693'	-02°59.805'	Trig point
19	057	51°54.949'	-02°59.898'	Stone marker for Oldcastle
19	058	51°55.399'	-03°00.036'	Stone marker for Cwmyoy
20	059	51°56.228'	-03°00.510'	Path junction for Longtown and Llanthony
21	060	51°57.645'	-03°02.156'	Stone marker to Llanthony
21	061	51°57.811'	-03°02.271'	Stone marker for Red Daren
22	062	51°58.327'	-03°03.091'	Trig point
22	063	51°58.875'	-03°03.832'	Junction with path to Capel-y-ffin
24	064	52°01.372'	-03°06.166'	Stone marker
25	065	52°01.676'	-03°06.128'	Brecon Beacon National Park sign
25	066	52°01.953'	-03°06.532'	Path joins/leaves road by guidepost
26	067	52°03.009'	-03°06.778'	Gate
26	068	52°03.153'	-03°06.891'	Track meets path / Path meets track
27	069	52°04.586'	-03°07.649'	Hay Bridge, Hay-on-Wye
27	070	52°05.372'	-03°07.414'	Track crossroads
28	071	52°06.215'	-03°07.438'	Cross the A438
28	072	52°06.678'	-03°08.458'	Path joins/leaves road by steps
29	073	52°07.233'	-03°07.804'	Path leaves/meets road by stile
29	074	52°08.630'	-03°08.457'	Track/road junction by Gilfach Farm
30	075	52°08.955'	-03°08.825'	St Mary's Church, Newchurch
30	076	52°09.213'	-03°08.148'	Summit of Disgwylfa Hill
31	077	52°10.014'	-03°07.321'	Path leaves/joins road at Grove Farm
31	078	52°10.983'	-03°07.034'	Path joins/leaves road at Dutch barn
32	079	52°11.351'	-03°07.401'	The Royal Oak, Gladestry
33	080	52°12.074'	-03°05.581'	Path crossroads near trig point
33	081	52°12.245'	-03°05.017'	Chilean pine trees on Hergest Ridge
33	082	52°12.253'	-03°03.400'	Five-barred gate at end of lane
34	083	52°12.282'	-03°02.412'	Turn right/left after St Mary's Church, Kington
34	084	52°12.392'	-03°02.052'	Cross the A44
35	085	52°12.906'	-03°02.366'	Gate by cattle grid on golf course
35	086	52°13.759'	-03°02.167'	Corner of path on Rushock Hill
35	087	52°14.145'	-03°03.555'	Path joins/leaves main road (B4362)
36	088	52°14.464'	-03°03.506'	Track leaves/meets road
36	089	52°15.277'	-03°04.203'	Cross lane by Granner Wood sign
37	090	52°16.106'	-03°04.373'	Cross a farm lane
37	091	52°16.946'	-03°03.331'	Join/leave the B4356
38	092	52°18.032'	-03°03.084'	Gate by disintegrated barn
38	093	52°18.794'	-03°03.235'	Cross the B4355
39	094	52°19.250'	-03°03.532'	Leave/join road at Rhos-y-Meirch

MAP	REF	GPS WAYPOINT		DESCRIPTION
40	095	52°20.534'	-03°03.048'	Cross the A488 in Knighton
40	096	52°20.989'	-03°03.359'	Cross railway line at footbridge
40	097	52°21.452'	-03°03.510'	Cairn on Panpunton Hill
41	098	52°22.368'	-03°04.381'	Trig point – Cwm-Sanaham Hill
41	099	52°22.953'	-03°04.755'	Cross road at Selley Cross
42	100	52°23.928'	-03°05.780'	Trig point
42	101	52°24.663'	-03°06.192'	Join/leave road to join track near Llanfair Hill
43	102	52°25.243'	-03°05.779'	Road joins track / Track joins road
43	103	52°26.236'	-03°05.733'	Road near Newcastle-on-Clun; cross track between stiles
44	104	52°27.100'	-03°05.283'	Road junction
44	105	52°27.724'	-03°05.323'	Cross road by Hergan
45	106	52°28.733'	-03°05.093'	Cross road at Churchtown
46	107	52°29.957'	-03°05.655'	Cross road at Kerry Ridgeway
46	108	52°30.872'	-03°05.652'	Path leaves/joins road before/after steps and stile
47	109	52°31.920'	-03°06.427'	Brompton Crossroads
48	110	52°32.754'	-03°06.856'	Path crosses lane
49	111	52°34.173'	-03°07.798'	Cross the B4386
50	112	52°35.138'	-03°08.148'	Bridge over River Camlad
51	113	52°36.645'	-03°07.587'	Junction of A490 and B4388
52	114	52°37.332'	-03°06.770'	Cattle grid by Greenwood Lodge
52	115	52°38.380'	-03°05.998'	Path joins/leaves road
53	116	52°38.924'	-03°05.153'	Stile at edge of forest
53	117	52°39.382'	-03°05.849'	Junction; path leaves track
55	118	52°40.360'	-03°06.938'	Bridge at Buttington
55	119	52°41.088'	-03°06.737'	Cross the A483
56	120	52°41.750'	-03°06.081'	Pool Quay; lane leaves A483
57	121	52°44.155'	-03°04.081'	Footbridge
58	122	52°45.609'	-03°04.987'	Four Crosses
59	123	52°46.150'	-03°06.422'	Aqueduct
59	124	52°46.906'	-03°05.340'	Bridge in Llanymynech
59	125	52°47.288'	-03°05.907'	Gate on Llanymynech Hill
60	126	52°48.319'	-03°05.860'	Cross road by postbox at Porth-y-waen
61	127	52°48.603'	-03°07.033'	Path leaves/joins Cefn Lane at Nant-Mawr
61	128	52°49.251'	-03°07.369'	Moelydd summit
61	129	52°49.946'	-03°06.096'	Trefonen
62	130	52°50.780'	-03°06.412'	Crossroads in Tyn-y-coed
63	131	52°52.286'	-03°06.189'	Join/leave road at crossroads after Baker's Hill
63	132	52°52.936'	-03°06.751'	Carreg-y-big
64	133	52°53.722'	-03°06.849'	Path crosses Orseddwen Farm track
64	134	52°54.592'	-03°06.679'	Road junction above Craignant
65	135	52°55.835'	-03°05.805'	Bridge at Castle Mill
66	136	52°56.575'	-03°05.863'	Tyn-y-Groes; path joins/leaves road by kissing gate
67	137	52°57.568'	-03°03.866'	Irish Bridge
68	138	52°58.231'	-03°05.267'	Pontcysyllte aqueduct; path goes under it
68	139	52°58.308'	-03°06.002'	Junction with A539
68	140	52°58.630'	-03°07.355'	Path joins/leaves lane
70	141	52°59.024'	-03°10.846'	Path leaves/meets road near Rock Farm
70a	142	53°00.222'	-03°10.851'	Farm track leaves/meets A542
70a	143	52°59.959'	-03°09.987'	Path meets/leaves road
71	144	53°01.308'	-03°08.710'	Bend in road – 'World's End'

MAP	REF	GPS WAYPOINT	DESCRIPTION
71	145	53°02.270' -03°08.451'	Path leaves/meets road
71	146	53°02.575' -03°09.569'	Cyrn-y-Brain path junction
72	147	53°03.454' -03°11.604'	Llandegla (south)
73	148	53°03.790' -03°12.055'	Llandegla (north)
73	149	53°04.351' -03°12.908'	Cross the B5431
73	150	53°04.348' -03°14.133'	Path joins/leaves road
74	151	53°05.136' -03°14.591'	Path to Llyn Gweryd
74	152	53°06.083' -03°14.819'	Join/leave track; leave/join path on Moel Llanfair
75	153	53°06.885' -03°14.818'	Clwyd Gate
75	154	53°07.566' -03°14.218'	Corner of field
75	155	53°07.773' -03°14.888'	Path junction; sign Moel Fenlli
76/77	156	53°08.148' -03°15.254'	Cross road at Bwlch Penbarra
77	157	53°09.266' -03°15.358'	Jubilee Tower
78	158	53°10.049' -03°16.775'	Cilcain path junction by Moel Famau Country Park sign
78	159	53°10.943' -03°16.664'	Cross road on south side of Moel Arthur
79	160	53°11.508' -03°17.411'	Cross road after leaving / and go through car park on north side of Moel Arthur
80	161	53°12.631' -03°19.049'	Track junction
80	162	53°13.108' -03°20.658'	Path joins/leaves road by Grove Goch
81	163	53°13.221' -03°21.206'	Kissing gate, Bodfari
81	164	53°14.436' -03°21.139'	Lane and path meet by Cefn Du hill
82	165	53°14.866' -03°21.535'	Corner of lane; continue straight
82	166	53°15.381' -03°21.791'	Turn left off / right onto lane
83	167	53°15.916' -03°22.999'	Footbridge over A55
84	168	53°17.269' -03°23.345'	Cross road at Tai-Marian/Marian Cwm; steps
84	169	53°17.761' -03°23.788'	Path crosses lane
84	170	53°18.333' -03°23.637'	Cross A5151
84	171	53°18.666' -03°24.229'	Bend in lane
85	172	53°19.745' -03°23.697'	Path meets/leaves road on edge of Prestatyn

Note: Where two instructions are given above (eg 'Turn onto/off road'), the first is for walkers travelling from Chepstow north and the second for walkers travelling from Prestatyn south.

APPENDIX C – TAKING A DOG

Many are the rewards that await those prepared to make the extra effort required to bring their best friend along the trail. But you shouldn't underestimate the amount of work involved. Indeed, just about every decision you make will be influenced by the fact that you've got a dog: how you plan to travel to the start of the trail, where you're going to stay, how far you're going to walk each day, where you're going to rest and where you're going to eat in the evening etc.

But if you're sure your dog can cope with (and will enjoy) walking 10 miles or more a day for several days in a row, and you can cope with the responsibility of looking after him or her, then you need to start preparing accordingly.

Looking after your dog
To begin with, you need to make sure that your own dog is fully **inoculated** against the usual doggy illnesses, and also up to date with regard to **worm pills** (eg Drontal) and **flea**

preventatives such as Frontline – they are, after all, following in the pawprints of many a dog before them, some of whom may well have left fleas or other parasites on the trail that now lie in wait for their next meal to arrive. **Pet insurance** is also a very good idea; if you've already got insurance, do check that it will cover a trip such as this.

On the subject of looking after your dog's health, perhaps the most important implement you can take with you is a **plastic tick remover**, available from vets for a couple of quid. These removers, while fiddly, help you to remove ticks safely (ie without leaving the head behind buried under the dog's skin).

Being in unfamiliar territory also makes it more likely that you and your dog could become separated. All dogs now have to be microchipped but make sure yours also has a tag with your contact details on it (a mobile phone number would be best if you have one).

When to keep your dog on a lead
● **On ridges, escarpments and cliff tops** It's a sad fact that, every year, a few dogs lose their lives falling over the edge of steep slopes. It usually occurs when they are chasing rabbits (which know where the edge is and are able, unlike your poor pooch, to stop in time).
● **When crossing farmland** This is particularly important in the lambing season (March to May) when your dog can scare the sheep, causing them to lose their young. Farmers are allowed by law to shoot at and kill any dogs that they consider are worrying their sheep. During lambing, most farmers would prefer it if you didn't take your dog at all. The exception is if your dog is being attacked by cows. Some years ago there were three deaths in the UK caused by walkers being trampled as they tried to rescue their dogs from the attentions of cattle. The advice in this instance is to let go of the lead, head speedily to a position of safety (usually the other side of the field gate or stile) and call your dog to you.
● **On National Trust land**, where it is compulsory to keep your dog on a lead.
● **Around ground-nesting birds** It's important to keep your dog under control when crossing an area where certain species of birds nest on the ground. Most dogs love foraging around in the woods but make sure you have permission to do so; some woods are used as 'nurseries' for game birds and dogs are only allowed through them if they are on a lead.
● **By roads etc** For obvious reasons.

What to pack
You've probably already got a good idea of what to bring to keep your dog alive and happy, but the following is a checklist:
● **Food/water bowl** Foldable cloth bowls are popular with walkers, being light and taking up little room in a rucksack. You can get also get a water-bottle-and-bowl combination, where the bottle folds into a 'trough' from which the dog can drink.
● **Lead and collar** An extendable one is probably preferable for this sort of trip. Make sure both lead and collar are in good condition – you don't want either to snap on the trail, or you may end up carrying your dog through sheep fields until a replacement can be found.
● **Medication** You'll know if you need to bring any lotions or potions.
● **Bedding** A simple blanket may suffice, or you can opt for something more elaborate if you aren't carrying your own luggage.
● **Poo bags** Essential.
● **Hygiene wipes** For cleaning your dog after it's rolled in, errm, stuff.
● **A favourite toy** Helps prevent your dog from pining for the entire walk.
● **Food/water** Remember to bring treats as well as regular food to keep up the mutt's morale. That said, if your dog is anything like mine the chances are they'll spend most of the walk dining on rabbit droppings and sheep poo anyway.
● **Corkscrew stake** Available from camping or pet shops, this will help you to keep your dog secure in one place while you set up camp/doze.
● **Tick remover** See above
● **Raingear** It can rain!   ● **Old towels** For drying your dog.

When it comes to packing, I always leave an exterior pocket of my rucksack empty so I can put used poo bags in there (for deposit at the first bin I come to). I always like to keep all the dog's kit together and separate from the other luggage (usually inside a plastic bag inside my rucksack). I have also seen several dogs sporting their own 'doggy rucksack', so they can carry their own food, water, poo etc – which certainly reduces the burden on their owner!

Cleaning up after your dog

It is extremely important that dog owners behave in a responsible way when walking the path. Dog excrement should be cleaned up. In towns, villages and fields where animals graze or which will be cut for silage, hay etc, you need to pick up and bag the excrement.

Staying (and eating) with your dog

In this guide we have used the symbol 🐾 to denote where a place welcomes dogs. However, this always needs to be arranged in advance and some places may charge extra (the fee being anything from nothing to a whopping £20). Many B&B-style places have only one or two rooms suitable for people with dogs; hostels do not permit them unless they are an assistance (guide) dog; smaller campsites tend to accept them, but some of the larger holiday parks do not – however, in either case it is likely the dog will have to be on a lead. Before you turn up always double check whether the place you would like to stay accepts dogs and whether there is space for them.

When it comes to **eating**, some cafés accept dogs and most landlords allow dogs in at least a section of their pubs, though few restaurants do. Make sure you always ask first and ensure your dog is on a lead and secured to your table or a radiator so it doesn't run around.

APPENDIX D – GLOSSARY OF WELSH WORDS

aber	river mouth	*dinas*	hill-fortress, city	*mynach*	monk
afon	river	*disgwylfa*	viewpoint, lookout	*mynydd*	mountain
allt	steep hillside			*nant*	brook
bach	little	*dol, dolau*	meadow	*newydd*	new
betws	church	*ffin*	boundary	*pandy*	fulling mill
blaen	head, source	*ffridd*	lower part of hill	*pen*	head, top
bran	crow	*ffynnon*	spring	*pentre*	village
bryn	hillside	*gwaun*	moorland, pasture	*plas*	hall, mansion
bwlch	pass	*hafod*	summer dwelling	*pont*	bridge
cae	field	*hen*	old	*porth*	gateway
caer	fortress	*hendre*	winter dwelling	*pwll*	pool
carreg	stone, rock	*heol*	road or street	*rhos*	moorland
castell	castle	*isaf*	lower	*rhyd*	ford
cefn	ridge	*llan*	enclosure, church	*tref*	homestead, hamlet
celli	grove, copse	*llanerch*	glade	*twyn*	hillock
clawdd	dyke, bank, hedge	*llech*	slab, stone	*ty*	house
coch	red	*llwyd*	grey or brown	*tyddyn*	smallholding
coed	wood	*maes*	field	*uchaf*	higher, upper
cwm	valley	*mawr*	great	*ynys*	island
cwrt	court	*moel*	bare hill	*ystrad*	vale, valley

INDEX

Page references in **bold** type refer to maps

❏ Offa's Dyke Walkers' Passport

If you'd like to collect inked stamps from stamping stations to form a souvenir of your progress along the Path, the **Offa's Dyke Association** (☎ 01547-528753, 💻 offas dyke.org.uk, see p44) have announced that from spring 2019 you can buy these passports from their website or by phoning the number above. They cost £5 plus 99p for postage. You can also get a new achievers' certificate and badge. The passport has been developed with the support of Cadw, Historic England and Natural Resources Wales. It's in an excellent cause as proceeds from the sales will go to a fund to be used on the conservation of the Dyke.

The **12 stamping stations** have been confirmed, as follows, from north to south:

- **Prestatyn** Nova (NOVA) Sports Centre*
- **Bodfari** community notice board
- **Llandegla** community shop
- **Carreg y Big** Oswestry Equestrian Centre
- **Beacon Ring** hillfort
- **Mellingon Lodge** – at the gates
- **Knighton** Offa's Dyke Centre*
- **Hergest Croft Gardens**
- **Hay-on-Wye** Tourist Information Centre
- **Llangattock-Lingoed** church
- **Redbrook** village store
- **Chepstow** Tourist Information Centre*

* You can also buy the passport from these centres

Every one sold will help to look after the Dyke

'The Passport has two aims: we want it to be a great deal of fun for walkers and every one sold will help to look after the Dyke. The more Passports that we sell the more projects that we will be able to support. We want to help Rob Dingle the National Trail Officer manage the Trail and Dyke sustainably and in a way that protects our heritage for this and future generations. ... The Offa's Dyke Passport is seasonal, operating each year between 1st May and 31st October. The season has been carefully chosen based on data published by Natural Resources Wales and the Environment Agency which shows that the Dyke's soils tend to be driest in this six month period. When soils are drier the risk of damage and erosion to the Dyke is reduced'. **David McGlade** (ODA Chairman)

Stamping stations provide a stamp and an ink pad, sometimes housed in a green wooden box

Tour du Mont Blanc
Jim Manthorpe, 2nd edn, £13.99
ISBN 978-1-905864-92-8, 204pp, 60 maps, 50 colour photos
At 4807m (15,771ft), Mont Blanc is the highest mountain in western Europe. The trail (105 miles, 168km) that circumnavigates the massif, passing through France, Italy and Switzerland, is the most popular long-distance walk in Europe. Includes day walks. Plus – Climbing guide to Mont Blanc

Kilimanjaro – the trekking guide
Henry Stedman, 5th edn, £14.99
ISBN 978-1-905864-95-9, 368pp, 40 maps, 50 colour photos
At 5895m (19,340ft) Kilimanjaro is the world's tallest freestanding mountain and one of the most popular destinations for hikers visiting Africa. Route guides & maps – the 6 major routes. City guides – Nairobi, Dar-es-Salaam, Arusha, Moshi & Marangu.

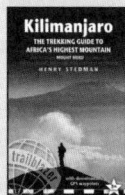

The Inca Trail, Cusco & Machu Picchu
Alex Stewart & Henry Stedman, 6th edn, £14.99
ISBN 978-1-905864-88-1, 370pp, 70 maps, 30 colour photos
The Inca Trail from Cusco to Machu Picchu is South America's most popular trek. This guide includes hiking options from two days to three weeks. Plus plans of Inca sites, guides to Lima, Cusco and Machu Picchu. Includes the High Inca Trail, Salkantay Trek and the Choquequirao Trail. New 6th edition adds two Sacred Valley treks: Lares Trail and Ausangate Circuit.

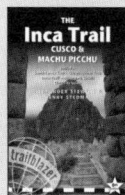

Peru's Cordilleras Blanca & Huayhuash
The Hiking & Biking Guide
Neil & Harriet Pike, 1st edn, £15.99
ISBN 978-1-905864-63-8, 242pp, 50 maps, 40 colour photos
This region, in northern Peru, boasts some of the most spectacular scenery in the Andes, and most accessible high mountain trekking and biking in the world. This practical guide contains 60 detailed route maps and descriptions covering 20 hiking trails and more than 30 days of paved and dirt road cycling.

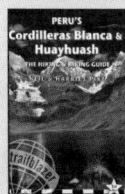

Moroccan Atlas – the trekking guide
Alan Palmer, 2nd edn, £14.99
ISBN 978-1-905864-59-1, 420pp, 86 maps, 40 colour photos
The High Atlas in central Morocco is the most dramatic and beautiful section of the entire Atlas range. Towering peaks, deep gorges and huddled Berber villages enchant all who visit. With 73 detailed maps, 13 town and village guides including Marrakech.

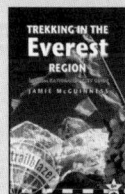

Trekking in the Everest Region
Jamie McGuinness 6th edn, £15.99
ISBN 978-1-905864-81-2, 320pp, 95 maps, 30 colour photos
Sixth edition of this popular guide to the world's most famous trekking region. Covers not only the classic treks but also the wild routes. Written by a Nepal-based trek and mountaineering leader. Includes: 27 detailed route maps and 52 village plans. Plus: Kathmandu city guide

TRAILBLAZER'S LONG-DISTANCE PATH (LDP) WALKING GUIDES

We've applied to destinations which are closer to home Trailblazer's proven formula for publishing definitive practical route guides for adventurous travellers. Britain's network of long-distance trails enables the walker to explore some of the finest landscapes in the country's best walking areas. These are guides that are user-friendly, practical, informative and environmentally sensitive.

'The same attention to detail that distinguishes its other guides has been brought to bear here'.

THE
SUNDAY TIMES

● **Unique mapping features** In many walking guidebooks the reader has to read a route description then try to relate it to the map. Our guides are much easier to use because walking directions, tricky junctions, places to stay and eat, points of interest and walking times are all written onto the maps themselves in the places to which they apply. With their uncluttered clarity, these are not general-purpose maps but fully edited maps drawn by walkers for walkers.

● **Largest-scale walking maps** At a scale of just under 1:20,000 (8cm or 3¹/₈ inches to one mile) the maps in these guides are bigger than even the most detailed British walking maps currently available in the shops.

● **Not just a trail guide – includes where to stay, where to eat and public transport** Our guidebooks cover the complete walking experience, not just the route. Accommodation options for all budgets are provided (pubs, hotels, B&Bs, campsites, bunkhouses, hostels) as well as places to eat. Detailed public transport information for all access points to each trail means that there are itineraries for all walkers, for hiking the entire route as well as for day or weekend walks.

● **Includes dowloadable GPS waypoints** – Marked on our maps and downloadable from the Trailblazer website.

Cleveland Way *Henry Stedman*, 1st edn, ISBN 978-1-905864-91-1, 208pp, 58 maps
Coast to Coast *Henry Stedman*, 8th edn, ISBN 978-1-905864-96-6, 268pp, 110 maps
Cornwall Coast Path (SW Coast Path Pt 2) *Stedman & Newton*, 6th edn,
ISBN 978-1-912716-05-0, 352pp, 142 maps
Cotswold Way *Tricia & Bob Hayne,* 4th edn, ISBN 978-1-912716-04-3, 204pp, 53 maps,
Dales Way *Henry Stedman,* 1st edn, ISBN 978-1-905864-78-2, 192pp, 50 maps
Dorset & South Devon (SW Coast Path Pt 3) *Stedman & Newton*, 2nd edn,
ISBN 978-1-905864-94-2, 336pp, 88 maps
Exmoor & North Devon (SW Coast Path Pt I) *Stedman & Newton*, 2nd edn,
ISBN 978-1-905864-86-7, 224pp, 68 maps
Great Glen Way *Jim Manthorpe*, 1st edn, ISBN 978-1-905864-80-5, 192pp, 55 maps
Hadrian's Wall Path *Henry Stedman*, 5th edn, ISBN 978-1-905864-85-0, 224pp, 60 maps
Norfolk Coast Path & Peddars Way *Alexander Stewart*, 1st edn,
ISBN 978-1-905864-98-0, 224pp, 75 maps,
North Downs Way *Henry Stedman*, 2nd edn, ISBN 978-1-905864-90-4, 240pp, 98 maps
Offa's Dyke Path *Keith Carter*, 5th edn, ISBN 978-1-912716-03-6, 256pp, 98 maps
Pembrokeshire Coast Path *Jim Manthorpe*, 5th edn, ISBN 978-1-905864-84-3, 236pp, 96 maps
Pennine Way *Stuart Greig*, 5th edn, ISBN 978-1-912716-02-9, 272pp, 138 maps
The Ridgeway *Nick Hill*, 4th edn, ISBN 978-1-905864-79-9, 208pp, 53 maps
South Downs Way *Jim Manthorpe*, 6th edn, ISBN 978-1-905864-93-5, 204pp, 60 maps
Thames Path *Joel Newton*, 2nd edn, ISBN 978-1-905864-97-3, 256pp, 99 maps
West Highland Way *Charlie Loram*, 7th edn, ISBN 978-1-912716-01-2, 218pp, 60 maps

'The Trailblazer series stands head, shoulders, waist and ankles above the rest.
They are particularly strong on mapping ...'
THE SUNDAY TIMES

TRAILBLAZER
British Walking Guides

Scottish Highlands
THE HILLWALKING GUIDE

West Highland
WAY

Pembrokeshire
COAST PATH

Cleveland
WAY

Scottish Highlands Hillwalking Guide

Great Glen Way

West Highland Way

Pennine Way

Hadrian's Wall Path

Coast to Coast

Dales Way

Cleveland Way

Pennine Way

Norfolk Coast Path & Peddars Way

Offa's Dyke Path

Cotswold Way

The Ridgeway

Pembrokeshire Coast Path

Thames Path

Exmoor & N Devon Coast Path

North Downs Way

Cornwall Coast Path

South Downs Way

Dorset & S Devon Coast Path

SCOTLAND

N. IRELAND

REP. OF IRELAND

ENGLAND

WALES

IRISH SEA

ENGLISH CHANNEL

Orkney

Thurso

Stornoway

Skye

Inverness

Aberdeen

Fort William

Mull

Arran

Milngavie

Glasgow

Edinburgh

Berwick upon Tweed

Kirk Yetholm

Bowness-on-Solway

Carlisle

Wallsend

Newcastle upon Tyne

Robin Hood's Bay

St Bees

Bowness-on-Windermere

Filey

Helmsley

Ilkley

York

Hull

Leeds

Edale

Lincoln

Belfast

Isle of Man

Dublin

Liverpool

Prestatyn

Manchester

Anglesey

Bangor

Crewe

Nottingham

Cromer

Norwich

Great Yarmouth

Knettishall Heath

Birmingham

Cambridge

Cardigan

Chipping Campden

Amroth

Kemble

Ivinghoe Beacon

London

Chepstow

Bristol

Cardiff

Bath

Overton Hill

Canterbury

Dover

Minehead

Winchester

Farnham

Salisbury

Eastbourne

Brighton

Bude

Portsmouth

Isle of Wight

Exeter

Poole

Plymouth

Isles of Scilly

Outer Hebrides

0   50   100km
0   25   50 miles

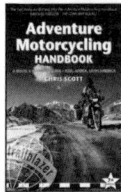

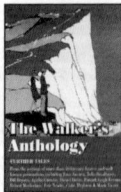

For more information about Trailblazer and our
expanding range of guides, for guidebook updates or
for credit card mail order sales visit our website:

www.trailblazer-guides.com

0 3 miles
0 5km

trailblazer

PRESTATYN MAP 86

Talacre

Gronant

Pe n-y-ffordd

MAP 85

RHYL

Meliden Gwaenysgor

Mostyn

MAP 84

Kinmel Bay

Dyserth Trelawynd Berthengam

Towyn

A548

A547

Rhuddlan

A525

Tai-marian/
Marian Cwm

A5151

Greenfield

Holway

A55

Gorsedd

Milwr

MAP 83

Rhuallt

Bodelwyddan

A55

St Asaph/
Llanelwy

B5381

Tremeirchion

MAP 82

Brynford

Caerwys

Pentre
Halkyn

B5121

A55

A541

Llannefydd

Sodom

MAP 81

Bodfari

Nannerch

B5123

Trefnant

B5428

A525

B5429

Henllan

MAP 80

MAP 79

B5382

B5428

Pen-y-Cloddiau

MAP 78

DENBIGH

Llangwyfan

Pantymwyn

Groes

Lawnt

Llandyrnog

Elevation profile

700m
600
500
400
300
200

Tai-marian/
Marian Cwm

Sodom

Prestatyn

Bodfari Rhuallt

0 miles 2 3 4 5 6 7 8 9 10 11 12 13

Prestatyn
Rhuallt
Bodfari

Chepstow

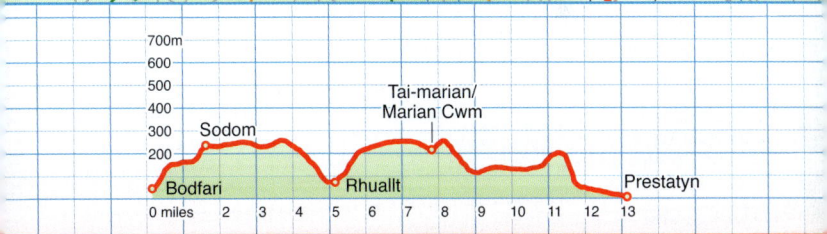

N Maps 81-83, Bodfari to Rhuallt
5 miles/8km – 2hrs 20mins-2hrs 40mins

Maps 83-86, Rhuallt to Prestatyn
8 miles/13km – 3hrs 50mins-4hrs 35mins

S Maps 86-83, Prestatyn to Rhuallt
8 miles/13km – 3½-4¼hrs

Maps 83-81, Rhuallt to Bodfari
5 miles/8km – 1hr 50mins-2hrs 10mins

NOTE: Add 20-30% to these times to allow for stops

Tremeirchion Caerwys Pentre Halkyn

Trefnant Sodom MAP 81 Bodfari Nannerch CONNAH'S QUAY

Northop

DENBIGH MAP 80 MAP 79 Pen-y-Cloddiau MAP 78 Pantymwyn MOLD BUCKLE

Llangwyfan

Lawnt Llandyrnog

Prion Moel Famau/ Jubilee Tower MAP 77 Loggerheads

Llanferres

Llanbedr- Dyffryn-Clwyd MAP 76

Cyffylliog Ruthin Treuddyn

Bontuchel Clwyd Gate MAP 75 MAP 74a Llanarmon-yn-Ial

Llanfair Dyffryn Clwyd MAP 74

Pwll-glas Graig Bwlchgwyn

Clawdd newydd MAP 73 Pant Coedpoeth

Llandegla MAP 72

Llanelidan MAP 71

0 — 3 miles
0 — 5km

trailblazer

Elevation profile:

700m 600 500 400 300 200 100

Turns for Llanarmon-yn-Ial

Moel Famau/Jubilee Tower 555m/1820ft

Pen-y-Cloddiau 440m/1442ft

Llandegla Llanarmon-yn-Ial Clwyd Gate Llanarmon-yn-Ial Bodfari

0 miles 2 3 4 5 6 7 8 9 10 11 12 13 14 15 16 17

Prestatyn
Bodfari
Clwyd Gate
Llandegla

Chepstow

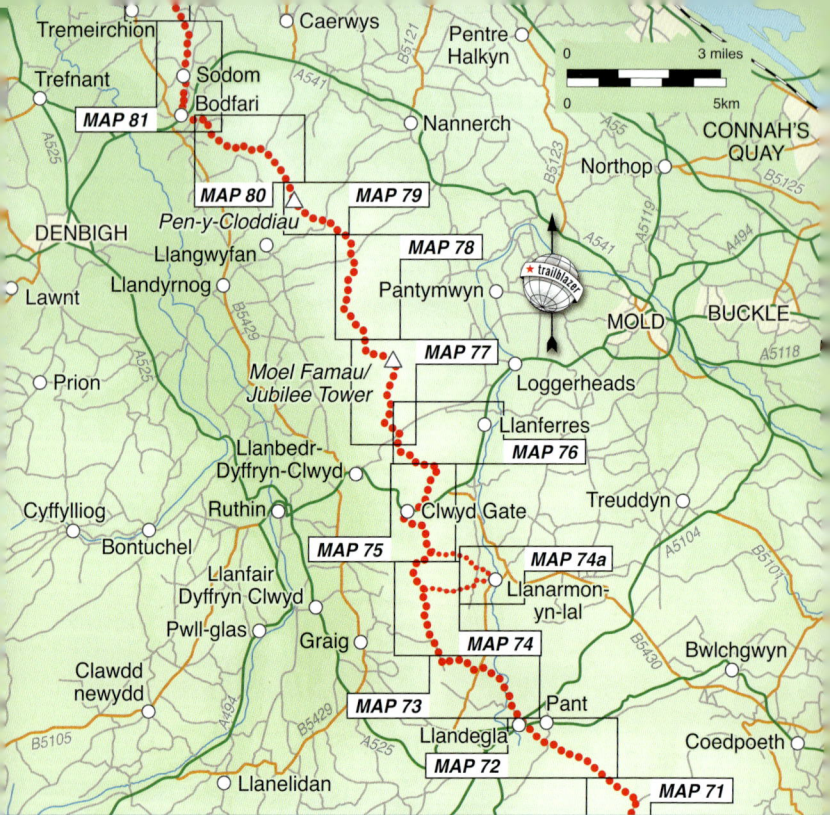

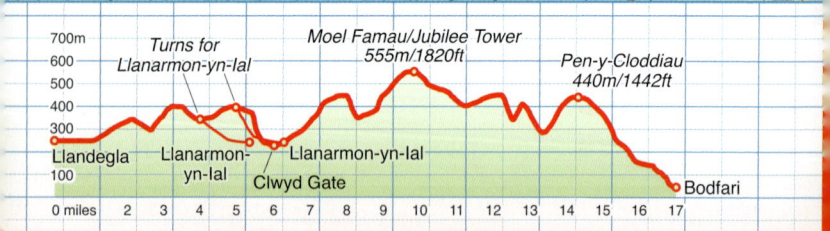

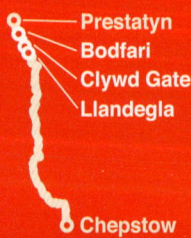

N ↑ Maps 73-75, Llandegla to Clwyd Gate
6 miles/10km – 2hrs 50mins-3hrs 20mins

Maps 75-81, Clwyd Gate to Bodfari
11 miles/18km – 5½hrs-6hrs 20mins

S ↓ Maps 81-75, Bodfari to Clwyd Gate
11 miles/18km – 5¾-6½hrs

Maps 75-73, Clwyd Gate to Llandegla
6 miles/10km – 2¾-3hrs 10mins

NOTE: Add 20-30% to these times to allow for stops

Map locations (top map)

Llanelidan
Llandegla
Pant
Coedpoeth
WREXHAM
MAP 72
Bryneglwys
MAP 71
Rhosllanerchrugog
MAP 70a
Eyton
MAP 70
Carrog
MAP 69
Ruabon
Garth
Trevor
Glyndyfrdwy
MAP 68
Llangollen
MAP 70b
Froncysyllte
MAP 67
Ty'n-y-groes
MAP 66
Glyn Ceiriog
Pontfadog
Castle Mill
Chirk
Pentre Cilgwyn
MAP 65
St Martin's
Craignant
Weston Rhyn
Tregeiriog
MAP 64
Selattyn
Gobowen
Llanmarmon Dyffryn Ceiriog
MAP 63
Racecourse Common
Whittington

0   3 miles
0   5km

trailblazer

Elevation profile

500m
400
200
100

Racecourse Common
Craignant
Castle Mill
Ty'n-y-groes
Froncysyllte
Trevor
Turns for Llangollen Map 69 / Map 70
Llangollen
Llandegla

0 miles 2 3 4 5 6 7 8 9 10 11 12 13 14 15 16 17 18 19 20 21

Prestatyn
Llandegla
Llangollen
Castle Mill
Racecourse Common

Chepstow

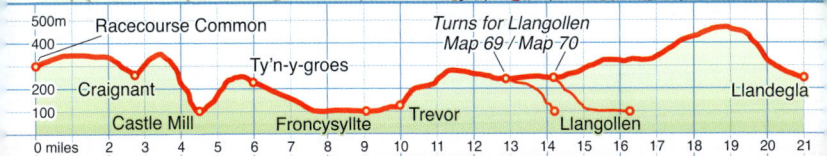

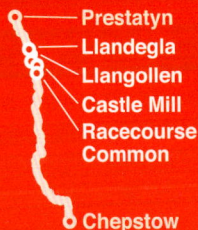

N↑ **Maps 63-65, Racecourse Common to Castle Mill** 4½ miles/7km – 1hr 50mins-2hrs 20mins

Maps 65-69, Castle Mill to Dinas Bran (& Llangollen) 8½ miles/14km – 3hrs 50mins-4½hrs

Maps 69-73, Dinas Bran (& Llangollen) to Llandegla 8 miles/13km – 3hrs 55mins-4½hrs

S↓ **Maps 73-69, Llandegla to Dinas Bran (& Llangollen)** 8 miles/13km – 3¾-4hrs 20mins

Maps 69-65, (Llangollen &) Dinas Bran to Castle Mill 8½ miles/14km – 3hrs 50mins-4½hrs

Maps 65-63, Castle Mill to Racecourse Common 4½ miles/7km – 2hrs-2hrs 35mins

NOTE: Add 20-30% to these times to allow for stops

MAP 63
Racecourse Common
Whittington
OSWESTRY
Ty'n-y-coed
Llansilin
MAP 62
Morda
Queen's Head
Trefonen
B5009
Maesbury
Moelydd
Treflach
MAP 61
Nant-Mawr
Weirbrook
B4580
A5
B4580
Porth-y-waen
MAP 60
Crickheath
Rhos-y-brithdir
Pant
Knockin
Llanfechain
Llanymynech
Kinnerly
B4398
Llanfyllin
MAP 59
Wilcott
B4398
Bryn Mawr
Four Crosses
A490
A495
Llandrinio
MAP 58
Arddleen
B4393
Crewgreen
MAP 57
Alberbury
B4393
Meifod
A490
Pool Quay
MAP 56
Wattlesborough Heath
MAP 55
Buttington
Westbury
B4392
WELSHPOOL
MAP 54
trailblazer
A495

600m
500
400
300
200
100

Moelydd 285m/934ft
Nant-Mawr
Racecourse Common
Porth-y-waen
Trefonen
Welshpool
Llanymynech
Pool Quay
Four Crosses
Buttington
Ty'n-y-coed

0 1 2 3 4 5 6 7 8 9 10 11 12 13 14 15 16 17 18 19 20

Prestatyn
Racecourse Common
Llanymynech
Buttington

Chepstow

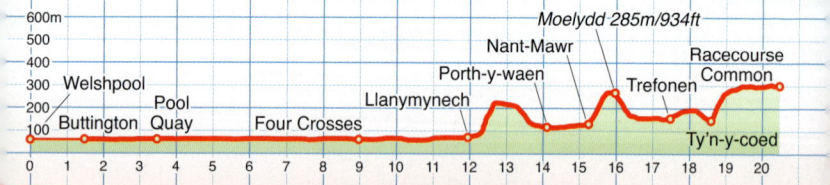

N **Maps 55-59, Buttington (for Welshpool) to Llanymynech** 10½ miles/17km – 4hrs-4hrs 40mins
Maps 59-63, Llanymynech to Racecourse Common 8½ miles/14km – 4¾hrs-5½hrs

S **Maps 63-59, Racecourse Common to Llanymynech** 8½ miles/14km – 4½hrs-5hrs 25mins
Maps 59-55, Llanymynech to Buttington (for Welshpool) 10½ miles/17km – 4hrs-4hrs 40mins
NOTE: Add 20-30% to these times to allow for stops

Pool Quay

MAP 56

Wattlesborough Heath

MAP 55

Westbury

Buttington

WELSHPOOL

MAP 54

MAP 54a

A458

△ *Beacon Ring*

Castle Caereinion

MAP 53

Brockton

Worthen

MAP 52

B4390

MAP 51

Kingswood

Forden

0   3 miles

0   5km

MAP 50

Chirbury

Bettws Cedewain

MAP 49a

Montgomery

Priest Weston

MAP 49

MAP 48

Abermule

Churchstoke

Norbury

MAP 47

Brompton Crossroads

Llanmerewig

Pontglas

MAP 46

Bishop's Castle

Kerry

trailblazer

700m
600
500
400
300
200

Brompton Crossroads

Turn for Montgomery

Kingswood

Beacon Ring

Montgomery

Forden

Buttington

Welshpool

0 miles   2   3   4   5   6   7   8   9   10   11   12   13   14

Prestatyn

Buttington

Brompton Crossroads

Chepstow

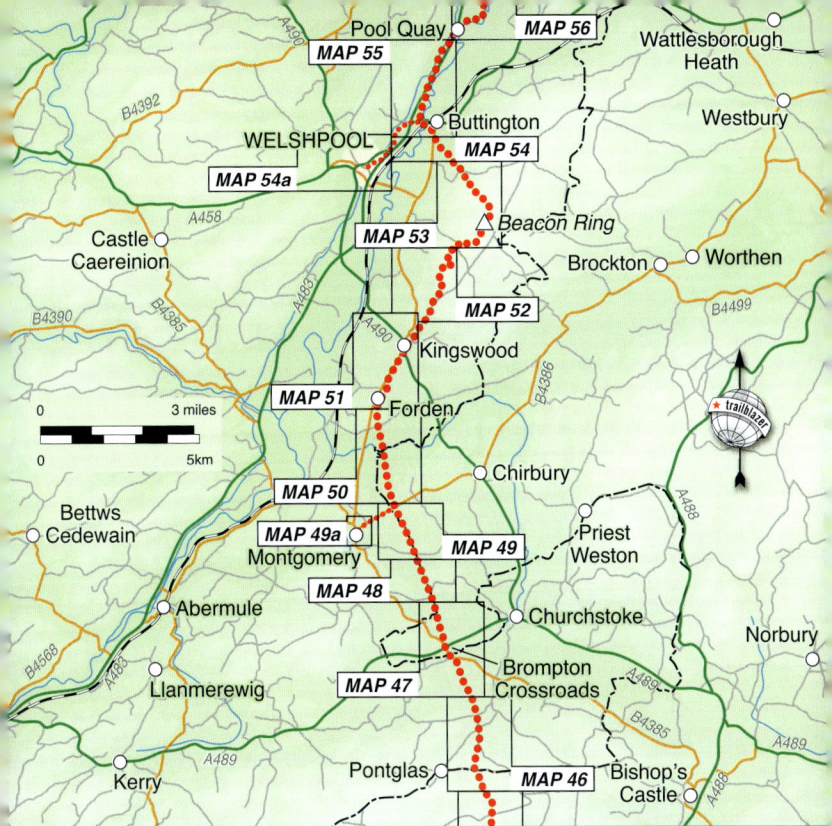

N↑ **Maps 47-55, Brompton Crossroads to Buttington (for Welshpool)**
12½ miles/20km – 4hrs 55mins-5hrs 40mins

S↓ **Maps 55-47, Buttington (for Welshpool) to Brompton Crossroads**
12½ miles/20km – 5¼hrs-5hrs 55mins

NOTE: Add 20-30% to these times to allow for stops

Abermule
Churchstoke
Norbury
Llanmerewig
Brompton Crossroads
MAP 47
A489
B4385
Kerry
A489
Pontglas
MAP 46
Bishop's Castle
Mainstone
Eyton
Churchtown
MAP 45
A488
trailblazer
Lydbury North
B4368
MAP 44
Kempton
B4355
Newcastle-on-Clun
Clunton
B4355
Clun
MAP 43
MAP 43a
430m/1408ft Highest point on Offa's Dyke
MAP 42
Hopton Castle
Selley Cross
Bedstone
Crossways
Skyborry Green
MAP 41
Bucknell
B4356
A4113
MAP 40
Knighton
Brampton Bryan

700m
600
500
400
300
Highest point of Offa's Dyke 430m/1408ft
Churchtown
Brompton Crossroads
Knighton
Turn for Clun
Clun
0 miles 2 3 4 5 6 7 8 9 10 11 12 13 14

0   3 miles
0   5km

Prestatyn

Brompton Crossroads

Knighton

Chepstow

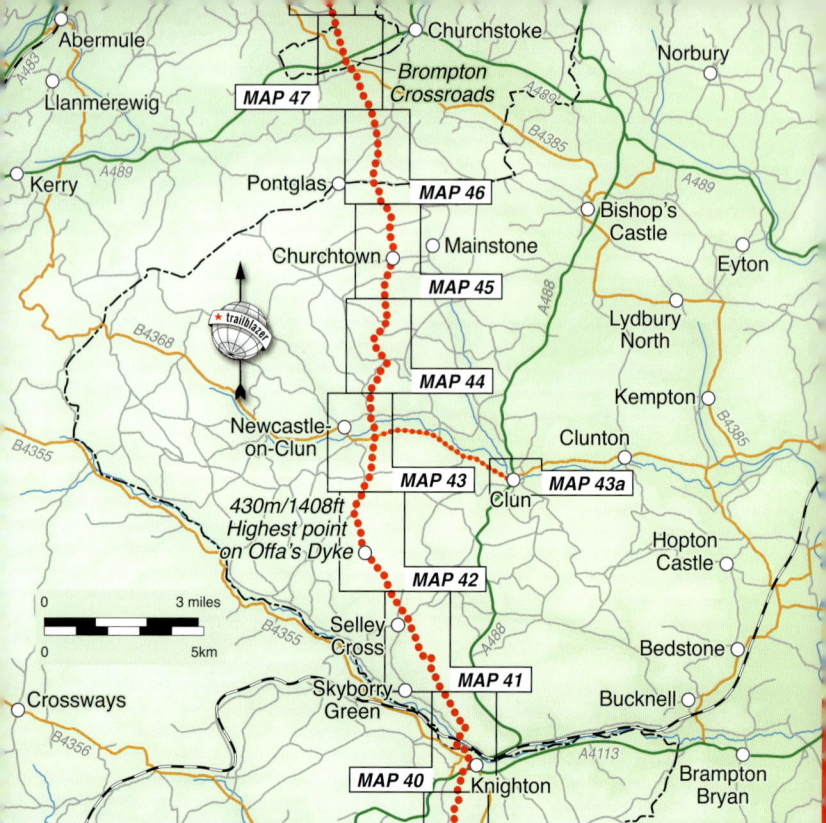

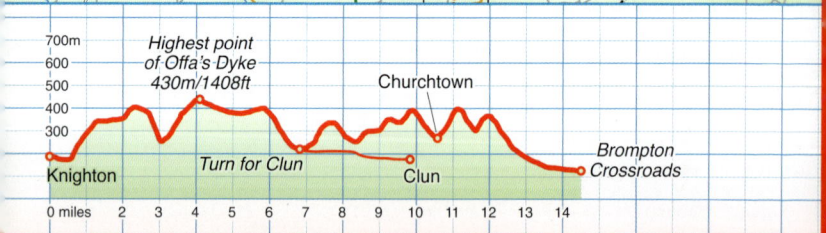

N↑ Maps 40-47, Knighton to Brompton Crossroads
14½ miles/23km – 8hrs-9¼hrs

S↓ Maps 47-40, Brompton Crossroads to Knighton
14½ miles/23km – 7hrs-8¼hrs

NOTE: Add 20-30% to these times to allow for stops

Crossways

B4355
Selley
Cross
Skyborry
Green

MAP 41

Bedstone
Bucknell

B4356

MAP 40
Knighton

A4113

Brampton
Bryan

Rhos-y-
meirch

MAP 39

A488

B4356

Norton

MAP 38
Dolley
Green

MAP 37
Discoed

Presteigne

B4362

Evenjobb

New Radnor

MAP 36

Walton

MAP 35

B4355

A44

MAP 33

MAP 34
Kington

MAP 32
Gladestry

MAP 31

Kingswood

A480

0 — 3 miles
0 — 5km

★ trailblazer

700m
600
500
400
300
200

*Turn for
Evenjobb*

Dolley Green

Knighton

Kington

0 miles 2   3   4   5   6   7   8   9   10   11   12   13

Prestatyn

Knighton
Kington

Chepstow

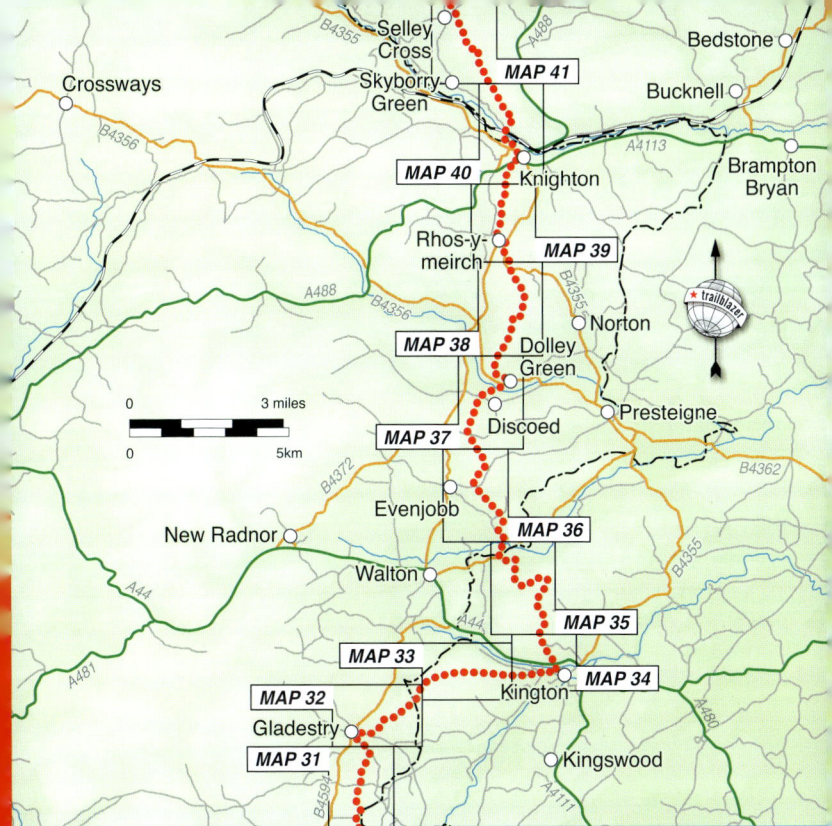

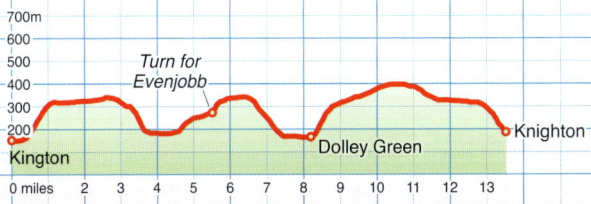

N↑ Maps 34-40, Kington to Knighton
13½ miles/22km – 6hrs-6hrs 55mins

S↓ Maps 40-34, Knighton to Kington
13½ miles/22km – 5hrs 55mins-6hrs 40mins

NOTE: Add 20-30% to these times to allow for stops

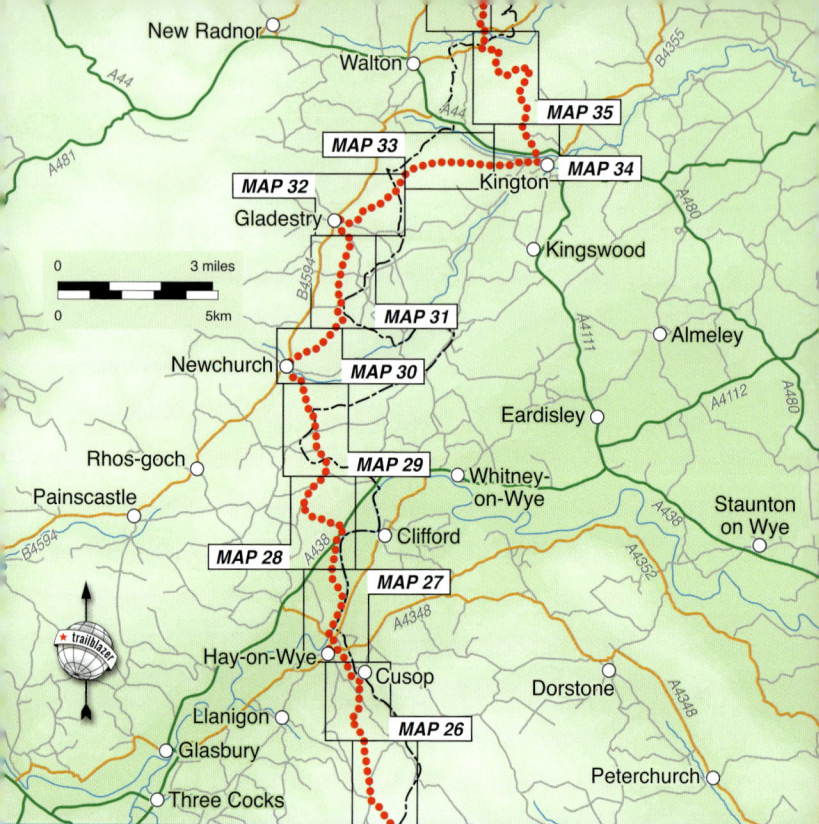

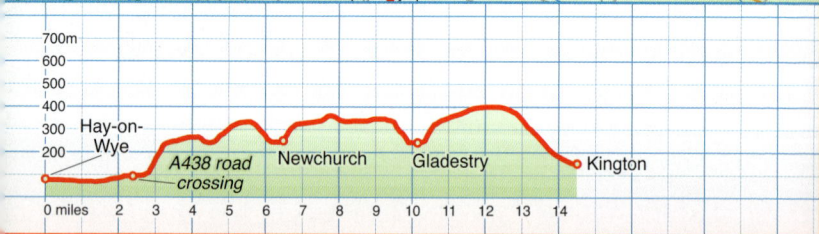

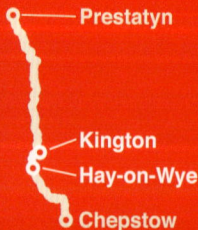

Maps 27-34, Hay-on-Wye to Kington
14½ miles/23km – 7¼hrs-8hrs 25mins

Maps 34-27, Kington to Hay-on-Wye
14½ miles/23km – 6hrs 20mins-7hrs 20mins

NOTE: Add 20-30% to these times to allow for stops

Hay-on-Wye
MAP 27
Cusop
Llanigon
Dorstone
Preston-on-Wye
A4348
Glasbury
A438
Peterchurch
A4352
MAP 26
Three Cocks
Felinore
MAP 25
MAP 24
Upper Maes-coed
703m/2306ft
Michaelchurch Escley
Middle Maes-coed
A4347
A4348
MAP 23
Lower Maes-coed
Capel-y-ffin
MAP 22
Abbey Dore
MAP 21
Turns for Llanthony
Longtown
Ewyas Harold
MAP 20a
0   3 miles
0   5km
★trailblazer
Llanthony
MAP 20
Waun Fach
Trig point 464m/1522ft
Oldcastle
A465
MAP 19
Cwmdu
MAP 18
Pandy
MAP 17
Llangattock-lingoed
Llanbedr
Llanvihangel Crucorney

700m
600
500
400
300
200

Trig point 464m 1522ft
Turns for Llanthony
Hatterrall Ridge – highest point 703m/2306ft
Turn for Capel-y-ffin
Turn for Longtown
Capel-y-ffin
Longtown
Pandy
Hay-on-Wye
0 miles   2   3   4   5   6   7   8   9   10   11   12   13   14   15   16   17

Prestatyn

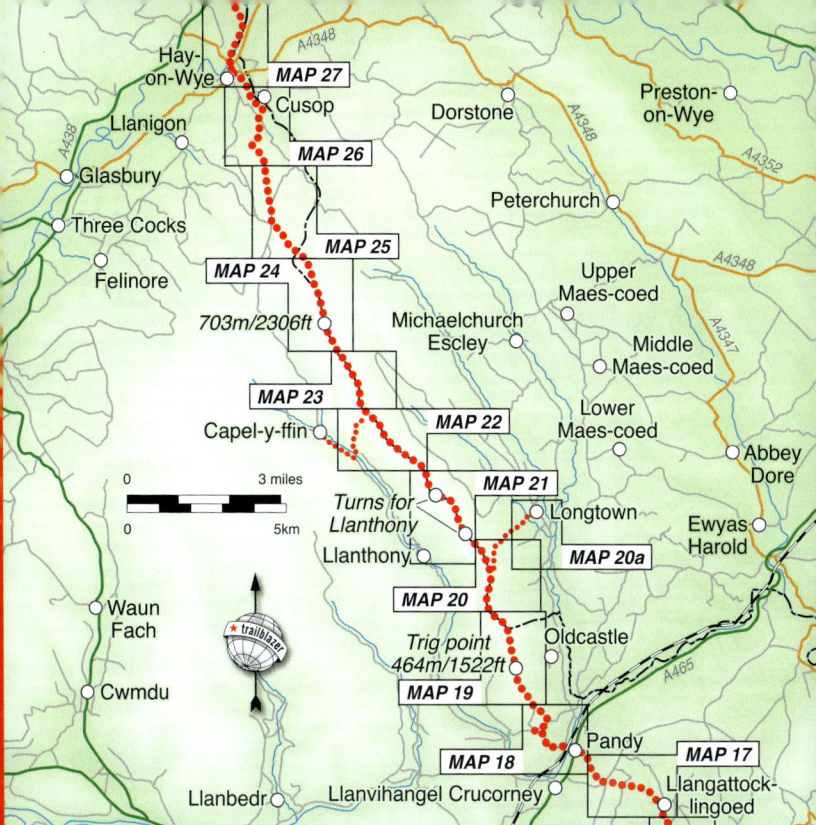

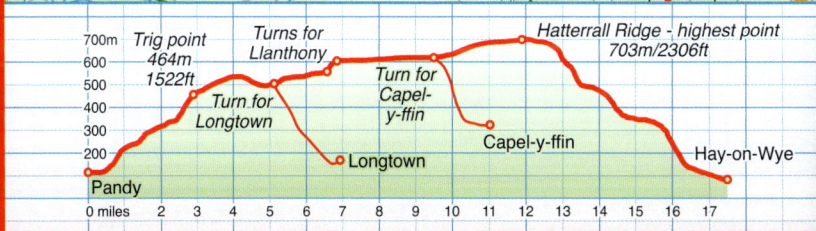

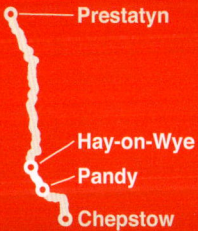

N Maps 18-27, Pandy to Hay-on-Wyc
17½ miles/28km – 8¾hrs-9¾hrs

S Maps 27-18, Hay-on-Wye to Pandy
17½ miles/28km – 8¾-10hrs

NOTE: Add 20-30% to these times to allow for stops

Hay-on-Wye
Pandy
Chepstow

Longtown
MAP 20a

Ewyas
Harold

Orcop Hill

Llanwarne

St Owen's
Cross

MAP 19

Oldcastle

A465

Groes-
lwyd

MAP 18

Pandy

MAP 17

Llanvihangel
Crucorney

Llangattock-
lingoed

Skenfrith

Llangarron

B4521

Llangrove

Whitchurch

Caggle
Street

MAP 16

Newcastle

Llanvetherine

White Castle

MAP 14

MAP 15

Llantilio-
Crossenny

Llanvihangel-
Ystern-Llewern

MONMOUTH

MAP 10

ABERGAVENNY

MAP 13

MAP 12

MAP 11

A466

Llanellen

Dingestown

A449

Upper/Lower
Redbrook

MAP 9

Llanover

B4293

Whitebrook

MAP 8

Bettws
Newydd

Raglan

trailblazer

N

0   3 miles
0   5km

A466

B4347

A4137

A465

B4598

B4042

700m
600
500
400
300
200
100

Llanvihangel-
Ystern-Llewern

Llantilio-
Crossenny

White
Castle

Caggle
Street

Llangattock-lingoed

Monmouth

Pandy

0 miles   2   3   4   5   6   7   8   9   10   11   12   13   14   15   16

Prestatyn

Pandy
Llantilio
Crossenny
Monmouth
Chepstow

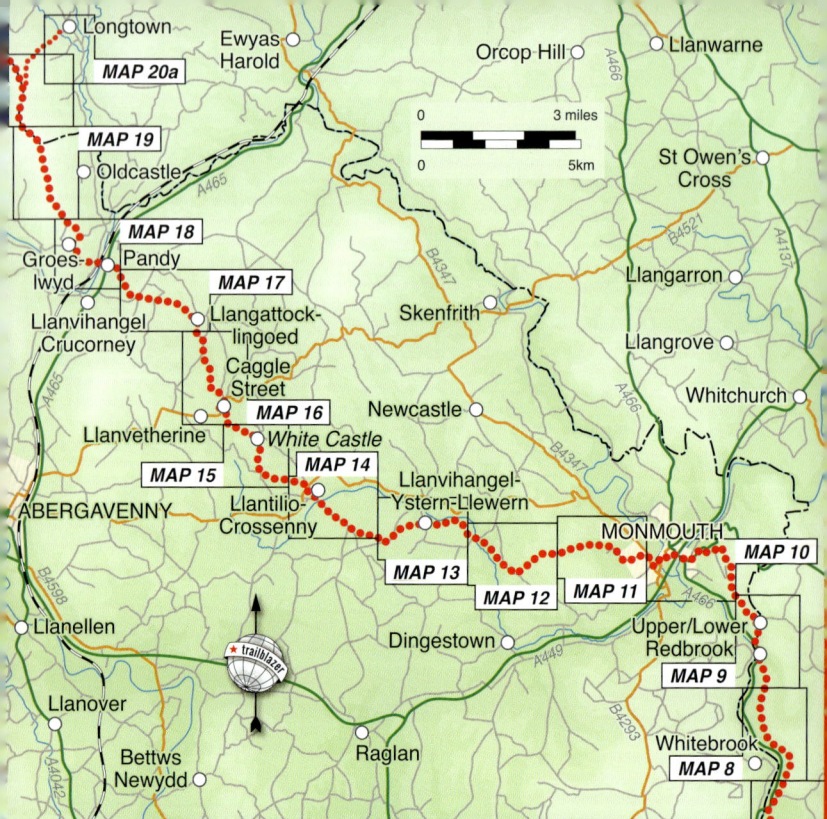

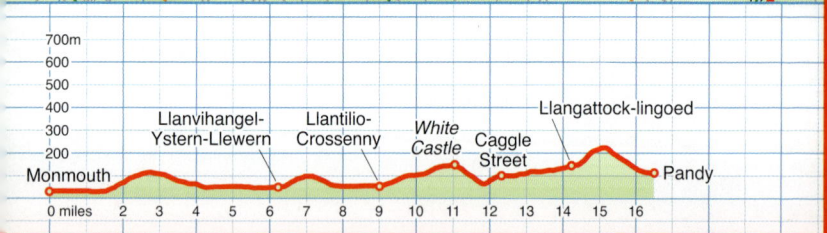

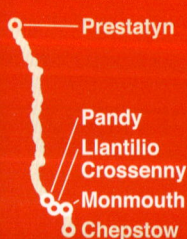

N ↑ Maps 10-14, Monmouth to Llantilio Crossenny
9 miles/14km – 4½hrs-5¼hrs
Maps 14-18, Llantilio Crossenny to Pandy
7½ miles/12km – 3½-4¼hrs

S ↓ Maps 18-14, Pandy to Llantilio Crossenny
7½ miles/12km – 3½-4½hrs
Maps 14-10, Llantilio Crossenny to Monmouth
9 miles/14km – 3hrs 55mins-4hrs 25mins

NOTE: Add 20-30% to these times to allow for stops

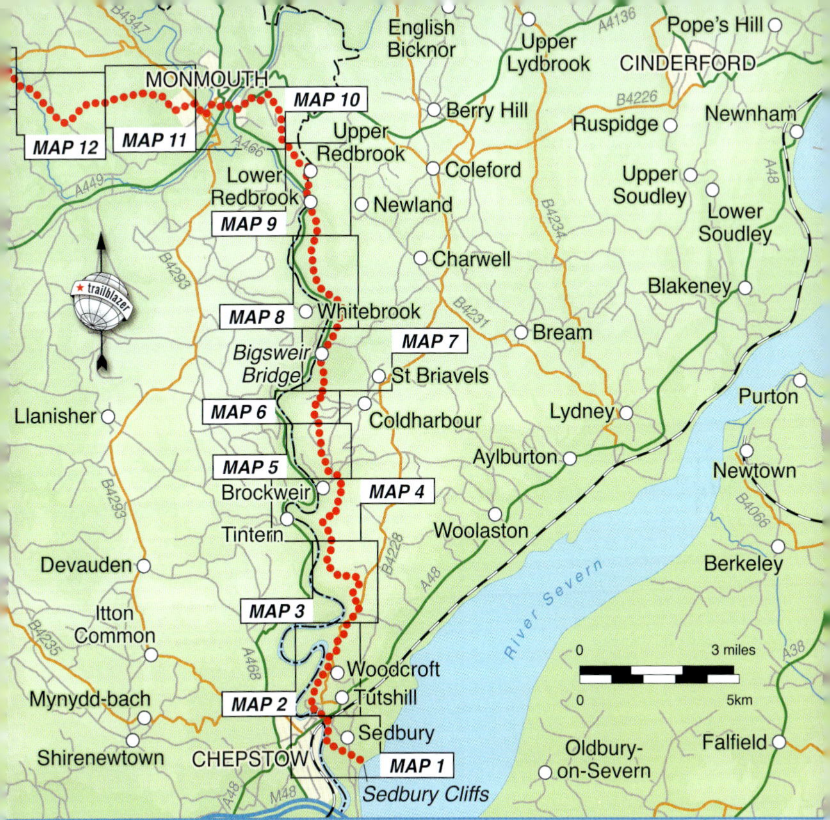
MONMOUTH
MAP 12
MAP 11
MAP 10
MAP 9
MAP 8
MAP 7
MAP 6
MAP 5
MAP 4
MAP 3
MAP 2
MAP 1
English Bicknor
Upper Lydbrook
Pope's Hill
CINDERFORD
Berry Hill
Ruspidge
Newnham
Upper Redbrook
Lower Redbrook
Coleford
Newland
Upper Soudley
Lower Soudley
Charwell
Blakeney
Whitebrook
Bream
Bigsweir Bridge
St Briavels
Llanisher
Coldharbour
Lydney
Purton
Aylburton
Newtown
Brockweir
Tintern
Woolaston
Devauden
Berkeley
Itton Common
River Severn
Woodcroft
Tutshill
Mynydd-bach
Sedbury
Shirenewtown
CHEPSTOW
Oldbury-on-Severn
Falfield
Sedbury Cliffs
0 3 miles
0 5km
trailblazer
B4347
A4136
B4226
A466
A449
A48
B4234
B4293
B4231
B4228
B4066
B4235
A468
A38
M48

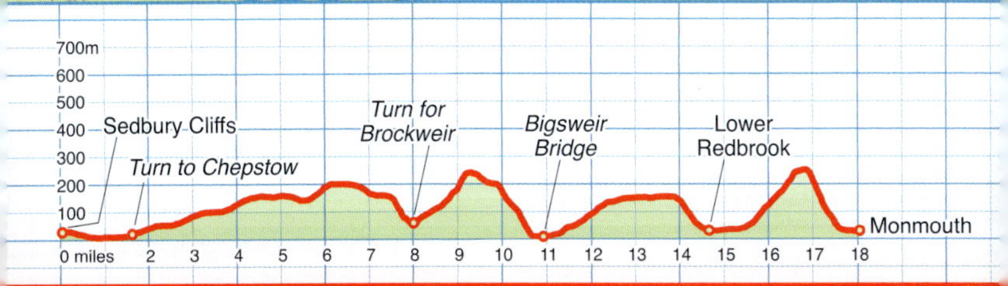
700m
600
500
400
300
200
100
Sedbury Cliffs
Turn to Chepstow
Turn for Brockweir
Bigsweir Bridge
Lower Redbrook
Monmouth
0 miles
2
3
4
5
6
7
8
9
10
11
12
13
14
15
16
17
18

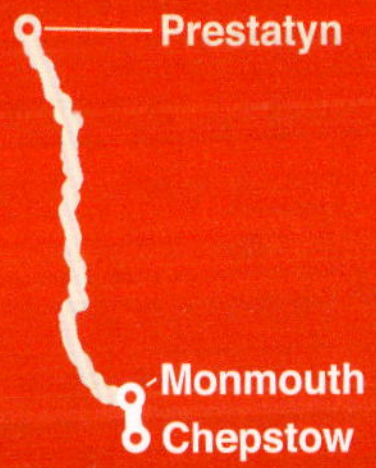
Prestatyn
Monmouth
Chepstow

N

Map 1, Sedbury to Chepstow
1½ miles/2km – 30-45mins

Maps 1-10, Chepstow to Monmouth
16½ miles/27km – 9hrs 25mins-10hrs 10mins

S

Maps 10-1, Monmouth to Chepstow
16½ miles/27km – 8½hrs-9¼hrs

Map 1, Chepstow to Sedbury
1½ miles/2km – 30-45mins

NOTE: Add 20-30% to these times to allow for stops

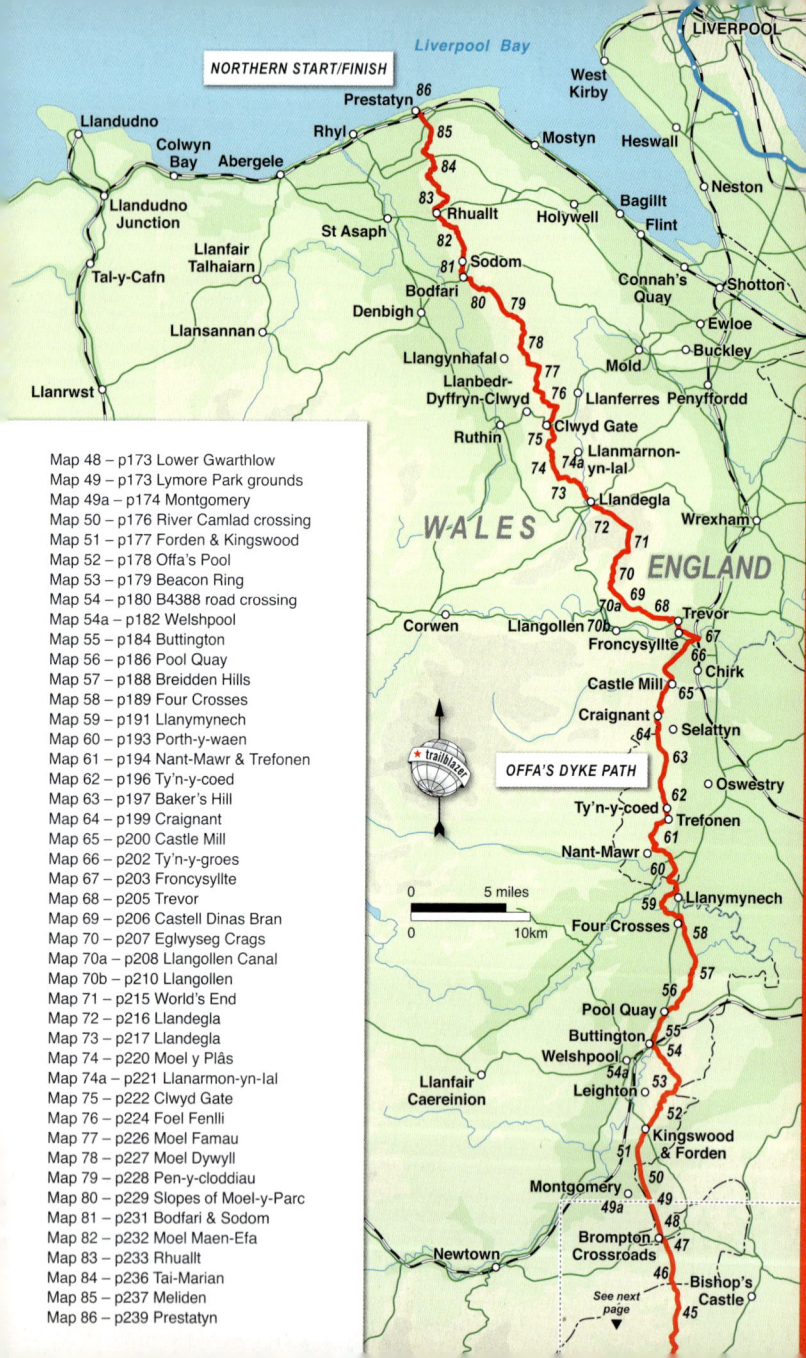

NORTHERN START/FINISH

OFFA'S DYKE PATH

★ trailblazer

0   5 miles

0   10km

See next
page
▼